Podman for DevOps

Containerization reimagined with Podman and its companion tools

Alessandro Arrichiello

Gianni Salinetti

BIRMINGHAM—MUMBAI

Podman for DevOps

Copyright © 2022 Packt Publishing

Group Product Manager: Rahul Nair
Publishing Product Manager: Niranjan Naikwadi
Senior Editor: Sangeeta Purkayastha
Content Development Editor: Nihar Kapadia
Technical Editor: Nithik Cheruvakodan
Copy Editor: Safis Editing
Project Coordinator: Shagun Saini
Proofreader: Safis Editing
Indexer: Sejal Dsilva
Production Designer: Sinhayna Bais
Marketing Coordinator: Nimisha Dua

First published: May 2022

Production reference: 1080422

Published by Packt Publishing Ltd.
Livery Place
35 Livery Street
Birmingham
B3 2PB, UK.

ISBN 978-1-80324-823-3

www.packt.com

To my son, Giovanni, for allowing me to steal time from our playtime. To my wife, Tecla, for being my loving partner and supporting me.

– Alessandro Arrichiello

To my son, Filippo, who teaches me to learn every day and enjoy the little things in life. To my beloved wife, Anna Veronica, for all the strength and inspiration she brings to our family.

– Gianni Salinetti

Foreword

Containers, their various runtimes, and Kubernetes are seeing fierce momentum in the technology and computing worlds. They are no longer just the darling of system administrators and Kubernetes distributed workloads. Containers are now endemic in **Continuous Integration** (**CI**) tasks, cloud workloads, and microservices. Starting with programmers, containers have even broken into the desktop space, where **Integrated Development Environments** (**IDEs**) can be the backend into containers for things such as testing language versions or compiling code. We can attribute the latest invigoration to the simplification of container images and the ability to distribute them in container registries. Not bad for a decades-old technology that used to simply focus on the isolation of a computing process.

Podman for DevOps begins with a detailed exploration of container history, from its inception to now. It then transitions into the various container technologies and arrives at the two most common ones: Docker and **Podman** (short for **Pod Manager**). The early chapters provide a comprehensive examination of Docker and Podman and describe the pros and cons of both. These comparisons demonstrate Podman's novelty and strengths.

Gianni and Alessandro then settle on Podman, beginning with an exploration of its architecture. They then follow the architecture by illustrating the various applications in the Podman stack, such as conmon and network tooling. After laying the groundwork for how Podman works, they meticulously review each Podman command in an example-oriented approach. Finally, Gianni and Alessandro provide a thorough review of Buildah, Podman's best friend and a best-of-breed application for building container images.

When I write about containers and Podman, one of my challenges when explaining concepts can be providing too many details or oversimplifying things. Gianni and Alessandro have found a perfect medium between both ends by supplying ample amounts of detail. I appreciated the carefully crafted explanations when the topic required them. Not only was the level of detail appropriate, but they also used a very wide scope when writing about Podman and containers. As I read the book, I was able to relate to their superb use of examples and they did not add layers of abstraction that can make learning difficult. *Podman for DevOps* was a pleasure to read. As a subject matter expert, I am certain it will be a perfect resource for those both new to and experienced with Podman and containers.

Brent J. Baude, Senior Principal Software Engineer

Podman Architect

Contributors

About the authors

Alessandro Arrichiello is a solution architect for Red Hat Inc. with a special focus on telco technologies. He has a passion for GNU/Linux systems, which began at age 14 and continues today. He has worked with tools for automating enterprise IT: configuration management and continuous integration through virtual platforms. Alessandro is also a writer for the Red Hat Developer Blog, on which he has authored several articles about container architecture and technology. He now helps telecommunication customers with adopting container orchestration environments such as Red Hat OpenShift and Kubernetes, infrastructure as a service such as OpenStack, edge computing, and data center automation.

Gianni Salinetti is a solution architect from Rome working for Red Hat Inc. with a special focus on cloud-native computing and hybrid cloud strategies. He started working with GNU/Linux back in 2001 and developed a passion for open source software. His main fields of interest are application orchestration, automation, and systems performance tuning. He is also an advocate of DevSecOps and GitOps practices. He is a former Red Hat instructor, having taught many classes about GNU/Linux, OpenStack, JBoss middleware, Ansible, Kubernetes, and Red Hat OpenShift. He won Red Hat EMEA awards as the best DevOps, cloud, and middleware instructor. He is also an author for the Red Hat Developer Blog and actively contributes to webinars and events.

About the reviewers

Nicolò Amato has over 20 years of experience working in the field of IT, 16 of which were at Hewlett Packard Enterprise, Accenture, DXC, and Red Hat Inc. Working in both technical and development roles has given him a broad base of skills and the ability to work with a diverse range of clients. His time was spent designing and implementing complex infrastructures for clients with the aim to migrate traditional services to hybrid, multi-cloud, and edge environments, evolving them into cloud-native services. He is enthusiastic about new technologies and he likes to be up to date – in particular with open source, which he considers one of the essences of technology that regulates the evolution of information technology.

Pierluigi Rossi is a solution architect for Red Hat Inc. His passion for GNU/Linux systems began 20 years ago and continues today. He has built a strong business and technical know-how on enterprise and cutting-edge technologies, working for many companies on different verticals and roles in the last 20 years. He has worked with virtualization and containerization tools (open source and not). He has also participated in several projects for corporate IT automation. He is now working on distributed on-premises and cloud environments involving IaaS, PaaS (OpenShift and Kubernetes), and automation. He loves open source in all its shades, and he enjoys sharing ideas and solutions with customers, colleagues, and community members.

Marco Alessandro Fagotto has been in the IT industry for 13 years, ranging across frontend and backend support, administration, system configuration, and security roles. Working in both technical and development roles has given him a broad base of skills and the ability to work with a diverse range of clients. He is a Red Hat Certified Professional, always looking for new technology and solutions to explore due to his interest in the fast evolution of the open source world.

Table of Contents

2
Comparing Podman and Docker

3
Running the First Container

4
Managing Running Containers

5
Implementing Storage for the Container's Data

Section 2: Building Containers from Scratch with Buildah

6

Meet Buildah – Building Containers from Scratch

7

Integrating with Existing Application Build Processes

8

Choosing the Container Base Image

9

Pushing Images to a Container Registry

Section 3: Managing and Integrating Containers Securely

10
Troubleshooting and Monitoring Containers

11
Securing Containers

Preface

DevOps best practices encourage the adoption of containers as the foundation of cloud-native ecosystems. As containers have become the new de facto standard for packaging applications and their dependencies, understanding how to implement, build, and manage them is now an essential skill for developers, system administrators, and SRE/operations teams. Podman and its companion tools, Buildah and Skopeo, make a great toolset to boost the development, execution, and management of containerized applications. Starting from the basic concepts of containerization and its underlying technologies, this book will help you get your first container up and running with Podman. The book explores the complete toolkit and illustrates the development of new containers, their life cycle management, troubleshooting, and security aspects.

By the end of *Podman for DevOps*, you'll have the skills needed to be able to build and package your applications inside containers as well as deploy, manage, and integrate them with system services.

Who this book is for

The book is for cloud developers looking to learn how to build and package applications inside containers, and system administrators who want to deploy, manage, and integrate containers with system services and orchestration solutions. This book provides a detailed comparison between Docker and Podman to aid you in learning Podman quickly.

What this book covers

Chapter 1, *Introduction to Container Technology*, covers the key concepts of container technology, a bit of history, and the underlying foundational elements that make things work.

Chapter 2, *Comparing Podman and Docker*, takes you through the architectures of Docker versus Podman, looking at high-level concepts and the main differences between them.

Chapter 3, Running the First Container, teaches you how to set up the prerequisites for running and managing your first container with Podman.

Chapter 4, Managing Running Containers, helps you understand how to manage the life cycles of your containers, starting/stopping/killing them to properly manage the services.

Chapter 5, Implementing Storage for the Container's Data, covers the basics of storage requirements for containers, the various offerings available, and how to use them.

Chapter 6, Meet Buildah – Building Containers from Scratch, is where you begin to learn the basic concepts of Buildah, Podman's companion tool that is responsible for assisting system administrators as well as developers during the container creation process.

Chapter 7, Integrating with Existing Application Build Processes, teaches you techniques and methods to integrate Buildah into a build process for your existing applications.

Chapter 8, Choosing the Container Base Image, covers more about the container base image format, trusted sources, and their underlying features.

Chapter 9, Pushing Images to a Container Registry, teaches you what a container registry is, how to authenticate them, and how to work with images by pushing and pulling them.

Chapter 10, Troubleshooting and Monitoring Containers, shows you how to inspect running or failing containers, search for issues, and monitor the health status of containers.

Chapter 11, Securing Containers, goes into more detail on security in containers, the main issues, and the important step of updating container images during runtime.

Chapter 12, Implementing Container Networking Concepts, teaches you about **Containers Network Interface** (**CNI**), how to expose a container to the external world, and finally, how to interconnect two or more containers running on the same machine.

Chapter 13, Docker Migration Tips and Tricks, sees you learn how to migrate from Docker to Podman in the easiest way by using some of the built-in features of Podman, as well as some tricks that may help in the process.

Chapter 14, Interacting with systemd and Kubernetes, shows you how to integrate a container as a system service in the underlying operating host, enabling its management with the common sysadmin's tools. Podman interaction features with Kubernetes will also be explored.

To get the most out of this book

In this book, we will guide you through the installation and use of Podman 3 or later, and its companion tools, Buildah and Skopeo. The default Linux distribution used in the book is Fedora Linux 34 or later but any other Linux distribution can be used. All commands and code examples have been tested using Fedora 34 or 35 and Podman 3 or 4, but they should work also with future version releases.

Software/hardware covered in the book	Operating system requirements
Podman 3 or later	Fedora Linux 34 or later (preferred) or any other Linux distribution
Buildah 1.x or later	
Skopeo 1.x or later	

If you are using the digital version of this book, we advise you to type the commands yourself or access the code from the book's GitHub repository (a link is available in the next section).

Doing so will help you avoid any potential errors related to the copying and pasting of code.

Download the example code files

You can download the example code files for this book from GitHub at `https://github.com/PacktPublishing/Podman-for-DevOps`. If there's an update to the code, it will be updated in the GitHub repository.

We also have other code bundles from our rich catalog of books and videos available at `https://github.com/PacktPublishing/`. Check them out!

Download the color images

We also provide a PDF file that has color images of the screenshots and diagrams used in this book. You can download it here: `https://static.packt-cdn.com/downloads/9781803248233_ColorImages.pdf`.

Conventions used

There are a number of text conventions used throughout this book.

`Code in text`: Indicates code words in text, database table names, folder names, filenames, file extensions, pathnames, dummy URLs, user input, and Twitter handles. Here is an example: "We just defined a name for our repo, `ubi8-httpd`, and we chose to link this repository to a GitHub repository push."

A block of code is set as follows:

```
[Unit]
Description=Podman API Socket
Documentation=man:podman-system-service(1)
```

When we wish to draw your attention to a particular part of a code block, the relevant lines or items are set in bold:

```
$ podman ps
CONTAINER ID IMAGE
COMMAND CREATED STATUS PORTS
NAMES
685a339917e7 registry.fedoraproject.org/f29/httpd:latest /
usr/bin/run-http... 3 minutes ago Up 3 minutes ago
clever_zhukovsky
```

Any command-line input or output is written as follows:

```
$ skopeo login -u admin -p p0dman4Dev0ps# --tls-verify=false
localhost:5000
Login Succeeded!
```

Bold: Indicates a new term, an important word, or words that you see onscreen. For instance, words in menus or dialog boxes appear in **bold**. Here is an example: "... and prints a crafted HTML page with the **Hello World!** message when it receives a GET / request."

> **Tips or important notes**
> Appear like this.

Get in touch

Feedback from our readers is always welcome.

General feedback: If you have questions about any aspect of this book, email us at customercare@packtpub.com and mention the book title in the subject of your message.

Errata: Although we have taken every care to ensure the accuracy of our content, mistakes do happen. If you have found a mistake in this book, we would be grateful if you would report this to us. Please visit www.packtpub.com/support/errata and fill in the form.

Piracy: If you come across any illegal copies of our works in any form on the internet, we would be grateful if you would provide us with the location address or website name. Please contact us at copyright@packt.com with a link to the material.

If you are interested in becoming an author: If there is a topic that you have expertise in and you are interested in either writing or contributing to a book, please visit authors.packtpub.com.

Share Your Thoughts

Once you've read , we'd love to hear your thoughts! Scan the QR code below to go straight to the Amazon review page for this book and share your feedback.

https://packt.link/r/1-803-24823-8

Your review is important to us and the tech community and will help us make sure we're delivering excellent quality content.

Section 1:
From Theory to Practice: Running Containers with Podman

This chapter will take you through the basic concepts of container technology, the main features of Podman and its companion tools, the main differences between Podman and Docker, and finally, will put the theory of running and managing containers into practice.

This part of the book comprises the following chapters:

- *Chapter 1, Introduction to Container Technology*
- *Chapter 2, Comparing Podman and Docker*
- *Chapter 3, Running the First Container*
- *Chapter 4, Managing Running Containers*
- *Chapter 5, Implementing Storage for the Container's Data*

1
Introduction to Container Technology

Container technology has old roots in operating system history. For example, do you know that part of container technology was born back in the 1970s? Despite their simple and intuitive approach, there are many concepts behind containers that deserve a deeper analysis to fully grasp and appreciate how they made their way in the IT industry.

We're going to explore this technology to better understand how it works under the hood, the theory behind it, and its basic concepts. Knowing the mechanics and the technology behind the tools will let you easily approach and learn the whole technology's key concepts.

Then, we will also explore container technology's purpose and why it has spread to every company today. Do you know that 50% of the world's organizations are running half of their application base as containers in production nowadays?

Let's dive into this great technology!

In this chapter, we're going to ask the following questions:

- What are containers?
- Why do I need a container?

- Where do containers come from?

- Where are containers used today?

Technical requirements

This chapter does not require any technical prerequisites, so feel free to read it without worrying about installing or setting up any kind of software on your workstation!

Anyway, if you are new to containers, you will find here many technical concepts useful to understand the next chapters. We recommend going through it carefully and coming back when needed. Previous knowledge of the Linux operating system would be helpful in understanding the technical concepts covered in this book.

Book conventions

In the following chapters, we will learn many new concepts with practical examples that will require active interaction with a Linux shell environment. In the practical examples, we will use the following conventions:

- For any shell command that will be anticipated by the $ character, we will use a standard user (not root) for the Linux system.

- For any shell command that will be anticipated by the # character, we will use the root user for the Linux system.

- Any output or shell command that would be too long to display in a single line for the code block will be interrupted with the \ character, and then it will continue to a new line.

What are containers?

This section describes the container technology from the ground up, beginning from basic concepts such as processes, filesystems, system calls, the process isolation up to container engines, and runtimes. The purpose of this section is to describe how containers implement process isolation. We also describe what differentiates containers from virtual machines and highlight the best use case of both scenarios.

Before asking ourselves what a container is, we should answer another question: what is a process?

According to *The Linux Programming Interface*, an enjoyable book by *Michael Kerrisk*, a *process* is an instance of an executing program. A program is a file holding information necessary to execute the process. A program can be dynamically linked to external libraries, or it can be statically linked in the program itself (the Go programming language uses this approach by default).

This leads us to an important concept: a process is executed in the machine CPU and allocates a portion of memory containing program code and variables used by the code itself. The process is instantiated in the machine's user space and its execution is orchestrated by the operating system kernel. When a process is executed, it needs to access different machine resources such as I/O (disk, network, terminals, and so on) or memory. When the process needs to access those resources, it performs a system call into the kernel space (for example, to read a disk block or send packets via the network interface).

The process indirectly interacts with the host disks using a filesystem, a multi-layer storage abstraction, that facilitates the write and read access to files and directories.

How many processes usually run in a machine? A lot. They are orchestrated by the OS kernel with complex scheduling logics that make the processes behave like they are running on a dedicated CPU core, while the same is shared among many of them.

The same program can instantiate many processes of its kind (for example, multiple web server instances running on the same machine). Conflicts, such as many processes trying to access the same network port, must be managed accordingly.

Nothing prevents us from running a different version of the same program on the host, assuming that system administrators will have the burden of managing potential conflicts of binaries, libraries, and their dependencies. This could become a complex task, which is not always easy to solve with common practices.

This brief introduction was necessary to set the context.

Containers are a simple and smart answer to the need of running isolated process instances. We can safely affirm that containers are a form of application isolation that works on many levels:

- **Filesystem isolation**: Containerized processes have a separated filesystem view, and their programs are executed from the isolated filesystem itself.

- **Process ID isolation**: This is a containerized process run under an independent set of **process IDs (PIDs)**.

- **User isolation**: **User IDs (UIDs)** and **group IDs (GIDs)** are isolated to the container. A process' UID and GID can be different inside a container and run with a privileged UID or GID inside the container only.

- **Network isolation**: This kind of isolation relates to the host network resources, such as network devices, IPv4 and IPv6 stacks, routing tables, and firewall rules.

- **IPC isolation**: Containers provide isolation for host IPC resources, such as POSIX message queues or System V IPC objects.

- **Resource usage isolation**: Containers rely on Linux **control groups** (**cgroups**) to limit or monitor the usage of certain resources, such as CPU, memory, or disk. We will discuss more about cgroups later in this chapter.

From an adoption point of view, the main purpose of containers, or at least the most common use case, is to run applications in isolated environments. To better understand this concept, we can look at the following diagram:

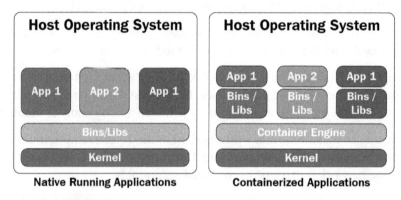

Figure 1.1 – Native applications versus containerized ones

Applications running natively on a system that does not provide containerization features share the same binaries and libraries, as well as the same kernel, filesystem, network, and users. This could lead to many issues when an updated version of an application is deployed, especially conflicting library issues or unsatisfied dependencies.

On other hand, containers offer a consistent layer of isolation for applications and their related dependencies that ensures seamless coexistence on the same host. A new deployment only consists of the execution of the new containerized version, as it will not interact or conflict with the other containers or native applications.

Linux containers are enabled by different native kernel features, with the most important being **Linux namespaces**. Namespaces abstract specific system resources (notably, the ones described before, such as network, filesystem mount, users, and so on) and make them appear as unique to the isolated process. In this way, the process has the illusion of interacting with the host resource, for example, the host filesystem, while an alternative and isolated version is being exposed.

Currently, we have a total of eight kinds of namespaces:

- **PID namespaces**: These isolate the process ID number in a separate space, allowing processes in different PID namespaces to retain the same PID.

- **User namespaces**: These isolate user and group IDs, root directory, keyrings, and capabilities. This allows a process to have a privileged UID and GID inside the container while simultaneously having unprivileged ones outside the namespace.

- **UTS namespaces**: These allow the isolation of hostname and NIS domain name.

- **Network namespaces**: These allow isolation of networking system resources, such as network devices, IPv4 and IPv6 protocol stacks, routing tables, firewall rules, port numbers, and so on. Users can create virtual network devices called **veth pairs** to build tunnels between network namespaces.

- **IPC namespaces**: These isolate IPC resources such as System V IPC objects and POSIX message queues. Objects created in an IPC namespace can be accessed only by the processes that are members of the namespace. Processes use IPC to exchange data, events, and messages in a client-server mechanism.

- **cgroup namespaces**: These isolate cgroup directories, providing a virtualized view of the process's cgroups.

- **Mount namespaces**: These provide isolation of the mount point list that is seen by the processes in the namespace.

- **Time namespaces**: These provide an isolated view of system time, letting processes in the namespace run with a time offset against the host time.

Now's, let's move on to resource usage.

Resource usage with cgroups

cgroups are a native feature of the Linux kernel whose purpose is to organize processes in a hierarchical tree and limit or monitor their resource usage.

The kernel cgroups interface, similar to what happens with /proc, is exposed with a cgroupfs pseudo-filesystem. This filesystem is usually mounted under /sys/fs/cgroup in the host.

cgroups offer a series of controllers (also called subsystems) that can be used for different purposes, such as limiting the CPU time share of a process, memory usage, freeze and resume processes, and so on.

The organizational hierarchy of controllers has changed through time, and there are currently two versions, V1 and V2. In cgroups V1, different controllers could be mounted against different hierarchies. Instead, cgroups V2 provide a unified hierarchy of controllers, with processes residing in the leaf nodes of the tree.

cgroups are used by containers to limit CPU or memory usage. For example, users can limit CPU quota, which means limiting the number of microseconds the container can use the CPU over a given period, or limit CPU shares, the weighted proportion of CPU cycles for each container.

Now that we have illustrated how process isolation works (both for namespaces and resources), we can illustrate a few basic examples.

Running isolated processes

A useful fact to know is that GNU/Linux operating systems offer all the features necessary to run a container manually. This result can be achieved by working with a specific system call (notably unshare() and clone()) and utilities such as the unshare command.

For example, to run a process, let's say /bin/sh, in an isolated PID namespace, users can rely on the unshare command:

```
# unshare --fork --pid --mount-proc /bin/sh
```

The result is the execution of a new shell process in an isolated PID namespace. Users can try to monitor the process view and will get an output such as the following:

```
sh-5.0# ps aux
USER         PID %CPU %MEM    VSZ    RSS TTY      STAT START
TIME COMMAND
root           1  0.0  0.0 226164   4012 pts/4    S     22:56
0:00 /bin/sh
root           4  0.0  0.0 227968   3484 pts/4    R+    22:56
0:00 ps aux
```

Interestingly, the shell process of the preceding example is running with PID 1, which is correct, since it is the very first process running in the new isolated namespace.

Anyway, the PID namespace will be the only one to be abstracted, while all the other system resources still remain the original host ones. If we want to add more isolation, for example on a network stack, we can add the --net flag to the previous command:

```
# unshare --fork --net --pid --mount-proc /bin/sh
```

The result is a shell process isolated on both PID and network namespaces. Users can inspect the network IP configuration and realize that the host native devices are no longer directly seen by the unshared process:

```
sh-5.0# ip addr show
1: lo: <LOOPBACK> mtu 65536 qdisc noop state DOWN group default
qlen 1000
    link/loopback 00:00:00:00:00:00 brd 00:00:00:00:00:00
```

The preceding examples are useful to understand a very important concept: containers are strongly related to Linux native features. The OS provided a solid and complete interface that helped container runtime development, and the capability to isolate namespaces and resources was the key that unlocked containers adoption. The role of the container runtime is to abstract the complexity of the underlying isolation mechanisms, with the mount point isolation being probably the most crucial of them. Therefore, it deserves a better explanation.

Isolating mounts

We have seen so far examples of unsharing that did not impact mount points and the filesystem view from the process side. To gain the filesystem isolation that prevents binary and library conflicts, users need to create another layer of abstraction for the exposed mount points.

This result is achieved by leveraging mount namespaces and bind mounts. First introduced in 2002 with the Linux kernel 2.4.19, mount namespaces isolate the list of mount points seen by the process. Each mount namespace exposes a discrete list of mount points, thus making processes in different namespaces aware of different directory hierarchies.

With this technique, it is possible to expose to the executing process an alternative directory tree that contains all the necessary binaries and libraries of choice.

Despite seeming a simple task, the management of a mount namespace is all but straightforward and easy to master. For example, users should handle different archive versions of directory trees from different distributions, extract them, and bind mount on separate namespaces. We will see later that the first approaches with containers in Linux followed this approach.

The success of containers is also bound to an innovative, multi-layered, copy-on-write approach of managing the directory trees that introduced a simple and fast method of copying, deploying, and using the tree necessary to run the container – container images.

Container images to the rescue

We must thank Docker for the introduction of this smart method of storing data for containers. Later, images would become an **Open Container Initiative (OCI)** standard specification (`https://github.com/opencontainers/image-spec`).

Images can be seen as a filesystem bundle that is downloaded (pulled) and unpacked in the host before running the container for the first time.

Images are downloaded from repositories called **image registries**. Those repositories can be seen as specialized object storages that hold image data and related metadata. There are both public and free-to-use registries (such as `quay.io` or `docker.io`) and private registries that can be executed in the customer private infrastructure, on-premises, or in the cloud.

Images can be built by DevOps teams to fulfill special needs or embed artifacts that must be deployed and executed on a host.

During the image build, process developers can inject pre-built artifacts or source code that can be compiled in the build container itself. To optimize image size, it is possible to create multi-stage builds with a first stage that compiles the source code using a base image with the necessary compilers and runtimes, and a second stage where the built artifacts are injected into a minimal, lightweight image, optimized for fast startup and minimal storage footprint.

The *recipe* of the build process is defined in a special text file called a **Dockerfile**, which defines all the necessary steps to assemble the final image.

After building them, users can push their own images on public or private registries for later use or complex, orchestrated deployments.

The following diagram summarizes the build workflow:

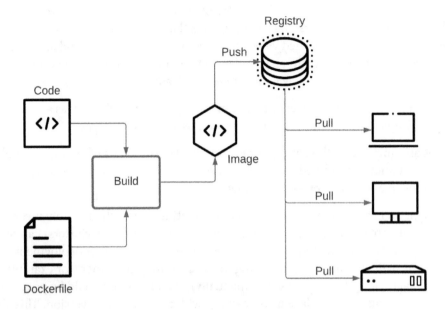

Figure 1.2 – Image build workflow

We will cover the build topic more extensively later in this book.

What makes a container image so special? The smart idea behind images is that they can be considered as a packaging technology. When users build their own image with all the binaries and dependencies installed in the OS directory tree, they are effectively creating a self-consistent object that can be deployed everywhere with no further software dependencies. From this point of view, container images are an answer to the long-debated sentence, *It works on my machine.*

Developer teams love them because they can be certain of the execution environment of their applications, and operations teams love them because they simplify the deployment process by removing the tedious task of maintaining and updating a server's library dependencies.

Another smart feature of container images is their copy-on-write, multi-layered approach. Instead of having a single bulk binary archive, an image is made up of many `tar` archives called *blobs* or *layers*. Layers are composed together using image metadata and squashed into a single filesystem view. This result can be achieved in many ways, but the most common approach today is by using **union filesystems**.

OverlayFS (`https://www.kernel.org/doc/html/latest/filesystems/overlayfs.html`) is the most used union filesystem nowadays. It is maintained in the kernel tree, despite not being completely POSIX-compliant.

According to kernel documentation, *"An overlay filesystem combines two filesystems – an 'upper' filesystem and a 'lower' filesystem."* This means that it can combine more directory trees and provide a unique, squashed view. The directories are the layers and are referred to as `lowerdir` and `upperdir` to respectively define the low-level directory and the one stacked on top of it. The unified view is called *merged*. It supports up to 128 layers.

OverlayFS is not aware of the concept of container image; it is merely used as a foundation technology to implement the multi-layered solution used by OCI images.

OCI images also implement the concept of **immutability**. The layers of an image are all read-only and cannot be modified. The only way to change something in the lower layers is to rebuild the image with appropriate changes.

Immutability is an important pillar of the cloud computing approach. It simply means that an infrastructure (such as an instance, container, or even complex clusters) can only be replaced by a different version and not modified to achieve the target deployment. Therefore, we usually do not change anything inside a running container (for example, installing packages or updating config files manually), even though it could be possible in some contexts. Rather, we replace its base image with a new updated version. This also ensures that every copy of the running containers stays in sync with others.

When a container is executed, a new read/write thin layer is created on top of the image. This layer is ephemeral, thus any changes on top of it will be lost after the container is destroyed:

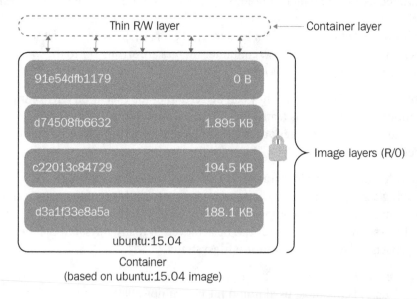

Figure 1.3 – A container's layers

This leads to another important statement: we do not store anything inside containers. Their only purpose is to offer a working and consistent runtime environment for our applications. Data must be accessed externally, by using bind mounts inside the container itself or network storage (such as **Network File System (NFS)**, **Simple Storage Service (S3)**, **Internet Small Computer System Interface (iSCSI)**, and so on).

Containers' mount isolation and images layered design provide a consistent immutable infrastructure, but more security restrictions are necessary to prevent processes with malicious behaviors escape the container sandbox to steal the host's sensitive information or use the host to attack other machines. The following subsection introduces security considerations to show how container runtimes can limit those behaviors.

Security considerations

From a security point of view, there is a hard truth to share: if a process is running inside a container, it simply does not mean it is more secure than others.

A malicious attacker can still make its way through the host filesystem and memory resources. To achieve better security isolation, additional features are available:

- **Mandatory access control**: *SELinux* or *AppArmor* can be used to enforce container isolation against the parent host. These subsystems, and their related command-line utilities, use a policy-based approach to better isolate the running processes in terms of filesystem and network access.

- **Capabilities**: When an unprivileged process is executed in the system (which means a process with an effective UID different from 0), it is subject to permission checking based on the process credentials (its effective UID). Those permissions, or privileges, are called capabilities and can be enabled independently, assigning to an unprivileged process limited privileged permissions to access specific resources. When running a container, we can add or drop capabilities.

- **Secure Computing Mode (Seccomp)**: This is a native kernel feature that can be used to restrict the syscall that a process is able to make from user space to kernel space. By identifying the strictly necessary privileges needed by a process to run, administrators can apply seccomp profiles to limit the attack surface.

Applying the preceding security features manually is not always easy and immediate, as some of them require a shallow learning curve. Instruments that automate and simplify (possibly in a declarative way) these security constraints provide a high value.

We will discuss security topics in further detail later in this book.

Container engines and runtimes

Despite being feasible and particularly useful from a learning point of view, running and securing containers manually is an unreliable and complex approach. It is too hard to reproduce and automate on production environments and can easily lead to configuration drift among different hosts.

This is the reason container engines and runtimes were born – to help automate the creation of a container and all the related tasks necessary that culminate with a running container.

The two concepts are quite different and tend to be often confused, thus requiring a clearance:

- A **container engine** is a software tool that accepts and processes requests from users to create a container with all the necessary arguments and parameters. It can be seen as a sort of orchestrator, since it takes care of putting in place all the necessary actions to have the container up and running; yet it is not the effective executor of the container (the container runtime's role).

  Engines usually solve the following problems:

  - Providing a command line and/or REST interface for user interaction

  - Pulling and extracting container images (discussed later in this book)

  - Managing container mount point and bind-mounting the extracted image

  - Handling container metadata

  - Interacting with the container runtime

  We have already stated that when a new container is instantiated, a thin R/W layer is created on top of the image; this task is achieved by the container engine, which takes care of presenting a working stack of the merged directories to the container runtime.

The container ecosystem offers a wide choice of container engines. **Docker** is, without doubt, the most well-known (despite not being the first) engine implementation, along with **Podman** (the core subject of this book), **CRI-O**, **rkt**, and **LXD**.

A **container runtime** is a low-level piece of software used by container engines to run containers in the host. The container runtime provides the following functionalities:

Starting the containerized process in the target mount point (usually provided by the container engine) with a set of custom metadata

Managing the cgroups' resource allocation

Managing mandatory access control policies (SELinux and AppArmor) and capabilities

There are many container runtimes nowadays, and most of them implement the **OCI runtime spec** reference (`https://github.com/opencontainers/runtime-spec`). This is an industry standard that defines how a runtime should behave and the interface it should implement.

The most common OCI runtime is **runc**, used by most notable engines, along with other implementations such as **crun**, **kata-containers**, **railcar**, **rkt**, and **gVisor**.

This modular approach lets container engines swap the container runtime as needed. For example, when Fedora 33 came out, it introduced a new default cgroups hierarchy called cgroups V2. runc did not support cgroups V2 in the beginning, and Podman simply swapped runc with another OCI-compatible container runtime (**crun**) that was already compliant with the new hierarchy. Now that runc finally supports cgroups V2, Podman will be able to safely use it again with no impact for the end user.

After introducing container runtimes and engines, it's time for one of the most debated and asked questions during container introductions – the difference between containers and virtual machines.

Containers versus virtual machines

Until now, we have talked about isolation achieved with native OS features and enhanced with container engines and runtimes. Many users could be tricked into thinking that containers are a form of virtualization.

There is nothing farther from the truth; containers are not virtual machines.

So, what is the main difference between a container and a virtual machine? Before answering, we can look at the following diagram:

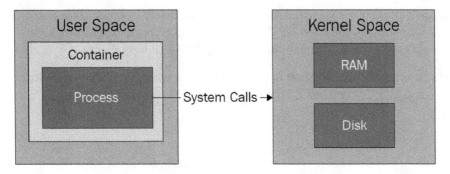

Figure 1.4 – A system call to a kernel from a container

A container, despite being isolated, holds a process that directly interacts with the host kernel using system calls. The process may not be aware of the host namespaces, but it still needs to context-switch into kernel space to perform operations such as I/O access.

On the other hand, a virtual machine is always executed on top of a **hypervisor**, running a guest operating system with its own filesystem, networking, storage (usually as image files), and kernel. The hypervisor is software that provides a layer of hardware abstraction and virtualization to the guest OS, enabling a single bare-metal machine running on capable hardware to instantiate many virtual machines. The hardware seen by the guest OS kernel is mostly virtualized hardware, with some exceptions:

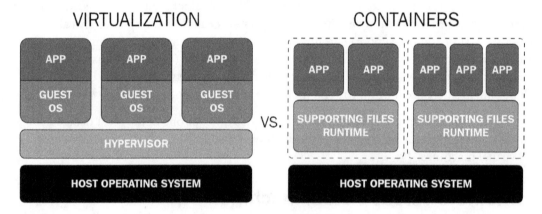

Figure 1.5 – Architecture – virtualization versus containers

This means that when a process performs a system call inside a virtual machine, it is always directed to the guest OS kernel.

To recap, we can affirm that containers share the same kernel with the host, while virtual machines have their own guest OS kernel.

This statement implies a lot of considerations.

From a security point of view, virtual machines provide better isolation from potential attacks. Anyway, some of the latest CPU-based attacks (Spectre or Meltdown, most notably) could exploit CPU vulnerabilities to access VMs' address spaces.

Containers have refined the isolation features and can be configured with strict security policies (such as CIS Docker, NIST, HIPAA, and so on) that make them quite hard to exploit.

From a scalability point of view, containers are faster to spin up than VMs. Running a new container instance is a matter of milliseconds if the image is already available in the host. These fast results are also achieved by the kernel-less nature of the container. Virtual machines must boot a kernel and initramfs, pivot into the root filesystem, run some kind of init (such as `systemd`), and start a variable number of services.

A VM will usually consume more resources than a container. To spin up a guest OS, we usually need to allocate more RAM, CPU, and storage than the resources needed to start a container.

Another great differentiator between VMs and containers is the focus on workloads. The best practice for containers is to spin up a container for every specific workload. On the other hand, a VM can run different workloads together.

Imagine a LAMP or WordPress architecture: on non-production or small production environments, it would not be strange to have everything (Apache, PHP, MySQL, and WordPress) installed on the same virtual machine. This design would be split into a multi-container (or multi-tier) architecture, with one container running the frontend (Apache-PHP-WordPress) and one container running the MySQL database. The container running MySQL could access storage volumes to persist the database files. At the same time, it would be easier to scale up/down the frontend containers.

Now that we understand how containers work and what differentiates them from virtual machines, we can move on to the next big question: why do I need a container?

Why do I need a container?

This section describes the benefits and the value of containers in modern IT systems, and how containers can provide benefits for both technology and business.

The preceding question could be rephrased as, what is the value of adopting containers in production?

IT has become a fast, market-driven environment where changes are dictated by business and technological enhancements. When adopting emerging technologies, companies are always looking to their **Return of Investment** (**ROI**) while striving to keep the **Total Cost of Ownership** (**TCO**) under reasonable thresholds. This is not always easy to attain.

This section will try to uncover the most important ones.

Open source

The technologies that power container technology are open source and became open standards widely adopted by many vendors or communities. Open source software, today adopted by large companies, vendors, and cloud providers, has many advantages, and provides great value for the enterprise. Open source is often associated with high-value and innovative solutions – that's simply the truth!

First, community-driven projects usually have a great evolutionary boost that helps mature the code and bring new features continuously. Open source software is available to the public and can be inspected and analyzed. This is a great transparency feature that also has an impact on software reliability, both in terms of robustness and security.

One of the key aspects is that it promotes an evolutionary paradigm where only the best software is adopted, contributed, and supported; container technology is a perfect example of this behavior.

Portability

We have already stated that containers are a technology that enables users to package and isolate applications with their entire runtime environment, which means all the files necessary to run. This feature unlocks one key benefit – portability.

This means that a container image can be pulled and executed on any host that has a container engine running, regardless of the OS distribution underneath. A CentOS or nginx image can be pulled indifferently from a Fedora or Debian Linux distribution running a container engine and executed with the same configuration.

Again, if we have a fleet of many identical hosts, we can choose to schedule the application instance on one of them (for example, using load metrics to choose the best fit) with the awareness of having the same result when running the container.

Container portability also reduces vendor lock-ins and provides better interoperability between platforms.

DevOps facilitators

As stated before, containers help solve the old *it works on my machine* pattern between development and operations teams when it comes to deploying applications for production.

As a smart and easy packaging solution for applications, they meet the developers' need to create self-consistent bundles with all the necessary binaries and configurations to run their workloads seamlessly. As a self-consistent way to isolate processes and guarantee separation of namespaces and resource usage, they are appreciated by operations teams who are no more forced to maintain complex dependencies constraints or segregate every single application inside VMs.

From this point of view, containers can be seen as facilitators of DevOps best practices, where developers and operators work closer to deploy and manage applications without rigid separations.

Developers who want to build their own container images are expected to be more aware of the OS layer built into the image and work closely with operations teams to define build templates and automations.

Cloud readiness

Containers are built for the cloud, designed with an immutable approach in mind. The immutability pattern clearly states that changes in the infrastructure (be it a single container or a complex cluster) must be applied by redeploying a modified version and not by patching the current one. This helps to increase a system's predictability and reliability.

When a new application version must be rolled out, it is built into a new image and a new container is deployed in place of the previous version. Build pipelines can be implemented to manage complex workflows, from application build and image creation, image registry push and tagging, until deployment in the target host. This approach drastically shortens provisioning time while reducing inconsistencies.

We will see later in this book that dedicated container orchestration solutions such as Kubernetes also provide ways to automate the scheduling patterns of large fleets of hosts and make containerized workloads easy to deploy, monitor, and scale.

Infrastructure optimization

Compared to virtual machines, containers have a lightweight footprint that drives much greater efficiency in the consumption of compute and memory resources. By providing a way to simplify workload execution, container adoption brings great cost savings.

IT resources optimization is achieved by reducing the computational cost of applications; if an application server that was running on top of a virtual machine can be containerized and executed on a host along with other containers (with dedicated resource limits and requests), computing resources can be saved and reused.

Whole infrastructures can be re-modulated with this new paradigm in mind; a bare-metal machine previously configured as a hypervisor can be reallocated as a worker node of a container orchestration system that simply runs more granular containerized applications as containers.

Microservices

Microservice architectures split applications into multiple services that perform fine-grained functions and are part of the application as a whole.

Traditional applications have a monolithic approach where all the functions are part of the same instance. The purpose of microservices is to break the monolith into smaller parts that interact independently.

Monolithic applications fit well into containers, but microservice applications have an ideal match with them.

Having one container for every single microservice helps to achieve important benefits, such as the following:

- Independent scalability of microservices
- More defined responsibilities for development teams' cloud access program
- Potential adoption of different technology stacks over the different microservices
- More control over security aspects (such as public-facing exposed services, mTLS connections, and so on)

Orchestrating microservices can be a daunting task when dealing with large and articulated architectures. The adoption of orchestration platforms such as **Kubernetes**, service mesh solutions such as **Istio** or **Linkerd**, and tracing tools such as **Jaeger** and **Kiali** becomes crucial to achieving control over complexity.

Where do containers come from? Containers' technology is not a new topic in the computer industry, as we will see in the next paragraphs. It has deep roots in OS history, and we'll discover that it could be even older than us!

This section rewinds the tape and recaps the most important milestones of containers in OS history, from Unix to GNU/Linux machines. A useful glance in the past to understand how the underlying idea evolved through the years.

Chroot and Unix v7

If we want to create an events timeline for our travel time in the containers' history, the first and older destination is 1979 – the year of Unix V7. At that time, way back in 1979, an important system call was introduced in the Unix kernel – the *chroot* system call.

> **Important Note**
>
> A system call (or syscall) is a method used by an application to request something from the OS's kernel.

This system call allows the application to change the root directory of the running copy of itself and its children, removing any capability of the running software to escape that jail. This feature allows you to prohibit the running application access to any kind of files or directory outside the given subtree, which was really a game changer for that time.

After some years, way back in 1982, this system call was then introduced, also in BSD systems.

Unfortunately, this feature was not built with security in mind, and over the years, OS documentation and security literature strongly discouraged the use of *chroot* jails as a security mechanism to achieve isolation.

Chroot was only the first milestone in the journey towards complete process isolation in *nix systems. The next was, from a historic point of view, the introduction of FreeBSD jails.

FreeBSD jails

Making some steps forward in our history trip, we jump back (or forward, depending on where we're looking from) to 2000, when the FreeBSD OS approved and released a new concept that extends the old and good *chroot* system call – FreeBSD jails.

> **Important Note**
>
> FreeBSD is a free and open source Unix-like operating system first released in 1993, born from the Berkeley Software Distribution, which was originally based on Research Unix.

As we briefly reported previously, *chroot* was a great feature back in the '80s, but the jail it creates can easily be escaped and has many limitations, so it was not adequate for complex scenarios. For that reason, FreeBSD jails were built on top of the *chroot* syscall with the goal of extending and enlarging its feature set.

In a standard *chroot* environment, a running process has limitations and isolation only at the filesystem level; all the other stuff, such as running processes, system resources, the networking subsystem, and system users, is shared by the processes inside the *chroot* and the host system's processes.

Looking at FreeBSD jails, its main feature is the virtualization of the networking subsystem, system users, and its processes; as you can imagine, this improves so much the flexibility and the overall security of the solution.

Let's schematize the four key features of a FreeBSD jail:

- **A directory subtree**: This is what we already saw also for the *chroot* jail. Basically, once defined as a subtree, the running process is limited to that, and it cannot escape from it.

- **An IP address**: This is a great revolution; finally, we can define an independent IP address for our jail and let our running process be isolated even from the host system.

- **A hostname**: Used inside the jail, this is, of course, different from the host system.

- **A command**: This is the running executable and has an option to be run inside the system jail. The executable has a relative path that is self-contained in the jail.

One plus of this kind of jail is that every instance has also its own users and root account that has no kind of privileges or permissions over the other jails or the underlying host system.

Another interesting feature of FreeBSD jails is that we have two ways of installing/creating a jail:

- From binary-reflecting the ones we might install with the underlying OS

- From the source, building from scratch what's needed by the final application

Solaris Containers (also known as Solaris Zones)

Moving back to our time machine, we must jump forward only a few years, to 2004 to be exact, to finally meet the first wording we can recognize – Solaris Containers.

Important Note

Solaris is a proprietary Unix OS born from SunOS in 1993, originally developed by Sun Microsystems.

To be honest, Solaris Containers was only a transitory naming of **Solaris Zones**, a virtualization technology built-in Solaris OS, with help also from a special filesystem, ZFS, that allows storage snapshots and cloning.

A *zone* is a virtualized application environment, built from the underlying operating system, that allows complete isolation between the base host system and any other applications running inside other *zones*.

The cool feature that Solaris Zones introduced is the concept of a branded zone. A branded zone is a completely different environment compared to the underlying OS, and can container different binaries, toolkits, or even a different OS!

Finally, for ensuring isolation, a Solaris zone can have its own networking, its own users, and even its own time zone.

Linux Containers (LXC)

Let's jump forward four years more and meet **Linux Containers** (**LXC**). We're in 2008, when Linux's first complete container management solution was released.

LXC cannot just be simplified as a manager for one of the first container implementations of Linux containers, because its authors developed a lot of the kernel features that now are also used for other container runtimes in Linux.

LXC has its own low-level container runtime, and its authors made it with the goal of offering an isolated environment as close as possible to VMs but without the overhead needed for simulating the hardware and running a brand-new kernel instance. LXC achieves this a goal and isolation thanks to the following kernel functionalities:

- Namespaces
- Mandatory access control
- Control groups (also known as cgroups)

Let's recap the kernel functionalities that we saw earlier in the chapter.

Linux namespaces

A namespace isolates processes that abstract a global system resource. If a process makes changes to a system resource in a namespace, these changes are visible only to other processes within the same namespace. The common use of the namespaces feature is to implement containers.

Mandatory access control

In the Linux ecosystem, there are several MAC implementations available; the most well-known project is **Security Enhanced Linux (SELinux)**, developed by the USA's **National Security Agency (NSA)**.

Important Note

SELinux is a mandatory access control architecture implementation used in Linux operating systems. It provides role-based access control and multi-level security through a labeling mechanism. Every file, device, and directory has an associated label (often described as a security context) that extends the common filesystem's attributes.

Control groups

Control groups (cgroups) is a built-in Linux kernel feature that can help to organize in hierarchical groups various types of resources, including processes. These resources can then be limited and monitored. The common interface used for interacting with cgroups is a pseudo-filesystem called **cgroupfs**. This kernel feature is really useful for tracking and limiting processes' resources, such as memory, CPU, and so on.

The main and greatest LXC feature coming from these three kernels' functionalities is, for sure, the *unprivileged containers.*

Thanks to namespaces, MAC, and cgroups, in fact, LXC can isolate a certain number of UIDs and GIDs, mapping them with the underlying operating system. This ensures that a UID of 0 in the container is (in reality) mapped to a higher UID at the base system host.

Depending on the privileges and the feature set we want to assign to our container, we can choose from a vast set of pre-built namespace types, such as the following:

- Network: Offering access to network devices, stacks, ports, and so on
- Mount: Offering access to mount points
- PID: Offering access to PIDs

The next main evolution from LXC (and, without doubt, the one that triggered the success of container adoption) was certainly Docker.

Docker

After just 5 years, back in 2013, Docker arises in the container landscape, and it rapidly became so popular. But what features were used back in those days? Well, we can easily discover that one of the first Docker container engines was LXC!

Just after one year of development, Docker's team introduced *libcontainer* and finally replaced the LXC container engine with their own implementation. Docker, similar to its predecessor, LXC, requires a daemon running on the base host system to keep the containers running and working properly.

One most notable feature (apart from the use of namespaces, MAC, and cgroups) was, for sure, OverlayFS, an overlay filesystem that helps combine multiple filesystems in just one single filesystem.

> **Important Note**
> OverlayFS is a Linux union filesystem. It can combine multiple mount points into one, creating a single directory structure that contains all the underlying files and subdirectories from sources.

At a high level, the Docker team introduced the concept of container images and container registries, which really was the functionality game changer. The registry and image concepts enabled the creation of a whole ecosystem to which every developer, sysadmin, or tech enthusiast could collaborate and contribute with their own custom container images. They also created a special file format for creating brand-new container images (Dockerfile) to easily automate the steps needed for building the container images from scratch.

Along with Docker, there is another engine/runtime project that caught the interest of the communities – rkt.

rkt

Just a few years after Docker's arise, across 2014 and 2015, the CoreOS company (acquired then by Red Hat) launched its own implementation of a container engine that has a very particular main feature – it was **daemon-less**.

This choice had an important impact: instead of having a central daemon administering a bunch of containers, every container was on its own, like any other standard process we may start on our base host system.

But the rkt (pronounced *rocket*) project became very popular in 2017 when the young **Cloud Native Computing Foundation** (**CNCF**), which aims to help and coordinate container and cloud-related projects, decided to adopt the project under their umbrella, together with another project donated by Docker itself – *containerd*.

In a few words, the Docker team extracted the project's core runtime from its daemon and donated it to the CNCF, which was a great step that motivated and enabled a great community around the topic of containers, as well as helping to develop and improve rising container orchestration tools, such as Kubernetes.

> **Important Note**
> Kubernetes (from the Greek term **κυβερνήτης**, meaning "helmsman"), also abbreviated as K8s, is an open source container-orchestration system for simplifying the application deployment and management in a multi-hosts environment. It was released as an open source project by Google, but it is now maintained by the CNCF.

Even if this book's main topic is Podman, we cannot mention now and in the following chapters the rising need of orchestrating complex projects made of many containers on multi-machine environments; that's the scenario where Kubernetes rose as the ecosystem leader.

After Red Hat's acquisition of CoreOS, the rkt project was discontinued, but its legacy was not lost and influenced the development of the Podman project. But before introducing the main topic of this book, let's dive into the OCI specifications.

OCI and CRI-O

As mentioned earlier, the *extraction* of containerd from Docker and the consequent donation to the CNCF motivated the open source community to start working seriously on container engines that could be injected under an orchestration layer, such as Kubernetes.

On the same wave, in 2015, Docker, with the help of many other companies (Red Hat, AWS, Google, Microsoft, IBM, and so on), started a governance committee under the umbrella of the Linux Foundation, the **Open Container Initiative** (**OCI**).

Under this initiative, the working team developed the runtime specification (**runtime spec**) and the image specification (**image spec**) for describing how the API and the architecture for new container engines should be created in the future.

The same year, the OCI team also released the first implementation of a container runtime adhering to the OCI specifications; the project was named runc.

The OCI defined not only a specification for running standalone containers but also provided the base for linking the Kubernetes layer with the underlying container engine more easily. At the same time, the Kubernetes community released the **Container Runtime Interface** (**CRI**), a plugin interface to enable the adoption of a wide variety of container runtimes.

That's where CRI-O jumps to 2017; released as an open source project by Red Hat, it was one of the first implementations of the Kubernetes Container Runtime Interface, enabling the use of OCI compatible runtimes. CRI-O represents a lightweight alternative to using Docker, rkt, or any other engines as Kubernetes' runtime.

As the ecosystem continues to grow, standards and specifications become more and more adopted, leading to a wider container ecosystem. The OCI specifications showed previously were crucial to the development of the runc container runtime, adopted by the Podman project.

Podman

We finally arrive at the end of our time travel; we reached 2017 in the previous paragraph and, in the same year, the first commit of the Podman project was made on GitHub.

The project's name reveals a lot about its purpose – *PODMAN = POD MANager*. We are now ready to look at the basic definition of a *pod* in a container's world.

A pod is the smallest deployable computing unit that can be handled by Kubernetes; it can be made of one or more containers. In the case of multiple containers in the same pod, they are scheduled and run side by side in a shared context.

Podman manages containers and containers' images, their storage volumes, and pods made of one or multiple containers, and it was built from scratch to adhere to the OCI standards.

Podman, like its predecessor, rkt, has no central daemon managing the containers but starts them as standard system processes. It also defines a Docker-compatible CLI interface to ease the transition from Docker.

One of the great features introduced by Podman is *rootless containers*. Usually, when we think about Linux containers, we immediately think about a system administrator that should set up some prerequisites at the OS level to prepare the environment that lets our container get up and running.

Rootless containers can easily run as a normal user, without requiring root. Using Podman with a non-privileged user will start restricted containers without any privileges, such as the user running it.

Without a doubt, Podman introduced greater flexibility and is a highly active project whose adoption grows constantly. Every major release brings many new features; for example, the 3.0 release introduced support for Docker Compose, which was a highly requested feature. This is also a good health metric of the community support.

Let's close the chapter with an overview of the most common container adoption use cases.

Where are containers used today?

This is an open-ended section. The intent is to tell where and how containers are used today in a production environment. This section also introduces the concept of container orchestration with Kubernetes, the most used open source orchestrator solution, adopted by thousands of companies worldwide. Container adoption is spreading across every enterprise company in every business sector.

But if we investigate the success stories of companies already using containers or a Kubernetes distribution, we'll discover that containerization and container orchestration are accelerating the project development and delivery, speeding up the creation of new use cases in every kind of industry – from automotive to healthcare. And regardless of the economics, this is really has a great impact on computer technology in general.

Companies are shifting from the old VM deployment model to a container one for new applications. As we briefly introduced in the previous paragraphs, a container could be easily represented as a new way for packaging applications.

Taking a step back to the VMs, what was their main purpose? It was creating an isolated environment with a reserved number of resources for a target application to be run.

With the introduction of containers, the enterprise companies realized that they can better optimize their infrastructure, speeding up the development and the deployment of new services introducing some kind of innovation.

Looking back (again) to the history of containers' adoption and their usage, we can see that at the beginning, they were used as a packaging method for old-style, monolithic application runtimes, but then once the cloud-native wave rose and concepts such as microservices became popular, containers became the de facto standard for packaging next-generation, cloud-native applications.

> **Important Note**
> Cloud-native computing is a software development practice to build and deploy scalable applications in public, private, or hybrid clouds.

On the other hand, containers' format and orchestration tools were influenced by the rise of microservice development and deployment; that's why today we find in Kubernetes a lot of additional services and resources, such as a service mesh and serverless computing, which are useful in a **microservice architecture**.

> **Important Note**
> Microservice architecture is a practice to create applications based on loosely coupled, fine-grained services, using lightweight protocols.

From our daily job with customers adopting containers, we can confirm that customers started packaging only standard applications in containers and orchestrated them with a container orchestrator, such as Kubernetes, but once new development models arrived at the developers' teams, the containers and their orchestrators started to also manage this new type of service more and more:

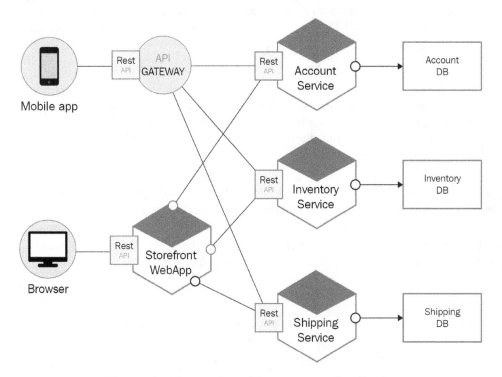

Figure 1.6 – Microservice architecture on a real application

Just to give us a bit more context around the microservice architecture topic, consider the previous picture, where we find a simple web store application built with microservices.

As we can see, depending on the type of client we're using (mobile phone or web browser), we'll then be able to interact with the three underlying services, all decoupled, communicating with a REST API. One of the great new features is also decoupling at the data level; every microservice has its own database and data structure, which makes them independent in every phase of development and deployment.

Now, if we match a container for every microservice shown in the architecture and we also add an orchestrator, such as Kubernetes, we'll find that the solution is almost complete! Thanks to the containers' technology, every service could have its own container base image with just the needed runtimes on board, which ensures a lightweight pre-built package with all the resources needed by the service once started.

On the other hand, looking at the various automated processes around application development and their maintenance, an architecture based on containers could also be easily fitted on the tools of **CI/CD** for automating all the needed steps to develop, test, and run an application.

> **Important Note**
>
> CI/CD stands for **continuous integration and continuous delivery/ deployment**. These practices try to fill the gap between development and operation activities, increasing the automation in the process of building, testing, and deployment applications.

We can say that containers' technology was born to fulfill system administrator needs but ended up being the beloved tool of developers! This technology represented in many companies the conjunction ring between the developers team and the operations one, which enabled and speeded up the adoption of DevOps practices that were previously isolated to increase collaboration between these two teams.

> **Important Note**
>
> DevOps is the group of practices that help link software development (Dev) and IT operations (Ops). The goal of DevOps is to shorten an application's development life cycle and to increase an application's delivery release.

Even though microservices and containers love to live together, enterprise companies have a lot of applications, software, and solutions that are not based on microservices architecture but previous monolithic approaches, for example, using clustered application servers! But we don't have to worry too much, as containers and their orchestrators evolved at the same time to support this kind of workload too.

Containers technology can be considered an evolved application packaging format that can be optimized for containing all the necessary libraries and tools, even complex monolithic applications. Over the years, the base container images evolved to optimize the size and content for creating smaller runtimes, capable of improving the overall management, even for complex monolithic applications.

If we look at the size of a Red Hat Enterprise Linux container base image in its minimal flavor, we can see that the image is around 30 MB during download and only 84 MB once extracted (through Podman, of course) in the target base system.

Even the orchestrators adopted internal features and resources for handling monolithic applications, too far from the cloud-native concepts. Kubernetes, for example, introduced in the platform's core some features for ensuring the statefulness of containers, as well as the concepts of persistent storage for saving locally cached data or important stuff for the application.

Summary

In this chapter, we discovered the underlying functionalities of container technology, from process isolation to container runtimes. Then, we looked at the main purposes and advantages of containers against VMs. After that, we started our time machines, looking into container history from 1979 to the current day. Finally, we discovered today's market trends and current container adoption in enterprise companies.

This chapter provided an introduction to container technology and its history. Podman is very close to Docker in terms of usability and CLI, and the next chapter will cover the differences between the two projects, from an architectural point of view and a user experience point of view.

After introducing Docker high-level architecture, Podman daemon-less architecture will be described in detail to understand how this container engine can manage containers without the need for a running daemon.

Further reading

For more information on the topics covered in this chapter, please refer to the following:

- *The Linux Programming Interface, Michael Kerrisk* (ISBN 978-1-59327-220-3)

- *Demystifying namespaces and containers in Linux*: `https://opensource.com/article/19/10/namespaces-and-containers-linux`

- *OCI Runtime Specs*: `https://github.com/opencontainers/runtime-spec`

- *OCI Image Specs*: `https://github.com/opencontainers/image-spec`

- *Container Runtime Interface announcement*: `https://kubernetes.io/blog/2016/12/container-runtime-interface-cri-in-kubernetes/`

2
Comparing Podman and Docker

As we learned from the previous chapter, container technology is not as new as we may think and therefore its implementation and architecture has been influenced over the years to reach its current status.

In this chapter, we'll go through a bit of the history and the main architecture of Docker and Podman container engines, completing the picture with a side-by-side comparison to let readers with some Docker experience easily get on board and learn the main differences before going into a deep exploration of Podman.

If you don't have much experience with Docker, you can easily jump to the next chapter and return to this one once you feel it is time to learn the differences between Podman and Docker container engines.

In this chapter, we're going to cover the following main topics:

- Docker container daemon architecture
- Podman daemonless architecture
- The main differences between Docker and Podman

Technical requirements

This chapter does not require any technical prerequisites; feel free to read it without worrying too much about installing or setting up any kind of software on your workstation!

If you want to replicate some of the examples that will be described in this chapter, you'll need to install and configure Podman and Docker on your workstation. As we described before, you can easily jump to the next chapter and come back to this one once you feel it's time to learn the differences between Podman and Docker container engines.

Please consider that in the next chapter, you'll be introduced to Podman's installation and configuration, so you'll be soon able to replicate any example you'll see in this chapter and in the following ones.

Docker container daemon architecture

Containers are a simple and smart answer to the need to run isolated process instances. We can safely affirm that containers are a form of application isolation that works at many levels, such as filesystem, network, resource usage, process, and so on.

As we saw in *Chapter 1*, *Introduction to Container Technology*, in the *Containers versus virtual machines* section, containers also differ from virtual machines because containers share the same kernel with the host, while virtual machines have their own guest OS kernel. From a security point of view, virtual machines provide better isolation from potential attacks, but a virtual machine will usually consume more resources than a container. To spin up a guest OS, we usually need to allocate more RAM, CPU, and storage than the resources needed to start a container.

Back in 2013, the Docker container engine appeared in the container landscape, and it rapidly became very popular.

As we explained before, a container engine is a software tool that accepts and processes requests from users to create a container; it can be seen as a sort of orchestrator. On the other hand, a container runtime is a lower-level piece of software used by container engines to run containers in the host, managing isolation, storage, networking, and so on.

In the early stages, the Docker container engine used LXC as a container runtime but then replaced it after a while with their own implementation, *libcontainer*.

The Docker container engine consists of three fundamental pillars:

- Docker daemon
- Docker REST API
- Docker CLI

These three pillars are represented in the following architecture:

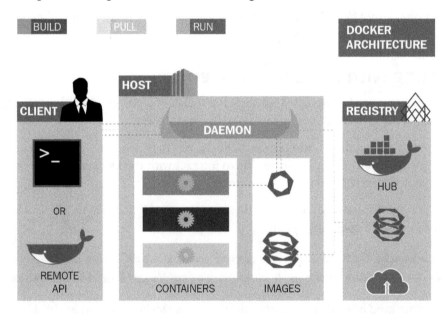

Figure 2.1 – Docker architecture

Once a Docker daemon is running, as shown in the preceding diagram, you can interact with it through a Docker client or a remote API. The Docker daemon is responsible for many local container activities as well as interacting with external registries to pull or push container images.

The Docker daemon is the most critical piece of the architecture, and it should always be up and running, otherwise your beloved containers will not survive for long! Let's see its details in the next section.

The Docker daemon

A daemon is a process that runs in the background; it supervises the system or provides functionality to other processes.

The Docker daemon is the background process that is responsible for the following:

- Listening for Docker API requests
- Handling, managing, and checking for running containers
- Managing Docker images, networks, and storage volumes
- Interacting with external/remote container image registries

All these actions should be instructed to the daemon through a client or by calling its API, but let's see how to communicate with it.

Interacting with the Docker daemon

The Docker daemon can be contacted through the socket of a process, usually available in the filesystem of the host machine: `/var/run/docker.sock`.

Depending on the Linux distribution of your choice, you may need to set the right permission for your non-root users to be able to interact with the Docker daemon or simply add your non-privileged users to the `docker` group.

As you can see in the following command, these are the permissions set for the Docker daemon in a Fedora 34 operating system:

```
[root@fedora34 ~]# ls -la /var/run/docker.sock
srw-rw----. 1 root docker 0 Aug 25 12:48 /var/run/docker.sock
```

There is no other kind of security or authentication for a Docker daemon enabled by default, so be careful not to publicly expose the daemon to untrusted networks.

The Docker REST API

Once a Docker daemon is up and running, you can communicate through a client or directly through the REST API. Through the Docker API, you can do every kind of activity you can perform through the command-line tool, such as the following:

- List containers
- Create a container
- Inspect a container
- Get container logs
- Export a container
- Start or stop a container

- Kill a container

- Rename a container

- Pause a container

The list goes on. Looking at one of these APIs, we can easily discover how they work and what the sample output returned by the daemon is.

In the following command, we are going to use the Linux command line tool `curl` for making an HTTP request to get details about any container image already stored in the daemon's local cache:

```
[root@fedora34 ~]# curl --unix-socket /var/run/docker.sock \
http://localhost/v1.41/images/json | jq
[
  {
    "Containers": -1,
    "Created": 1626187836,
    "Id": "sha256:be72532cbd81ba4adcef7d8f742abe7632e6f5b35
bbd53251e5751a88813dd5f",
    "Labels": {
      "architecture": "x86_64",
      "build-date": "2021-07-13T14:50:13.836919",
      "com.redhat.build-host": "cpt-1005.osbs.prod.upshift.
rdu2.redhat.com",
      "com.redhat.component": "ubi7-minimal-container",
      "com.redhat.license_terms": "https://www.redhat.com/en/
about/red-hat-end-user-license-agreements#UBI",
      "description": "The Universal Base Image Minimal is a
stripped down image that uses microdnf as a package manager.
This base image is freely redistributable, but Red Hat only
supports Red Hat technologies through subscriptions for Red
Hat products. This image is maintained by Red Hat and updated
regularly.",
      "distribution-scope": "public",
      "io.k8s.description": "The Universal Base Image Minimal
is a stripped down image that uses microdnf as a package
manager. This base image is freely redistributable, but Red
Hat only supports Red Hat technologies through subscriptions
for Red Hat products. This image is maintained by Red Hat and
updated regularly.",
```

```
       "io.k8s.display-name": "Red Hat Universal Base Image 7
Minimal",
       "io.openshift.tags": "minimal rhel7",
       "maintainer": "Red Hat, Inc.",
       "name": "ubi7-minimal",
       "release": "432",
       "summary": "Provides the latest release of the minimal
Red Hat Universal Base Image 7.",
       "url": "https://access.redhat.com/containers/#/registry.
access.redhat.com/ubi7-minimal/images/7.9-432",
       "vcs-ref": "8c60d5a9644707e7c4939980a221ec2927d9a88a",
       "vcs-type": "git",
       "vendor": "Red Hat, Inc.",
       "version": "7.9"
     },
     "ParentId": "",
     "RepoDigests": [
        "registry.access.redhat.com/ubi7/ubi-minimal@sha256:
73b4f78b569d178a48494496fe306dbefc3c0434c4b
872c7c9d7f23eb4feb909"
     ],
     "RepoTags": [
        "registry.access.redhat.com/ubi7/ubi-minimal:latest"
     ],
     "SharedSize": -1,
     "Size": 81497870,
     "VirtualSize": 81497870
   }
]
```

As you can see in the preceding command, the output is in JSON format, very detailed with multiple metadata information, from container image name to its size. In this example, we pre-fetched a **RHEL Universal Base Image** version 7 in its minimal flavour that is only 80 MB!

Of course, APIs are not made for human consumption or interaction; they fit well with machine-to-machine interaction and so they are commonly used for software integration. For this reason, let's now explore how the command-line client works and which options are available.

Docker client commands

The Docker daemon has its own companion that instructs and configures it – a command-line client.

The Docker command-line client has more than 30 commands with respective options that will enable any system administrator or Docker user to instruct and control the daemon and its containers. The following is an overview of the most common commands:

- `build`: Build an image from a Dockerfile
- `cp`: Copy files/folders between a container and the local filesystem
- `exec`: Run a command in a running container
- `images`: List images
- `inspect`: Return low-level information on Docker objects
- `kill`: Kill one or more running containers
- `load`: Load an image from a TAR archive or stdin
- `login`: Log in to a Docker registry
- `logs`: Fetch the logs of a container
- `ps`: List running containers
- `pull`: Pull an image or a repository from a registry
- `push`: Push an image or a repository to a registry
- `restart`: Restart one or more containers
- `rm`: Remove one or more containers
- `rmi`: Remove one or more images
- `run`: Run a command in a new container
- `save`: Save one or more images to a TAR archive (streamed to stdout by default)
- `start`: Start one or more stopped containers
- `stop`: Stop one or more running containers
- `tag`: Create a `TARGET_IMAGE` tag that refers to `SOURCE_IMAGE`

The list goes on. As you can see from this subset, there are many commands available for managing the container images and the running containers, even exporting a container image or building a new one.

Once you launch the Docker client with one of these commands and its respective options, the client will contact the Docker daemon, where it'll instruct it in what is needed, and which action must be performed. Again, the daemon here is the key element of the architecture and it needs to be up and running, so ensure this before trying to use the Docker client as well as any of its REST APIs.

Docker images

A Docker image is a format introduced by Docker for managing binary data and metadata as a template for container creation. Docker images are packages for shipping and transferring runtimes, libraries, and all the stuff needed for a given process to be up and running.

As we mentioned in *Chapter 1, Introduction to Container Technology*, in the *Where do containers come from?* section, the creation of this format was really a game changer and significantly different from the various other container technologies that arose in the past.

Starting from version 1.12, Docker started adopting an image specification that has over the years evolved into the current version that adheres to the **OCI Image Format Specification**.

The first Docker Image Specification included many concepts and fields that are now part of the OCI Image Format Specification, such as the following:

- A list of layers
- Creation date
- Operating system
- CPU architecture
- Configuration parameters for use within a container runtime

A Docker image's content (binaries, libraries, filesystem data) is organized in layers. A layer is just a set of filesystem changes that does not contain any environment variable or default arguments for a given command. This data is stored in the **Image Manifest** that owns the configuration parameters.

But how are these layers created and then aggregated in a Docker image? The answer is not so simple. The layers in a container image are composed together using image metadata and merged into a single filesystem view. This result can be achieved in many ways, but as anticipated in the previous chapter, the most common approach today is by using union filesystems – combining two filesystems and providing a unique, *squashed* view. Finally, when a container is executed, a new, *read/write* ephemeral layer is created on top of the image, which will be lost after the container is destroyed.

As we said earlier in this chapter, container images and their distribution were the killer feature of Docker containers. So, in the next section, let's look at the key element for container distribution, **Docker registries**.

Docker registries

A Docker registry is just a repository of Docker container images that holds the metadata and the layers of container images for making them available to several Docker daemons.

A Docker daemon acts as a client to a Docker registry through an HTTP API, pushing and pulling container images depending on the action that the Docker client instructs.

Using a container registry could really help the use of containers on many independent machines that could be configured to ask to a registry some container images if they are not present in the Docker daemon local cache. The default registry that is preconfigured in Docker daemon settings is **Dockerhub**, a **Software-as-a-Service** container registry hosted by Docker company in the cloud. However, Dockerhub is not the only registry; many other container registries have appeared in recent years.

Almost every company or community working with containers created their own container registry with a different web interface. One of the free alternative services to Dockerhub is **Quay.io**, a Software-as-a-Service container registry hosted by the Red Hat company.

One great alternative to cloud services is the on-premises Docker registry, which can be created through a container on a machine running the Docker daemon with just one command:

```
$ docker run -d -p 5000:5000 --restart=always --name registry
registry:2
```

It is not the objective of this book to go through the various Docker options and configuration, but if you want to know more about the Docker registry, you can refer to the main Docker documentation at `https://docs.docker.com/registry/deploying/`.

We have looked at a lot of stuff so far, namely the Docker API, client, daemon, images, and finally the registry, but, as we mentioned earlier, it's all dependent on the correct usage of the Docker daemon that should be always healthy and up and running. So, let's explore now what happens in the event that it stops working.

What does a running Docker architecture look like?

The Docker daemon is the central key element of the whole Docker architecture. We will explore in this section what a Docker daemon and a bunch of running containers look like.

We will not dive into the steps needed for installing and setting up the Docker daemon; instead, we will directly analyze a preconfigured operating system with it:

```
[root@fedora34 ~]# systemctl status docker
● docker.service - Docker Application Container Engine
     Loaded: loaded (/usr/lib/systemd/system/docker.service;
disabled; vendor preset: disabled)
     Active: active (running) since Tue 2021-08-31 19:46:57
UTC; 1h 39min ago
TriggeredBy: ● docker.socket
       Docs: https://docs.docker.com
   Main PID: 20258 (dockerd)
      Tasks: 12
     Memory: 31.1M
        CPU: 1.946s
     CGroup: /system.slice/docker.service
             └─20258 /usr/bin/dockerd -H fd:// --containerd=/
run/containerd/containerd.sock
```

As you can see from the preceding command, we just verified that the Docker daemon is up and running, but it's not the only container service running on the system. The Docker daemon has a companion that we skipped in the previous part to keep the description easy to understand: **Containerd**.

To better understand the workflow, have a look at the following diagram:

Figure 2.2 – Running a Docker container

Containerd is the project that decouples the container management (kernel interaction included) from the Docker daemon, and it also adheres to the OCI standard using runc as container runtime.

So, let's check the status of Containerd in our preconfigured operating system:

```
[root@fedora34 ~]# systemctl status containerd
● containerd.service - containerd container runtime
     Loaded: loaded (/usr/lib/systemd/system/containerd.
service; disabled; vendor preset: disabled)
     Active: active (running) since Wed 2021-08-25 12:48:17
UTC; 6 days ago
       Docs: https://containerd.io
    Process: 4267 ExecStartPre=/sbin/modprobe overlay
(code=exited, status=0/SUCCESS)
   Main PID: 4268 (containerd)
      Tasks: 43
     Memory: 44.1M
        CPU: 8min 36.291s
     CGroup: /system.slice/containerd.service
             ├─ 4268 /usr/bin/containerd
             ├─20711 /usr/bin/containerd-
shim-runc-v2 -namespace moby -id
3901d2600732ae1f2681cde0074f290c1839b1a4b0c63ac
9aaccdba4f646e06a -address /run/containerd/containe>
             ├─20864 /usr/bin/containerd-
shim-runc-v2 -namespace moby -id
78dc2eeb321433fc67cf910743c0c53e54d9f45cfee8d183
19d03a622dc56666 -address /run/containerd/containe>
             └─21015 /usr/bin/containerd-
shim-runc-v2 -namespace moby -id
7433c0613412349833b927efa79a4f589916b12c942003cd
616d45ed7611fc31 -address /run/containerd/containe>
```

As you can see from the preceding console output, the service is up and running and it has started three child processes: /usr/bin/containerd-shim-runc-v2. This matches perfectly what we just saw in *Figure 2.2*!

Now, let's check our running containers interacting with the Docker CLI:

```
[root@fedora34 ~]# docker ps
CONTAINER ID    IMAGE                                    COMMAND
CREATED              STATUS           PORTS             NAMES
7433c0613412    centos/httpd-24-centos7:latest       "container-
entrypoin…"    26 minutes ago    Up 26 minutes    8080/tcp, 8443/
tcp    funny_goodall
78dc2eeb3214    centos/httpd-24-centos7:latest       "container-
entrypoin…"    26 minutes ago    Up 26 minutes    8080/tcp, 8443/
tcp    wonderful_rubin
3901d2600732    centos/httpd-24-centos7:latest       "container-
entrypoin…"    26 minutes ago    Up 26 minutes    8080/tcp, 8443/
tcp    relaxed_heisenberg
```

As you can see, the Docker client confirms that we have three running containers on our system, all started through the runc container runtime, managed by the Containerd system service and configured through a Docker daemon.

Now that we have introduced this new element, Containerd, let's look at it in more depth in the next section.

Containerd architecture

Containerd architecture is composed of several components that are organized in subsystems. Components that link different subsystems are also referred to as modules in the Containerd architecture, as can be seen in the following diagram:

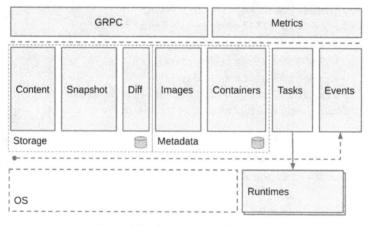

Figure 2.3 – Containerd architecture

The two main subsystems available are the following:

- The bundle service that extracts bundles from disk images
- The runtime service that executes the bundles, creating the runtime containers

The main modules that make the architecture fully functional are the following:

- The `Executor` module, which implements the container runtime that is represented in the preceding architecture as the **Runtimes** block
- The `Supervisor` module, which monitors and reports container state that is part of the **Containers** block in the preceding architecture
- The `Snapshot` module, which manages filesystem snapshots
- The `Events` module, which collects and consumes events
- The `Metrics` module, which exports several metrics via the metrics API

The steps needed by Containerd to place a container in a running state are too complex to be described in this section, but we can sum them up as follows:

1. Pull metadata and content through a **Distribution Controller**.
2. Use the **Bundle Controller** to unpack the retrieved data, creating snapshots that will compose bundles.
3. Execute the container through the bundle just created through the **Runtime Controller**:

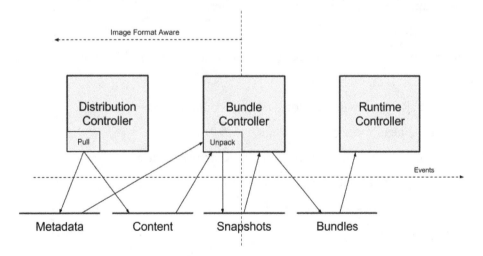

Figure 2.4 – Containerd data flow diagram

In this section, we have described the key features and design principles of the Docker container engine, with its daemon-centric approach. We can now move on to analyze the Podman daemonless architecture.

Podman daemonless architecture

Podman (short for *POD MANager*) is a daemonless container engine that enables users to manage containers, images, and their related resources such as storage volumes or network resources. First-time users installing Podman soon realize that there is no service to start after the installation is complete. No background running daemon is required to run containers with Podman!

Once installed, the Podman binary acts both as a **command-line interface** (**CLI**) and as a container engine that orchestrates the container runtime execution. The following subsections will explore the details of the Podman behavior and building blocks.

Podman commands and REST API

The Podman CLI provides a growing set of commands. The curated list is available at `https://docs.podman.io/en/latest/Commands.html`.

The following list explores a subset of the most commonly used commands:

- `build`: Build an image from a Containerfile or Dockerfile
- `cp`: Copy files/folders between a container and the local filesystem
- `exec`: Run a command in a running container
- `events`: Show Podman events
- `generate`: Generate structured data such as Kubernetes YAML or systemd units
- `images`: List local cached images
- `inspect`: Return low-level information on containers or images
- `kill`: Kill one or more running containers
- `load`: Load an image from a container TAR archive or stdin
- `login`: Log in to a container registry
- `logs`: Fetch the logs of a container
- `pod`: Manage pods

- `ps`: List running containers
- `pull`: Pull an image or a repository from a registry
- `push`: Push an image or a repository to a registry
- `restart`: Restart one or more containers
- `rm`: Remove one or more containers
- `rmi`: Remove one or more images
- `run`: Run a command in a new container
- `save`: Save one or more images to a TAR archive (streamed to stdout by default)
- `start`: Start one or more stopped containers
- `stop`: Stop one or more running containers
- `system`: Manage Podman (disk usage, container migration, REST API services, storage management, and pruning)
- `tag`: Create a `TARGET_IMAGE` tag that refers to `SOURCE_IMAGE`
- `unshare`: Run a command in a modified user namespace
- `volume`: Manage container volumes (list, pruning, creation, inspection)

In the upcoming chapters of the book, we will cover the preceding commands in greater detail and understand how to use them to manage the full container life cycle.

Users who have already worked with Docker will immediately spot the same commands they used to execute with the Docker CLI. Podman CLI commands are compatible with Docker ones to help a smooth transition between the two tools.

Differently from Docker, Podman does not need a running Docker daemon listening on a Unix socket to execute the preceding commands. Users can still choose to run a Podman service and make it listen to a Unix socket to expose native REST APIs.

By running the following command, Podman will create a socket endpoint on a path of preference and listen to API calls:

```
$ podman system service --time 0 unix://tmp/podman.sock
```

If not provided, the default socket endpoint is `unix://run/podman/podman.sock` for rootful services and `unix://run/user/<UID>/podman/podman.sock` for rootless containers.

As a result, users can then make REST API calls to the socket endpoint. The following example queries Podman for the available local images:

```
curl --unix-socket /tmp/podman.sock \ http://d/v3.0.0/libpod/
images/json | jq .
```

The Podman project maintains OpenAPI-compliant documentation of available REST API calls at `https://docs.podman.io/en/latest/_static/api.html`.

The piped `jq` command in the preceding example is useful to produce a more readable JSON-pretty output. We will explore the Podman REST API and systemd socket-based activation in greater detail in the post-installation customization section of *Chapter 3, Running the First Container*. Let's now describe Podman building blocks in greater detail.

Podman building blocks

Podman aims to adhere to open standards as much as possible; therefore, most of the runtime, build, storage, and networking components rely on community projects and standards. The components described in the following list can be seen as the main Podman building blocks:

- The container life cycle is managed with the **libpod** library, already included in the Podman main repository: `https://github.com/containers/podman/tree/main/libpod`.

- The container runtime is based on the OCI specs implemented by OCI-compliant runtimes, such as **crun** and **runc**. We will see in this chapter how container runtimes work and the main difference between the above-mentioned ones.

- At the same time, image management implements the **containers/image** library (`https://github.com/containers/image`). This is a set of Go libraries used both by container engines and container registries.

- Container and image storage is implemented adopting the **containers/storage** library (`https://github.com/containers/storage`), another Go library to manage filesystem layers, container images, and container volumes at runtime.

- Image builds are implemented with Buildah (`https://github.com/containers/buildah`), which is both a binary tool and a library for building OCI images. We will cover Buildah later in this book.

- Container runtime monitoring and communication with the engine is implemented with **Conmon**, a tool for monitoring OCI runtimes, used by both Podman and **CRI-O** (`https://github.com/containers/conmon`).

Container networking support is implemented through the Kubernetes **Container Network Interface** (**CNI**) specs. This also helps shape Podman networking with a plugin-oriented approach. By default, Podman uses the basic `bridge` CNI plugin. An extended list of plugins is available in the following repository: `https://github.com/containernetworking/plugins`.

As stated earlier, Podman orchestrates the container life cycle thanks to the libpod library, described in the next subsection.

The libpod library

Podman core foundations are based on the libpod library, which is also adopted by other open source projects such as CRI-O. This library contains all the necessary logic to orchestrate the container life cycle and we can safely say that the development of this library was the key to the birth of the Podman project as we know it today.

The library is written in Go and is thus accessed as a **Go package** and is intended to implement all the high-level functionalities of the engine. According to the libpod and Podman documentation, its scope includes the following:

- Managing container image format, which includes both OCI and Docker images. This includes the full image life cycle management, from authenticating and pulling from a container registry, and local storage of the image layers and metadata, to the building of new images and pushing to remote registries.

- Container life cycle management – from container creation (with all the necessary preliminary steps involved) and running the container to all the other runtime functionalities such as stop, kill, resume, and delete, process execution on running containers, and logging.

- Managing both simple containers and **pods**, which are groups of sandboxed containers that share namespaces together (notably UTC, IPC, Network, and recently Pid) and are also managed together as a whole.

- Supporting **rootless** containers and pods that can be executed by standard users with no need for privilege escalation.

- Managing container resource isolation. This is achieved at a low level with CGroup but Podman users can interact using CLI options during container execution to manage memory and CPU reservation or limit read/write rate on a storage device.

- Supporting a CLI that can be used as a Docker-compatible alternative. Most Podman commands are the same as in the Docker CLI.

- Providing a Docker-compatible REST API with local Unix sockets (not enabled by default). Libpod REST APIs provide all the functionalities provided by the Podman CLI.

The lidpod package interacts, at a lower level, with container runtimes, Conmon, and packages such as container/storage, container/image, Buildah, and CNI. In the next section, we will focus on the container runtime execution.

The runc and crun OCI container runtimes

As illustrated in the previous chapter, a container engine takes care of the high-level orchestration of the container life cycle, while the low-level actions necessary to create and run the container are delivered by a container runtime.

An industry standard has emerged in the last few years, with the help of the major container environment contributors: the **OCI Runtime Specification**. The full specification is available at `https://github.com/opencontainers/runtime-spec`.

From this repository, the *Runtime and Lifecycle* document provides a full description of how the container runtime should handle the container creation and execution: `https://github.com/opencontainers/runtime-spec/blob/master/runtime.md`.

Runc (`https://github.com/opencontainers/runc`) is currently the most widely adopted OCI container runtime. Its history leads back to 2015, when Docker announced the spin out of all its infrastructure plumbing into a dedicated project called runC.

RunC fully supports Linux containers and OCI runtime specs. The project repository includes the **libcontainer** package, which is a Go package for creating containers with namespaces, cgroups, capabilities, and filesystem access controls. Libcontainer was an independent Docker project before, and when the runC project was created, it was moved inside its main repository for the sake of consistence and clarity.

The libcontainer package defines the inner logic and the low-level system interaction to bootstrap a container from scratch, from the initial isolation of namespaces to the execution as PID 1 of the binary program inside the container itself.

The runtime recalls the libcontainer library to fulfil the following tasks:

- Consume the container mount point and the container metadata provided by Podman
- Interact with the kernel to start the container and execute the isolated process using the `clone()` and `unshare()` syscalls
- Set up CGroup resource reservations
- Set up SELinux Policy, Seccomp, and App Armor rules

Along with running processes, libcontainer handles the initialization of namespaces and file descriptors, the creation of the container rootFS and bind mounts, exporting logs from container processes, managing security restrictions with seccomp, SELinux and AppArmor, and creating and mapping users and groups

The libcontainer architecture is quite a complex topic for this book and obviously needs further investigation to better understand its internals.

For readers interested in viewing the code and understanding Podman internals, the container interface that adheres to the OCI runtime specs is defined in the `https://github.com/opencontainers/runc/blob/master/libcontainer/container.go` source file.

The methods for the Linux OS that implement the interface are defined in `https://github.com/opencontainers/runc/blob/master/libcontainer/container_linux.go`.

The low-level execution of `clone()` and `unshare()` syscall to isolate the process namespaces is handled by the **nsenter** package, more precisely by the `nsexec()` function. This is a C function embedded in the Go code thanks using **cgo**.

The code of `nsexec()` can be found here:

```
https://github.com/opencontainers/runc/blob/master/
libcontainer/nsenter/nsexec.c
```

Along with `runC`, many other container runtimes have been created. An alternative runtime we will discuss in this book is **crun** (`https://github.com/containers/crun`), a fast and low-memory-footprint OCI container runtime fully written in C. The idea behind `crun` was to provide an improved OCI runtime that could leverage the C design approach for a cleaner and lightweight runtime. Since they are both OCI runtimes, `runC` and `crun` can be used interchangeably by a container engine.

For example, in 2019, the Fedora project made a brave move and chose to release Fedora 31 with CGroup V2 as the default (`https://www.redhat.com/sysadmin/fedora-31-control-group-v2`). At the time of this choice, `runC` was not yet capable of managing containers under CGroup V2.

Consequently, the Podman release for Fedora adopted `crun` as the default runtime since it was already capable of managing both CGroup V1 and V2. This switch was almost seamless for end users, who continued to use Podman in the same way with the same commands and behaviors. Later, `runC` finally introduced support for CGroup V2, from v1.0.0-rc93, and can now be used on newer distributions seamlessly.

However, the CGroup topic was not the only differentiator between `runC` and `crun`.

`crun` provides some interesting advantages against `runC`, such as the following:

- **Smaller binary**: A `crun` build is approximately 50 times smaller than a `runC` build.
- **Faster execution**: `crun` is faster on instrumenting the container than `runC` under the same execution conditions.
- **Less memory usage**: `crun` consumes less than half the memory of `runC`. A smaller memory footprint is extremely helpful when dealing with massive container deployments or IoT appliances.

`crun` can also be used as a library and integrated in other OCI-compliant projects. Both `crun` and `runC` provide a CLI but are not meant to be used manually by end users, who are supposed to use a container engine such as Podman or Docker to manage the container life cycle.

How easy is it to switch between the two runtimes in Podman? Let's see the following examples. Both examples run a container using the `--runtime` flag to provide an OCI runtime binary path. The first one runs the container using `runC`:

```
podman --runtime /usr/bin/runc run --rm fedora echo "Hello
World"
```

The second line runs the same container with the `crun` binary:

```
podman --runtime /usr/bin/crun run --rm fedora echo "Hello
World"
```

The examples assume that both runtimes are already installed in the system.

Both `crun` and `runC` support **eBPF** and **CRIU**.

eBPF stands for **Extended Berkeley Packet Filter** and is a kernel-based technology that allows the execution of user-defined programs in the Linux kernel to add extra capabilities to the system without the need to recompile the kernel or load extra modules. All eBPF programs are executed inside a sandbox virtual machine and their execution is secure by design. Today, eBPF is gaining momentum and attracting industry interest, leading to wide adoption in different use cases, most notably networking, security, observability, and tracing.

Checkpoint Restore in Userspace (CRIU) is a piece of software that enables users to freeze a running container and save its state to disk for further resume. Data structures saved in memory are dumped and restored accordingly.

Another important architectural component used by Podman is Conmon, a tool for monitoring container runtime status. Let's investigate this in more detail in the next subsection.

Conmon

We may still have some questions about runtime execution.

How do Podman (the container engine) and `runC/crun` (the OCI container runtime) interact with each other? Which is responsible for launching the container runtime process? Is there a way to monitor the container execution?

Let's introduce the Conmon project (`https://github.com/containers/conmon`). Conmon is a monitoring and communication tool that sits between the container engine and the runtime.

Every time a new container is created, a new instance of Conmon is launched. It detaches from the container manager process and runs daemonized, launching the container runtime as a child process.

If we attach a tracing tool to a Podman container, we can see in the following the order it's written in:

1. The container engine runs the Conmon process, which detaches and daemonizes itself.
2. The Conmon process runs a container runtime instance that starts the container and exits.
3. The Conmon process continues to run to provide a monitoring interface, while the manager/engine process has exited or detached.

The following diagram shows the logical workflow, from Podman execution to the running container:

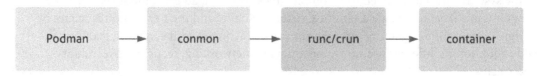

Figure 2.5 – Running a Podman container

On a system with many running containers, users will find many instances of the Conmon process, one for every container created. In other words, Conmon acts as a small, dedicated daemon to the container.

Let's look at the following example, where a simple shell loop is used to create three identical nginx containers:

```
[root@fedora34 ~]# for i in {1..3}; do podman run -d --rm
docker.io/library/nginx; done
592f705cc31b1e47df18f71ddf922ea7e6c9e49217f00d1af8
cf18c8e5557bde
4b1e44f512c86be71ad6153ef1cdcadcdfa8bcfa8574f606a0832
c647739a0a2
4ef467b7d175016d3fa024d8b03ba44b761b9a75ed66b2050de3fe
c28232a8a7
[root@fedora34 ~]# ps aux | grep conmon
root       21974  0.0  0.1  82660   2532
?          Ssl  22:31   0:00 /usr/bin/conmon --api-version 1 -c
592f705cc31b1e47df18f71ddf922ea7e6c9e49217f00d1af8
cf18c8e5557bde -u
592f705cc31b1e47df18f71ddf922ea7e6c9e49217f00d1af8
cf18c8e5557bde -r /usr/bin/crun [..omitted output]
root       22089  0.0  0.1  82660   2548
?          Ssl  22:31   0:00 /usr/bin/conmon --api-version 1 -c
4b1e44f512c86be71ad6153ef1cdcadcdfa8bcfa8574f606a0832
c647739a0a2 -u
4b1e44f512c86be71ad6153ef1cdcadcdfa8bcfa8574f606a0832
c647739a0a2 -r /usr/bin/crun [..omitted output]
root       22198  0.0  0.1  82660   2572
?          Ssl  22:31   0:00 /usr/bin/conmon --api-version 1 -c
4ef467b7d175016d3fa024d8b03ba44b761b9a75ed66b2050de3f
ec28232a8a7 -u
4ef467b7d175016d3fa024d8b03ba44b761b9a75ed66b2050de3f
ec28232a8a7 -r /usr/bin/crun [..omitted output]
```

After running the containers, a simple regular expression pattern applied to the output of the `ps aux` command shows three Conmon process instances.

Even if Podman is not running anymore (since there is no daemon), it is still possible to connect to the Conmon process and attach to the container. At the same time, Conmon exposes console sockets and container logs to log files or the systemd journal.

Conmon is a lightweight project written in C. It also provides Go language bindings to pass config structures between the manager and the runtime.

Rootless containers

One of the most interesting features of Podman is the capability to run rootless containers, which means that users without elevated privileges can run their own containers.

Rootless containers provide better security isolation and let different users run their own container instances independently and, thanks to **fork/exec**, a daemonless approach adopted by Podman, rootless containers are amazingly easy to manage. A rootless container is simply run by the standard user with the usual commands and arguments, as in the following example:

```
$ podman run -d --rm docker.io/library/nginx
```

When this command is issued, Podman creates a new user namespace and maps UIDs between the two namespaces using a **uid_map** file (see `man user_namespaces`). This method allows you to have, for example, a root user inside the container mapped to an ordinary user in the host.

Rootless containers and image data are stored under the user home directory, usually under `$HOME/.local/share/containers/storage`.

Podman manages network connectivity for rootless containers in a different way than rootful containers. An in-depth technical comparison between rootless and rootful containers, especially from the network and security point of view, will be covered later in this book.

After an in-depth analysis of the runtime workflow, it is useful to provide an overview of the OCI image specs used by Podman.

OCI images

Podman and the container/image package implement the **OCI Image Format Specification**. The full specification is available on GitHub at the following link and pairs with the OCI runtime specification: `https://github.com/opencontainers/image-spec`.

An OCI image is made of the following elements:

1. Manifest
2. An image index (optional)
3. An image layout
4. A filesystem layer changeset archive that will be unpacked to create a final filesystem
5. An image configuration document to define layer ordering, as well as application arguments and environments

Let's see in detail what kinds of information and data are managed by the most relevant of the preceding elements.

Manifest

An image manifest specification should provide content-addressable images. The image manifest contains image layers and configurations for a specific architecture and operating system, such as Linux x86_64.

Specification: `https://github.com/opencontainers/image-spec/blob/main/manifest.md`

Image index

An image index is an object that contains a list of manifests related to different architectures (for example, amd64, arm64, or 386) and operating systems, along with custom annotations.

Specification: `https://github.com/opencontainers/image-spec/blob/main/image-index.md`

Image layout

The OCI image layout represents the directory structure of image blobs. The image layout also provides the necessary manifest location references as well as image index (in JSON format) and the image configuration. The image `index.json` contains the reference to the image manifest, stored as a blob in the OCI image bundle.

Specification: `https://github.com/opencontainers/image-spec/blob/main/image-layout.md`

Filesystem layers

Inside an image, one or more layers are applied on top of each other to create a filesystem that the container can use.

At a low level, layers are packaged as TAR archives (with compression options with gzip and zstd). The filesystem layer implements the logic of layers stacking and how the changeset layers (layers containing file changes) are applied.

As described in the previous chapter, a copy-on-write or union filesystem has become a standard to manage stacking in a graph-like approach. To manage layers stacking, Podman uses **overlayfs** by default as a graph driver.

Specification: `https://github.com/opencontainers/image-spec/blob/main/layer.md`

Image configuration

An image configuration defines the image layer composition and the corresponding execution parameters such as entry points, volumes, execution arguments, or environment variables, as well as additional image metadata.

The image JSON holding the configurations is an **immutable** object; changing it means creating a new derived image.

Specification: `https://github.com/opencontainers/image-spec/blob/main/config.md`

The following diagram represents an OCI image implementation, composed of image layer(s), image index, and image configuration:

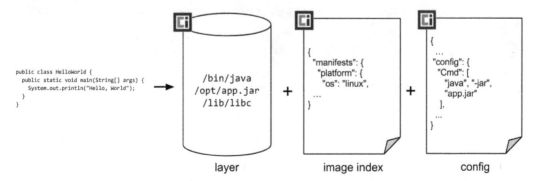

Figure 2.6 – OCI image implementation

Let's inspect a realistic example from a basic, lightweight **alpine** image:

```
# tree alpine/
alpine/
├── blobs
│   └── sha256
│       ├── 03014f0323753134bf6399ffbe26dcd75e89c6a7429adfab
392d64706649f07b
│       ├── 696d33ca1510966c426bdcc0daf05f75990d68c4eb820f615
edccf7b971935e7
│       └──
a0d0a0d46f8b52473982a3c466318f479767577551a53ffc9074
c9fa7035982e
├── index.json
└── oci-layout
```

The directory layout contains an `index.json` file, with the following content:

```
{
  "schemaVersion": 2,
  "manifests": [
    {
      "mediaType": "application/vnd.oci.image.manifest.
v1+json",
      "digest":
"sha256:03014f0323753134bf6399ffbe26dcd75e89c6a7429adfab
392d64706649f07b",
      "size": 348,
      "annotations": {
        "org.opencontainers.image.ref.name": "latest"
      }
    }
  ]
}
```

The index contains a manifests array with only one item inside. The object digest is a SHA256 and corresponds to filename as one of the blobs listed previously. The file is the image manifest and can be inspected:

```
# cat alpine/blobs/
sha256/03014f0323753134bf6399ffbe26dcd75e89c6a7429adfab392
d64706649f07b | jq
{
  "schemaVersion": 2,
  "config": {
    "mediaType": "application/vnd.oci.image.config.v1+json",
    "digest": "sha256:696d33ca1510966c426bdcc0daf05f75990d
68c4eb820f615edccf7b971935e7",
    "size": 585
  },
  "layers": [
    {
      "mediaType": "application/vnd.oci.image.layer.
v1.tar+gzip",
      "digest": "sha256:a0d0a0d46f8b52473982a3c466318f47976
7577551a53ffc9074c9fa7035982e",
      "size": 2814446
    }
  ]
}
```

The manifest contains references to the image configuration and layers. In this particular case, the image has only one layer. Again, their digests correspond to the blob filenames listed before.

The config file shows image metadata, environment variables, and command execution. At the same time, it contains DiffID references to the layers used by the image and image creation information:

```
# cat alpine/blobs/sha256/696d33ca1510966c426bdcc0daf05f75990
d68c4eb820f615edccf7b971935e7 | jq
{
  "created": "2021-08-27T17:19:45.758611523Z",
  "architecture": "amd64",
  "os": "linux",
```

```
   "config": {
     "Env": [
        "PATH=/usr/local/sbin:/usr/local/bin:/usr/sbin:/usr/bin:/
sbin:/bin"
     ],
     "Cmd": [
        "/bin/sh"
     ]
   },
   "rootfs": {
     "type": "layers",
     "diff_ids": [
        "sha256:e2eb06d8af8218cfec8210147357a68b7e13f7c485b991c
288c2d01dc228bb68"
     ]
   },
   "history": [
     {
        "created": "2021-08-27T17:19:45.553092363Z",
        "created_by": "/bin/sh -c #(nop) ADD file:aad4290d27580
cc1a094ffaf98c3ca2fc5d699fe695dfb8e6e9fac
20f1129450 in / "
     },
     {
        "created": "2021-08-27T17:19:45.758611523Z",
        "created_by": "/bin/sh -c #(nop)  CMD [\"/bin/sh\"]",
        "empty_layer": true
     }
   ]
}
```

The image layer is the third blob file. This is a TAR archive that could be exploded and inspected. For space reasons, in this book the example is limited to an inspection of the file type:

```
# file alpine/blobs/sha256/a0d0a0d46f8b52473982a3c466318f47
9767577551a53ffc9074c9fa7035982e
alpine/blobs/sha256/a0d0a0d46f8b52473982a3c466318f479767577
```

```
551a53ffc9074c9fa7035982e: gzip compressed data, original size
modulo 2^32 5865472
```

The result demonstrates that the file is a TAR gzipped archive.

The main differences between Docker and Podman

In the previous sections, we went through the key features of Docker and Podman, looking into the underlying layer, discovering the companion open source projects that made these two tools unique in their container engine role, but now it's time to compare them.

As we saw earlier, the significant difference between the two is that Docker has a daemon-centric approach while Podman instead has a daemonless architecture. The Podman binary acts as CLI as well as a container engine and uses Conmon to orchestrate and monitor the container runtime.

Looking under the hood into the internals of both projects, we will also find many other differences but, in the end, once the container has started, they both leverage OCI standard container runtimes but with some differences: Docker uses `runc` while Podman uses `crun` in most distributions, with some exceptions; for example, it still uses `runc` in the most conservative Red Hat Enterprise Linux 8 with `crun` as an option.

Despite the `crun` performance advantages described in the previous section, it is not the objective of this book to make a detailed performance comparison between the two. Anyway, readers interested in the topic will easily find literature about the performance differences between the two runtimes.

Another big gap that was recently filled by the Docker team was the rootless container. Podman was the first container engine to bring out this excellent feature that increases security and improve the usage of containers in many contexts but, as we mentioned, this feature is now available in Docker too.

But let's go more practical in the next sections, by comparing them side by side through the command line first and then by running a container.

Command-line interface comparison

In this section, we will go through a side-by-side comparison looking at the Docker and Podman CLIs.

Looking at the available commands for both CLIs, it is easy to spot the many similarities. The following table was truncated to improve readability:

Docker	Podman
attach	attach
build	auto-update
commit	build
cp	commit
create	container
diff	cp
events	create
exec	diff
export	events
history	exec
images	export
import	generate
info	healthcheck
inspect	help
kill	history
load	image
login	images
logout	import
logs	info
pause	init
port	inspect
...	...

Table 2.1 – Comparison of Docker and Podman commands

As we stated many times in the preceding section, as well as in the previous chapter, Docker was born in 2013 while Podman only arrived 4 years later in 2017. Podman was built keeping in mind how experienced container administrators were with the most famous container engine available at that time: Docker. For this reason, the Podman development team decided to not change too much the *look and feel* of the command-line tools for improving Docker users' migration to the new-born Podman.

There was a claim, in fact, at the beginning of the distribution of Podman that if you have any existing scripts that run Docker you can create an alias and it should work (`alias docker=podman`). It was also created a package that places a *fake* Docker command under `/usr/bin` that points to *Podman* binary instead. For this reason, if you are a Docker user, you can expect a smooth transition to Podman once you are ready.

Another important point is that the images created with Docker are compatible with the OCI standard, so you can easily migrate or pull again any image you previously used with Docker.

If we take a deep look into the command options available for Podman, you will notice that there are some additional commands that are not present in Docker, while some others are missing.

For example, Podman can manage, along with containers, **pods** (the name Podman is quite telling here). The pod concept was introduced with Kubernetes and represents the smallest execution unit in a Kubernetes cluster.

With Podman, users can create empty pods and then run containers inside them easily using the following command:

```
$ podman pod create --name mypod
$ podman run --pod mypod -d docker.io/library/nginx
```

This is not as easy with Docker, where users must first run a container and then create new ones attaching to the network namespace of the first container.

Podman has additional features that could help users to move their containers in Kubernetes environments. Using the command `podman generate kube`, Podman can create a Kubernetes YAML file for a running container that can be used to create a pod inside a Kubernetes cluster.

Running containers as systemd services is equally easy with the `podman generate systemd` command, which takes a running container or pod and generates a systemd unit file that can be used to automatically run services at system startup.

A notable example: the **OpenStack** project, an open source cloud computing infrastructure, adopted Podman as the default manager for its containerized services when deployed with TripleO. All the services are executed by Podman and orchestrated by systemd in the control plane and compute nodes.

Having checked the surface of these container engines and having looked at their command lines, let's recap the under-the-hood differences in the next section.

Running a container

Running a container in a Docker environment, as we mentioned earlier, consists of using the Docker command-line client to communicate with the Docker daemon that will do the actions required to get the container up and running. Just to summarize the concepts we explained in this chapter, we can take a look the following diagram:

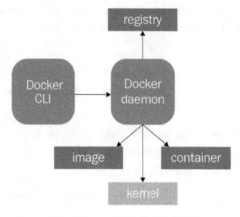

Figure 2.7 – Docker simplified architecture

Podman, instead, interacts directly with the image registry, storage, and with the Linux kernel through the container runtime process (not a daemon), with Conmon as a monitoring process executed between Podman and the OCI runtime, as we can schematize in the following diagram:

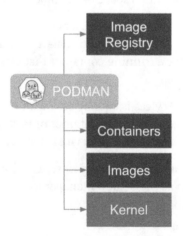

Figure 2.8 – Podman simplified architecture

The core difference between the two architectures is the daemon-centric Docker vision versus the fork/exec approach of Podman.

This book does not get into the pros and cons of the Docker daemon architecture and features. Anyway, we safely can tell that a significant number of Docker users were concerned about this daemon-centric approach for many reasons, for example:

- The daemon could be a single point of failure.

- If for some reason a failure occurs, then there will be orphaned processes.

- The daemon owns all the running containers as child processes.

Despite the architectural differences, and the aliasing solutions described before to easily migrate projects without changing any script, running a container from the command line with Docker or Podman is pretty much the same thing for the end user:

```
$ docker run -d --rm docker.io/library/nginx
$ podman run -d --rm docker.io/library/nginx
```

For the same reason, most of the command-line arguments of CLI commands have been kept as close as possible to the original version in Docker.

Summary

In this chapter, we have discussed the main differences between Podman and Docker, both from architectural and usage points of view. We described the main building blocks of the two container engines and highlighted the different community projects that fuel the Podman project, especially OCI specifications and the runC and crun runtimes.

The purpose of this book is not to debate why and how Podman could be a better choice than Docker. We think that everybody who works with containers should be extremely grateful to the Docker company and community for the great work they did in bringing containers to the masses and freeing them from niche adoption.

At the same time, the evolutionary approach of open source software facilitates the birth of new projects that try to compete to be adopted. Ever since it was born, the Podman project has grown exponentially and gained a wider user base day by day.

Understanding the engine internals is still an important task, anyway. For troubleshooting, performance tuning, or even just curiosity, investing time in understanding how each component relates to each other, reading the code, and testing builds is a smart choice that will pay back someday.

In the next chapters, we will uncover in detail the features and behavior of this great container engine.

Further reading

For more information about the topics covered in this chapter, you can refer to the following:

- `https://developers.redhat.com/blog/2020/09/25/rootless-containers-with-podman-the-basics`
- `https://developers.redhat.com/blog/2020/11/19/transitioning-from-docker-to-podman`
- `https://github.com/opencontainers/runc/blob/master/docs/cgroup-v2.md`
- `https://www.redhat.com/sysadmin/introduction-crun`
- `https://ebpf.io/what-is-ebpf/`

3
Running the First Container

In the previous chapters, we discussed the history of containers, their adoption, and the various technologies that contribute to their spread, while also looking at the main differences between **Docker** and **Podman**.

Now, it's time to start working with real examples: in this chapter, we will learn about how to get Podman up and running on your preferred Linux operating system so that we can start our first container. We will discover the various installation methods, all the prerequisites, and then start a container.

In this chapter, we're going to cover the following main topics:

- Choosing an operating system and installation method
- Preparing your environment
- Running your first container

Technical requirements

Having good technical experience in administering a Linux operating system would be preferable for understanding the key concepts provided in this chapter.

We will go through the main steps of installing new software on various Linux distributions, so having some experience as a Linux sysadmin could be helpful in troubleshooting possible issues during installation.

In addition, some of the theoretical concepts that were explained in the previous chapters could help you understand the procedures described in this chapter.

Choosing an operating system and installation method

Podman is supported on different distributions and operating systems. It is very easy to install, and the various distributions now provide their own maintained packages that can be installed with their specific package managers.

In this section, we will cover the different installation steps for the most common GNU/Linux distributions, as well as on macOS and Windows, despite the focus of this book being on Linux-based environments.

As a bonus topic, we will also learn how to build Podman directly from source.

Choosing between Linux distributions and another OS

The choice between the different distributions of the GNU/Linux operating system is something that is dictated by the user's preferences and needs, which are usually influenced by several factors that are outside the scope of this book.

Many advanced users today choose Linux distributions as their main operating systems. However, there is a large quota, especially among developers, who stick to macOS as their standard operating system. Microsoft Windows still retains the largest market share on desktop workstations and laptops.

Today, we have a huge ecosystem of Linux distributions that have evolved from a smaller subset of core, historical distributions such as Debian, Fedora, Red Hat Enterprise Linux, Gentoo, Arch, and openSUSE. Specialized websites such as **DistroWatch** (https://distrowatch.com) keep track of the many releases of Linux and BSD-based distributions.

Despite running a Linux kernel, the various distributions have different architectural approaches for userspace behavior, such as filesystem structure, libraries, or packaging systems used to deliver software releases.

Another significant difference is related to security and mandatory access control subsystems: for example, Fedora, CentOS, Red Hat Enterprise Linux, and all the derivates lean on **SELinux** as their mandatory access control subsystem. On the other hand, Debian, Ubuntu, and their derivates are based on a similar solution called **AppArmor**.

Podman interacts with both SELinux and AppArmor to provide better container isolation, but the underlying interfaces are different.

> **Important Note**
> All this book's examples and source code has been written and tested using **Fedora Workstation 34** as the reference OS.

Those of you who want to reproduce an environment as close as possible to the book in their lab have different options:

- Use the Fedora 34 Vagrant Box (`https://app.vagrantup.com/fedora/boxes/34-cloud-base`). **Vagrant** is a software solution developed by **Hashicorp** to create fast, lightweight VMs, especially suitable for development use. See `https://www.vagrantup.com/` for further details about Vagrant and how to use it on your operating system of choice.

- Directly download the cloud image (`https://alt.fedoraproject.org/cloud/`) and create instances on the public/private cloud or just deploy it on a hypervisor of your choice.

- Manually install Fedora Workstation. In this case, the official installation guide (`https://docs.fedoraproject.org/en-US/fedora/f34/install-guide/`) provides detailed instructions on deploying the OS.

Running instances on public clouds is the best option for users who are not able to run virtual machines locally.

Providers such as Amazon Web Services, Google Cloud Platform, Microsoft Azure, and DigitalOcean also offer ready-to-use Fedora-based cloud instances with low monthly prices for smaller sizes.

Prices can vary in time and across tiers and keeping track of them is beyond the purpose of this book. Almost all providers offer free plans for learning or basic use, with small/micro tiers at very low prices.

Containers are Linux-based, and the different container engines and runtimes interact with the Linux kernel and libraries to operate. Windows has recently introduced support for native containers with an approach to isolation that's quite close to the Linux namespace concepts described previously. However, only Windows-based images can run natively and not all container engines support native execution.

The same considerations are valid for macOS: its architecture is not based on Linux but on a hybrid Mach/BSD kernel called **XNU**. For this reason, it does not offer the Linux kernel features necessary to run containers natively.

For both Windows and macOS, a virtualization layer that abstracts the Linux machine is necessary to run native Linux containers.

Podman offers remote client functions for Windows and macOS, enabling users to connect to a local or remote Linux box.

Windows users can also benefit from an alternative approach based on the **Windows Subsystem for Linux (WSL) 2.0**, a compatibility layer that runs a lightweight VM to expose Linux kernel interfaces along with Linux userspace binaries, thanks to Hyper-V virtualization support.

The following sections will cover the necessary steps for installing Podman on the most popular Linux distributions, as well as macOS and Windows.

Installing Podman on Fedora

Fedora packages are maintained by its wide community and managed with the **DNF** package manager. To install Podman, run the following command from a terminal:

```
# dnf install -y podman
```

This command installs Podman and configures the environment with config files (covered in the next section). It also installs systemd units to provide additional features such as REST API services or container auto-updates.

Installing Podman on CentOS

Podman can be installed on CentOS 7, CentOS 8, and CentOS Stream (https://www.centos.org/). Users installing on CentOS 7 must have the **Extras** repository enabled, while users installing on CentOS 8 and Stream must have the Podman package available from the already enabled **AppStream** repository.

To install Podman, run the following command from a terminal:

```
# yum install -y podman
```

Like in Fedora, this command installs Podman and all its dependencies, including config files and `systemd` unit files.

Installing Podman on RHEL

To install Podman on **Red Hat Enterprise Linux** (**RHEL**) (`https://www.redhat.com/en/technologies/linux-platforms/enterprise-linux`), users should follow two different procedures on RHEL 7 and RHEL 8.

On RHEL 7, users must enable the extra channel and then install the Podman package:

```
# subscription-manager repos \
--enable=rhel-7-server-extras-rpms
# yum -y install podman
```

On RHEL 8, the Podman package is available on a dedicated module called **container-tools**. Modules are custom sets of RPM packages that can be organized in streams with independent release cycles:

```
# yum module enable -y container-tools:rhel8
# yum module install -y container-tools:rhel8
```

The `container-tools` module installs, along with Podman, two useful tools, both of which will be covered later in this book:

- **Skopeo**, a tool for managing OCI images and registries
- **Buildah**, a specialized tool for building custom OCI images from Dockerfiles and from scratch

(Not) Installing Podman on Fedora CoreOS and Fedora Silverblue

The title of this subsection is a bit of a joke. The reality is that Podman is already installed on both distributions and is a crucial tool for running containerized workloads.

The **Fedora CoreOS** and **Fedora SilverBlue** distributions are immutable, atomic operating systems aimed to be used on server/cloud and desktop environments, respectively.

Fedora CoreOS (`https://getfedora.org/en/coreos/`) is the upstream of Red Hat CoreOS, the operating system used to run Red Hat OpenShift and the base OS of **OpenShift Kubernetes Distribution** (**OKD**), the community-based Kubernetes distribution used as the upstream of Red Hat OpenShift.

Fedora Silverblue (`https://silverblue.fedoraproject.org/`) is a desktop-focused immutable operating system that aims to provide a stable and comfortable desktop user experience, especially for developers working with containers.

So, on both Fedora CoreOS and Fedora Silverblue, just open a terminal and run Podman.

Installing Podman on Debian

The Podman package is available on **Debian** (`https://www.debian.org/`) since version 11, codename Bullseye (named after the famous toy horse from the Toy Story 2 and 3 movies).

Debian uses the `apt-get` package handling utility to install and upgrade system packages.

To install Podman on a Debian system, run the following command from the terminal:

```
# apt-get -y install podman
```

The preceding command installs the Podman binary and its dependencies, along with its config files, `systemd` units, and man pages.

Installing Podman on Ubuntu

Being built on Debian, **Ubuntu** (`https://ubuntu.com/`) behaves in an analogous way for package management. To install Podman on Ubuntu 20.10 or later, run the following commands:

```
# apt-get -y update
# apt-get -y install podman
```

These two commands update the system packages and then install the Podman binaries and related dependencies.

Installing Podman on openSUSE

The **openSUSE** distribution (`https://www.opensuse.org/`) is backed by SUSE and is available in two different flavors – the rolling release known as **Tumbleweed,** and the LTS distribution known as **Leap**. Podman is available in the openSUSE repositories and can be installed with the following command:

```
# zypper install podman
```

The Zypper package manager will download and install all the necessary packages and dependencies.

Installing Podman on Gentoo

Gentoo (`https://www.gentoo.org/`) is a clever distribution that is characterized by building installed packages directly on the target machine with the optional extra user customizations. To achieve this, it uses the **Portage** package manager, inspired by FreeBSD ports.

To install Podman on Gentoo, run the following command:

```
# emerge app-emulation/podman
```

The `emerge` utility will download and automatically build the Podman sources on the system.

Installing Podman on Arch Linux

Arch Linux (`https://archlinux.org/`) is a rolling Linux distribution that shines for being highly customizable. It uses the **pacman** package manager to install and update packages from official and users' custom repositories.

To install Podman on Arch Linux and derivate distributions, run the following command from the terminal:

```
# pacman -S podman
```

By default, Podman's installation on Arch Linux does not permit rootless containers. To enable them, follow the official Arch wiki instructions: `https://wiki.archlinux.org/title/Podman#Rootless_Podman`.

Installing Podman on Raspberry Pi OS

The famous Raspberry Pi single-board computer has achieved enormous success among developers, makers, and hobbyists.

It runs the Raspberry Pi OS (`https://www.raspberrypi.org/software/operating-systems/#raspberry-pi-os-32-bit`), which is based on Debian.

Podman's arm64 build is available and can be installed by following the same steps described previously for the Debian distribution.

Installing Podman on macOS

Apple users who develop and run Linux containers can install and use Podman as a remote client, while the containers are executed on a remote Linux box. The Linux machine can also be a VM that's executed on macOS and directly managed by Podman.

To install Podman using the Homebrew package manager, run the following command from the terminal:

```
$ brew install podman
```

To initialize the VM running the Linux box, run the following commands:

```
$ podman machine init
$ podman machine start
```

Alternatively, users can create and connect to an external Linux host.

Another valid approach on macOS to creating fast, lightweight VMs for development use is Vagrant. When the Vagrant machine is created, users can manually or automatically provision additional software such as Podman and start using the customized instance using the remote client.

Installing Podman on Windows

To run Podman as a remote client, simply download and install the latest release from the GitHub releases page (`https://github.com/containers/podman/releases/`). Extract the archive in a suitable location and edit the TOML-encoded `containers.conf` file to configure a remote URI for the Linux machine or pass additional options.

The following code snippet shows an example configuration:

```
[engine]
remote_uri= " ssh://root@10.10.1.9:22/run/podman/podman.sock"
```

The remote Linux machine exposes Podman on a UNIX socket managed by a `systemd` unit. We will cover this topic in greater detail later in this book.

To run Podman on WSL 2.0, users must first install a Linux distribution from the Microsoft Store on their Windows host. There is a variety of available distributions under the Microsoft catalog.

The following example is based on Ubuntu 20.10:

```
# apt-get -y install podman
# mkdir -p /etc/containers
# echo -e "[registries.search]\nregistries = \
['docker.io', 'quay.io']" | tee \ /etc/containers/registries.
conf
```

The preceding commands install the latest Podman stable release and configure the /etc/containers/registries.conf file to provide a registries whitelist.

After its installation, some minor customizations are necessary to adapt it to the WSL 2.0 environment:

```
# cp /usr/share/containers/libpod.conf /etc/containers
# sed -i 's/ cgroup_manager = "systemd"/ cgroup_manager =
"cgroupfs"/g' /etc/containers/libpod.conf
# sed -i 's/ events_logger = "journald"/ events_logger =
"file"/g' /etc/containers/libpod.conf
```

The preceding command configures logging and CGroup management to successfully run rootful containers in the subsystem.

Building Podman from source

Building an application from source has many advantages: users can inspect and customize code before building, cross-compile for different architectures, or selectively build only a subset of binaries. It is also a great learning opportunity to get into the project's structure and understand its evolution. Last but not least, building from source lets the users get the latest development versions with cool new features, bugs included.

The following steps assume that the building machine is a Fedora distribution. First, we must install the necessary dependencies needed to compile Podman:

```
# dnf install -y \
  btrfs-progs-devel \
  conmon \
  containernetworking-plugins \
  containers-common \
  crun \
  device-mapper-devel \
  git \
```

```
    glib2-devel \
    glibc-devel \
    glibc-static \
    go \
    golang-github-cpuguy83-md2man \
    gpgme-devel \
    iptables \
    libassuan-devel \
    libgpg-error-devel \
    libseccomp-devel \
    libselinux-devel \
    make \
    pkgconfig
```

This command will take a while to install all the packages and their cascading dependencies.

When the installation is complete, choose a working directory and clone the Podman repository using the git command:

```
$ git clone https://github.com/containers/podman.git
```

This command will clone the entire repository in the working directory.

Change to the project directory and start the build:

```
$ cd podman
$ make package-install
```

The make package-install command compiles the source code, builds the RPM files, and installs the packages locally. Remember that the RPM format is associated with Fedora/CentOS/RHEL distributions and managed by the dnf and yum package managers.

The build process will take a few minutes to complete. To test the successful installation of the packages, simply run the following code:

```
$ podman version
Version:      4.0.0-dev
API Version:  4.0.0-dev
Go Version:   go1.16.6
Git Commit:   cffc747fccf38a91be5cd106d2e507afaaa23e14
```

```
Built:          Sat Aug  4 00:00:00 2018
OS/Arch:        linux/amd64
```

Sometimes, it is useful to build the binaries on a dedicated build host and then deploy them on other machines, using either package managers or simple archives. To only build the binaries, run the following command:

```
$ make
```

At the end of the build, the binaries will be available under the bin/ folder. To install the compiled binaries and config files locally by simply copying them into the target directories defined in the Makefile, run the following command:

```
$ make install
```

To create a binary release similar to the .tar.gz archive, which is available on the GitHub release page, run the following command:

```
$ make podman-release.tar.gz
```

Bonus tip: Building a different version is very easy – just switch to the tag of the target release using the git command. For example, to build v3.3.1, use the following command:

```
$ git checkout v3.3.1
```

In this section, we learned how to install binary releases of Podman on different distributions using their respective package managers. We also learned how to install the Podman remote client on macOS and Windows, along with Windows WSL 2.0 mode. We closed this section by showing you how to build from source.

In the next section, we will learn how to configure Podman for the first run by preparing the system environment.

Preparing your environment

Once the Podman packages have been installed, Podman is ready to be used *out of the box*. However, some minor customizations can be useful to provide better interoperability with external registries or to customize runtime behaviors.

Customizing the container registries search list

Podman searches for and downloads images from a list of trusted container registries. The `/etc/containers/registries.conf` file is a TOML config file that can be used to customize whitelisted registries that are allowed to be searched and used as image sources, as well as registry mirroring and insecure registries without TLS termination.

In this config file, the `unqualified-search-registries` key is populated with an array of unqualified registries with no specification regarding images repositories and tags.

On a Fedora system, with a new installation of Podman, this key has the following content:

```
unqualified-search-registries = ["registry.fedoraproject.org",
 "registry.access.redhat.com", "docker.io", "quay.io"]
```

Users can add or remove registries from this array to let Podman search and pull from them.

> **Important Note**
>
> Be very cautious when adding registries and use only trusted registries to avoid pulling images containing malicious code.

The default list is adequate to search for and run all the book examples. Those of you who are already running private registries can try to add them to the unqualified search registries array.

Since registries are both private and public, please keep in mind that private registries usually require additional authentication to be accessed. This can be accomplished with the `podman login` command, which will be covered later in this book.

If the `$HOME/.config/containers/registries.conf` file is found in the user home, it overrides the `/etc/containers/registries.conf` file. In this way, different users on the same system will be able to run Podman with their custom registry whitelists and mirrors.

Optional – enable socket-based services

This is an optional step and, in the absence of specific needs, this section's contents can be safely skipped.

As we mentioned previously, Podman is a daemonless container manager that needs no background service to run containers. However, users may need to interact with the Libpod APIs exposed by Podman, especially when migrating from a Docker-based environment.

Podman can expose its APIs using a UNIX socket (default behavior) or a TCP socket. The latter option is less secure because it makes Podman accessible from the outside world, but it is necessary in some cases, such as when it should be accessed by a Podman client on a Windows or macOS workstation.

> **Important Note**
> Be careful when running the API service using a TCP endpoint on a machine exposed to the internet since the service will be globally accessible.

The following command exposes the Podman APIs on a UNIX socket:

```
$ sudo podman system service --time=0 \
  unix:///run/podman/podman.sock
```

After running this command, users can connect to the API service.

Having to run this command on a terminal window is not a handy approach. Instead, the best approach is to use a **systemd socket** (see man systemd.socket).

Socket units in systemd are special kinds of service activators: when a request reaches the pre-defined endpoint of the socket, systemd immediately spawns the homonymous service.

When Podman is installed, the podman.socket and podman.service unit files are created. podman.socket has the following content:

```
# cat /usr/lib/systemd/system/podman.socket
[Unit]
Description=Podman API Socket
Documentation=man:podman-system-service(1)
[Socket]
ListenStream=%t/podman/podman.sock
SocketMode=0660


[Install]
WantedBy=sockets.target
```

The `ListenStream` key holds the relative path of the socket, which is expanded to `/run/podman/podman.sock`:

The podman.service has the following content:

```
# cat /usr/lib/systemd/system/podman.service
[Unit]
Description=Podman API Service
Requires=podman.socket
After=podman.socket
Documentation=man:podman-system-service(1)
StartLimitIntervalSec=0

[Service]
Type=exec
KillMode=process
Environment=LOGGING="--log-level=info"
ExecStart=/usr/bin/podman $LOGGING system service

[Install]
WantedBy=multi-user.target
```

The `ExecStart=` field indicates the command to be launched by the service, which is the same `podman system service` command we showed previously.

The `Requires=` field indicates that the `podman.service` unit needs `podman.socket` to be activated.

So, what happens when we enable and start the `podman.socket` unit? `systemd` handles the socket and waits for a connection to the socket endpoint. When this event happens, it immediately starts the `podman.service` unit. After a period of inactivity, the service is stopped again.

To enable and start the socket unit, run the following command:

```
# systemctl enable --now podman.socket
```

We can test the results with a simple `curl` command:

```
# curl --unix-socket /run/podman/podman.sock \
  http://d/v3.0.0/libpod/info
```

The printed output will be a JSON payload that contains the container engine configuration.

What happened when we hit the URL? Under the hood, the service unit was immediately started and triggered by the socket when the connection was issued. Some of you may have noticed a slight delay (in the order of a 1/10th of a second) the very first time the command was executed.

After 5 seconds of inactivity, `podman.service` deactivates again. This is due to the default behavior of the `podman system service` command, which runs for 5 seconds only by default unless the `-time` option is passed to provide a different timeout (a value of 0 means forever).

Optional – customize Podman's behavior

Podman's default configuration works out of the box for most use cases, but its configuration is highly flexible. The following configuration files are available for customizing its behavior:

- `containers.conf`: This TOML-formatted file holds Podman runtime configurations, as well as search paths for conmon and container runtime binaries. It is installed by default under the `/usr/share/containers/` path and can be overridden by the `/etc/containers/containers.conf` and `$HOME/.config/containers/containers.conf` files for system-wide and user-wide settings, respectively.

  This file can be used to customize the behavior of the engine. Users can influence how the container is created and its life cycle by customizing settings such as logging, DNS resolution, environment variables, shared memory usage, Cgroup management, and many others.

  For a full list of settings, check out the related man page, which was installed along with the Podman package. (`man containers.conf`)

- `storage.conf`: This TOML-formatted file is used to customize the storage settings that are used by the container engine. In particular, this file enables you to customize the default storage driver, as well as the read/write directory of the container storage (also known as the graph root), which is an additional driver storage option. By default, the driver is set to **overlay**.

  The default path of this file is `/usr/share/containers/storage.conf` and overrides can be found or created under `/etc/containers/storage.conf` for system-wide customizations.

User-scoped configurations that impact rootless containers can be found under `$XDG_CONFIG_HOME/containers/storage.conf` or `$HOME/.config/containers/storage.conf`.

- `mounts.conf`: This file defines the volume mounts that should be automatically mounted inside a container when it is started. This is useful, for example, to automatically pass secrets such as keys and certificates inside a container.

  It can be found under `/usr/share/containers/mounts.conf` and overridden by a file located at `/etc/containers/mounts.conf`.

  In rootless mode, the override file can be placed under `$HOME/.config/containers/mounts.conf`.

- `seccomp.json`: This is a JSON file that lets users customize the allowed `syscalls` that a process inside a container can perform and define the blocked ones at the same time. This topic will be covered again in *Chapter 11, Securing Containers*, which will provide a deeper understanding of the security constraints of containers.

  The default path for this file is `/usr/share/containers/seccomp.json`. The seccomp man page (`man seccomp`) provides an overview of how seccomp works on a Linux system.

- `policy.json`: This is a JSON file that defines how Podman will perform signature verification. The default path of this file is `/etc/containers/policy.json` and can be overridden by the user-scoped `$HOME/.config/containers/policy.json`.

  This config file accepts three kinds of policies:

  - **insecureAcceptAnything**: Accept any image from the specified registry.

  - **reject**: Reject any image from the specified registry.

  - **signedBy**: Accept only images signed by a specific, known entity.

  The default configuration is to accept every image (the `insecureAcceptAnything` policy), but it can be modified to pull only trusted images that can be verified by a signature. Users can define custom GPG keys to verify the signatures and the identity that signed them. For extra details about the possible policies and configuration examples, please refer to the related man page (`man containers-policy.json`).

In this section, we discussed some basic configurations of Podman that are useful to know from when Podman is first installed. In the next section, we will cover our first container execution examples.

Running your first container

Now, it's time to finally run our first container.

In the previous section, we uncovered how to install Podman on our favorite Linux distribution, as well as what's included in the base packages once installed. Now, we can start using our daemonless container engine.

Running containers in Podman is handled through the `podman run` command, which accepts many options for controlling the behavior of the just ran container, its isolation, its communication, its storage, and so on.

The easiest and shortest Podman command for running a brand-new container is as follows:

```
$ podman run <imageID>
```

We have to replace the `imageID` string with the image name/location/tag we want to run. If the image is not present in the cache or we have not downloaded it before, Podman will pull the image for us from the respective container registry.

Interactive and pseudo-tty

To introduce this command and its options, let's start simple and run the following command:

```
$ podman run -i -t fedora /bin/bash
Resolved "fedora" as an alias (/etc/containers/registries.
conf.d/000-shortnames.conf)
Trying to pull registry.fedoraproject.org/fedora:latest...
Getting image source signatures
Copying blob ecfb9899f4ce done
Copying config 37e5619f4a done
Writing manifest to image destination
Storing signatures
[root@ec444ad299ab /]#
```

Let's see what Podman did once we executed the previous command:

1. It recognized the image's name, `fedora`, as an alias for the latest Fedora container image.

2. It then realized that the image was missing from the local cache because it was the first time that we tried to run it.

3.　It pulled down the image from the right registry. It chose the Fedora Project registry because it matched the aliases contained in the registries' configurations.

4.　Finally, it started the container and presented us with an interactive shell, executing the Bash shell program that we requested.

The previous command prompted an interactive shell thanks to the two options that we can analyze, as follows:

- `--tty, -t`: With this option, Podman allocates a **pseudo-tty** (see `man pty`) and attaches it to the container's standard input.

- `--interactive, -i`: With this option, Podman keeps `stdin` open and ready to be attached to the previous pseudo-tty.

As stated in the previous chapters, when a container is created, the isolated processes inside it will run on a writable root filesystem, as a result of a layered overlay.

This allows any process to write files, but don't forget that they will last until the container is running, as containers are ephemeral by default.

Now, you can execute any command and check its output in the console we just brought up:

```
[root@ec444ad299ab /]# dnf install -y iputils iproute
Last metadata expiration check: 0:01:50 ago on Mon Sep 13
08:54:20 2021.
Dependencies resolved.
================================================================
================================================================
=================================================
Package                                          Architecture
Version                                          Repository
Size
================================================================
================================================================
=================================================

Installing:
iproute                                                x86_64
5.10.0-2.fc34                                          fedora
679 k
iputils                                                x86_64
20210202-2.fc34                                        fedora
170 k
```

```
Installing dependencies:
...
[root@ec444ad299ab /]# ip r
default via 10.0.2.2 dev tap0
10.0.2.0/24 dev tap0 proto kernel scope link src 10.0.2.100
[root@ec444ad299ab /]# ping -c2 10.0.2.2
PING 10.0.2.2 (10.0.2.2) 56(84) bytes of data.
64 bytes from 10.0.2.2: icmp_seq=1 ttl=255 time=0.030 ms
64 bytes from 10.0.2.2: icmp_seq=2 ttl=255 time=0.200 ms

--- 10.0.2.2 ping statistics ---
2 packets transmitted, 2 received, 0% packet loss, time 1034ms
rtt min/avg/max/mdev = 0.030/0.115/0.200/0.085 ms
```

As you can see, in the previous example, we just installed two packages for inspecting the container's network configuration and then executing a ping to the default router that's assigned to the virtual networking of our running container. Again, if we stop this container, any changes will be lost.

To exit this interactive shell, we can just press *Ctrl + D* or execute the exit command. By doing this, the container will be terminated because the main running process we requested to execute (/bin/bash) will stop!

Now, let's look at some other nice and useful options we can use with the podman run command.

Detaching from a running container

As we learned previously, Podman gives us the chance to attach an interactive shell to our running container. However, we will soon discover that this is not the preferred way to run our containers.

Once a container has been started, we can easily detach from it, even if we start it with an interactive tty attached:

```
$ podman run -i -t registry.fedoraproject.org/f29/httpd
Trying to pull registry.fedoraproject.org/f29/httpd:latest...
Getting image source signatures
Copying blob aaf5ad2e1aa3 done
Copying blob 7692efc5f81c done
```

```
Copying blob d77ff9f653ce done

Copying config 25c76f9dcd done

Writing manifest to image destination

Storing signatures

=> sourcing 10-set-mpm.sh ...

=> sourcing 20-copy-config.sh ...

=> sourcing 40-ssl-certs.sh ...

AH00558: httpd: Could not reliably determine the server's fully
qualified domain name, using 10.0.2.100. Set the 'ServerName'
directive globally to suppress this message

[Tue Sep 14 09:26:05.691906 2021] [ssl:warn] [pid 1:tid
140416655523200] AH01882: Init: this version of mod_ssl was
compiled against a newer library (OpenSSL 1.1.1b FIPS  26 Feb
2019, version currently loaded is OpenSSL 1.1.1 FIPS  11 Sep
2018) - may result in undefined or erroneous behavior

[Tue Sep 14 09:26:05.692610 2021] [ssl:warn] [pid 1:tid
140416655523200] AH01909: 10.0.2.100:8443:0 server certificate
does NOT include an ID which matches the server name

AH00558: httpd: Could not reliably determine the server's fully
qualified domain name, using 10.0.2.100. Set the 'ServerName'
directive globally to suppress this message

[Tue Sep 14 09:26:05.752028 2021] [ssl:warn] [pid 1:tid
140416655523200] AH01882: Init: this version of mod_ssl was
compiled against a newer library (OpenSSL 1.1.1b FIPS  26 Feb
2019, version currently loaded is OpenSSL 1.1.1 FIPS  11 Sep
2018) - may result in undefined or erroneous behavior

[Tue Sep 14 09:26:05.752806 2021] [ssl:warn] [pid 1:tid
140416655523200] AH01909: 10.0.2.100:8443:0 server certificate
does NOT include an ID which matches the server name

[Tue Sep 14 09:26:05.752933 2021] [lbmethod_heartbeat:notice]
[pid 1:tid 140416655523200] AH02282: No slotmem from mod_
heartmonitor

[Tue Sep 14 09:26:05.755334 2021] [mpm_event:notice] [pid 1:tid
140416655523200] AH00489: Apache/2.4.39 (Fedora) OpenSSL/1.1.1
configured -- resuming normal operations

[Tue Sep 14 09:26:05.755346 2021] [core:notice] [pid 1:tid
140416655523200] AH00094: Command line: 'httpd -D FOREGROUND'
```

What now? To detach from our running container, we just need to press these special keyboard shortcuts: *Ctrl + P*, *Ctrl + Q*. With this sequence, we will return to our shell prompt while the container will keep running.

To recover our detached container's `tty`, we must get the list of running containers:

```
$ podman ps
CONTAINER ID   IMAGE
COMMAND                  CREATED        STATUS          PORTS
NAMES
685a339917e7   registry.fedoraproject.org/f29/httpd:latest    /
usr/bin/run-http...   3 minutes ago   Up 3 minutes ago
clever_zhukovsky
```

We will explore this command in more detail in the next chapter, but for the moment, just take note of `Container ID` and then execute the following command to re-attach to the previous `tty`:

```
$ podman attach 685a339917e7
```

Note that we can easily start a container in *detached* mode by simply adding the `-d` option to `podman run`, like this:

```
$ podman run -d -i -t registry.fedoraproject.org/f29/httpd
```

In the next section, we'll learn how to use the detach option for special purposes.

Network port publishing

As we mentioned in the previous chapters, Podman, like any other container engine, attaches a virtual network to a container in a running state that has been isolated from the original host network. For this reason, if we want to easily reach our container or even expose it outside our host network, we need to instruct Podman to do port mapping.

The Podman `-p` option publishes a container's port to the host:

```
-p=ip:hostPort:containerPort
```

Both `hostPort` and `containerPort` could be a range of ports, and if the host IP is not set or it is set to `0.0.0.0`, then the port will be bound to all the IP addresses of the host.

If we take back the command we used in the previous section, it becomes the following:

```
$ podman run -p 8080:8080 -d -i -t \ registry.fedoraproject.
org/f29/httpd
```

Now, we can take note of what `Container ID` has been assigned to our running container:

```
$ podman ps
CONTAINER ID   IMAGE
COMMAND            CREATED           STATUS           PORTS
NAMES
fc9d97642801   registry.fedoraproject.org/f29/httpd:latest   /
usr/bin/run-http... 10 minutes ago  Up 10 minutes ago
0.0.0.0:8080->8080/tcp  confident_snyder
```

Then, we can look at the port mapping we just defined:

```
$ podman port fc9d97642801
8080/tcp -> 0.0.0.0:8080
```

Next, we can test whether this port mapping works using `curl`, an easy-to-use HTTP web client. Alternatively, you can point your favorite web browser to the same URL, as follows:

```
$ curl -s 127.0.0.1:8080 | head
  % Total    % Received % Xferd  Average Speed   Time     Time
Time  Current
                                 Dload  Upload   Total    Spent
Left  Speed
100  <!DOCTYPE html PUBLIC "-//W3C//DTD XHTML 1.1//EN" "http://
www.w3.org/TR/xhtml11/DTD/xhtml11.dtd">
4
6<html xmlns="http://www.w3.org/1999/xhtml" xml:lang="en"
lang="en">
5    <head>
0        <title>Test Page for the Apache HTTP Server on
Fedora</title>
         <meta http-equiv="Content-Type" content="text/html;
charset=UTF-8" />
         <style type="text/css">
1            /*<![CDATA[*/
0            body {
0                background-color: #fff;
```

Before concluding this chapter, let's take a look at other interesting options that could be useful for managing configuration and container behavior at runtime.

Configuration and environment variables

The `podman run` command has tons of options for letting us configure the container behavior at runtime – we are talking about around 120 options at the time of writing this book.

For example, we have an option for changing the time zone of our running containers; that is, `--tz`:

```
$ date
Tue Sep 14 17:44:59 CEST 2021
$ podman run --tz=Asia/Shanghai fedora date
Tue Sep 14 23:45:11 CST 2021
```

We can change the DNS of our brand-new container with the `--dns` option:

```
$ podman run --dns=1.1.1.1 fedora cat /etc/resolv.conf
search lan
nameserver 1.1.1.1
```

We can also add a host to the `/etc/hosts` file to override a local internal address:

```
$ podman run --add-host=my.server.local:192.168.1.10 \
fedora cat /etc/hosts
127.0.0.1    localhost localhost.localdomain localhost4
localhost4.localdomain4
::1          localhost localhost.localdomain localhost6
localhost6.localdomain6
192.168.1.10 my.server.local
```

We can even add an HTTP proxy to let our container use a proxy for HTTP requests. The default Podman behavior is to pass many environment variables from the host, some of which are `http_proxy`, `https_proxy`, `ftp_proxy`, and `no_proxy`.

On the other hand, we can also define custom environment variables that we can pass to our container thanks to the `–env` option:

```
$ podman run --env MYENV=podman fedora printenv
PATH=/usr/local/sbin:/usr/local/bin:/usr/sbin:/usr/bin:/sbin:/
bin
TERM=xterm
container=oci
DISTTAG=f34container
```

```
FGC=f34
MYENV=podman
HOME=/root
HOSTNAME=93f2541180d2
```

Adding and using environment variables with our containers is a best practice for passing configuration parameters to the application and influencing the service's behavior from the operating system host. As we saw in *Chapter 1, Introduction to Container Technology*, containers are immutable and ephemeral by default. So, for this reason, we should leverage environment variables, as we did in the preceding example, to configure a container at runtime.

Summary

In this chapter, we started playing around with Podman's basic commands, we learned how to run a container by looking at the most interesting options available, and we are now ready to move on to the next level: container management. To work as a system administrator in the container world, we must understand and learn about the management commands that let us inspect and check the health of our running containerized services; that's what we saw in this chapter.

In the next chapter, which is deeply focused on container management, we are going to learn how to manage image and container life cycles with Podman. We will learn how to inspect and extract logs from running containers and will also introduce pods, how to create them, and how to run containers within them.

Further reading

For more information about the topics that were covered in this chapter, you can refer to the following resources:

- Installing Podman on MacOS: `https://podman.io/blogs/2021/09/06/podman-on-macs.html`

- Installing Podman on Windows: `https://www.redhat.com/sysadmin/podman-windows-wsl2`

- Managing container registries: `https://www.redhat.com/sysadmin/manage-container-registries`

- Podman API documentation: `https://docs.podman.io/en/latest/_static/api.html`

- Systemd socker manual: `https://www.freedesktop.org/software/systemd/man/systemd.socket.html`

- Podman and seccomp profiles: `https://podman.io/blogs/2019/10/15/generate-seccomp-profiles.html`

4

Managing Running Containers

In the previous chapter, we learned how to set up the environment to run containers with Podman, covering binary installation for the major distributions, system configuration files, and a first example container run to verify that our setup was correct. This chapter will offer a more detailed overview of container execution, how to manage and inspect running containers, and how to group containers in pods. This chapter is important for gaining the right knowledge and expertise to start our experience as a system administrator for container technologies.

In this chapter, we're going to cover the following main topics:

- Managing container images
- Operations with running containers
- Inspecting container information
- Capturing logs from containers
- Executing processes in a running container
- Running containers in pods

Technical requirements

Before proceeding with this chapter and its exercises, a machine with a working Podman instance is required. As stated in *Chapter 3*, *Running the First Container*, all the examples in the book are executed on a Fedora 34 system, but can be reproduced on an **operating system (OS)** of your choice.

Finally, a good understanding of the topics covered in the previous chapters is useful to easily grasp concepts regarding **Open Container Initiative (OCI)** images and container execution.

Managing container images

In this section, we will see how to find and pull (download) an image in the local system, as well as inspect its contents. When a container is created and run for the first time, Podman takes care of pulling the related image automatically. However, being able to pull and inspect images in advance gives some valuable advantages, the first being that a container executes faster when images are already available in the machine's local store.

As we stated in the previous chapters, containers are a way to isolate processes in a sandboxed environment with separate namespaces and resource allocation.

The filesystem mounted in the container is provided by the OCI image described in *Chapter 2*, *Comparing Podman and Docker* .

OCI images are stored and distributed by specialized services called **container registries**. A container registry stores images and metadata and exposes simple **REpresentational State Transfer (REST) application programming interface (API)** services to enable users to push and pull images.

There are essentially two types of registries: public and private. A public registry is accessible as a public service (with or without authentication). The main public registries such as docker.io, gcr.io, or quay.io are also used as the image repositories of larger open source projects.

Private registries are deployed and managed inside an organization and can be more focused on security and content filtering. The main container registry projects nowadays are graduated under the **Cloud Native Computing Foundation (CNCF)** (https://landscape.cncf.io/card-mode?category=container-registry&grouping=category) and offer advanced enterprise features to manage multitenancy, authentication, and **role-based access control (RBAC)**, as well as image vulnerability scanning and image signing.

In *Chapter 9, Pushing Images to a Container Registry*, we will provide more details and examples of interaction with container registries.

The largest part of public and private registries expose Docker Registry HTTP API V2 (`https://docs.docker.com/registry/spec/api/`). Being a **HyperText Transfer Protocol (HTTP)**-based REST API, users could interact with the registry with a simple `curl` command or design their own custom clients.

Podman offers a **command-line interface (CLI)** to interact with public and private container registries, manage logins when registry authentication is required, search for image repositories by passing a string pattern, and handle locally cached images.

Searching for images

The first command we will learn to use to search images across multiple registries is the `podman search` command. The following example shows how to search an nginx image:

```
# podman search nginx
```

The preceding command will produce an output with many entries from all the whitelisted registries (see the *Preparing your environment | Customizing container registries' search lists* section of *Chapter 3, Running the First Container*). The output will be a little clumsy, with many entries from unknown and unreliable repositories.

In general, the `podman search` command accepts the following pattern:

```
podman search [options] TERM
```

Here, `TERM` is the search argument. The resulting output of a search has the following fields:

- `INDEX`: The registry indexing the image
- `NAME`: The full name of the image, including the registry name and associated namespaces
- `DESCRIPTION`: A short description of the image role
- `STARS`: The number of stars given by users (available only on registries supporting this feature, such as `docker.io`)
- `OFFICIAL`: A Boolean for specifying whether the image is official
- `AUTOMATED`: A field set to `OK` if the image is automated

> **Important Note**
>
> Never trust unknown repositories and always prefer official images. When pulling images from a niche project, try to understand the content of the image before running it. Remember that an attacker could hide malicious code that could be executed inside containers.
>
> Even trusted repositories can be compromised in some cases. In enterprise scenarios, implement image signature verification to avoid image tampering.

It is possible to apply filters to the search and refine the output. For example, to refine the search and print only official images, we can add the following filtering option that only prints out images with the `is-official` flag:

```
# podman search nginx --filter=is-official
```

This command will print one line pointing to `docker.io/library/nginx:latest`. This official image is maintained by the nginx community and can be used more confidently.

Users can refine the output format of the command. The following example shows how to print only the image registry and the image name:

```
# podman search fedora  \
  --filter is-official \
  --format "table {{.Index}} {{.Name}}"


INDEX        NAME
docker.io    docker.io/library/fedora
```

The output image name has a standard naming pattern that deserves a detailed description. The standard format is shown here:

```
<registry>[:<port>]/[<namespace>/]<name>:<tag>
```

Let's describe the preceding fields in detail, as follows:

- `registry`: This contains the registry the image is stored in. The nginx image in our example is stored in the `docker.io` public registry. Optionally, it is possible to specify a custom port number for the registry. By default, registries expose the `5000` **Transmission Control Protocol** (**TCP**) port.

- `namespace`: This field provides a hierarchy structure that is useful for distinguishing the image context from the provider. The namespace could represent the parent organization, the username of the owner of the repository, or the image role.

- `name`: This contains the name of the private/public image repository where all the tags are stored. It is often referred to as the application name (that is, nginx).

- `tag`: Every image stored in the registry has a unique tag, mapped to a **Secure Hash Algorithm 256 (SHA256)** digest. The generic `:latest` tag can be omitted in the image name.

The generic search hides the image tags by default. To show all available tags for a given repository, we can use the `-list-tags` option to a given image name, as follows:

```
# podman search quay.io/prometheus/prometheus --list-tags
NAME                              TAGquay.io/prometheus/prometheus
v2.5.0
quay.io/prometheus/prometheus    v2.6.0-rc.0
quay.io/prometheus/prometheus    v2.6.0-rc.1
quay.io/prometheus/prometheus    v2.6.0
quay.io/prometheus/prometheus    v2.6.1
quay.io/prometheus/prometheus    v2.7.0-rc.0
quay.io/prometheus/prometheus    v2.7.0-rc.1
quay.io/prometheus/prometheus    v2.7.0-rc.2
quay.io/prometheus/prometheus    v2.7.0
quay.io/prometheus/prometheus    v2.7.1
[...output omitted...]
```

This option is really useful for finding a specific image tag in the registry, often associated with a release version of the application/runtime.

> **Important Note**
>
> Using the `:latest` tag can lead to image versioning issues since it is not a descriptive tag. Also, it is usually expected to point to the latest image version. Unfortunately, this is not always true since an untagged image could retain the latest tag while the latest pushed image could have a different tag. It is up to the repository maintainer to apply tags correctly. If the repository uses semantic versioning, the best option is to pull the most recent version tag.

Pulling and viewing images

Once we have found our desired image, it can be downloaded using the `podman pull` command, as follows:

```
# podman pull docker.io/library/nginx:latest
```

Notice the root user for running the Podman command. In this case, we are pulling the image as root, and its layers and metadata are stored in the `/var/lib/containers/storage` path.

We can run the same command as a standard user by executing the command in a standard user's shell, like this:

```
$ podman pull docker.io/library/nginx:latest
```

In this case, the image will be downloaded in the user home directory under `$HOME/.local/share/containers/storage/` and will be available to run rootless containers.

Users can inspect all locally cached images with the `podman images` command, as illustrated here:

```
# podman images
```

REPOSITORY SIZE	TAG	IMAGE ID	CREATED
docker.io/library/nginx ago 138 MB	latest	ad4c705f24d3	2 weeks
docker.io/library/fedora ago 184 MB	latest	dce66322d647	2 months
[...omitted output...]			

The output shows the image repository name, its tag, the image **identifier** (**ID**), the creation date, and the image size. It is very useful to keep an updated view of the images available in the local store and understand which ones are obsolete.

The `podman images` command also supports many options (a complete list is available by executing the `man podman-images` command). One of the more interesting options is `-sort`, which can be used to sort images by size, date, ID, repository, or tag. For example, we could print images sorted by creation date to find out the most obsolete ones, as follows:

```
# podman images --sort=created
```

Another couple of very useful options are the –all (or –a) and –quiet (or –q) options. Together, they can be combined to print only the image IDs of all the locally stored images, even intermediate image layers. The command will print output similar to the following example:

```
# podman images -qa
ad4c705f24d3
a56f85702a94
b5c5125e3fee
4d7fc5917f3e
625707533167
f881f1aa4d65
96ab2a326180
```

Listing and showing the images already pulled on a system it is not the most interesting part of the job! Let's discover how to inspect images with their configuration and contents in the next section.

Inspecting images' configurations and contents

To inspect the configuration of a pulled image, the podman image inspect (or the shorter podman inspect) command comes to help us, as illustrated here:

```
# podman inspect docker.io/library/nginx:latest
```

The printed output will be a **JavaScript Object Notation** (**JSON**)-formatted object containing the image config, architecture, layers, labels, annotation, and the image build history.

The image history shows the creation history of every layer and is very useful for understanding how the image was built when the Dockerfile or the Containerfile is not available.

Since the output is a JSON object, we can extract single fields to collect specific data or use them as input parameters for other commands.

The following example prints out the command executed when a container is created upon this image:

```
# podman inspect docker.io/library/nginx:latest \
--format "{{ .Config.Cmd }}"
[nginx -g daemon off;]
```

Notice that the formatted output is managed as a Go template.

Sometimes, the inspection of an image must go further than a simple configuration check. On occasions, we need to inspect the filesystem content of an image. To achieve this result, Podman offers the useful `podman image mount` command.

The following example mounts the image and prints its mount path:

```
# podman image mount docker.io/library/nginx
/var/lib/containers/storage/overlay/
ba9d21492c3939befbecd5ec32f6f1b9d564ccf8b1b279e0fb5c186e8b7
967f2/merged
```

If we run a simple `ls` command in the provided path, we will see the image filesystem, composed from its various merged layers, as follows:

```
# ls -al /var/lib/containers/storage/overlay/
ba9d21492c3939befbecd5ec32f6f1b9d564ccf8b1b279e0fb5c186e8b7
967f2/merged
total 92
dr-xr-xr-x. 1 root root 4096 Sep 25 22:30 .
drwx------. 5 root root 4096 Sep 25 22:53 ..
drwxr-xr-x. 2 root root 4096 Sep  2 02:00 bin
drwxr-xr-x. 2 root root 4096 Jun 13 12:30 boot
drwxr-xr-x. 2 root root 4096 Sep  2 02:00 dev
drwxr-xr-x. 1 root root 4096 Sep  9 20:26 docker-entrypoint.d
-rwxrwxr-x. 1 root root 1202 Sep  9 20:25 docker-entrypoint.sh
drwxr-xr-x. 1 root root 4096 Sep  9 20:26 etc
drwxr-xr-x. 2 root root 4096 Jun 13 12:30 home
drwxr-xr-x. 1 root root 4096 Sep  9 20:26 lib
drwxr-xr-x. 2 root root 4096 Sep  2 02:00 lib64
drwxr-xr-x. 2 root root 4096 Sep  2 02:00 media
drwxr-xr-x. 2 root root 4096 Sep  2 02:00 mnt
drwxr-xr-x. 2 root root 4096 Sep  2 02:00 opt
drwxr-xr-x. 2 root root 4096 Jun 13 12:30 proc
drwx------. 2 root root 4096 Sep  2 02:00 root
drwxr-xr-x. 3 root root 4096 Sep  2 02:00 run
drwxr-xr-x. 2 root root 4096 Sep  2 02:00 sbin
drwxr-xr-x. 2 root root 4096 Sep  2 02:00 srv
```

```
drwxr-xr-x. 2 root root 4096 Jun 13 12:30 sys
drwxrwxrwt. 1 root root 4096 Sep  9 20:26 tmp
drwxr-xr-x. 1 root root 4096 Sep  2 02:00 usr
drwxr-xr-x. 1 root root 4096 Sep  2 02:00 var
```

To unmount the image, simply run the podman image unmount command, as follows:

```
# podman image unmount docker.io/library/nginx
```

Mounting images in rootless mode is a bit different since this execution mode only supports manual mounting of the **Virtual File System** (**VFS**) storage driver. Since we are working with a default OverlayFS storage driver, the mount/unmount commands would not work. A workaround is to run the podman unshare command first. It executes a new shell process inside a new namespace where the current **user ID** (**UID**)/**globally unique ID** (**GID**) are mapped to UID 0 and GID 0, respectively. From now on, we have elevated privileges to run the podman mount command. Let's see an example here:

```
$ podman unshare
# podman image mount docker.io/library/nginx:latest \
/home/<username>/.local/share/containers/storage/overlay/
ba9d21492c3939befbecd5ec32f6f1b9d564ccf8b1b279e0fb5c186e8b7967
f2/merged
```

Notice that the mount point is now in the <username> home directory.

To unmount, simply run the podman unmount command, as follows:

```
# podman image unmount docker.io/library/nginx:latest
ad4c705f24d392b982b2f0747704b1c5162e45674294d5640cca7076eba2
865d
# exit
```

The exit command is necessary to exit the temporary unshared namespace.

Deleting images

To delete a local store image, we can use the podman rmi command. The following example deletes the nginx image pulled before:

```
# podman rmi docker.io/library/nginx:latest
Untagged: docker.io/library/nginx:latest
```

```
Deleted: ad4c705f24d392b982b2f0747704b1c5162e45674294d5640cca7
076eba2865d
```

The same command works in rootless mode when executed by a standard user against their home local store.

To remove all the cached images, use the following example, which relies on shell command expansion to get a full list of image IDs:

```
# podman rmi $(podman images -qa)
```

Notice the sharp symbol at the beginning of the line that tells us that the command is executed as root.

The next command removes all images in a regular user local cache (notice the dollar symbol at the beginning of the line):

```
$ podman rmi $(podman images -qa)
```

> **Important Note**
>
> The `podman rmi` command fails to remove images that are currently in use from a running container. First, stop the containers using the blocked images and then run the command again.

Podman also offers a simpler way to clean up dangling or unused images—the `podman image prune` command. It does not delete images from containers in use, so if you have running or stopped containers, the correspondent container image will be not deleted.

The following example deletes all unused images without asking for confirmation:

```
$ sudo podman image prune -af
```

The same command applies in rootless mode, deleting only images in the user home local store, as illustrated in the following code snippet:

```
$ podman image prune -af
```

With this, we have learned how to manage container images on our machine. Let's now learn how to handle and check running containers.

Operations with running containers

In *Chapter 2, Comparing Podman and Docker* , we learned in the *Running your first container* section how to run a container with basic examples, involving the execution of a Bash process inside a Fedora container and an `httpd` server that was also helpful for learning how to expose containers externally.

We will now explore a set of commands used to monitor and check our running containers and gain insights into their behavior.

Viewing and handling container status

Let's start by running a simple container and exposing it on port `8080` to make it accessible externally, as follows:

```
$ podman run -d -p 8080:80 docker.io/library/nginx
```

The preceding example is run in rootless mode, but the same can be applied as a root user by prepending the `sudo` command. In this case, it was simply not necessary to have a container executed in that way.

> **Important Note**
>
> Rootless containers give an extra security advantage. If a malicious process breaks the container isolation, maybe leveraging a vulnerability on the host, it will at best gain the privileges of the user who started the rootless container.

Now that our container is up and running and ready to serve, we can test it by running a `curl` command on the localhost, which should produce a **HyperText Markup Language (HTML)** default output like this:

```
$ curl localhost:8080
<!DOCTYPE html>
<html>
<head>
<title>Welcome to nginx!</title>
<style>
html { color-scheme: light dark; }
body { width: 35em; margin: 0 auto;
```

```
font-family: Tahoma, Verdana, Arial, sans-serif; }
</style>
</head>
<body>
<h1>Welcome to nginx!</h1>
<p>If you see this page, the nginx web server is successfully
installed and
working. Further configuration is required.</p>
<p>For online documentation and support please refer to
<a href="http://nginx.org/">nginx.org</a>.<br/>
Commercial support is available at
<a href="http://nginx.com/">nginx.com</a>.</p>


<p><em>Thank you for using nginx.</em></p>
</body>
</html>
```

Obviously, an empty nginx server without contents to serve is useless, but we will learn how to serve custom contents by using volumes or building custom images later in the next chapters.

The first command we can use to check our container is podman ps. This simply prints out useful information from the running containers, with the option of customizing and sorting the output. Let's run the command in our host and see what is printed, as follows:

```
$ podman ps
CONTAINER ID    IMAGE                           COMMAND
CREATED         STATUS              PORTS                   NAMES
d8bbd5da64d0    docker.io/library/nginx:latest  nginx -g daemon
o...   13 minutes ago  Up 13 minutes ago   0.0.0.0:8080->80/tcp
unruffled_saha
```

The output produces some interesting information about running containers, as detailed here:

- CONTAINER ID: Every new container gets a unique hexadecimal ID. The full ID has a length of 64 characters, and a shortened portion of 12 characters is printed in the podman ps output.

- IMAGE: The image used by the container.

- COMMAND: The command executed inside the container.

- CREATED: The creation date of the container.

- STATUS: The current container status.

- PORTS: The network ports opened in the container. When a port mapping is applied, we can see one or more host ip:port pairs mapped to the container ports with an arrow sign. For example, the 0.0.0.0:8080->80/tcp string means that the 8080/tcp host port is exposed on all the listening interfaces and is mapped to the 80/tcp container port.

- NAMES: The container name. This can be assigned by the user or be randomly generated by the container engine.

> **Tip**
>
> Notice the randomly generated name in the last column of the output. Podman continues the Docker *tradition* to generate random names using adjectives in the left part of the name and notable scientists and hackers in the right part. Indeed, Podman still uses the same github.com/docker/docker/namesgenerator Docker package, included in the vendor directory of the project.

To get a full list of both running and stopped containers, we can add an -a option to the command. To demonstrate this, we first introduce the podman stop command. This changes the container status to stopped and sends a SIGTERM signal to the processes running inside the container. If the container becomes unresponsive, it sends a SIGKILL signal after a given timeout of 10 seconds.

Let's try to stop the previous container and check its state by executing the following code:

```
$ podman stop d8bbd5da64d0
$ podman ps
```

This time, podman ps produced an empty output. This is because the container state is stopped. To get a full list of both running and stopped containers, run the following command:

```
$ podman ps -a
CONTAINER ID   IMAGE   COMMAND   CREATED   STATUS   PORT   NAMES
d8bbd5da64d0   docker.io/library/nginx:latest   nginx -g daemon
o...   About a minute ago   Exited (0) About a minute ago
0.0.0.0:8080->80/tcp   unruffled_saha
```

Notice the status of the container, which states that the container has exited with a 0 exit code.

The stopped container can be resumed by running the `podman start` command, as follows:

```
$ podman start d8bbd5da64d0
```

This command simply starts again the container we stopped before.

If we now check the container status again, we will see it is up and running, as indicated here:

```
$ podman ps
CONTAINER ID   IMAGE   COMMAND   CREATED    STATUS    PORT    NAMES

d8bbd5da64d0  docker.io/library/nginx:latest   nginx -g daemon
o...   8 minutes ago  Up 1 second ago  0.0.0.0:8080->80/tcp
unruffled_saha
```

Podman keeps the container configuration, storage, and metadata as long as it is in a stopped state. Anyway, when we resume the container, we start a new process inside it.

For more options, see the related **manual (man)** page (`man podman-start`).

If we simply need to restart a running container, we can use the `podman restart` command, as follows:

```
$ podman restart <Container_ID_or_Name>
```

This command has the effect of immediately restarting the processes inside the container with a new **process ID (PID)**.

The `podman start` command can also be used to start containers that have been previously created but not run. To create a container without starting it, use the `podman create` command. The following example creates a container but does not start it:

```
$ podman create -p 8080:80 docker.io/library/nginx
```

To start it, run `podman start` on the created container ID or name, as follows:

```
$ podman start <Container_ID_or_Name>
```

This command is very useful for preparing an environment without running it or for mounting a container filesystem, as in the following example:

```
$ podman unshare
$ podman container mount <Container_ID_or_Name>
/home/<username>/.local/share/containers/storage/overlay/
bf9d8df299436d80dece200a23e1b8b957f987a254a656ef94cdc5666982
3b5c/merged
```

Let's now introduce a very frequently used command: podman rm. As the name indicates, it is used to remove containers from the host. By default, it removes stopped containers, but it can be forced to remove running containers with the -f option.

Using the container from the previous example, if we stop it again and issue the podman rm command, as illustrated in the following code snippet, all the container storage, configs, and metadata will be discarded:

```
$ podman stop d8bbd5da64d0
$ podman rm d8bbd5da64d0
```

If we now run a podman ps command again, even with the -a option, we will get an empty list, as illustrated here:

```
$ podman ps -a
CONTAINER ID    IMAGE        COMMAND        CREATED       STATUS
PORTS           NAMES
```

For more details, please inspect the command man page (man podman-rm).

Sometimes, it is useful—just as with images—to print only the container ID with the -q option. This one, combined with the -a option, can print a list of all stopped and running containers in the host. Let's try another example here:

```
$ for i in {1..5}; do podman run -d docker.io/library/nginx;
done
```

It's interesting to notice that we have used a shell loop to start five identical containers, this time without any port mapping—just plain nginx containers. We can inspect their IDs with the following command:

```
$ podman ps -qa
b38ebfed5921
6204efc6d6b2
```

```
762967d87657
269f1affb699
1161072ec559
```

How can we stop and remove all our running containers quickly? We can use shell expansion to combine it with other commands and reach the desired result. Shell expansion is a powerful tool that runs the command inside round parentheses and lets us pass the output string as arguments to the external command, as illustrated in the following code snippet:

```
$ podman stop $(podman ps -qa)
$ podman rm $(podman ps -qa)
```

The two commands stopped all the running containers, identified by their IDs, and removed them from the host.

The podman ps command enables users to refine their output by applying specific filters. A full list of all applicable filters is available on the podman-ps man page. A simple but useful application is the status filter, which enables users to print only containers in a specific condition. Possible statuses are created, exited, paused, running, and unknown.

The following example only prints containers in an exited status:

```
$ podman ps --filter status=exited
```

Again, we can leverage the power of shell expansion to remove nothing but the exited containers, as follows:

```
$ podman rm $(podman ps -qa --filter status=exited)
```

A similar result can be achieved with the simpler-to-remember podman container prune command shown here, which removes (prunes) all stopped containers from the host:

```
$ podman container prune
```

Sorting is another useful option for producing ordered output when listing containers. The following example shows how to sort by container ID:

```
$ podman ps -q --sort id
```

The podman ps command support formatting using a Go template to produce custom output. The next example prints only the container IDs and the commands executed inside them:

```
$ podman ps -a --format "{{.ID}}  {{.Command}}" --no-trunc
```

Also, notice the --no-trunc option is added to avoid truncating the command output. This is not mandatory but is useful when we have long commands executed inside the containers.

If we simply wish to extract the host PID of the process running inside the running containers, we can run the following example:

```
$ podman ps --format "{{ .Pid }}"
```

Instead, if we need to also find out information about the isolated namespaces, podman ps can print details about the cloned namespaces of the running containers. This is a useful starting point for advanced troubleshooting and inspection. You can see the command being run here:

```
$ podman ps --namespace
CONTAINER ID   NAMES                        PID        CGROUPNS      IPC
MNT            NET            PIDNS          USERNS     UTS
f2666ed4a46a   unruffled_hofstadter   437764         4026533088
4026533086   4026533083   4026532948   4026533087   4026532973
4026533085
```

This subsection covered many common operations to control and view the status of containers. In the next section, we will learn how to pause and resume running containers.

Pausing and unpausing containers

This short section covers the podman pause and podman unpause commands. Despite being a section related to container status handling, it is interesting to understand how Podman and the container runtime leverage **control groups** (**cgroups**) to achieve specific purposes.

Simply put, the pause and unpause commands have the purpose of pausing and resuming the processes of a running container. Now, the reader could legitimately need clearance about the difference between pause and stop commands in Podman.

While the `podman stop` command simply sends a `SIGTERM/SIGKILL` signal to the parent process in the container, the `podman pause` command uses cgroups to pause the process without terminating it. When the container is unpaused, the same process is resumed transparently.

> **Tip**
>
> The pause/unpause low-level logic is implemented in the container runtime—for the most curious, this was the implementation in `crun` at the time of writing:
>
> `https://github.com/containers/crun/blob/7ef74c9330033cb884507c28fd8c267861486633/src/libcrun/cgroup.c#L1894-L1936`

The following example demonstrates the podman `pause` and `unpause` commands. First, let's start a Fedora container that prints a date and time string every 2 seconds in an endless loop, as follows:

```
$ podman run --name timer docker.io/library/fedora bash -c
"while true; do echo $(date); sleep 2; done"
```

We intentionally leave the container running in a window and open a new window/tab to manage its status. Before issuing the `pause` command, let's inspect the PID by executing the following code:

```
$ podman ps --format "{{ .Pid }}" --filter name=timer
816807
```

Now, let's pause the running container with the following command:

```
$ podman pause timer
```

If we go back to the `timer` container, we see that the output just paused but the container has not exited. The `unpause` action seen here will bring it back to life:

```
$ podman unpause timer
```

After the `unpause` action, the timer container will start printing date outputs again. Looking at the PID here, nothing has changed, as expected:

```
$ podman ps --format "{{ .Pid }}" --filter name=timer
816807
```

We can check the cgroups status of the paused/unpaused container. In a third tab, open a terminal with a root shell and access the `cgroupfs` controller hierarchy after replacing the correct container ID, as follows:

```
$ sudo -i
$ cd /sys/fs/cgroup/user.slice/user-1000.slice/user@1000.
service/user.slice/libpod-<CONTAINER_ID>.scope/container
```

Now, look at the `cgroup.freeze` file content. This file holds a Boolean value and its state changes as we pause/unpause the container from 0 to 1 and vice versa. Try to pause and unpause the container again to test the changes.

> **Cleanup Tip**
>
> Since the echo loop was issued with a `bash -c` command, we need to send a `SIGKILL` signal to the process. To do this, we can stop the container and wait for the 10-second timeout, or simply run a `podman kill` command, as follows:
>
> ```
> $ podman kill timer
> ```

In this subsection, we covered in detail the most common commands for watching and modifying a container's status. We can now move on to inspect the processes running inside the running containers.

Inspecting processes inside containers

When a container is running, processes inside it are isolated at the namespace level, but users still own total control of the processes running and can inspect their behavior. There are many levels of complexity in process inspection, but Podman offers tools that can speed up this task.

Let's start with the `podman top` command: this provides a full view of the processes running inside a container. The following example shows the processes running inside an nginx container:

```
$ podman top  f2666ed4a46a
```

USER	PID	PPID	%CPU	ELAPSED
TTY	TIME	COMMAND		
root	1	0	0.000	3m26.540290427s
?	0s	nginx: master process nginx -g daemon		
off;				

nginx ?	26 0s	1 nginx: worker process	0.000	3m26.540547429s
nginx ?	27 0s	1 nginx: worker process	0.000	3m26.540788803s
nginx ?	28 0s	1 nginx: worker process	0.000	3m26.540914386s
nginx ?	29 0s	1 nginx: worker process	0.000	3m26.541040023s
nginx ?	30 0s	1 nginx: worker process	0.000	3m26.541161213s
nginx ?	31 0s	1 nginx: worker process	0.000	3m26.541297546s
nginx ?	32 0s	1 nginx: worker process	0.000	3m26.54141773s
nginx ?	33 0s	1 nginx: worker process	0.000	3m26.541564289s
nginx ?	34 0s	1 nginx: worker process	0.000	3m26.541685475s
nginx ?	35 0s	1 nginx: worker process	0.000	3m26.541808977s
nginx ?	36 0s	1 nginx: worker process	0.000	3m26.541932099s
nginx ?	37 0s	1 nginx: worker process	0.000	3m26.54205111s

The result is very similar to the `ps` command output rather than the interactive one produced by the Linux `top` command.

It is possible to apply custom formatting to the output. The following example only prints PIDs, commands, and arguments:

```
$ podman top f2666ed4a46a pid comm args
```

PID	COMMAND	COMMAND
1 off;	nginx	nginx: master process nginx -g daemon
26	nginx	nginx: worker process
27	nginx	nginx: worker process
28	nginx	nginx: worker process
29	nginx	nginx: worker process

```
30          nginx          nginx: worker process
31          nginx          nginx: worker process
32          nginx          nginx: worker process
33          nginx          nginx: worker process
34          nginx          nginx: worker process
35          nginx          nginx: worker process
36          nginx          nginx: worker process
37          nginx          nginx: worker process
```

We may need to inspect container processes in greater detail. As we discussed earlier in *Chapter 1, Introduction to Container Technology*, once a brand-new container is started, it will start assigning PIDs from number 0, while under the hood, the container engine will map this container's PIDs with the real ones on the host. So, we can use the output of the `podman ps --namespace` command to extract the process's original PID in the host for a given container. With that information, we can conduct advanced analysis. The following example shows how to attach the `strace` command, used to inspect processes' **system calls (syscalls)**, to the process running inside the container:

```
$ sudo strace -p <PID>
```

Details about the usage of the `strace` command are beyond the scope of this book. See `man strace` for more advanced examples and a more in-depth explanation of the command options.

Another useful command that can be easily applied to processes running inside a container is `pidstat`. Once we have obtained the PID, we can inspect the resource usage in this way:

```
$ pidstat -p <PID> [<interval> <count>]
```

The integers applied at the end represent, respectively, the execution interval of the command and the number of times it must print the usage stats. See `man pidstat` for more usage options.

When a process in a container becomes unresponsive, it is possible to handle its abrupt termination with the `podman kill` command. By default, it sends a `SIGKILL` signal to the process inside the container. The following example creates an `httpd` container and then kills it:

```
$ podman run --name custom-webserver -d docker.io/library/httpd
$ podman kill custom-webserver
```

We can optionally send custom signals (such as SIGTERM or SIGHUP) with the --signal option. Notice that a killed container is not removed from the host but continues to exist, is stopped, and is in an exited status.

In *Chapter 10, Troubleshooting and Monitoring Containers*, we will again deal with container troubleshooting and learn how to use advanced tools such as nsenter to inspect container processes. We now move on to basic container statistics commands that can be useful for monitoring the overall resource usage by all containers running in a system.

Monitoring container stats

When multiple containers are running in the same host, it is crucial to monitor the amount of **central processing unit** (**CPU**), memory, disk, and network resources they are consuming in a given interval of time. The first, simpler command that an administrator can use is the podman stats command, shown here:

```
$ podman stats
```

Without any options, the command will open a top-like, self-refreshing window with the stats of all the running containers. The default printed values are listed here:

- ID: The running container ID
- NAME: The running container name
- CPU %: The total CPU usage as a percentage
- MEM USAGE / LIMIT: Memory usage against a given limit (dictated by system capabilities or by cgroups-driven limits)
- MEM %: The total memory usage as a percentage
- NET IO: Network **input/output** (**I/O**) operations
- BLOCK IO: Disk I/O operations
- PIDS: The number of PIDs inside the container
- CPU TIME: Total consumed CPU time
- AVG CPU %: Average CPU usage as a percentage

In case a redirect is needed, it is possible to avoid streaming a self-refreshing output with the --no-stream option, as follows:

```
$ podman stats --no-stream
```

Anyway, having a static output of this type is not very useful for parsing or ingestion. A better approach is to apply a JSON or Go template formatter. The following example prints out stats in a JSON format:

```
$ podman stats --format=json
[
  {
    "id": "e263f68bbb83",
    "name": "infallible_sinoussi",
    "cpu_time": "33.518ms",
    "cpu_percent": "2.05%",
    "avg_cpu": "2.05%",
    "mem_usage": "19.3MB / 33.38GB",
    "mem_percent": "0.06%",
    "net_io": "-- / --",
    "block_io": "-- / --",
    "pids": "13"
  }
]
```

In a similar way, it is possible to customize the output fields using a Go template. The following example only prints out the container ID, CPU percentage usage, total memory usage in bytes, and PIDs:

```
$ podman stats -a --no-stream --format "{{ .ID }} {{ .CPUPerc }} {{ .MemUsageBytes }} {{ .PIDs }}"
```

In this section, we have learned how to monitor running containers and their isolated processes. The next section shows how to inspect container configurations for analysis and troubleshooting.

Inspecting container information

A running container exposes a set of configuration data and metadata ready to be consumed. Podman implements the `podman inspect` command to print all the container configurations and runtime information. In its simplest form, we can simply pass the container ID or name, like this:

```
$ podman inspect <Container_ID_or_Name>
```

This command prints a JSON output with all the container configurations. For the sake of space, we will list some of the most notable fields here:

- `Path`: The container entry point path. We will dig deeper into entry points later when we analyze Dockerfiles.

- `Args`: The arguments passed to the entry point.

- `State`: The container's current state, including crucial information such as the executed PID, the common PID, the OCI version, and the health check status.

- `Image`: The ID of the image used to run the container.

- `Name`: The container name.

- `MountLabel`: Container mount label for **Security-Enhanced Linux (SELinux)**.

- `ProcessLabel`: Container process label for SELinux.

- `EffectiveCaps`: Effective capabilities applied to the container.

- `GraphDriver`: The type of storage driver (default is `overlayfs`) and a list of overlay upper, lower, and merged directories.

- `Mounts`: The actual bind mounts in the container.

- `NetworkSettings`: The overall container network settings, including its internal **Internet Protocol (IP)** address, exposed ports, and port mappings.

- `Config`: Container runtime configuration, including environment variables, hostname, command, working directory, labels, and annotations.

- `HostConfig`: Host configuration, including cgroups' quotas, network mode, and capabilities.

This is a huge amount of information that most of the time is too much for our needs. When we need to extract specific fields, we can use the `--format` option to print only selected ones. The following example prints only the host-bound PID of the process executed inside the container:

```
$ podman inspect <ID or Name> --format "{{ .State.Pid }}"
```

The result is in a Go template format. This allows for flexibility to customize the output string as we desire.

The `podman inspect` command is also useful for understanding the behavior of the container engine and for gaining useful information during troubleshooting tasks.

For example, when a container is launched, we learn that the `resolv.conf` file is mounted inside the container from a path that is defined in the `{{ .ResolvConfPath }}` key. The target path is `/run/user/<UID>/containers/overlay-containers/<Container_ID>/userdata/resolv.conf` when the container is executed in rootless mode, and `/var/run/containers/storage/overlay-containers/<Container_ID>/userdata/resolv.conf` when in rootful mode.

Other interesting information is the list of all the merged layers managed by `overlayfs`. Let's try to run a new container, this time in rootful mode, and find out information about the merged layers, as follows:

```
# podman run --name logger -d docker.io/library/fedora bash -c
"while true; do echo test >> /tmp/test.log; sleep 5; done"
```

This container runs a simple loop that writes a string on a text file every 5 seconds. Now, let's run a `podman inspect` command to find out information about `MergedDir`, which is the directory where all layers are merged by `overlayfs`. The code is illustrated in the following snippet:

```
# podman inspect logger --format "{{ .GraphDriver.Data.
MergedDir
 }}"
/var/lib/containers/storage/
overlay/27d89046485db7c775b108a80072eafdf9aa63d14ee1205946d746
23fc195314/merged
```

Inside this directory, we can find the `/tmp/test.log` file, as indicated here:

```
# cat /var/lib/containers/storage/
overlay/27d89046485db7c775b108a80072eafdf9aa63d14ee1205946d746
23fc195314/merged/tmp/test.log
test
test
test
test
test
[...]
```

We can dig deeper—the `LowerDir` directory holds a list of the base image layers, as shown in the following code snippet:

```
# podman inspect logger \
--format "{{ .GraphDriver.Data.LowerDir}}"
 /var/lib/containers/storage/
overlay/4c85102d65a59c6d478bfe6bc0bf32e8c79d9772689f62451c7196
380675d4af/diff
```

In this example, the base image is made up of only one layer. Are we going to find the log file here? Let's have a look:

```
# cat /var/lib/containers/storage/
overlay/4c85102d65a59c6d478bfe6bc0bf32e8c79d9772689f62451c7196
380675d4af/diff/tmp/test.log
cat: /var/lib/containers/storage/
overlay/4c85102d65a59c6d478bfe6bc0bf32e8c79d9772689f62451c7196
380675d4af/diff/tmp/test.log: No such file or directory
```

We are missing the log file in this layer. This is because the `LowerDir` directory is not written and represents the read-only image layers. It is merged with an `UpperDir` directory that is the read-write layer of the container. With `podman inspect`, we can find out where it resides, as illustrated here:

```
# podman inspect logger --format "{{ .GraphDriver.Data.UpperDir }}"
/var/lib/containers/storage/
overlay/27d89046485db7c775b108a80072eafdf9aa63d14ee1205946d746
23fc195314/diff
```

The output directory will contain only a bunch of files and directories, written since the container startup, including the `/tmp/test.log` file, as illustrated in the following code snippet:

```
# cat /var/lib/containers/storage/
overlay/27d89046485db7c775b108a80072eafdf9aa63d14ee1205946d746
23fc195314/diff/tmp/test.log
test
test
test
test
```

```
test
[...]
```

We can now stop and remove the logger container by running the following command:

```
# podman stop logger && podman rm logger
```

This example was in anticipation of the container storage topic that will be covered in *Chapter 5, Implementing Storage for the Container's Data*. The `overlayfs` mechanisms, with the lower, upper, and merged directory concepts, will be analyzed in more detail.

In this section, we learned how to inspect running containers and collect runtime information and configurations. The next section is going to cover best practices for capturing logs from containers.

Capturing logs from containers

As described earlier in this chapter, containers are made of one or more processes that can fail, printing errors and describing their current state in a log file. But where are these logs stored?

Well, of course, a process in a container could write its log messages inside a file somewhere in a temporary filesystem that the container engine has made available to it (if any). But what about a read-only filesystem or any permission constraints in the running container?

A container's best practice for exposing relevant logs outside the container's shield actually leverages the use of standard streams: **standard output** (`STDOUT`) and **standard error** (`STDERR`).

> **Good to Know**
>
> Standard streams are communication channels interconnected to a running process in an OS. When a program is run through an interactive shell, these streams are then directly connected to the user's running terminal to let input, output, and error flow between the terminal and the process, and vice versa.

Depending on the options we use for running a brand-new container, Podman will act appropriately by attaching the `STDIN`, `STDOUT`, and `STDERR` standard streams to a local file for storing the logs.

In *Chapter 3*, *Running the First Container*, we saw how to run a container in the background, detaching from a running container. We used the -d option to start a container in *detached* mode through the podman run command, as illustrated here:

```
$ podman run -d -i -t registry.fedoraproject.org/f29/httpd
```

With the previous command, we are instructing Podman to start a container in detached mode (-d), with a pseudo-terminal attached to the STDIN stream (-t) keeping the standard input stream open even if there is no terminal attached yet (-i).

The standard Podman behavior is to attach to STDOUT and STDERR streams and store any container's published data in a log file on the host filesystem.

If we are working with Podman as a *root* user, we can take a look at the log file available on the host system, executing the following steps:

1. First, we need to start our container and take note of the ID returned by Podman, or ask Podman for a list of containers and take note of their ID. The code to accomplish this is shown in the following snippet:

    ```
    # podman run -d -i -t registry.fedoraproject.org/f29/
    httpd
    c6afe22eac7c22c35a303d5fed45bc1b6442a4cec4a9060f392362bc
    4cecb25d
    # .
    CONTAINER ID
          IMAGE                                          COMMAND
             CREATED          STATUS          PORTS
    NAMES
    c6afe22eac7c22c35a303d5fed45bc1b6442a4cec4a9060f392362bc4
    cecb25d  registry.fedoraproject.org/f29/httpd:latest   /
    usr/bin/run-httpd  27 minutes ago  Up 27 minutes ago
        gifted_allen
    ```

2. After that, we can take a look under the /var/lib/containers/storage/ overlay-containers/ directory and search for a folder with a name that matches our container's ID, as follows:

    ```
    # cd /var/lib/containers/storage/overlay-containers/
    c6afe22eac7c22c35a303d5fed45bc1b6442a4cec4a9060f392362bc4
    cecb25d/
    ```

3. Finally, we can check the logs of our running container by taking a look at the file named `ctr.log` in the `userdata` directory, as follows:

```
# cat userdata/ctr.log
2021-09-27T15:42:46.925288013+00:00 stdout P => sourcing
10-set-mpm.sh ...
2021-09-27T15:42:46.925604590+00:00 stdout F
2021-09-27T15:42:46.926882725+00:00 stdout P => sourcing
20-copy-config.sh ...
2021-09-27T15:42:46.926920142+00:00 stdout F
2021-09-27T15:42:46.929405654+00:00 stdout P => sourcing
40-ssl-certs.sh ...
2021-09-27T15:42:46.929460531+00:00 stdout F
2021-09-27T15:42:46.987174441+00:00 stdout P AH00558:
httpd: Could not reliably determine the server's
fully qualified domain name, using 10.88.0.9. Set the
'ServerName' directive globally to suppress this message
2021-09-27T15:42:46.987242961+00:00 stdout F
2021-09-27T15:42:46.996989350+00:00 stdout F [Mon
Sep 27 15:42:46.996748 2021] [ssl:warn] [pid 1:tid
139708367605120] AH01882: Init: this version of mod_ssl
was compiled against a newer library (OpenSSL 1.1.1b FIPS
26 Feb 2019, version currently loaded is OpenSSL 1.1.1
FIPS  11 Sep 2018) - may result in undefined or erroneous
behavior
...
2021-09-27T15:42:47.101066096+00:00 stdout F [Mon Sep
27 15:42:47.099445 2021] [core:notice] [pid 1:tid
139708367605120] AH00094: Command line: 'httpd -D
FOREGROUND'
```

We just discovered the secret place where Podman saves all logs of our containers!

Please note that the procedure we just introduced will work properly if the `log_driver` field for the `containers.conf` file is set to the `k8s-file` value. For example, in the Fedora Linux distribution starting from version 35, the maintainers decided to switch from `k8s-file` to `journald`. In this case, you could look for the logs directly using the `journalctl` command-line utility.

If you want to take a look at the default `log_driver` field, you can look in the following path:

```
# grep log_driver /usr/share/containers/containers.conf
```

Does this mean that we need to perform this entire complex procedure every time we need to analyze the logs of our containers? Of course not!

Podman has a `podman logs` built-in command that can easily discover, grab, and print the latest container logs for us. Considering the previous example, we can easily check the logs of our running container by executing the following command:

```
# podman logs c6afe22eac7c22c35a303d5fed45bc1b6442a4cec4a9060f
392362bc4cecb25d
=> sourcing 10-set-mpm.sh ...
=> sourcing 20-copy-config.sh ...
=> sourcing 40-ssl-certs.sh ...
AH00558: httpd: Could not reliably determine the server's fully
qualified domain name, using 10.88.0.9. Set the 'ServerName'
directive globally to suppress this message
[Mon Sep 27 15:42:46.996748 2021] [ssl:warn] [pid 1:tid 13970
8367605120] AH01882: Init: this version of mod_ssl was compiled
 against a newer library (OpenSSL 1.1.1b FIPS  26 Feb 2019,
version currently loaded is OpenSSL 1.1.1 FIPS  11 Sep 2018)
- may result in undefined or erroneous behavior
...
[Mon Sep 27 15:42:47.099445 2021] [core:notice] [pid 1:tid
139708367605120] AH00094: Command line: 'httpd -D FOREGROUND'
```

We can also get the short ID for our running container and pass this ID to the `podman logs` command, as follows:

```
# podman ps
CONTAINER ID   IMAGE
COMMAND             CREATED         STATUS
PORTS       NAMES
c6afe22eac7c   registry.fedoraproject.org/f29/httpd:latest
/usr/bin/run-http...  40 minutes ago  Up 40 minutes ago
        gifted_allen
# podman logs --tail 2 c6afe22eac7c
[Mon Sep 27 15:42:47.099403 2021] [mpm_event:notice] [pid 1:tid
139708367605120] AH00489: Apache/2.4.39 (Fedora) OpenSSL/1.1.1
```

```
configured -- resuming normal operations
[Mon Sep 27 15:42:47.099445 2021] [core:notice] [pid 1:tid 1397
08367605120] AH00094: Command line: 'httpd -D FOREGROUND'
```

In the previous command, we also used a nice option of the `podman logs` command: the `--tail` option, which lets us output only the latest needed rows of the container's log. In our case, we requested the latest two.

As we saw earlier in this section, Podman saves the container logs into the host filesystem. These files, by default, are not limited in size, so it could happen that for long-living containers that might produce a lot of logs, these files could become very large.

For this reason, as we usually talk about logs and log files, one important configuration parameter that could help reduce the log files' size is available through the Podman global configuration file available at this location: `/etc/containers/containers.conf`.

If this configuration file is missing, you can easily create a new one, inserting the following rows to apply the configuration:

```
# vim /etc/containers/containers.conf
[containers]
log_size_max=10000000
```

Through the previous configuration, we are limiting every log file for our future running containers to 10 **megabytes (MB)**. If you have some running containers, you have to restart them to apply this new configuration.

We are now ready to move to the next section, where we will discover another useful command.

Executing processes in a running container

In the *Podman daemonless architecture* section of *Chapter 2, Comparing Podman and Docker*, we talked about the fact that Podman, as with any other container engine, leverages the Linux namespace functionality to correctly isolate running containers from each other and from the OS host as well.

So, just because Podman creates a brand-new namespace for every running container, it should not be a surprise that we can attach to the same Linux namespace of a running container, executing other processes just as in a full operating environment.

Podman gives us the ability to execute a process in a running container through the `podman exec` command.

Once executed, this command will find internally the right Linux namespace to which the target running container is attached. Having found the Linux namespace, Podman will execute the respective process, passed as an argument to the podman exec command, attaching it to the target Linux namespace. The final process will be in the same environment as the original process companion and it will be able to interact with it.

To understand how this works in practice, we can consider the following example whereby we will first run a container and then execute a process beside the existing processes:

```
# podman run -d -i -t registry.fedoraproject.org/f29/httpd
47fae73e4811a56d799f258c85bc50262901bec2f9a9cab19c01af89713
a1248
# podman exec -ti
47fae73e4811a56d799f258c85bc50262901bec2f9a9cab19c01af89713
a1248 /bin/bash
bash-4.4$ ps aux
USER          PID %CPU %MEM    VSZ    RSS TTY       STAT START
    TIME COMMAND
default         1  0.6  0.6  20292 13664 pts/0      Ss+  13:37
    0:00 httpd -D FOREGROUND
...
```

As you can see from the previous commands, we grabbed the container ID provided by Podman once the container was started and we passed it to the podman exec command as an argument.

The podman exec command could be really useful for troubleshooting, testing, and working with an existing container. In the preceding example, we attached an interactive terminal running the Bash console, and we launched the ps command for inspecting the running processes available in the current Linux namespace assigned to the container.

The podman exec command has many options available, similar to the ones provided by the podman run command. As you saw from the previous example, we used the option for getting a pseudo-terminal attached to the STDIN stream (-t), keeping the standard input stream open even if there is no terminal attached yet (-i).

For more details on the available options, we can check the manual with the respective command, as illustrated here:

```
# man podman exec
```

We are moving forward in our journey to the container management world, and in the next section, we will also take a look at some of the capabilities that Podman offers to enable containerized workloads in the Kubernetes container orchestration world.

Running containers in pods

As we mentioned in the *Docker versus Podman main differences* section of *Chapter 2, Comparing Podman and Docker* , Podman offers capabilities to easily start adopting some basic concepts of the de facto container orchestrator named Kubernetes (also sometimes referred to as k8s).

The pod concept was introduced with Kubernetes and represents the smallest execution unit in a Kubernetes cluster. With Podman, users can create empty pods and then run containers inside them easily.

Grouping two or more containers inside a single pod can have many benefits, such as the following:

- Sharing the same network namespace, IP address included
- Sharing the same storage volumes for storing persistent data
- Sharing the same configurations

In addition, placing two or more containers in the same pod will actually enable them to share the same **inter-process communication** (**IPC**) Linux namespace. This could be really useful for applications that need to communicate with each other using shared memory.

The simplest way to create a pod and start working with it is to use this command:

```
# podman pod create --name myhttp
3950703adb04c6bca7f83619ea28c650f9db37fd0060c1e263cf7ea34
dbc8dad
# podman pod ps
POD ID          NAME        STATUS      CREATED         INFRA ID
        # OF CONTAINERS
3950703adb04  myhttp        Created     6 seconds ago   1bdc82
e77ba2   1
```

As shown in the previous example, we create a new pod named myhttp and then check the status of the pod on our host system: there is just one pod in a created state.

We can now start the pod as follows and check what will happen:

```
# podman pod start myhttp
3950703adb04c6bca7f83619ea28c650f9db37fd0060c1e263cf7ea34
dbc8dad
```

```
# podman pod ps
```

POD ID	NAME	STATUS	CREATED	INFRA ID	# OF CONTAINERS
3950703adb04	myhttp	Running	About a minute ago	1bdc82e77ba2	1

The pod is now running, but what is Podman actually running? We created an empty pod without containers inside! Let's take a look at the running container by executing the podman ps command, as follows:

```
# podman ps
```

CONTAINER ID	IMAGE	COMMAND	CREATED	STATUS	PORTS	NAMES
1bdc82e77ba2	k8s.gcr.io/pause:3.5		About a minute ago	Up 6 seconds ago		3950703adb04-infra

The podman ps command is showing a running container with an image named pause. This container is run by Podman by default as an infra container. This kind of container does nothing—it just holds the namespace and lets the container engine connect to any other running container inside the pod.

Having demystified the role of this special container inside our pods, we can now take a brief look at the steps required to start a multi-container pod.

First of all, let's start by running a new container inside the existing pod we created in the previous example, as follows:

```
# podman run --pod myhttp -d -i -t registry.fedoraproject.org/
f29/httpd
Cb75e65f10f6dc37c799a3150c1b9675e74d66d8e298a8d19eadfa125d
ffdc53
```

Then, we can check whether the existing pod has updated the number of containers it contains, as illustrated in the following code snippet:

```
# podman pod ps
POD ID          NAME         STATUS        CREATED          INFRA ID
      # OF CONTAINERS
3950703adb04    myhttp       Running       21 minutes ago
1bdc82e77ba2    2
```

Finally, we can ask Podman for a list of running containers with the associated pod name, as follows:

```
# podman ps -p
CONTAINER ID    IMAGE
COMMAND                 CREATED         STATUS              PORTS
NAMES                   POD ID          PODNAME
1bdc82e77ba2    k8s.gcr.io/pause:3.5
22 minutes ago  Up 20 minutes ago                      3950703adb04-
infra    3950703adb04    myhttp
cb75e65f10f6    registry.fedoraproject.org/f29/httpd:latest    /
usr/bin/run-http...   4 minutes ago   Up 4 minutes ago
determined_driscoll    3950703adb04    myhttp
```

As you can see, the two containers running are both associated with the pod named myhttp!

Important Note

Please consider periodically cleaning up the lab environment after completing all the examples contained in this chapter. This could help you save resources and avoid any errors when moving to the next chapter's examples. For this reason, you can refer to the code provided in the AdditionalMaterial folder in the book's GitHub repository: https://github.com/ PacktPublishing/Podman-for-DevOps/tree/main/ AdditionalMaterial.

With the same approach, we can add more and more containers to the same pod, letting them share all the data we described before.

Please note that placing containers in the same pod can be beneficial in some cases, but this represents an anti-pattern for the container technology. In fact, as mentioned before, Kubernetes considers the **pod** the smallest computing unit to run on top of the distributed nodes' part of one cluster. This means that once you group two or more containers under the same pod, they will be executed together on the same node and the orchestrator cannot balance or distribute their workload on multiple machines.

We will explore more about Podman's features that can enable you to enter the container orchestration world through Kubernetes in the next chapters!

Summary

In this chapter, we started developing experience in managing containers, starting with container images, and then working with running containers. Once our containers were running, we also explored the various commands available in Podman to inspect and check the logs and troubleshoot our containers. The operations needed to monitor and look after running containers are really important for any container administrator. Finally, we also took a brief look at the Kubernetes concepts available in Podman that let us group two or more containers under the same Linux namespace. All the concepts and the examples we just went through will help us start our experience as a system administrator for container technologies.

We are now ready to explore another important topic in the next chapter: managing storage for our containers!

5
Implementing Storage for the Container's Data

In the previous chapters, we explored how to run and manage our containers using Podman, but we will soon come to realize in this chapter that these operations aren't useful in certain scenarios where the applications included in our containers need to store data in a persistent mode. Containers are ephemeral by default, and this is one of their main features, as we described in the first chapter of this book, and for this reason, we need a way to attach persistent storage to a running container to preserve the container's important data.

In this chapter, we're going to cover the following main topics:

- Why does storage matter for containers?
- Containers' storage features
- Copying files into and out of a container
- Attaching host storage to a container

Technical requirements

Before proceeding with the chapter's lecture and examples, a machine with a working Podman installation is required. As stated in *Chapter 3*, *Running the First Container*, all the examples in the book are executed on a Fedora 34 system or later but can be reproduced on the reader's OS of choice.

Finally, a good understanding of the topics covered in *Chapter 4*, *Managing Running Containers*, is useful in terms of being able to easily grasp concepts regarding OCI images and container execution.

Why does storage matter for containers?

Before moving forward in the chapter and answering this interesting question, we need to distinguish between two kinds of storage for containers:

- External storage attached to running containers to store data, making it persistent on a container's restart
- Underlying storage for root filesystems of our containers and container images

Talking about external storage, as we described in *Chapter 1*, *Introduction to Container Technology*, containers are stateless, ephemeral, and often with a read-only filesystem. This is because the theory behind the technology states that containers should be used for spawning scalable and distributed applications that have to scale horizontally instead of vertically.

Scaling an application horizontally means that in case we require additional resources for our running services, we will not increase CPU or RAM for a single running container, but we will instead launch a brand new container that will handle the incoming requests along with the existing container. This is the same well-known paradigm adopted in the public cloud. The container in principle should be ephemeral because any additional copy of the existing container image should be run at any time for empowering the existing running service.

Of course, exceptions exist, and it could happen that a running container cannot be scaled horizontally or that it simply needs to share configurations, cache, or any other data relevant to other copies of the same container images at startup time or during runtime.

Let's understand this with the help of a real-life example. Using a car-sharing service to get a new car for every destination inside a city can be a useful and smart way to move around without worrying about parking fees, fuel, and other things. However, at the same time, this service cannot allow you to store or leave your stuff inside of a parked car. Therefore, when using a car-sharing service, we can unpack our stuff once we get into a car, but we must pack it back before we leave that car. The same applies similarly to containers, where we must attach to them some storage for letting our container write data down but then, once our container stops, we should detach that storage so that a brand-new container can use it when needed.

Here's another more technical example: let's consider a standard three-tier application with a web, a backend, and a database service. Every layer of this application may need storage, which it will use in a variety of ways. The web service may need a place to save a cache, store rendered web pages, some customized images at runtime, and so on. The backend service will need a place to store configuration and synchronization data between the other running backend services, if any, and so on. The database service will surely need a place to store the DB data.

Storage is often associated with low-level infrastructure, but in a container, the storage becomes important even for developers, who should plan where to attach the storage, and the features needed for their application.

If we extend the topic to container orchestration, then the storage inherits a strategic role because it should be as elastic and feasible as the Kubernetes orchestrator that we might use it with. The container storage in this case should become more like software-defined storage – able to provide storage resources in a self-service way to developers, and to containers in general.

Although this book will talk about local storage, it's important to note that this is not enough for the Kubernetes orchestrator because containers should be portable from one host to another depending on the availability and scaling rules defined. This is where software-defined storage could be the solution!

As we can deduct from the previous examples, external storage matters in containers. The usage may vary depending on the running application inside our container, but it is required. At the same time, another key role is driven by the underlying container storage that is responsible for handling the correct storage of containers and the container images' root filesystem. Choosing the right, stable, and performing underlying local storage will ensure better and correct management of our containers.

So, let's first explore a bit of the theory of container storage and then discuss how to work with it.

Containers' storage features

Before going into a real example and use cases, we should first dig into the main differences between container storage and a **container storage interface (CSI)**.

Container storage, previously referred to as *underlying container storage*, is responsible for handling container images on **Copy-on-Write (COW)** filesystems. Container images need to be transferred and move around until a container engine is instructed to run them, so we need a way to store that image until it is run. That's the role of container storage.

Once we start using an orchestrator such as Kubernetes, CSI instead is responsible for providing container block or file storage that containers need to write data to.

In the next section of this chapter, we will concentrate on container storage and its configuration. Later, we will talk about external storage for containers and the options we have in Podman to expose the host local storage to the running containers.

A great innovation introduced with Podman is the *containers/storage* project (https://github.com/containers/storage), a great way to share an underlying common method for accessing container storage on a host. With the arrival of Docker, we were forced to pass through the Docker daemon to interact with container storage. With no other way to directly interact with the underlying storage, the Docker daemon just hid it from the user as well as the system administrator.

With the *containers/storage* project, we now have an easy way to use multiple tools for analyzing, managing, or working with container storage at the same time.

The configuration of this low-level piece of software is so important for Podman as well as for other companion tools of Podman and can be inspected or edited through its configuration file available at /etc/containers/storage.conf.

Looking at the configuration file, we can easily discover that we can change a lot of options in terms of how our containers interact with the underlying storage. Let's inspect the most important option – the storage driver.

Storage driver

The configuration file, as one of its first options, gives the opportunity to choose the default **Copy On Write (COW)** container storage driver. The configuration file in the current version, at the time of writing this book, supports the following COW drivers:

- overlay
- vfs

- devmapper

- aufs

- btrfs

- zfs

These are also often referred to as **graph drivers** because most of them organize the layers they handle in a graph structure.

Using Podman on Fedora 34 or later, the container's storage configuration file is shipped with overlay as the default driver.

Another important thing to mention is that, at the time of writing this book, there are two versions of the overlay filesystem – version 1 and version 2.

The original overlay filesystem version 1 was initially used by the Docker container engine, but was later abandoned in favor of version 2. That's why Podman and the container's storage configuration file refers generically to the name overlay, but it instead uses the new version 2.

Before going into detail regarding the other options and, finally, the practical examples contained in this chapter, let's further explore how one of these COW filesystem drivers works.

The overlay union filesystem has been present in a Linux kernel since version 3.18. It is usually enabled by default and activated dynamically once a mount is initiated with this filesystem.

The mechanism behind this filesystem is really simple but powerful – it allows a directory tree to be overlaid on another, storing only the differences, but showing the latest updated, *squashed* tree of directories.

Usually, in the world of containers, we start using a read-only filesystem, adding one or more layers, read-only again, until a running container will use this bunch of *squashed* layers as its root filesystem. This is where the last read-write layer will be created as an overlay of the others.

Let's see what happens under the hood once we pull down a brand-new container image with Podman:

> **Important Note**
> If you wish to proceed with testing the following example on your test machine, ensure that you remove any running container and container images to easily match the image with the layers that Podman will download for us.

```
# podman pull quay.io/centos7/httpd-24-centos7:latest
Trying to pull quay.io/centos7/httpd-24-centos7:latest...
Getting image source signatures
Copying blob 5f2e13673ac2 done
Copying blob 8dd5a5013b51 done
Copying blob b2cc5146c9c7 done
Copying blob e17e89f32035 done
Copying blob 1b6c93aa6be5 done
Copying blob 6855d3fe68bc done
Copying blob f974a2323b6c done
Copying blob d620f14a5a76 done
Copying config 3b964f33a2 done
Writing manifest to image destination
Storing signatures
3b964f33a2bf66108d5333a541d376f63e0506aba8ddd4813f9d4e104
271d9f0
```

We can see from the previous command output that multiple layers have been downloaded. That's because the container image we pulled down is composed of many layers.

Now we can start inspecting just the downloaded layers. First of all, we have to locate the right directory, which we can search for inside the configuration file. Alternatively, we can use an easier technique. Podman has a command dedicated to displaying its running configuration and other useful information – `podman info`. Let's see how it works:

```
# podman info | grep -A19 "store:"
store:
  configFile: /etc/containers/storage.conf
```

```
containerStore:
  number: 0
  paused: 0
  running: 0
  stopped: 0
graphDriverName: overlay
graphOptions:
  overlay.mountopt: nodev,metacopy=on
graphRoot: /var/lib/containers/storage
graphStatus:
  Backing Filesystem: btrfs
  Native Overlay Diff: "false"
  Supports d_type: "true"
  Using metacopy: "true"
imageStore:
  number: 1
runRoot: /run/containers/storage
volumePath: /var/lib/containers/storage/volumes
```

To reduce the output of the `podman info` command, we used the `grep` command to only match the `store` section that contains the current configuration in place for container storage.

As we can see, the driver used is `overlay`, and the root directory to search our layers is reported as the `graphRoot` directory: `/var/lib/containers/storage`; for rootless containers, the equivalent is `$HOME/.local/share/containers/storage`. We also have other paths reported, but we will talk about these later in this section. The keyword `graph` is a term derived from the category of drivers we just introduced earlier.

Let's take a look into that directory to see what the actual content is:

```
# cd /var/lib/containers/storage
# ls
libpod  mounts  overlay  overlay-containers  overlay-images
overlay-layers  storage.lock  tmp  userns.lock
```

We have several directories available for which the names are pretty self-explanatory. The ones we are looking for are as follows:

- `overlay-images`: This contains the metadata of the container images downloaded.

- `overlay-layers`: This contains the archives for all the layers of every container image.

- `overlay`: This is the directory containing the unpacked layers of every container image.

Let's check the content of the first directory, `overlay-images`:

```
# ls -l overlay-images/
total 8
drwx------. 1 root root   630 15 oct 18.36
3b964f33a2bf66108d5333a541d376f63e0506aba8ddd4813f9d4e10427
1d9f0
-rw-------. 1 root root 1613 15 oct 18.36 images.json
-rw-r--r--. 1 root root   64 15 oct 18.36 images.lock
```

As we can imagine, in this directory, we can find the metadata of the only container image we pulled down and, in the directory with a very long ID, we will find the manifest file describing the layers that make up our container image.

Let's now check the content of the second directory, `overlay-layers`:

```
# ls -l overlay-layers/
total 1168
-rw-------. 1 root root   2109 15 oct 18.35
0099baae6cd3ca0ced38d658d7871548b32bd0e42118b788d818b76131ec
8e75.tar-split.gz
-rw-------. 1 root root 795206 15 oct 18.35
53498d66ad83a29fcd7c7bcf4abbcc0def4fc912772aa8a4483b51e232309
aee.tar-split.gz
-rw-------. 1 root root  52706 15 oct 18.35
6c26feaaa75c7bac1f1247acc06e73b46e8aaf2e741ad1b8bacd6774bffdf6
ba.tar-split.gz
-rw-------. 1 root root   1185 15 oct 18.35
74fa1495774e94d5cdb579f9bae4a16bd90616024a6f4b1ffd13344c367df1
f6.tar-split.gz
-rw-------. 1 root root 308144 15 oct 18.36
```

```
ae314017e4c2de17a7fb007294521bbe8ac1eeb004ac9fb57d1f1f03090f78
c9.tar-split.gz
-rw-------. 1 root root    1778 15 oct 18.36
beba3570ce7dd1ea38e8a1b919a377b6dc888b24833409eead446bff401d8f
6e.tar-split.gz
-rw-------. 1 root root     697 15 oct 18.36
e59e7d1e1874cc643bfe6f854a72a39f73f22743ab38eff78f91dc019cca91
f5.tar-split.gz
-rw-------. 1 root root    5555 15 oct 18.36
e5a13564f9c6e233da30a7fd86489234716cf80c317e52ff8261bf0cb34dc
7b4.tar-split.gz
-rw-------. 1 root root    3716 15 oct 18.36 layers.json
-rw-r--r--. 1 root root      64 15 oct 19.06 layers.lock
```

As we can see, we just found all the layers' archives downloaded for our container image, but where they have been unpacked? The answer is easy – in the third folder, `overlay`:

```
# ls -l overlay
total 0
drwx------. 1 root root  46 15 oct 18.35
0099baae6cd3ca0ced38d658d7871548b32bd0e42118b788d818b76131ec
8e75
drwx------. 1 root root  46 15 oct 18.35
53498d66ad83a29fcd7c7bcf4abbcc0def4fc912772aa8a4483b51e23230
9aee
drwx------. 1 root root  46 15 oct 18.35
6c26feaaa75c7bac1f1247acc06e73b46e8aaf2e741ad1b8bacd6774bffd
f6ba
drwx------. 1 root root  46 15 oct 18.35
74fa1495774e94d5cdb579f9bae4a16bd90616024a6f4b1ffd13344c367d
f1f6
drwx------. 1 root root  46 15 oct 18.35
ae314017e4c2de17a7fb007294521bbe8ac1eeb004ac9fb57d1f1f03090f
78c9
drwx------. 1 root root  46 15 oct 18.36
beba3570ce7dd1ea38e8a1b919a377b6dc888b24833409eead446bff401d
8f6e
drwx------. 1 root root  46 15 oct 18.36
e59e7d1e1874cc643bfe6f854a72a39f73f22743ab38eff78f91dc019cca
91f5
drwx------. 1 root root  46 15 oct 18.36
```

```
e5a13564f9c6e233da30a7fd86489234716cf80c317e52ff8261bf0cb34d
c7b4
```
```
drwx------. 1 root root 416 15 oct 18.36 l
```

The first question that could arise when looking at the latest directory content is, what's the purpose of the l (L in lowercase) directory?

To answer this question, we have to inspect the content of a layer directory. We can start with the first one on the list:

```
# ls -la
overlay/0099baae6cd3ca0ced38d658d7871548b32bd0e42118b788d818b
76131ec8e75/
```
```
total 8
```
```
drwx------. 1 root root   46 15 oct 18.35 .
```
```
drwx------. 1 root root 1026 15 oct 18.36 ..
```
```
dr-xr-xr-x. 1 root root   24 15 oct 18.35 diff
```
```
-rw-r--r--. 1 root root   26 15 oct 18.35 link
```
```
-rw-r--r--. 1 root root   86 15 oct 18.35 lower
```
```
drwx------. 1 root root    0 15 oct 18.35 merged
```
```
drwx------. 1 root root    0 15 oct 18.35 work
```

Let's understand the purpose of these files and directories:

- diff: This directory represents the upper layer of the overlay, and is used to store any changes to the layer.

- lower: This file reports all the lower layer mounts, ordered from uppermost to lowermost.

- merged: This directory is the one that the overlay is mounted on.

- work: This directory is used for internal operations.

- link: This file contains a unique string for the layer.

Now, coming back to our question, what's the purpose of the l (L in lowercase) directory?

Under the l directory, there are symbolic links with unique strings pointing to the diff directory for every layer. The symbolic links reference lower layers in the lower file. Let's check it:

```
# ls -la overlay/l/
```
```
total 32
```

```
drwx------. 1 root root   416 15 oct 18.36 .
drwx------. 1 root root  1026 15 oct 18.36 ..
lrwxrwxrwx. 1 root root    72 15 oct 18.35 A4ZYMM4AK5NM6JYJA7
EK2DLTGA -> ../74fa1495774e94d5cdb579f9bae4a16bd90616024a6f4
b1ffd13344c367df1f6/diff
lrwxrwxrwx. 1 root root    72 15 oct 18.35 D2WVDYIWL6I77ZOIXR
VQKCXNG2 -> ../
ae314017e4c2de17a7fb007294521bbe8ac1eeb004ac9fb57d1f1f03090
f78c9/diff
lrwxrwxrwx. 1 root root    72 15 oct 18.36 G4KXMAOCE56TIB252
ZMWEFRFHU -> ../
beba3570ce7dd1ea38e8a1b919a377b6dc888b24833409eead446bff401
d8f6e/diff
lrwxrwxrwx. 1 root root    72 15 oct 18.35 JHHF5QA7YSKDSKRSC
HNADBVKDS ->
../53498d66ad83a29fcd7c7bcf4abbcc0def4fc912772aa8a4483b51e2
32309aee/diff
lrwxrwxrwx. 1 root root    72 15 oct 18.36 KNCK5EDUAQJDAIDWQ6
TWDFQF5B -> ../
e59e7d1e1874cc643bfe6f854a72a39f73f22743ab38eff78f91dc019cca
91f5/diff
lrwxrwxrwx. 1 root root    72 15 oct 18.35 LQUM7XDVWHIJRLIWAL
CFKSMJTT ->
../0099baae6cd3ca0ced38d658d7871548b32bd0e42118b788d818b76131
ec8e75/diff
lrwxrwxrwx. 1 root root    72 15 oct 18.35 V6OV3TLBBLTATIJDCTU
6N72XQ5 ->
../6c26feaaa75c7bac1f1247acc06e73b46e8aaf2e741ad1b8bacd6774bf
fdf6ba/diff
lrwxrwxrwx. 1 root root    72 15 oct 18.36 ZMKJYKM2VJEAYQHCI7SU
Q2R3QW -> ../
e5a13564f9c6e233da30a7fd86489234716cf80c317e52ff8261bf0cb34dc7
b4/diff
```

To double-check what we just learned, let's find the first layer of our container image and check whether there is a lower file for it.

Let's inspect the manifest file for our container image:

```
# cat overlay-images/3b964f33a2bf66108d5333a541d376f63e0506ab
a8ddd4813f9d4e104271d9f0/manifest | head -15
{
```

```
    "schemaVersion": 2,
    "mediaType": "application/vnd.docker.distribution.manifest.
v2+json",
    "config": {
        "mediaType": "application/vnd.docker.container.image.v1
+json",
        "size": 16212,
        "digest":
"sha256:3b964f33a2bf66108d5333a541d376f63e0506aba8ddd4813f9d4
e104271d9f0"
    },
    "layers": [
        {
            "mediaType": "application/vnd.docker.image.rootfs.
diff.tar.gzip",
            "size": 75867345,
            "digest":
"sha256:b2cc5146c9c7855cb298ca8b77ecb153d37e3e5c69916ef42361
3a46a70c0503"
        },
```

Then, we must compare the checksum of the compressed archive with the list of all the layers we downloaded:

> **Good to Know**
>
> SHA-256 is an algorithm used to produce a unique cryptographic hash that can be used to verify the integrity of a file (checksum).

```
# cat overlay-layers/layers.json | jq | grep -B3 -A10
"sha256:b2cc5"
  {
    "id":
"53498d66ad83a29fcd7c7bcf4abbcc0def4fc912772aa8a4483b51e23
2309aee",
    "created": "2021-10-15T16:35:49.782784856Z",
    "compressed-diff-digest":
"sha256:b2cc5146c9c7855cb298ca8b77ecb153d37e3e5c69916ef423
613a46a70c0503",
```

```
    "compressed-size": 75867345,
    "diff-digest":
"sha256:53498d66ad83a29fcd7c7bcf4abbcc0def4fc912772aa8a448
3b51e232309aee",
    "diff-size": 211829760,
    "compression": 2,
    "uidset": [
      0,
      192
    ],
    "gidset": [
      0,
```

The file we just analyzed, `overlay-layers/layers.json`, was not indented. For this reason, we used the `jq` utility to format it and make it human-readable.

> **Good to Know**
>
> If you cannot find the `jq` utility on your system, you can install it through the operating system default package manager. On Fedora, for example, you can run `dnf install jq`.

As you can see, we just found the ID of our root layer. Now, let's look at its content:

```
# ls -l
overlay/53498d66ad83a29fcd7c7bcf4abbcc0def4fc912772aa8a448
3b51e232309aee/
total 4
dr-xr-xr-x. 1 root root 158 15 oct 18.35 diff
drwx------. 1 root root   0 15 oct 18.35 empty
-rw-r--r--. 1 root root  26 15 oct 18.35 link
drwx------. 1 root root   0 15 oct 18.35 merged
drwx------. 1 root root   0 15 oct 18.35 work
```

As we can verify, there is not a `lower` file inside the layer's directory because this is the first layer of our container image!

The difference we might notice is the presence of a directory named `empty`. This is because if a layer has no parent, then the overlay system will create a dummy lower directory named `empty` and it will skip writing a `lower` file.

Finally, as the last stage of our practical example, let's run our container and verify that a new `diff` layer will be created. We expect that this layer will contain only the difference between the lower ones.

First, we run our container image we just analyzed:

```
# podman run -d quay.io/centos7/httpd-24-centos7
bd0eef7cd50760dd52c24550be51535bc11559e52eea7d782a1fa69
76524fa76
```

As you can see, we started it in the background through the `-d` option to continue working on the system host. After this, we will execute a new shell on the pod to actually check the container's root folder and create a new file on it:

```
# podman exec -ti
bd0eef7cd50760dd52c24550be51535bc11559e52eea7d782a1fa69
76524fa76 /bin/bash
bash-4.2$ pwd
/opt/app-root/src
bash-4.2$ echo "this is my NOT persistent data" > tempfile.txt
bash-4.2$ ls
tempfile.txt
```

This new file we just created will be temporary and will only last for the lifetime of the container. It is now time to find the `diff` layer that was just created by the overlay driver on our host system. The easiest way is to analyze the mount points used in the running container:

```
bash-4.2$ mount | head
overlay on / type overlay (rw,relatime,context="system_u:
object_r:container_file_t:s0:c300,c861",lowerdir=/var/lib/
containers/storage/overlay/l/ZMKJYKM2VJEAYQHCI7SUQ2R3QW:/var/
lib/containers/storage/overlay/l/G4KXMAOCE56TIB252ZMWEFRFHU:
/var/lib/containers/storage/overlay/l/KNCK5EDUAQJDAIDWQ6TWDF
QF5B:/var/lib/containers/storage/overlay/l/D2WVDYIWL6I77ZOIX
RVQKCXNG2:/var/lib/containers/storage/overlay/l/LQUM7XDVWHI
JRLIWALCFKSMJTT:/var/lib/containers/storage/overlay/l/
A4ZYMM4AK5NM6JYJA7EK2DLTGA:/var/lib/containers/storage/
overlay/l/V6OV3TLBBLTATIJDCTU6N72XQ5:/var/lib/containers/
storage/overlay/l/JHHF5QA7YSKDSKRSCHNADBVKDS,upperdir=/var/
lib/containers/storage/overlay/
b71e4bea5380ca233bf6b0c7a1c276179b841e263ee293e987c6cc54
af516f23/diff,workdir=/var/lib/containers/storage/overlay/
```

```
b71e4bea5380ca233bf6b0c7a1c276179b841e263ee293e987c6cc54af
516f23/work,metacopy=on)
```
```
proc on /proc type proc (rw,nosuid,nodev,noexec,relatime)
```
```
tmpfs on /dev type tmpfs (rw,nosuid,context="system_u:object
_r:container_file_t:s0:c300,c861",size=65536k,mode=755,inode64)
```

As you can see, the first mount point of the list shows a very long line full of layer paths divided by colons. In this long line, we can find the `upperdir` directory we are searching for:

```
upperdir=/var/lib/containers/storage/overlay/
b71e4bea5380ca233bf6b0c7a1c276179b841e263ee293e987c6cc54af5
16f23/diff
```

Now, we can inspect the content of this directory and navigate to the various paths available to find the container root directory where we wrote that file in the previous commands:

```
# ls -la /var/lib/containers/storage/overlay/
b71e4bea5380ca233bf6b0c7a1c276179b841e263ee293e987c6cc54af5
16f23/diff/opt/app-root/src/
```
```
total 12
```
```
drwxr-xr-x. 1 1001 root     58 16 oct 00.40 .
```
```
drwxr-xr-x. 1 1001 root     12 22 set 10.39 ..
```
```
-rw-------. 1 1001 root     81 16 oct 00.46 .bash_history
```
```
-rw-------. 1 1001 root   1024 16 oct 00.38 .rnd
```
```
-rw-r--r--. 1 1001 root     31 16 oct 00.39 tempfile.txt
```
```
# cat /var/lib/containers/storage/overlay/
b71e4bea5380ca233bf6b0c7a1c276179b841e263ee293e987c6cc54af5
16f23/diff/opt/app-root/src/tempfile.txt
```
```
this is my NOT persistent data
```

As we verified, the data is stored on the host operating system, but it is stored in a temporary layer that will sooner or later be removed once the container is removed!

Now, coming back to the original topic that sent us on this small trip under the hood of the overlay storage driver, we were talking about `/etc/containers/storage.conf`. This file holds all the configurations for the *containers/storage* project that is responsible for sharing an underlying common method to access container storage on a host.

The other options available in this file are related to the customization of the storage driver as well as changing the default path for the internal storage directories.

The last point we should briefly talk about is the `runroot` directory. In this folder, the container storage program will store all temporary writable content produced by the container.

If we inspect the folder on our running host where we started the container for the previous example, we will find that there is a folder named with its ID with various files that have been mounted on the container to replace the original files:

```
# ls -l /run/containers/storage/overlay-containers/
bd0eef7cd50760dd52c24550be51535bc11559e52eea7d782a1fa69765
24fa76/userdata
total 20
-rw-r--r--. 1 root root   6 16 oct 00.38 conmon.pid
-rw-r--r--. 1 root root  12 16 oct 00.38 hostname
-rw-r--r--. 1 root root 230 16 oct 00.38 hosts
-rw-r--r--. 1 root root   0 16 oct 00.38 oci-log
-rwx------. 1 root root   6 16 oct 00.38 pidfile
-rw-r--r--. 1 root root  34 16 oct 00.38 resolv.conf
drwxr-xr-x. 3 root root  60 16 oct 00.38 run
```

As you can see from the preceding output, the container's folder under the `runroot` path contains various files that have been mounted directly onto the container to customize it.

To wrap up, in the previous examples, we analyzed the anatomy of a container image and what happens once we run a new container from that image. The technology behind the scenes is amazing and we saw that a lot of features are related to the isolation capabilities offered by the operating system. Here, storage offers other important functionalities that have made containers the greatest technology that we all now know about.

Copying files in and out of a container

Podman enables users to move files into and out of a running container. This result is achieved using the `podman cp` command, which can move files and folders to and from a container. Its usage is quite simple and will be illustrated in the next example.

First, let's start a new Alpine container:

```
$ podman run -d --name alpine_cp_test alpine sleep 1000
```

Now, let's grab a file from the container – we have chosen the `/etc/os-release` file, which provides some information about the distribution and its version ID:

```
$ podman cp alpine_cp_test:/etc/os-release /tmp
```

The file has been copied to the host `/tmp` folder and can be inspected:

```
$ cat /tmp/os-release
NAME="Alpine Linux"
ID=alpine
VERSION_ID=3.14.2
PRETTY_NAME="Alpine Linux v3.14"
HOME_URL=https://alpinelinux.org/
BUG_REPORT_URL="https://bugs.alpinelinux.org/"
```

In the opposite direction, we can copy files or folders from the host to the running container:

```
$ podman cp /tmp/build_folder alpine_cp_test:/
```

This example copies the `/tmp/build_folder` folder, and all its content, under the root filesystem of the Alpine container. We can then inspect the result of the copy command by using `podman exec` with the `ls` utility command.

Interacting with overlayfs

There is another way to copy files from a container to the host, which is by using the `podman mount` command and interacting directly with the merged overlays.

To mount a running rootless container's filesystem, we first need to run the `podman unshare` command, which permits users to run commands inside a modified user namespace:

```
$ podman unshare
```

This command drops a root shell in a new user namespace configured with *UID 0* and *GID 0*. It is now possible to run the `podman mount` command and obtain the absolute path of the mount point:

```
# cd $(podman mount alpine_cp_test)
```

The preceding command uses shell expansion to change to the path of the `MergedDir`, which, as the name says, merges the `LowerDir` and `UpperDir` contents to provide a unified view of the different layers. From now on, it is possible to copy files to and from the container root filesystem.

The previous examples were based on rootless containers, but the same logic applies to rootful containers. Let's start a rootful Nginx container:

```
$ sudo podman run -d \
  --name rootful_nginx docker.io/library/nginx
```

To copy files in and out, we need to prepend the `sudo` command:

```
$ sudo podman cp \
  rootful_nginx:/usr/share/nginx/html/index.html /tmp
```

The preceding command copies the default `index.html` page to the host `/tmp` directory. Keep in mind that `sudo` elevates the user privileges to root, and therefore copied files will have *UID 0* and *GID 0* ownership.

The practice of copying files and folders from a container is especially useful for troubleshooting purposes. The opposite action of copying them inside a running container can be useful for updating and testing secrets or configuration files. In that case, we have the option of persisting those changes, as described in the next subsection.

Persisting changes with podman commit

The previous examples are not a method for permanently customizing running containers, since the immutable nature of containers implies that persistent modifications should go through an image rebuild.

However, if we need to preserve the changes and produce a new image without starting a new build, the `podman commit` command provides a way to persist the changes to a container into a new image.

The commit concept is of primary importance in Docker and OCI image builds. In fact, we can see the different steps of a Dockerfile as a series of commits applied during the build process.

The following example shows how to persist a file copied into a running container and produce a new image. Let's say we want to update the default index.html page of our Nginx container:

```
$ echo "Hello World!" > /tmp/index.html
$ podman run --name custom_nginx -d -p \
  8080:80 docker.io/library/nginx
$ podman cp /tmp/index.html \
  custom_nginx:/usr/share/nginx/html/
```

Let's test the changes applied:

```
$ curl localhost:8080
Hello World!
```

Now we want to persist the changed index.html file into a new image, starting from the running container with podman commit:

```
$ podman commit -p custom_nginx hello-world-nginx
```

The preceding command persists the changes by effectively creating a new image layer containing the updated files and folders.

The previous container can now be safely stopped and removed before testing the new custom image:

```
$ podman stop custom_nginx && podman rm custom_nginx
```

Let's test the new custom image and inspect the changed index.html file:

```
$ podman run -d -p 8080:80 --name hello_world \
  localhost/hello-world-nginx
$ curl localhost:8080
Hello World!
```

In this section, we have learned how to copy files to and from a running container and how to commit the changes on the fly by producing a new image.

In the next section, we are going to learn how host storage is attached to a container by introducing the concept of **volumes** and **bind mounts**.

Attaching host storage to a container

We have already talked about the immutable nature of containers. Starting from pre-built images, when we run a container, we instance a read/write layer on top of a stack of read-only layers using a copy-on-write approach.

Containers are ephemeral objects based on a stateful image. This implies that containers are not meant to store data inside them – if a container crashes or is removed, all the data would be lost. We need a way to store data in a separate location that is mounted inside the running container, preserved when the container is removed, and ready to be reused by a new container.

There is another important caveat that should not be forgotten – **secrets** and **config files**. When we build an image, we can pass all the files and folders we need inside it. However, sealing secrets like certificates or keys inside a build is not a good practice. If we need, for example, to rotate a certificate, we must rebuild the whole image from scratch. In the same way, changing a config file that resides inside an image implies a new rebuild every time we change a setting.

For these reasons, OCI specifications support **volumes** and **bind mounts** to manage storage attached to a container. In the next sections, we will learn how volumes and bind mounts work and how to attach them to a container.

Managing and attaching bind mounts to a container

Let's start with bind mounts since they leverage a native Linux feature. According to the official Linux man pages, a bind mount is *a way to remount a part of the filesystem hierarchy somewhere else*. This means that using bind mounts, we can replicate the view of a directory under another mount point in the host.

Before learning how containers use bind mounts, let's see a basic example where we simply bind mount the /etc directory under the /mnt directory:

```
$ sudo mount --bind /etc /mnt
```

After issuing this command, we will see the exact contents of /etc under /mnt. To unmount, simply run the following command:

```
$ sudo umount /mnt
```

The same concept can be applied to containers – Podman can bind mount host directories inside a container and offers dedicated CLI options to simplify the mount process.

Podman offers two options that can be used to bind mount: `-v | --volume` and `–mount`. Let's cover these in more detail.

-v|--volume option

This option uses a compact, single field argument to define the source host directory and the container mount point with the pattern `/HOST_DIR:/CONTAINER_DIR`. The following example mounts the `/host_files` directory on the `/mnt` mount point inside the container:

```
$ podman run -v /host_files:/mnt docker.io/library/nginx
```

It is possible to pass extra arguments to define mount behavior; for example, to mount the host directory as read-only:

```
$ podman run -v /host_files:/mnt:ro \
   docker.io/library/nginx
```

Other viable options for bind mounts using the `-v | --volume` option can be found in the run command man page (`man podman-run`).

--mount option

This option is more verbose since it uses a *key=value* syntax to define source and destinations as well as the mount type and extra arguments. This option accepts different mount types (bind mounts, volumes, tmpfs, images, and devpts) in the `type=TYPE,source=HOST_DIR,destination=CONTAINER_DIR` pattern. The source and destination keys can be replaced with the shorter `src` and `dst`, respectively. The previous example can be rewritten as follows:

```
$ podman run \
   --mount type=bind,src=/host_files,dst=/mnt \
   docker.io/library/nginx
```

We can also pass an extra option by adding an extra comma; for example, to mount the host directory as read-only:

```
$ podman run \
   --mount type=bind,src=/host_files,dst=/mnt,ro=true \
   docker.io/library/nginx
```

Despite being very simple to use and understand, bind mounts have some limitations that could impact the life cycle of the container in some cases. Host files and directories must exist before running the containers and permissions must be set accordingly to make them readable or writable. Another important caveat to keep in mind is that a bind mount always obfuscates the underlying mount point in the container if populated by files or directories. A useful alternative to bind mounts is **volumes**, described in the next subsection.

Managing and attaching volumes to a container

A volume is a directory created and managed directly by the container engine and mounted to a mount point inside the container. They offer a great solution for persisting data generated by a container.

Volumes can be managed using the `podman volume` command, which can be used to list, inspect, create, and remove volumes in the system. Let's start with a basic example, with a volume automatically created by Podman on top of the Nginx document root:

```
$ podman run -d -p 8080:80  --name nginx_volume1 -v /usr/share/
nginx/html docker.io/library/nginx
```

This time, the –v option has an argument with only one item – the document root directory. In this case, Podman automatically creates a volume and bind mounts it to the target mount point.

To prove that a new volume has been created, we can inspect the container:

```
$ podman inspect nginx_volume1
[...omitted output...]
"Mounts": [
            {
                "Type": "volume",
                "Name":
"2ed93716b7ad73706df5c6f56bda262920accec59e7b6642d36f938e936
d36d9",
                "Source": "/home/packt/.local/share/containers
/storage/volumes/2ed93716b7ad73706df5c6f56bda262920accec59e7b6
642d36f93
8e936d36d9/_data",
                "Destination": "/usr/share/nginx/html",
                "Driver": "local",
                "Mode": "",
                "Options": [
```

```
                    "nosuid",
                    "nodev",
                    "rbind"
                ],
                "RW": true,
                "Propagation": "rprivate"
            }
        ],
[...omitted output]
```

In the `Mounts` section, we have a list of objects mounted in the container. The only item is an object of the `volume` type, with a generated UID as its `Name` and a `Source` field that represents its path in the host, while the `Destination` field is the mount point inside the container.

We can double-check the existence of the volume with the `podman volume ls` command:

```
$ podman volume ls
DRIVER VOLUME NAME
local  2ed93716b7ad73706df5c6f56bda262920accec59e7b6642d36f93
8e936d36d9
```

Looking inside the source path, we will find the default files in the container document root:

```
$ ls -al
/home/packt/.local/share/containers/storage/
volumes/2ed93716b7ad73706df5c6f56bda262920accec59e7b6642d36f93
8e936d36d9/_data
total 16
drwxr-xr-x. 2 gbsalinetti gbsalinetti 4096 Sep  9 20:26 .
drwx------. 3 gbsalinetti gbsalinetti 4096 Oct 16 22:41 ..
-rw-r--r--. 1 gbsalinetti gbsalinetti  497 Sep  7 17:21 50x.
html
-rw-r--r--. 1 gbsalinetti gbsalinetti  615 Sep  7 17:21 index.
html
```

This demonstrated that when an empty volume is created, it is populated with the content of the target mount point. When a container stops, the volume is preserved along with all the data and can be reused when the container is restarted by another container.

The preceding example shows a volume with a generated UID, but it is possible to choose the name of the attached volume, as in the following example:

```
$ podman run -d -p 8080:80  --name nginx_volume2 -v nginx_vol:/
usr/share/nginx/html docker.io/library/nginx
```

In the preceding example, Podman creates a new volume named nginx_vol and stores it under the default volumes directory. When a named volume is created, Podman does not need to generate a UID.

The default volumes directory has different paths for rootless and rootful containers:

- For rootless containers, the default volume storage path is <USER_HOME>/.
  local/share/containers/storage/volumes.
- For rootful containers, the default volume storage path is /var/lib/
  containers/storage/volumes.

Volumes created in those paths are persisted after the container is destroyed and can be reused by other containers.

To manually remove a volume, use the podman volume rm command:

```
$ podman volume rm nginx_vol
```

When dealing with multiple volumes, the podman volume prune command removes all the unused volumes. The following example prunes all the volumes in the user default volume storage (the one used by rootless containers):

```
$ podman volume prune
```

The next example shows how to remove volumes used by rootful containers by using the sudo prefix:

```
$ sudo podman volume prune
```

> **Important Note**
>
> Do not forget to monitor volumes accumulating in the host since they consume disk space that could be reclaimed, and prune unused volumes periodically to avoid cluttering the host storage.

Users can also preliminarily create and populate volumes before running the container. The following example uses the `podman create volume` command to create the volume mounted to the Nginx document root and then populates it with a test `index.html` file:

```
$ podman volume create custom_nginx
$ echo "Hello World!" >> $(podman volume inspect custom_nginx -
format "{{ .Mountpoint }}")/index.html
```

We can now run a new Nginx container using the pre-populated volume:

```
$ podman run -d -p 8080:80  --name nginx_volume3 -v custom_
nginx:/usr/share/nginx/html docker.io/library/nginx
```

The HTTP test shows the updated contents:

```
$ curl localhost:8080
Hello World!
```

This time, the volume, which was not empty in the beginning, obfuscated the container target directory with its contents.

Mounting volumes with the --mount option

As with bind mounts, we can freely choose between the `-v|--volume` and the `--mount` options. The following example runs an Nginx container using the `--mount` flag:

```
$ podman run -d -p 8080:80  --name nginx_volume4 --mount
type=volume,src=custom_nginx,dst=/usr/share/nginx/html docker.
io/library/nginx
```

While the `-v|--volume` option is compact and widely adopted, the advantage of the `--mount` option is a more clear and expressive syntax, along with an exact statement of the mount type.

Volume drivers

The preceding volume examples are all based on the same **local** volume driver, which is used to manage volume in the local filesystem of the host. Additional volume drivers can be configured in the `/usr/share/containers/containers.conf` file in the `[engine.volume_plugins]` section by passing the plugin name followed by the file or socket path.

The local volume driver can also be used to mount **NFS** shares in the host running the container. This result cannot be achieved with rootless containers anyway. The following example shows how to create a volume backed by an NFS share and mount it inside a MongoDB container on its /data/db directory:

```
$ sudo podman volume create --driver local
--opt type=nfs --opt o=addr=nfs-host.example.
com,rw,context="system_u:object_r:container_file_t:s0" --opt
device=:/opt/nfs-export nfs-volume
$ sudo podman run -d -v nfs-volume:/data/db docker.io/library/
mongo
```

A prerequisite of the preceding example is the preliminary configuration of the NFS server, which should be accessible by the host running the container.

Volumes in builds

Volumes can be pre-defined during the image build process. This lets image maintainers define which container directories will be automatically attached to volumes. To understand this concept, let's inspect this minimal Dockerfile:

```
FROM docker.io/library/nginx:latest
VOLUME /usr/share/nginx/html
```

The only change made to the docker.io/library/nginx image is a **VOLUME** directive, which defines which directory should be externally mounted as an anonymous volume in the host. This is simply metadata, and the volume will be created only at runtime when a container is started from this image.

If we build the image and run a container based on the example Dockerfile, we can see an automatically created anonymous volume:

```
$ podman build -t my_nginx .
$ podman run -d --name volumes_from_build my_nginx
$ podman inspect volumes_from_build --format "{{ .Mounts }}"
[{volume 4d6ac7edcb4f01add205523b7733d61ae4a5772786eacca68e49
72b20fd1180c /home/packt/.local/share/containers/storage/
volumes/4d6ac7edcb4f01add205523b7733d61ae4a5772786eacca68e4972
b20fd1180c/_data /usr/share/nginx/html local  [nodev exec
nosuid rbind] true rprivate}]
```

Without an explicit volume creation option, Podman has already created and mounted the container volume. This automatic volume definition at build time is a common practice in all containers that are expected to persist data, like databases.

For example, the `docker.io/library/mongo` image is already configured to create two volumes, one for `/data/configdb` and one for `/data/db`. The same behavior can be identified in the most common databases, including PostgreSQL, MariaDB, and MySQL.

It is possible to define how pre-defined anonymous volumes should be mounted when the container is started. The default ID **bind**, which means that new volumes are created and bind-mounted in the container, but it is possible to use **tmpfs** or ignore the mount altogether with the `--image-volume` option. The following example starts a MongoDB container with its default volumes mounted as tmpfs:

```
$ podman run -d --image-volume tmpfs docker.io/library/mongo
```

In *Chapter 6, Meet Buildah – Building Containers from Scratch*, we will cover the build process in greater detail. We now close this subsection with an example of how to mount volumes across multiple containers.

Mounting volumes across containers

One of the greatest advantages of volumes is their flexibility. For example, a container can mount volumes from an already running container to share the same data. To accomplish this result, we can use the `--volumes-from` option. The following example starts a MongoDB container and then cross mounts its volumes on a Fedora container:

```
$ podman run -d --name mongodb01 docker.io/library/mongo
$ podman run -it --volumes-from=mongodb01 docker.io/library/
fedora
```

The second container drops an interactive root shell we can use to inspect the filesystem content:

```
[root@c10420016687 /]# ls -al /data
total 20
drwxr-xr-t.  4 root root 4096 Oct 17 15:36 .
dr-xr-xr-x. 19 root root 4096 Oct 17 15:36 ..
drwxr-xr-x.  2  999  999 4096 Sep 20 22:20 configdb
drwxr-xr-x.  4  999  999 4096 Oct 17 15:36 db
```

As expected, we can find the MongoDB volumes mounted in the Fedora container. If we stop and even remove the first `mongodb01` container, the volumes remain active and mounted inside the Fedora container.

Until now, we have seen basic use cases with no specific segregation between containers or mounted resources. If the host has SELinux enabled and in enforcing mode, some extra considerations must be applied.

SELinux considerations for mounts

SELinux recursively applies labels to files and directories to define their context. Those labels are usually stored as extended filesystem attributes. SELinux uses contexts to manage policies and define which processes can access a specific resource.

The `ls` command is used to see the type context of a resource:

```
$ ls -alZ /etc/passwd
-rw-r--r--. 1 root root system_u:object_r:passwd_file_t:s0 2965
Jul 28 21:00 /etc/passwd
```

In the preceding example, the `passwd_file_t` label defines the type context of the `/etc/passwd` file. Depending on the type context, a program can or cannot access a file while SELinux is running in enforcing mode.

Processes also have their type context – containers run with the label `container_t` and have read/write access to files and directories labeled with `container_file_t` type context, and read/execute access to `container_share_t` labeled resources.

Other host directories accessible by default are `/etc` as read-only and `/usr` as read/execute. Also, resources under `/var/lib/containers/overlay/` are labeled as `container_share_t`.

What happens if we try to mount a directory not correctly labeled?

Podman still executes the container without complaining about the wrong labeling, but the mounted directory or file will not be accessible from a process running inside the containers, which are labeled with the `container_t` context type. The following example tries to mount a custom document root for an Nginx container without respecting the labeling constraints:

```
$ mkdir ~/custom_docroot
$ echo "Hello World!" > ~/custom_docroot/index.html
```

```
$ podman run -d \
    --name custom_nginx \
  -p 8080:80 \
    -v ~/custom_docroot:/usr/share/nginx/html \
    docker.io/library/nginx
```

Apparently, everything went fine – the container started properly and the processes inside it are running, but if we try to contact the Nginx server, we see the error:

```
$ curl localhost:8080
<html>
<head><title>403 Forbidden</title></head>
<body>
<center><h1>403 Forbidden</h1></center>
<hr><center>nginx/1.21.3</center>
</body>
</html>
```

`403 - Forbidden` shows that the Nginx process cannot access the `index.html` page. To fix this error, we have two options – put SELinux in **permissive** mode or relabel the mounted resources. By putting SELinux in permissive mode, it continues to track down the violations without blocking them. Anyway, this is not a good practice and should be used only when we cannot correctly troubleshoot access issues and need to put SELinux out of the equation. The following command sets SELinux to permissive mode:

```
$ sudo setenforce 0
```

> **Important Note**
> Permissive mode is not equal to disabling SELinux entirely. When working in this mode, SELinux still logs AVC denials without blocking. System admins can immediately switch between permissive and enforcing modes without rebooting. Disabling, on the other hand, implies a full system reboot.

The second preferred option is to simply relabel the resources we need to mount. To achieve this result, we could use SELinux command-line tools. As a shortcut, Podman offers a simpler way – the :z and :Z suffixes applied to the volume mount arguments. The difference between the two suffixes is subtle:

- The :z suffix tells Podman to relabel the mounted resources in order to enable all containers to read and write it. It works with both volumes and bind mounts.

- The :Z suffix tells Podman to relabel the mounted resources in order to enable only the current container to read and write it exclusively. This also works with both volumes and bind mounts.

To test the difference, let's try to run the container again with the :z suffix and see what happens:

```
$ podman run -d \
  --name custom_nginx \
  -p 8080:80 \
  -v ~/custom_docroot:/usr/share/nginx/html:z \
  docker.io/library/nginx
```

Now, the HTTP calls return the expected results since the process was able to access the index.html file without being blocked by SELinux:

```
$ curl localhost:8080
Hello World!
```

Let's look at the SELinux file context automatically applied to the mounted directory:

```
$ ls -alZ ~/custom_docroot
total 20
drwxrwxr-x.  2 packt packt system_u:object_r:container_
file_t:s0  4096 Oct 16 15:53 .
drwxrwxr-x. 74 packt packt unconfined_u:object_r:user_home_
dir_t:s0 12288 Oct 16 16:32 ..
-rw-rw-r--.  1 packt packt system_u:object_r:container_
file_t:s0  13 Oct 16 15:53 index.html
```

Let's focus on the `system_u:object_r:container_file_t:s0` label. The final `s0` field is a **Multi-Level Security** (**MLS**) sensitivity level, which means that all processes with the same sensitivity level will have read/write access to the resource. Therefore, other containers that run with the `s0` sensitivity level will be able to mount the resource with read/write access privileges. This also represents a security issue since a malicious container on the same host would be able to attack other containers by stealing or overwriting data.

The solution to this problem is called **Multi-Category Security** (**MCS**). SELinux uses MCS to configure additional categories, which are plaintext labels applied to the resources along with the other SELinux labels. MCS-labeled objects are then accessible only to processes with the same categories assigned.

When a container is started, processes inside it are labeled with MCS categories, following the pattern **cXXX,cYYY**, where XXX and YYY are randomly picked integers.

Podman automatically applies MCS categories to mounted resources when Z (uppercase) is passed. To test this behavior, let's run the Nginx container again with the `:Z` suffix:

```
$ podman run -d \
   --name custom_nginx \
  -p 8080:80 \
   -v ~/custom_docroot:/usr/share/nginx/html:Z \
   docker.io/library/nginx
```

We can immediately see that the mounted folder has been relabeled with MCS categories:

```
$ ls -alZ ~/custom_docroot
total 20
drwxrwxr-x.  2 packt packt system_u:object_r:container_
file_t:s0:c16,c898  4096 Oct 16 15:53 .
drwxrwxr-x. 74 packt packt unconfined_u:object_r:user_home_
dir_t:s0        12288 Oct 16 21:12 ..
-rw-rw-r--.  1 packt packt system_u:object_r:container_
file_t:s0:c16,c898    13 Oct 16 15:53 index.html
```

A simple test will return the expected `Hello World!` text, proving that the processes inside the container are allowed to access the target resources:

```
$ curl localhost:8080
Hello World!
```

What happens if we run a second container with the same approach, by applying : z again to the same bind mount?

```
$ podman run -d \
   --name custom_nginx2 \
  -p 8081:80 \
  -v ~/custom_docroot:/usr/share/nginx/html:Z \
   docker.io/library/nginx
```

This time, we run the HTTP test on port 8081 and HTTP GET still works correctly:

```
$ curl localhost:8081
Hello World!
```

However, if we test once again the container mapped to port 8080, we will get an unexpected 403 Forbidden message:

```
$ curl localhost:8080
<html>
<head><title>403 Forbidden</title></head>
<body>
<center><h1>403 Forbidden</h1></center>
<hr><center>nginx/1.21.3</center>
</body>
</html>
```

Not surprisingly, the second container was executed with the : z suffix and relabeled the directory with a new pair of MCS categories, thus making the first container unable to access the previously available content.

> **Important Note**
> The previous examples were conducted with bind mounts, but applied to volumes in the same way. Use these techniques with caution to avoid unwanted relabels of a bind mounted system or home directories.

In this subsection, we demonstrated the power of SELinux to manage containers and resource isolation. Let's conclude this chapter with an overview of other types of storage that can be attached to containers.

Attaching other types of storage to a container

Along with bind mounts and volumes, it is possible to attach other types of storage to containers, more specifically, of the kinds **tmpfs**, **image**, and **devpts**.

Attaching tmpfs storage

Sometimes, we need to attach storage to containers that is not meant to be persistent (for example, cache usage). Using volumes or bind mounts would clutter the host local disk (or any other backend if using different storage drivers). In those particular cases, we can use a **tmpfs** volume.

tmpfs is a virtual memory filesystem, which means that all its contents are created inside the host virtual memory. A benefit of tmpfs is that it provides faster I/O since all the read/write operations mostly happen in the RAM.

To attach a tmpfs volume to a container, we can use the `--mount` option or the `--tmpfs` option.

The `--mount` flag has the great advantage of being more verbose and expressive regarding the storage type, source, destination, and extra mount options. The following example runs an `httpd` container with a tmpfs volume attached to the container:

```
$ podman run -d -p 8080:80 \
    --name tmpfs_example1 \
    --mount type=tmpfs,tmpfs-size=512M,destination=/tmp \
    docker.io/library/httpd
```

The preceding command creates a tmpfs volume of 512 MB and mounts it on the `/tmp` folder of the container. We can test the correct mount creation by running the `mount` command inside the container:

```
$ podman exec -it tmpfs_example1 mount | grep '\/tmp'
tmpfs on /tmp type tmpfs
(rw,nosuid,nodev,relatime,context="system_u:object_r:container_
file_t:s0:c375,c804",size=524288k,uid=1000,gid=1000,inode64
```

This demonstrates that the tmpfs filesystem has been correctly mounted inside the container. Stopping the container will automatically discard tmpfs:

```
$ podman stop tmpfs_example1
```

The following example mounts a tmpfs volume using the `--tmpfs` option:

```
$ podman run -d -p 8080:80 \
    --name tmpfs_example2 \
    --tmpfs /tmp:rw,size= 524288k,mode=1777 \
    docker.io/library/httpd
```

This example provides the same results as the previous one: a running container with a 512 MB tmpfs volume mounted on the `/tmp` directory in read/write mode and `1777` permissions.

By default, the tmpfs volume is mounted inside the container with the following mount options – **rw**, **noexec**, **nosuid**, and **nodev**.

Another interesting feature is the automatic MCS labeling from SELinux. This provides automatic segregation of the filesystem and prevents any other container from accessing the data in memory.

Attaching images

OCI images are the base that provides layers and metadata to start containers, but they can also be attached to a container filesystem at runtime. This can be useful for troubleshooting purposes or for attaching binaries that are available in a foreign image. When an OCI image is mounted inside a container, an extra overlay is created. This implies that even when the image is mounted with read/write permissions, users never alter the original image but the upper overlay only.

The following example mounts a `busybox` image with read/write permissions inside an Alpine container:

```
$ podman run -it \
    --mount type=image,src=docker.io/library/busybox,dst=/
mnt,rw=true \
    alpine
```

> **Important Note**
> The mounted image must already be cached in the host. Podman only pulls the base container image if it is available when a container is created, but it expects the mounted images to already be available. A preliminary pull of the images will solve the issue.

Attaching devpts

This option is useful for attaching a **pseudo terminal slave** (**PTS**) to a container. This feature was introduced in Podman 2.1.0 to support containers that need to mount / dev/ from the host into the container, while still creating a terminal. The /dev pseudo filesystem of the host enables containers to gain direct access to the machine's physical or virtual devices.

To create a container with the /dev filesystem and a devpts device attached, run the following command:

```
$ sudo podman run -it \
  -v /dev/:/dev:rslave \
  --mount type=devpts,destination=/dev/pts \
  docker.io/library/fedora
```

To check the result of the mount option, we require an extra tool inside the container. For this reason, we can install it with the following command:

```
[root@034c8a61a4fc /]# dnf install -y toolbox
```

The resulting container has an extra, non-isolated, devpts device mounted on /dev/pts:

```
# mount | grep '\/dev\/pts'
devpts on /dev/pts type devpts
(rw,nosuid,noexec,relatime,seclabel,gid=5,mode=620,ptmxmode=
000)
devpts on /dev/pts type devpts
(rw,nosuid,noexec,relatime,context="system_u:object_r:
container_file_t:s0:c299,c741",gid=5,mode=620,ptmxmode=666)
```

The preceding output was extracted by running the mount command inside the container.

Summary

In this chapter, we have completed a journey on container storage and Podman features offered to manipulate it. The material in this chapter is crucial to understanding how Podman manages both ephemeral and persistent data and provides best practices to users to manipulate their data.

In the first section, we learned why container storage matters and how it should be correctly managed both in single host and orchestrated, multi-host environments.

In the second section, we took a deep dive into container storage features and storage drivers, with a special focus on overlayfs.

In the third section, we learned how to copy files to and from a container. We also saw how changes could be committed to a new image.

The fourth section described the different possible scenarios of storage attached to a container, covering bind mounts, volumes, tmpfs, images, and devpts. This section was also a perfect fit to discuss SELinux interaction with storage management and see how we can use it to isolate storage resources across containers on the same host.

In the next chapter, we will learn a very important topic for both developers and operations teams, which is how to build OCI images with both Podman and **Buildah**, an advanced and specialized image-building tool.

Further reading

Refer to the following resources for more information:

- Containers Storage project page: `https://github.com/containers/storage`

- Container Labeling: `https://danwalsh.livejournal.com/81269.html`

- Why you should be using Multi-Category Security for your Linux containers: `https://www.redhat.com/en/blog/why-you-should-be-using-multi-category-security-your-linux-containers`

- Udica: Generate SELinux policies: `https://github.com/containers/udica`

- Overlay source code: `https://github.com/containers/storage/blob/main/drivers/overlay/overlay.go`

Section 2: Building Containers from Scratch with Buildah

In this part, you will learn the basics of the container creation process, applying the theory we saw in the previous chapter, and choosing the right secure base images to start building new container images from scratch.

This part of the book comprises the following chapters:

6

Meet Buildah – Building Containers from Scratch

The great appeal of containers is that they allow us to package applications inside immutable images that can be deployed on systems and run seamlessly. In this chapter, we will learn how to create images using different techniques and tools. This includes learning how an image build works under the hood and how to create images from scratch.

In this chapter, we're going to cover the following main topics:

- Basic image building with Podman
- Meet Buildah, Podman's companion tool for builds
- Preparing our environment
- Choosing our build strategy
- Building images from scratch
- Building images from a Dockerfile

Technical requirements

Before proceeding with this chapter, a machine with a working Podman installation is required. As stated in *Chapter 3*, *Running the First Container*, all the examples in the book are executed on a Fedora 34 system or later but can be reproduced on the reader's choice of OS.

A good understanding of the topics covered in *Chapter 4*, *Managing Running Containers*, is useful to easily grasp concepts regarding **Open Container Initiative** (**OCI**) images.

Basic image building with Podman

A container's OCI image is a set of immutable layers stacked together with a copy-on-write logic. When an image is built, all the layers are created in a precise order and then pushed to the container registry, which stores our layers as tar-based archives along with additional image metadata.

As we learned in the *OCI Images* section of *Chapter 2*, *Comparing Podman and Docker*, these manifests are necessary to correctly reassemble the image layers (the image manifest and the image index) and to pass runtime configurations to the container engine (the image configuration).

Before proceeding with the basic examples of image builds with Podman, we need to understand how image builds generally work to grasp the simple but very smart key concepts that lay beneath.

Builds under the hood

Container images can be built in different ways, but the most common approach, probably one of the keys to the huge success of containers, is based on Dockerfiles.

A **Dockerfile**, as the name suggests, is the main configuration file for Docker builds and is a plain list of actions to be executed in the build process.

Over time, Dockerfiles became a standard in OCI image builds and today are adopted in many use cases.

> **Important Note**
> To standardize and remove the association with the brand, Containerfiles were also introduced; they have the very same syntax as Dockerfiles and are supported natively by Podman. In this book, we will use the two terms *Dockerfile* and *Containerfile* interchangeably.

We will learn in detail Dockerfiles' syntax in the next subsection. For now, let's just focus on a concept – a Dockerfile is a set of build instructions that the build tool executes sequentially. Let's look at this example:

```
FROM docker.io/library/fedora
RUN dnf install -y httpd && dnf clean all -y
COPY index.html /var/www/html
CMD ["/usr/sbin/httpd", "-DFOREGROUND"]
```

This basic example of a Dockerfile holds only four instructions:

- The FROM instruction, which defines the base image that will be used
- The RUN instruction, which executes some actions during the build (in this example, installing packages with the dnf package manager)
- The COPY instruction, which copies files or directories from the build working directory to the image
- The CMD instruction, which defines the command to be executed when the container starts

When the RUN and the COPY actions of the example are executed, new layers that hold the changes are cached in intermediate layers, represented by temporary containers. This is a native feature in Docker that has the advantage of reusing cached layers on further builds when no changes are requested on a specific layer. All the intermediate containers will produce read-only layers merged by the overlay graph driver.

Users don't need to manually manage the cached layers – the engine automatically implements the necessary actions by creating the temporary containers, executing the actions defined by the Dockerfile instructions, and then committing. By repeating the same logic for all the necessary instructions, Podman creates a new image with additional layers on top of the ones of the base image.

It is possible to squash the image layers into a single one to avoid a negative impact on the overlay's performances. Podman offers the same features and lets you choose between caching intermediate layers or not.

Not all Dockerfile instructions change the filesystem, and only the ones that do it will create a new image layer; all the other instructions, such as the CMD instruction in the preceding example, produce an empty layer with metadata only and no changes in the overlay filesystem.

In general, the only instructions that create new layers by effectively changing the filesystem are the RUN, COPY, and ADD instructions. All the other instructions in a Dockerfile or Containerfile just create temporary intermediate images and do not impact the final image filesystem.

This is also a good reason to keep the number of Dockerfile RUN, COPY, and ADD instructions limited, since having images cluttered with too many layers is not a good pattern and impacts the graph driver performances.

We can inspect an image's history and the actions that have been applied to every layer. The following example shows an excerpt of the output from the podman inspect command, with the target image being a potential one created from the previous sample Dockerfile:

```
$ podman inspect myhttpd
[...omitted output]
        "History": [
            {
                "created": "2021-04-01T17:59:37.09884046Z",
                "created_by": "/bin/sh -c #(nop)    LABEL
maintainer=Clement Verna \u003ccverna@fedoraproject.org\
u003e",
                "empty_layer": true
            },
            {
                "created": "2021-04-01T18:00:19.741002882Z",
                "created_by": "/bin/sh -c #(nop)    ENV
DISTTAG=f34container FGC=f34 FBR=f34",
                "empty_layer": true
            },
            {
                "created": "2021-07-23T11:16:05.060688497Z",
                "created_by": "/bin/sh -c #(nop) ADD file:85d7
f2d8e4f31d81b27b8e18dfc5687b5dabfaafdb2408a3059e120e4c15307b in
/ "
            },
            {
                "created": "2021-07-23T11:16:05.833115975Z",
                "created_by": "/bin/sh -c #(nop)    CMD [\"/bin/
bash\"]",
```

```
                        "empty_layer": true
            },
            {
                        "created": "2021-10-24T21:27:18.783034844Z",
                        "created_by": "/bin/sh -c dnf install -y httpd
\u0026\u0026 dnf clean all -y  ",
                        "comment": "FROM docker.io/library/
fedora:latest"
            },
            {
                        "created": "2021-10-24T21:27:21.095937071Z",
                        "created_by": "/bin/sh -c #(nop) COPY file:
78c6e1dcd6f819581b54094fd38a3fd8f170a2cb768101e533c964e
04aacab2e in /var/www/html "
            },
            {
                        "created": "2021-10-24T21:27:21.182063974Z",
                        "created_by": "/bin/sh -c #(nop) CMD [\"/usr/
sbin/httpd\", \"-DFOREGROUND\"]",
                        "empty_layer": true
            }
        ]
[...omitted output]
```

Looking at the last three items of the image history, we can note the exact instructions defined in the Dockerfile, including the last CMD instruction that does not create any new layer but instead metadata that will persist in the image config.

With this deeper awareness of the image build logic in mind, let's now explore the most common Dockerfile instructions before proceeding with the Podman build examples.

Dockerfile and Containerfile instructions

As stated before, Dockerfiles and Containerfiles share the same syntax. The instruction in those files should be seen as (and truly are) commands passed to the container engine or build tool. This subsection provides an overview of the most frequently used instructions.

All Dockerfile/Containerfile instructions follow the same pattern:

```
# Comment
INSTRUCTION arguments
```

The following list provides a non-exhaustive list of the most common instructions:

- **FROM**: This is the first instruction of a build stage and defines the base image used as the starting point of the build. It follows the FROM `<image>[:<tag>]` syntax to identify the correct image to use.

- **RUN**: This instruction tells the engine to execute the commands passed as arguments inside a temporary container. It follows the RUN `<command>` syntax. The invoked binary or script must exist in the base image or a previous layer.

  As stated before, the RUN instruction creates a new image layer; therefore, it is a frequent practice to concatenate commands into the same RUN instruction to avoid cluttering too many layers.

  This example compacts three commands inside the same RUN instruction:

  ```
  RUN dnf upgrade -y && \
      dnf install httpd -y && \
      dnf clean all -y
  ```

- **COPY**: This instruction copies files and folders from the build working directory to the build sandbox. Copied resources are persisted in the final image. It follows the COPY `<src>… <dest>` syntax, and it has a very useful option that lets us define the destination user and group instead of manually changing ownership later – `--chown=<user>:<group>`.

- **ADD**: This instruction copies files, folders, and remote URLs to the build destination target. It follows the ADD `<src>… <dest>` syntax. This instruction also supports the automatic extraction of tar files from a source directly into the target path.

- **ENTRYPOINT**: The executed command in the container. It receives arguments from the command line (in the form of podman `run <image> <arguments>`) or from the CMD instruction.

  An ENTRYPOINT image cannot be overridden by command-line arguments. The supported forms are the following:

  - ENTRYPOINT `["command", "param1", "paramN"]` (also known as the *exec* form)

  - ENTRYPOINT `command param1 paramN` (the *shell* form)

If not set, its default value is bash -c. When set to the default value, commands are passed as an argument to the bash process. For example, if a ps aux command is passed as an argument at runtime or in a CMD instruction, the container will execute bash -c "ps aux".

A frequent practice is to replace the default ENTRYPOINT command with a custom **script** that behaves in the same way and offers more granular control of the runtime execution.

- **CMD**: The default argument(s) passed to the ENTRYPOINT instruction. It can be a full command or a set of plain arguments to be passed to a custom script or binary set as ENTRYPOINT. It supported forms are the following:

  - CMD ["command", "param1", "paramN"] (the *exec* form)

  - CMD ["param1, "paramN"] (the *parameter* form, used to pass arguments to a custom ENTRYPOINT)

  - CMD command param1 paramN (the *shell* form)

- **LABEL**: This instruction is used to apply custom labels to the image. Labels are used as metadata at build time or runtime. It follows the LABEL <key1>=<value1> ... <keyN>=<valueN> syntax.

- **EXPOSE**: This sets metadata about listening ports exposed by the processes running in the container. It supports the EXPOSE <port>/<protocol> format.

- **ENV**: This configures environment variables that will be available to the next build commands and at runtime when the container is executed. This instruction supports the ENV <key1>=<value1>... <keyN>=<valueN> format.

  Environment variables can also be set inside a RUN instruction with a scope limited to the instruction itself.

- **VOLUME**: This sets a volume that will be created at runtime during container execution. The volume will be automatically mapped by Podman inside the default volume storage directory. The supported formats are the following:

  - VOLUME ["/path/to/dir"]

  - VOLUME /path/to/dir

See also the *Attaching host storage to a container* section in *Chapter 5, Implementing Storage for the Containers' Data*, for more details about volumes.

- **USER**: This instruction defines the username and user group for the next `RUN`, `CMD`, and `ENTRYPOINT` instructions. The `GID` value is not mandatory.

  The supported formats are the following:
  - `USER <username>:[<groupname>]`
  - `USER <UID>:[<GID>]`

- **WORKDIR**: This sets the working directory during the build process. This value is retained during container execution. It supports the `WORKDIR /path/to/workdir` format.

- **ONBUILD**: This instruction defines a trigger command to be executed once an image build has been completed. In this way, the image can be used as a parent for a new build by calling it with the `FROM` instruction. Its purpose is to allow the execution of some final command on a child container image.

  The supported formats are the following:
  - `ONBUILD ADD . /opt/app`
  - `ONBUILD RUN /opt/bin/custom-build /opt/app/src`

Now that we have learned the most common instructions, let's dive into our first build examples with Podman.

Running builds with Podman

Good news – Podman provides the same build commands and syntax as Docker. If you are switching from Docker, there will be no learning curve to start building your images with it. Under the hood, there is a notable advantage in choosing Podman as a build tool – Podman can build containers in rootless mode, using a fork/exec model.

This is a step forward compared to Docker builds, where communication with the daemon listening on the Unix socket is necessary to run the build.

Let's start by running a simple build based on the `httpd` Dockerfile illustrated in the first *Builds under the hood subsection*. We will use the following `podman build` command:

```
$ podman build -t myhttpd .
STEP 1/4: FROM docker.io/library/fedora
STEP 2/4: RUN dnf install -y httpd && dnf clean all -y
[...omitted output]
--> 50a981094eb
STEP 3/4: COPY index.html /var/www/html
```

```
--> 73f8702c5e0
STEP 4/4: CMD ["/usr/sbin/httpd", "-DFOREGROUND"]
COMMIT myhttpd
--> e773bfee6f2
Successfully tagged localhost/myhttpd:latest
e773bfee6f289012b37285a9e559bc44962de3aeed001455231b5a8f2721b8f9
```

In the preceding example, the output of the dnf install command was omitted for the sake of clarity and space.

The command runs the instructions sequentially and persists the intermediate layers until the final image is committed and tagged. The build steps are numbered (1/4 to 4/4) and some of them (RUN and COPY here) produce non-empty layers, forming part of the image lowerDirs.

The first FROM instruction defines the base image, which is pulled automatically if not present in the host.

The second instruction is RUN, which executes the dnf command to install the httpd package and clean up the system upon completion. Under the hood, this line is executed as "bash -c 'dnf install -y httpd && dnf clean all -y'".

The third COPY instruction simply copies the index.html file in the default httpd document root.

Finally, the fourth step defines the default container CMD instruction. Since no ENTRYPOINT instructions were set, this will translate into the following command:

```
"bash -c '/usr/sbin/httpd -DFOREGROUND'"
```

The next example is a custom Dockerfile/Containerfile where a custom web server is built:

```
FROM docker.io/library/fedora
# Install required packages
RUN set -euo pipefail; \
    dnf upgrade -y; \
    dnf install httpd -y; \
    dnf clean all -y; \
    rm -rf /var/cache/dnf/*
# Custom webserver configs for rootless execution
RUN set -euo pipefail; \
    sed -i 's|Listen 80|Listen 8080|' \
        /etc/httpd/conf/httpd.conf; \
```

```
    sed -i 's|ErrorLog "logs/error_log"|ErrorLog /dev/stderr|' \
            /etc/httpd/conf/httpd.conf; \
    sed -i 's|CustomLog "logs/access_log" combined|CustomLog /dev/stdout combined|' \
            /etc/httpd/conf/httpd.conf; \
    chown 1001 /var/run/httpd


# Copy web content
COPY index.html /var/www/html
# Define content volume
VOLUME /var/www/html
# Copy container entrypoint.sh script
COPY entrypoint.sh /entrypoint.sh
# Declare exposed ports
EXPOSE 8080
# Declare default user
USER 1001
ENTRYPOINT ["/entrypoint.sh"]
CMD ["httpd"]
```

This example was designed for the purpose of this book to illustrate some peculiar elements:

- Packages installed with a package manager should be kept at a minimum. After installing the httpd package, necessary to run the web server, the cache is cleaned to save layer space.

- Multiple commands can be grouped together in a single RUN instruction. However, we don't want to continue the build if a single command fails. To provide a failsafe shell execution, the set -euo pipefail command was prepended. Also, to improve readability, the single commands were split into more lines using the \ character, which can work as a line break or escape character.

- To avoid running the isolated processes as the root user, a series of workarounds were implemented in order to have the httpd process running as the generic 1001 user. Those workarounds included updating files permissions and group ownership on specific directories that are expected to be accessed by non-root users. This is a security best practice that reduces the attack surface of the container.

- A common pattern in containers is the redirections of application logs to the container's `stdout` and `stderr`. The common httpd log streams have been modified for this purpose using regular expressions against the `/etc/httpd/conf/httpd.conf` file.

- The web server ports are declared as exposed with the `EXPOSE` instruction.

- The `CMD` instruction is a simple `httpd` command without any other argument. This was done to illustrate how the `ENTRYPOINT` can interact with the CMD arguments.

The container `ENTRYPOINT` instruction is modified with a custom script that brings more flexibility to the way the `CMD` instruction is managed. The `entrypoint.sh` file tests whether the container is executed as root and checks the first `CMD` argument – if the argument is `httpd`, it executes the `httpd -DFOREGROUND` command; otherwise, it lets you execute any other command (a shell, for example). The following code is the content of the `entrypoint.sh` script:

```
#!/bin/sh
set -euo pipefail
if [ $UID != 0 ]; then
    echo "Running as user $UID"
fi
if [ "$1" == "httpd" ]; then
    echo "Starting custom httpd server"
    exec $1 -DFOREGROUND
else
    echo "Starting container with custom arguments"
    exec "$@"
fi
```

Let's now build the image with the `podman build` command:

```
$ podman build -t myhttpd .
```

The newly built image will be available in the local host cache:

```
$ podman images | grep myhttpd
localhost/myhttpd latest 6dc90348520c 2 minutes ago   248 MB
```

After building, we can **tag** the image with the target registry name. The following example tags the image applying the v1.0 tag and the latest tag:

```
$ podman tag localhost/myhttpd quay.io/<username>/myhttpd:v1.0
```

After tagging, the image will be ready to be pushed to the remote registry. We will cover the interaction with registries in greater detail in *Chapter 9, Pushing Images to a Container Registry*.

The example image will be composed of five layers, including the base Fedora image layer. We can verify the number of layers by running the podman inspect command against the new image:

```
$ podman inspect myhttpd --format '{{ .RootFS.Layers }}'
[sha256:b6d0e02fe431db7d64d996f3dbf903153152a8f8b857cb4829
ab3c4a3e484a72
sha256:f41274a78d9917b0412d99c8b698b0094aa0de74ec8995c88e5
dbf1131494912
sha256:e57dde895085c50ea57db021bffce776ee33253b4b8cb0fe909b
bbac45af0e8c
sha256:9989ee85603f534e7648c74c75aaca5981186b787d26e0cae0bc
7ee9eb54d40d
sha256:ca402716d23bd39f52d040a39d3aee242bf235f626258958b889
b40cdec88b43]
```

It is possible to squash the current build layers into a single layer using the --layers=false option. The resulting image will have only two layers – the base Fedora layer and the squashed one. The following example rebuilds the image without caching the intermediate layers:

```
$ podman build -t myhttpd --layers=false .
```

Let's inspect the output image again:

```
$ podman inspect myhttpd --format '{{ .RootFS.Layers }}'
[sha256:b6d0e02fe431db7d64d996f3dbf903153152a8f8b857cb
4829ab3c4a3e484a72
sha256:6c279ab14837b30af9360bf337c7f9b967676a61831eee9
1012fa67083f5dcf1]
```

This time, the final image has the two expected layers only.

Reducing the number of layers can be useful to keep the image minimal in terms of overlays. The downside of this approach is that we will have to rebuild the whole image for every configuration change without taking advantage of cached layers.

In terms of isolation, Podman can safely build images in rootless mode. Indeed, this is considered a value since there should be no need to run builds with a privileged user such as root. If rootful builds are necessary, they are fully functional and supported. The following example runs a build as the root user:

```
# podman build -t myhttpd .
```

The resulting image will be available only in the system image cache and its layers stored under /var/lib/containers/storage/.

The flexible nature of Podman builds is strongly related to its companion tool, **Buildah**, a specialized tool to build OCI images that provides greater flexibility in builds. In the next section, we will describe Buildah's features and how it manages image builds.

Meet Buildah, Podman's companion tool for builds

Podman does an excellent job in plain builds with Dockerfiles/Containerfiles and helps teams to preserve their previously implemented build pipelines without the need for new investments.

However, when it comes to more specialized build tasks, or when users need more control on the build workflow, with the option of including scripting logic, the Dockerfile/Containerfile approach shows its limitations. Communities struggled to find alternative building approaches that can overcome the rigid, workflow-based logic of Dockerfiles/Containerfiles.

The same community that develops Podman brought to life the Buildah (pronounced *build-ah*) project, a tool to manage OCI builds with support for multiple building strategies. Images created with Buildah are fully portable and compatible with Docker, and all engines are compliant with the OCI image and runtime specs.

Buildah is an open source project released under the Apache 2.0 license. Sources are available on GitHub at the following URL: https://github.com/containers/buildah.

Buildah is complementary to Podman, which borrows its build logic by vendoring its libraries to implement basic build functionalities against Dockerfiles and Containerfiles. The final Podman binary, which is compiled in Go as a statically linked single file, embeds Buildah packages to manage the build steps.

Buildah uses the *containers/image* project (`https://github.com/containers/image`) to manage an image's life cycle and its interaction with registries, and the *containers/storage* project (`https://github.com/containers/storage`) to manage images and containers' filesystem layers.

The advanced build strategy of Buildah is based on the parallel support for traditional Dockerfile/Containerfile-based builds, and for builds driven by native Buildah commands that replicate the Dockerfile instructions.

By replicating Dockerfile instructions in standard commands, Buildah becomes a scriptable tool that can be interpolated with custom logic and native shell constructs such as conditionals, loops, or environment variables. For example, the RUN instruction in a Dockerfile can be replaced with a `buildah run` command.

If teams need to preserve the build logic implemented in previous Dockerfiles, Buildah offers the `buildah build` (or its alias, `buildah bud`) command, which builds the image reading from the provided Dockerfile/Containerfile.

Buildah can smoothly run in rootless mode to build images; this is a valuable, highly demanded feature from a security point of view. No Unix sockets are necessary to run a build. At the beginning of this chapter, we explained how builds are always based on containers; Buildah is not exempt from this behavior, and all its builds are executed inside working containers, starting on top of the base image.

The following list provides a non-exhaustive description of the most frequently used commands in Buildah:

- **buildah from**: Initializes a new working container on top of a base image. It accepts the `buildah from [options] <image>` syntax. An example of this command is `$ buildah from fedora`.

- **buildah run**: This is equivalent to the RUN instruction of a Dockerfile; it runs a command inside a working container. This command accepts the `buildah run [options] [--] <container> <command>` syntax. The `--` (double dash) option is necessary to separate potential options from the effective container command. An example of this command is `buildah run <containerID> -- dnf install -y nginx`.

- **buildah config**: This command configures image metadata. It accepts the `buildah config [options] <container>` format. The options available for this command are associated with the various Dockerfile instructions that do not modify filesystem layers but set some container metadata – for instance, the setup of the entrypoint container. An example of this command is `buildah config --entrypoint/entrypoint.sh <containerID>`.

- **buildah add**: This is equivalent to the ADD instruction of the Dockerfile; it adds files, directories, and even URLs to the container. It supports the `buildah add [options] <container> <src> [[src ...] <dst>` syntax and allows you to copy multiple files in one single command. An example of this command is `buildah add <containerID> index.php /var/www.html`.

- **buildah copy**: This is the same as the Dockerfile COPY instruction; it adds files, URLs, and directories to the container. It supports the `buildah copy [options] <container> <src> [[src ...] <dst>` syntax. An example of this command is `buildah copy <containerID> entrypoint.sh /`.

- **buildah commit**: This commits a final image out of a working container. This command is usually the last executed one. It supports the `buildah copy [options] <container> <image_name>` syntax. The container image created from this command can be later tagged and pushed to a registry. An example of this command is `buildah commit <containerID> <myhttpd>`.

- **buildah build**: The equivalent command of the classic Podman build. This command takes Dockerfiles or Containerfiles as arguments, along with the build directory path. It accepts the `buildah build [options] [context]` syntax and the `buildah bud` command alias. An example of this command is `buildah build -t <imageName> ..`.

- **buildah containers**: This lists the active working container involved in Buildah builds, along with the base image used as starting point. Equivalent commands are `buildah ls` and `buildah ps`. The supported syntax is `buildah containers [options]`. An example of this command is `buildah containers`.

- **buildah rm**: This is used to remove working containers. The `buildah delete` command is equivalent. The supported syntax is `buildah rm <container>`. This command has only one option, the `-all, -a` option, to remove all the working containers. An example of this command is `buildah rm <containerID>`.

- **buildah mount**: This command can be used to mount a working container root filesystem. The accepted syntax is `buildah mount [containerID ... ]`. When no argument is passed, the command only shows the currently mounted containers. An example of this command is `buildahmount<containerID>`.

- **buildah images**: This lists all the available images in the local host cache. The accepted syntax is `buildah images [options] [image]`. Custom output formats such as JSON are available. An example of this command is `buildah images --json`.

- **buildah tag**: This applies a custom name and tags to an image in the local store. The syntax follows the `buildah tag <name> <new-name>` format. An example of this command is `buildah tag myapp quay.io/packt/myapp:latest`.

- **buildah push**: This pushes a local image to a remote private or public register, or local directories in Docker or OCI format. This command offers greater flexibility when compared to equivalents in Podman or Docker. The command syntax is `buildah push [options] <image> [destination]`. Examples of this command include `buildah push quay.io/packt/myapp:latest`, `buildah push <imageID> docker://<URL>/repository:tag`, and `buildah push <imageID> oci:</path/to/dir>:image:tag`.

- **buildah pull**: This pulls an image from a registry, an OCI archive, or directory. Syntax includes `buildah pull [options] <image>`. Examples of this command include `buildah pull <imageName>`, `buildah pull docker://<URL>/repository:tag`, and `buildah pull dir:</path/to/dir>`.

All the commands described previously have their corresponding man page, with the man `buildah-<command>` pattern. For example, to read documentation details about the `buildah run` command, just type `man buildah-run` on the terminal.

The next example shows basic Buildah capabilities. A Fedora base image is customized to run an httpd process:

```
$ container=$(buildah from fedora)
$ buildah run $container -- dnf install -y httpd; dnf clean all
$ buildah config --cmd "httpd -DFOREGROUND" $container
$ buildah config --port 80 $container
$ buildah commit $container myhttpd
$ buildah tag myhttpd registry.example.com/myhttpd:v0.0.1
```

The preceding commands will produce an OCI-compliant, portable image with the same features of an image built from a Dockerfile, all in a few lines that can be included in a simple script.

We will now focus on the first command:

```
$ container=$(buildah from fedora)
```

The `buildah from` command pulls a Fedora image from one of the allowed registries and spins up a working container from it, returning the container name. Instead of simply having it printed on standard output, we will capture the name with shell expansion syntax. From now on, we can pass the `$container` variable, which holds the name of the generated container, to the subsequent commands. Therefore, the build commands will be executed inside this working container. This is quite a common pattern and is especially useful to automate Buildah commands in scripts.

> **Important Note**
>
> There is a subtle difference between the concept of container in Buildah and Podman. Both adopt the same technology to create containers, but Buildah containers are short-lived entities that are created to be modified and committed, while Podman containers are supposed to run long-living workloads.

The flexible and embeddable nature of this approach is remarkable – Buildah commands can be included anywhere, and users can choose between a fully automated build process and a more interactive one.

For example, Buildah can be easily integrated with **Ansible**, the open source automation engine, to provide automated builds using native connection plugins that enable communication with working containers.

You can choose to include Buildah inside a CI pipeline (such as **Jenkins**, **Tekton**, or **GitLab CI/CD**) to gain full control of the build and integration tasks.

Buildah is also included in larger projects of the cloud-native community, such as the **Shipwright** project (`https://github.com/shipwright-io/build`).

Shipwright is an extensible build framework for Kubernetes that provides the flexibility of customizing image builds using custom resource definitions and different build tools. Buildah is one of the available solutions that you can choose when designing your build processes with it.

We will see more detailed and richer examples in the next subsections. Now that we have seen an overview of Buildah's capabilities and use cases, let's dive into the installation and environment preparation steps.

Preparing our environment

Buildah is available on different distributions and can be installed using the respective package managers. This section provides a non-exhaustive list of installation examples on the major distributions. For the sake of clarity, it is important to reiterate that the book lab environments were all based on Fedora 34:

- **Fedora**: To install Buildah on Fedora, run the following `dnf` command:

```
$ sudo dnf -y install buildah
```

- **Debian**: To install Buildah on Debian Bullseye or later, run the following `apt-get` commands:

```
$ sudo apt-get update
$ sudo apt-get -y install buildah
```

- **CentOS**: To install Buildah on CentOS, run the following `yum` command:

```
$ sudo yum install -y buildah
```

- **RHEL8**: To install Buildah on RHEL8, run the following `yum module` commands:

```
$ sudo yum module enable -y container-tools:1.0
$ sudo yum module install -y buildah
```

- **RHEL7**: To install Buildah on RHEL7, enable the `rhel-7-server-extras-rpms` repository and install with `yum`:

```
$ sudo subscription-manager repos --enable=rhel-7-server-extras-rpms
$ sudo yum -y install buildah
```

- **Arch Linux**: To install Buildah on Arch Linux, run the following `pacman` command:

```
$ sudo pacman -S buildah
```

- **Ubuntu**: To install Buildah on Ubuntu 20.10 or later, run the following `apt-get` commands:

```
$ sudo apt-get -y update
$ sudo apt-get -y install buildah
```

- **Gentoo**: To install Buildah on Gentoo, run the following `emerge` command:

```
$ sudo emerge app-emulation/libpod
```

- **Build from source**: Buildah can also be built from the source. For the purpose of this book, we will keep the focus on simple deployment methods, but if you're curious, you will find the following guide useful to try out your own builds: `https://github.com/containers/buildah/blob/main/install.md#building-from-scratch`.

Finally, Buildah can be deployed as a container, and builds can be executed inside it with a nested approach. This process will be covered in greater detail in *Chapter 7, Integrating with Existing Application Build Processes*.

After installing Buildah to our host, we can move on to verifying our installation.

Verifying the installation

After installing Buildah, we can now run some basic test commands to verify the installation.

To see all the available images in the host local store, use the following commands:

```
$ buildah images
```
```
# buildah images
```

The image list will be the same as the one printed by the `podman images` command since they share the same local store.

Also note that the two commands are executed as an unprivileged user and as root, pointing respectively to the user rootless local store and the system-wide local store.

We can run a simple test build to verify the installation. This is a good chance to test a basic build script whose only purpose is to verify whether Buildah is able to fully run a complete build.

For the purpose of this book (and for fun), we have created the following simple test script that creates a minimal Python 3 image:

```
#!/bin/bash


BASE_IMAGE=alpine
TARGET_IMAGE=python3-minimal

```

```
if [ $UID != 0 ]; then
    echo "### Running build test as unprivileged user"
else
    echo "### Running build test as root"
fi


echo "### Testing container creation"
container=$(buildah from $BASE_IMAGE)
if [ $? -ne 0 ]; then
    echo "Error initializing working container"
fi


echo "### Testing run command"
buildah run $container apk add --update python3 py3-pip
if [ $? -ne 0 ]; then
    echo "Error on run build action"
fi


echo "### Testing image commit"
buildah commit $container $TARGET_IMAGE
if [ $? -ne 0 ]; then
    echo "Error committing final image"
fi


echo "### Removing working container"
buildah rm $container
if [ $? -ne 0 ]; then
    echo "Error removing working container"
fi


echo "### Build test completed successfully!"
exit 0
```

The same test script can be executed by a non-privileged user and by root.

We can verify the newly built image by running a simple container that executes a Python shell:

```
$ podman run -it python3-minimal /usr/bin/python3
Python 3.9.5 (default, May 12 2021, 20:44:22)
[GCC 10.3.1 20210424] on linux
Type "help", "copyright", "credits" or "license" for more
information.
>>>
```

After successfully testing our new Buildah installation, let's inspect the main configuration files used by Buildah.

Buildah configuration files

The main Buildah configuration files are the same ones used by Podman. They can be leveraged to customize the behavior of the working containers executed in builds.

On Fedora, these config files are installed by the containers-common package, and we already covered them in the *Prepare your environment* section in *Chapter 3, Running the First Container*.

The main config files used by Buildah are as follows:

- /usr/share/containers/mounts.conf: This config file defines the files and directories that are automatically mounted inside a Buildah working container.

- /etc/containers/registries.conf: This config file has the role of managing registries allowed to be accessed for image searches, pulls, and pushes.

- /usr/share/containers/policy.json: This JSON config file defines image signature verification behavior.

- /usr/share/containers/seccomp.json: This JSON config file defines the allowed and prohibited syscalls to a containerized process.

In this section, we have learned how to prepare the host environment to run Buildah. In the next section, we are going to identify the possible build strategies that can be implemented with Buildah.

Choosing our build strategy

There are basically three types of build strategies that we can use with Buildah:

- Building a container image starting from an existing base image

- Building a container image starting from scratch

- Building a container image starting from a Dockerfile

We have already provided an example of the build strategy from an existing base image in the *Meet Buildah, Podman's companion* section. Since this strategy is pretty similar from a workflow point of view to building from scratch, we will focus our practical examples on the last one, which provides great flexibility to create a small footprint and secure images.

Before going through the various technical details in the next section, let's start exploring all these strategies at a high level.

Even though we can find a lot of prebuilt container images available on the most popular public container registries, sometimes we might not be able to find a particular configuration, setup, or bundle of tools and services for our containers; that is why container image creation becomes a really important step that we need to practice.

Also, security constraints often require us to implement images with reduced attack surfaces, and therefore, DevOps teams must know how to customize every step of the build process to achieve this result.

With this awareness in mind, let's start with the first build strategy.

Building a container image starting from an existing base image

Let's imagine finding a well-done prebuilt container image for our favorite application server that our company is widely using. All the configurations for this container image are okay, and we can attach storage to the right mount points to persist the data and so on, but sooner or later, we may realize that some particular tools that we use for troubleshooting are missing in the container image, or that some libraries are missing that should be included!

In another scenario, we could be happy with the prebuilt image but still need to add custom contents to it – for example, the customer application.

What would be the solution in those cases?

In this first use case, we can extend the existing container image, adding stuff and editing the existing files to suit our purposes. In the previous basic examples, Fedora and Alpine images were customized to serve different purposes. Those images were generic OS filesystems with no specific purpose, but the same concept can be applied to a more complex image.

In the second use case, we can customize an image – for example, the default library Httpd. We can install PHP modules and then add our application's PHP files, producing a new image with our custom contents already built in.

We will see in the next sections how we can extend an existing container image.

Let's move on to the second strategy.

Building a container image starting from scratch

The previous strategy would be enough for many common situations, where we can find a prebuilt image to start working with, but sometimes it may be that the particular use case, application, or service that we want to containerize is not so common or widely used.

Imagine having a custom legacy application that requires some old libraries and tools that are no longer included on the latest Linux distribution or that may have been replaced by more recent ones. In this scenario, you might need to start from an empty container image and add piece by piece all the necessary stuff for your legacy application.

We have learned in this chapter that, actually, we will always start from a sort of initial container image, so this strategy and the previous one are pretty much the same.

Let's move on to the third and final strategy.

Building a container image starting from a Dockerfile

In *Chapter 1, Introduction to Container Technology*, we talked about container technology history and how Docker gained momentum in that context. Podman was born as an alternative evolution project of the great concepts that Docker helped to develop until now. One of the great innovations that Docker created in its own project history is, for sure, the Dockerfile.

Looking into this strategy at a high level, we can affirm that even when using a Dockerfile, we will arrive at one of the previous build strategies. The reality is not far away from the latest assumption we made, because Buildah under the hood will parse the Dockerfile, and it will build the container that we briefly introduced for previous build strategies.

So, in summary, are there any differences or advantages we need to consider when choosing our default build strategy? Obviously, there is no ultimate answer to this question. First of all, we should always look into the container communities, searching for some prebuilt image that could help our *build* process; on the other hand, we can always fall back on the *build from scratch* process. Last but not least, we can consider Dockerfile for easily distributing and sharing our build steps with our development group or the wider container communities.

This ends up our quick high-level introduction; we can now move on to the practical examples!

Building images from scratch

Before going into the details of this section and learning how to build a container image from scratch, let's make some tests to verify that the installed Buildah is working properly.

First of all, let's check whether our Buildah image cache is empty:

```
# buildah images
REPOSITORY    TAG    IMAGE ID    CREATED    SIZE
# buildah containers -a
CONTAINER ID  BUILDER   IMAGE ID      IMAGE NAME
CONTAINER NAME
```

> **Important Note**
> Podman and Buildah share the same container storage; for this reason, if you previously ran any other example shown in this chapter or book, you will find that your container storage cache is not that empty!

As we learned in the previous section, we can leverage the fact that Buildah will output the name of the just-created working container to easily store it in an environment variable and use it once needed. Let's create a brand-new container from scratch:

```
# buildah from scratch
# buildah images
REPOSITORY    TAG    IMAGE ID    CREATED    SIZE
# buildah containers
CONTAINER ID  BUILDER   IMAGE ID      IMAGE NAME
CONTAINER NAME
af69b9547db9     *                     scratch
working-container
```

As you can see, we used the special `from scratch` keywords that are telling Buildah to create an empty container with no data inside it. If we run the `buildah images` command, we will note that this special image is not listed.

Let's check whether the container really is empty:

```
# buildah run working-container bash
2021-10-26T20:15:49.000397390Z: executable file 'bash' not
found in $PATH: No such file or directory
error running container: error from crun creating container for
[bash]: : exit status 1
error while running runtime: exit status 1
```

No executable was found in our empty container – what a surprise! The reason is that the working container has been created on an empty filesystem.

Let's see how we can easily fill this empty container. In the following example, we will interact directly with the underlying storage, using the package manager of our host system to install the binaries and the libraries needed for running a `bash` shell in our container image.

First of all, let's instruct Buildah to mount the container storage and check where it resides:

```
# buildah mount working-container
/var/lib/containers/storage/overlay/b5034cc80252b6f4af2155f
9e0a2a7e65b77dadec7217bd2442084b1f4449c1a/merged
```

> **Good to Know**
>
> If you start the build in rootless mode, Buildah will run the mount in a different namespace, and for this reason, the mounted volume might not be accessible from the host when using a driver different than vfs.

Great! Now that we have found it, we can leverage the host package manager to install all the needed packages in this `root` folder, which will be the `root` path of our container image:

```
# scratchmount=$(buildah mount working-container)
# dnf install --installroot $scratchmount --releasever 34 bash
coreutils --setopt install_weak_deps=false -y
```

> **Important Note**
>
> If you are running the previous command on a Fedora release different than version 34, (for example, version 35), then you need to import the GPG public keys of Fedora 34 or use the `--nogpgcheck` option.

First of all, we will save the very long directory path in an environment variable and then execute the `dnf` package manager, passing the just-obtained directory path as the install root directory, setting the release version of our Fedora OS, specifying the packages that we want to install (`bash` and `coreutils`), and finally, disabling weak dependency, accepting all the changes to the system.

The command should end up with a `Complete!` statement; once done, let's try again with the same command that we saw failing earlier in this section:

```
# buildah run working-container bash
bash-5.1# cat /etc/fedora-release
Fedora release 34 (Thirty Four)
```

It worked! We just installed a Bash shell in our empty container. Let's see now how to finish our image creation with some other configuration steps. First of all, we need to add to our final container image a command to be run once it is up and running. For this reason, we will create a Bash script file with some basic commands:

```
# cat command.sh
#!/bin/bash
cat /etc/fedora-release
/usr/bin/date
```

We have created a Bash script file that prints the Fedora release of the container and the system date. The file must have execute permissions before being copied:

```
# chmod +x command.sh
```

Now that we have filled up our underlying container storage with all the needed base packages, we can unmount the `working-container` storage and use the `buildah copy` command to inject files from the host to the container:

```
# buildah unmount working-container
af69b9547db93a7dc09b96a39bf5f7bc614a7ebd29435205d358e09ac
99857bc
# buildah copy working-container ./command.sh /usr/bin
659a229354bdef3f9104208d5812c51a77b2377afa5ac819e3c3a1a2887eb9f7
```

The `buildah copy` command gives us the ability to work with the underlying storage without worrying about mounting it or handling it under the hood.

We are now ready to complete our container image by adding some metadata to it:

```
# buildah config --cmd /usr/bin/command.sh working-container
# buildah config --created-by "podman book example" working-container
# buildah config --label name=fedora-date working-container
```

We started with the `cmd` option, and after that, we added some descriptive metadata. We can finally commit our `working-container` into an image!

```
# buildah commit working-container fedora-date
Getting image source signatures
Copying blob 939ac17066d4 done
Copying config e24a2fafde done
Writing manifest to image destination
Storing signatures
e24a2fafdeb5658992dcea9903f0640631ac444271ed716d7f749eea7a651487
```

Let's clean up the environment and check the available container images into the host:

```
# buildah rm working-container
af69b9547db93a7dc09b96a39bf5f7bc614a7ebd29435205d358e09ac99857bc
```

We can now inspect the details of the just-created container image:

```
# podman images
REPOSITORY                    TAG              IMAGE ID        CREATED
SIZE
localhost/fedora-date    latest         e24a2fafdeb5   About a minute
ago   366 MB
# podman inspect localhost/fedora-date:latest
[...omitted output]            "Labels": {
          "io.buildah.version": "1.23.1",
          "name": "fedora-date"
       },
       "Annotations": {
          "org.opencontainers.image.base.digest": "",
          "org.opencontainers.image.base.name": ""
       },
       "ManifestType": "application/vnd.oci.image.manifest.
v1+json",
       "User": "",
       "History": [
          {
             "created": "2021-10-26T21:16:48.777712056Z",
             "created_by": "podman book example"
          }
       ],
       "NamesHistory": [
          "localhost/fedora-date:latest"
       ]
    }
]
```

As we can see from the previous output, the container image has a lot of metadata that can tell us many details. Some of them we set through the previous commands, such as the created_by, name, and Cmd tags; the other tags are populated automatically by Buildah.

Finally, let's run our brand-new container image with Podman!

```
# podman run -ti localhost/fedora-date:latest
Fedora release 34 (Thirty Four)
Tue Oct 26 21:18:29 UTC 2021
```

This ends our journey in creating a container image from scratch. As we saw, this is not a typical method for creating a container image; in many scenarios and for various use cases, it can be enough to start with an OS base image, such as `from fedora` or `from alpine`, and then add the required packages, using the respective package managers available in those images.

> **Good to Know**
>
> Some Linux distributions also provide base container images in a **minimal** flavor (for example, **fedora-minimal**) that reduce the number of packages installed, as well as the size of the target container image. For more information, refer to `https://www.docker.com/` and `https://quay.io/`!

Let's now inspect how to build images from Dockerfiles with Buildah.

Building images from a Dockerfile

As we described earlier in this chapter, the Dockerfile can be an easy option to create and share the build steps for creating a container image, and for this reason, it is really easy to find a lot of source Dockerfiles on the net.

The first step of this activity is to build a simple Dockerfile to work with. Let's create a Dockerfile for creating a containerized web server:

```
# mkdir webserver
# cd webserver/
[webserver]# vi Dockerfile
[webserver]# cat Dockerfile
# Start from latest fedora container base image
FROM fedora:latest
MAINTAINER podman-book  # this should be an email

# Update the container base image
RUN echo "Updating all fedora packages"; dnf -y update; dnf -y
```

```
clean all

# Install the httpd package
RUN echo "Installing httpd"; dnf -y install httpd

# Expose the http port 80
EXPOSE 80

# Set the default command to run once the container will be
started
CMD ["/usr/sbin/httpd", "-DFOREGROUND"]
```

Looking at the previous output, we first created a new directory, and inside, we created a text file named Dockerfile. After that, we inserted the various keywords and steps commonly used in the definition of a brand-new Dockerfile; every step and keyword has a dedicated description comment on top, so the file should be easy to read.

Just to recap, these are the steps contained in our brand-new Dockerfile:

1. Start from the latest Fedora container base image.
2. Update all the packages for the container base image.
3. Install the httpd package.
4. Expose HTTP port 80.
5. Set the default command to run once the container is started.

As seen previously in this chapter, Buildah provides a dedicated buildah build command to start a build from a Dockerfile.

Let's see how it works:

```
[webserver]# buildah build -f Dockerfile -t myhttpdservice .
STEP 1/6: FROM fedora:latest
Resolved "fedora" as an alias (/etc/containers/registries.
conf.d/000-shortnames.conf)
Trying to pull registry.fedoraproject.org/fedora:latest...
Getting image source signatures
Copying blob 944c4b241113 done
Copying config 191682d672 done
Writing manifest to image destination
```

```
Storing signatures
STEP 2/6: MAINTAINER podman-book  # this should be an email
STEP 3/6: RUN echo "Updating all fedora packages"; dnf -y
update; dnf -y clean all
Updating all fedora packages
Fedora 34 - x86_64                                16 MB/s |   74
MB     00:04

...

STEP 4/6: RUN echo "Installing httpd"; dnf -y install httpd
Installing httpd
Fedora 34 - x86_64                                20 MB/s |   74
MB     00:03

...

STEP 5/6: EXPOSE 80
STEP 6/6: CMD ["/usr/sbin/httpd", "-DFOREGROUND"]
COMMIT myhttpdservice
Getting image source signatures
Copying blob 7500ce202ad6 skipped: already exists
Copying blob 51b52d291273 done
Copying config 14a2226710 done
Writing manifest to image destination
Storing signatures
--> 14a2226710e
Successfully tagged localhost/myhttpdservice:latest
14a2226710e7e18d2e4b6478e09a9f55e60e0666dd8243322402ecf6fd1eaa0d
```

As we can see from the previous output, we pass the following options to the `buildah build` command:

- `-f`: To define the name of the Dockerfile. The default filename is `Dockerfile`, so in our case, we can omit this option because we named the file as the default one.

- `-t`: To define the name and the tag of the image we are building. In our case, we are only defining the name. The image will be tagged `latest` by default.

- Finally, as the last option, we need to set the directory where Buildah needs to work and search for the Dockerfile. In our case, we are passing the current `.` directory.

Of course, these are not the only options that Buildah gives us to configure the build; we will see some of them later in this section.

Coming back to the command we just executed, as we can see from the output, all the steps defined in the Dockerfile have been executed in the exact written order and printed with a given fractional number to show the intermediate steps against the total number. In total, six steps were executed.

We can check the result of our command by listing the images with the `buildah images` command:

```
[webserver]# buildah images
REPOSITORY                                          TAG        IMAGE ID
CREATED          SIZE
localhost/myhttpdservice                            latest
14a2226710e7    2 minutes ago     497 MB
```

As we can see, our container image has just been created with the `latest` tag; let's try to run it:

```
# podman run -d localhost/myhttpdservice:latest
133584ab526faaf7af958da590e14dd533256b60c10f08acba6c1209ca05a885
# podman logs
133584ab526faaf7af958da590e14dd533256b60c10f08acba6c1209ca05a885
AH00558: httpd: Could not reliably determine the server's fully
qualified domain name, using 10.88.0.4. Set the 'ServerName'
directive globally to suppress this message
# curl 10.88.0.4
<!doctype html>
<html>
  <head>
    <meta charset='utf-8'>
    <meta name='viewport' content='width=device-width, initial-
scale=1'>
    <title>Test Page for the HTTP Server on Fedora</title>
    <style type="text/css">
...
```

Looking at the output, we just ran our container in detached mode; after that, we inspected the logs to find out the IP address that we need to pass as an argument for the `curl` test command.

We just run the container as the root user on our workstation, and the container just received an internal IP address on Podman's container network interface. We can check that the IP address is part of that network by running the following commands:

```
# ip a show dev cni-podman0
14: cni-podman0: <BROADCAST,MULTICAST,UP,LOWER_UP> mtu 1500
qdisc noqueue state UP group default qlen 1000
    link/ether c6:bc:ba:7c:d3:0c brd ff:ff:ff:ff:ff:ff
    inet 10.88.0.1/16 brd 10.88.255.255 scope global cni-
podman0
       valid_lft forever preferred_lft forever
    inet6 fe80::c4bc:baff:fe7c:d30c/64 scope link
       valid_lft forever preferred_lft forever
```

As we can see, the container's IP address was taken from the network reported in the previous 10.88.0.1/16 output.

As we anticipated, the buildah build command has a lot of other options that can be useful while developing and creating brand-new container images. Let's explore one of them that is worth mentioning – --layers.

We already learned how to use this option with Podman earlier in this chapter. Starting from version 1.2 of Buildah, the development team added this great option that gives us the ability to enable or disable the layers' caching mechanism. The default configuration sets the --layers option to *false*, which means that Buildah will not keep intermediate layers, resulting in a build that squashes all the changes in a single layer.

It is also possible to set the management of the layers with an environment variable – for example, to enable layer caching, run export BUILDAH_LAYERS=true.

Obviously, the downside of this option is that the retained layers actually use storage space on the system host, but on the other hand, we can save computational power if we need to rebuild a given image, changing only the latest layers and without rebuilding the whole image!

Summary

In this chapter, we explored a fundamental topic of container management – their creation. This step is mandatory if we want to customize, keep updated, and manage our container infrastructure correctly. We learned that Podman is often partnered with another tool called Buildah that can help us in the process of container image building. This tool has a lot of options, like Podman, and shares a lot of them with it (storage included!). Finally, we went through the different strategies that Buildah offers us to build new container images, and one of them is actually inherited by the Docker ecosystem – the Dockerfile.

This chapter is only an introduction to the topic of container image building; we will discover more advanced techniques in the next chapter!

Further reading

- Buildah project tutorials: `https://github.com/containers/buildah/tree/main/docs/tutorials`

- How to use Podman inside of a container: `https://www.redhat.com/sysadmin/podman-inside-container`

- How to build tiny container images: `https://www.redhat.com/sysadmin/tiny-containers`

7

Integrating with Existing Application Build Processes

After learning how to create custom container images using Podman and Buildah, we can now focus on special use cases that can make our build workflows more efficient and portable. For instance, small images are a very common requirement in an enterprise environment, for performance and security reasons. We will explore how to achieve this goal by breaking down the build process into different stages.

This chapter will also try to uncover scenarios where Buildah is not expected to run directly on a developer machine but is driven instead by a container orchestrator or embedded inside custom applications that are expected to call its libraries or **command line interface (CLI)**.

In this chapter, we're going to cover the following main topics:

- Multistage container builds
- Running Buildah inside a container
- Integrating Buildah with custom builders

Technical requirements

Before proceeding with this chapter, a machine with a working Podman installation is required. As stated in *Chapter 3, Running the First Container*, all the examples in the book are executed on a Fedora 34 system or later versions but can be reproduced on the reader's OS of choice.

A good understanding of the topics covered in *Chapter 6, Meet Buildah – Building Containers from Scratch*, will be useful to easily grasp concepts regarding builds, both with native Buildah commands and from Dockerfiles.

Multistage container builds

We have learned so far how to create builds with Podman and Buildah using Dockerfiles or native Buildah commands that unleash potential advanced building techniques.

There is still an important point that we haven't already discussed – the size of the images.

When creating a new image, we should always take care of its final size, which is the result of the total number of layers and the number of changed files inside them.

Minimal images with a small size have the great advantage of being able to be pulled faster from registries. Nevertheless, a large image will eat a lot of precious disk space in the host's local store.

We already showed examples of some best practices to keep images compact in size, such as building from scratch, cleaning up package manager caches, and reducing the amount of RUN, COPY, and ADD instructions to the minimum necessary. However, what happens when we need to build an application from its source and create a final image with the final artifacts?

Let's say we need to build a containerized Go application – we should start from a base image that includes Go runtimes, copy the source code, and compile to produce the final binary with a series of intermediate steps, most notably downloading all the necessary Go packages inside the image cache. At the end of the build, we should clean up all the source code and the downloaded dependencies and put the final binary (which is statically linked in Go) in a working directory. Everything will work, but the final image will still include the Go runtimes included in the base image, which are no longer necessary at the end of the compilation process.

When Docker was introduced and Dockerfiles gained momentum, this problem was circumnavigated in different ways by DevOps teams who struggled to keep images minimal. For example, **binary builds** were a way to inject the final artifact compiled externally inside the built image. This approach solves the image size problem but removes the advantage of a standardized environment for builds provided by runtime/compiler images.

A better approach is to share volumes between containers and have the final container image grab the compiled artifacts from a first build image.

To provide a standardized approach, Docker, and then the OCI specifications, introduced the concept of **multistage builds**. Multistage builds, as the name says, allow users to create builds with multiple stages using different FROM instructions and have subsequent images grab contents from the previous ones.

In the next subsections, we will explore how to achieve this result with Dockerfiles/Containerfiles and with Buildah's native commands.

Multistage builds with Dockerfiles

The first approach to multistage builds is by creating multiple stages in a single Dockerfile/Containerfile, with each block beginning with a FROM instruction.

Build stages can copy files and folders from previous ones using the - -from option to specify the source stage.

The next examples show how to create a minimal multistage build for the Go application, with the first stage acting as a pure build context and the second stage copying the final artifact inside a minimal image:

Chapter07/http_hello_world/Dockerfile

```
# Builder image
FROM docker.io/library/golang


# Copy files for build
COPY go.mod /go/src/hello-world/
COPY main.go /go/src/hello-world/
```

```
# Set the working directory
WORKDIR /go/src/hello-world


# Download dependencies
RUN go get -d -v ./...


# Install the package
RUN go build -v


# Runtime image
FROM registry.access.redhat.com/ubi8/ubi-micro:latest
COPY --from=0 /go/src/hello-world/hello-world /
EXPOSE 8080


CMD ["/hello-world"]
```

The first stage copies the source `main.go` file and the `go.mod` file to manage the Go module dependencies. After downloading the dependency packages (`go get -d -v ./...`), the final application is built (`go build -v ./...`).

The second stage grabs the final artifact (`/go/src/hello-world/hello-world`) and copies it under the new image root. To specify that the source file should be copied from the first stage, the `--from=0` syntax is used.

In the first stage, we used the official `docker.io/library/golang` image, which includes the latest version of the Go programming language. In the second stage, we used the **ubi-micro** image, a minimal image from Red Hat with a reduced footprint, optimized for microservices and statically linked binaries. Universal Base Images will be covered in greater detail in *Chapter 8, Choosing the Container Base Image*.

The Go application listed as follows is a basic web server that listens on port `8080/tcp` and prints a crafted HTML page with the *"Hello World!"* message when it receives a `GET /` request:

> **Important Note**
>
> For the purpose of this book, it is not necessary to be able to write or understand the Go programming language. However, a basic understanding of the language syntax and logic will prove to be very useful, since the greatest part of container-related software (such as Podman, Docker, Buildah, Skopeo, Kubernetes, and OpenShift) is written in Go.

Chapter07/http_hello_world/main.go

```go
package main

import (
        "log"
    "net/http"
)

func handler(w http.ResponseWriter, r *http.Request) {
    log.Printf("%s %s %s\n", r.RemoteAddr, r.Method, r.URL)
    w.Header().Set("Content-Type", "text/html")
    w.Write([]byte("<html>\n<body>\n"))
    w.Write([]byte("<p>Hello World!</p>\n"))
    w.Write([]byte("</body>\n</html>\n"))
}

func main() {
    http.HandleFunc("/", handler)
    log.Println("Starting http server")
    log.Fatal(http.ListenAndServe(":8080", nil))
}
```

The application can be built using either Podman or Buildah. In this example, we choose to build the application with Buildah:

```
$ cd http_hello_world
$ buildah build -t hello-world .
```

Finally, we can check the resulting image size:

```
$ buildah images --format '{{.Name}} {{.Size}}' \
localhost/hello-world
localhost/hello-world    45 MB
```

The final image has a size of only 45 MB!

We can improve our Dockerfile by adding custom names to the base images using the keyword AS. The following example is a rework of the previous Dockerfile following this approach, with the key elements highlighted in bold:

```
# Builder image
FROM docker.io/library/golang AS builder

# Copy files for build
COPY go.mod /go/src/hello-world/
COPY main.go /go/src/hello-world/

# Set the working directory
WORKDIR /go/src/hello-world

# Download dependencies
RUN go get -d -v ./...

# Install the package
RUN go build -v ./...

# Runtime image
FROM registry.access.redhat.com/ubi8/ubi-micro:latest AS srv
COPY --from=builder /go/src/hello-world/hello-world /
EXPOSE 8080

CMD ["/hello-world"]
```

In the preceding example, the name of the builder image is set as builder, while the final image is named srv. Interestingly, the COPY instruction can now specify the builder as using the custom name with the --from=builder option.

Dockerfile/Containerfile builds are the most common approach but still lack some flexibility when it comes to implementing a custom build workflow. For those special use cases, Buildah native commands come to our rescue.

Multistage builds with Buildah native commands

As mentioned before, the multistage build feature is a great approach to produce images with a small footprint and a reduced attack surface. To provide greater flexibility during the build process, the Buildah native commands come to our rescue. As we mentioned earlier in *Chapter 6, Meet Buildah – Building Containers from Scratch*, Buildah offers a series of commands that replicate the behavior of the Dockerfile instructions, thus offering greater control over the build process when those commands are included in scripts or automations.

The same concept applies when working with multistage builds, where we can also apply extra steps between the stages. For instance, we can mount the build container overlay file system and extract the built artifact to release alternate packages, all before building the final runtime image.

The following example builds the same `hello-world` Go application by translating the previous Dockerfile instructions into native Buildah commands, with everything inside a simple shell script:

```bash
#!/bin/bash
# Define builder and runtime images
BUILDER=docker.io/library/golang
RUNTIME=registry.access.redhat.com/ubi8/ubi-micro:latest


# Create builder container
container1=$(buildah from $BUILDER)


# Copy files from host
if [ -f go.mod ]; then
    buildah copy $container1 'go.mod' '/go/src/hello-world/'
else
    exit 1
fi
if [ -f main.go ]; then
    buildah copy $container1 'main.go' '/go/src/hello-world/'
else
    exit 1
fi


# Configure and start build
buildah config --workingdir /go/src/hello-world $container1
```

```
buildah run $container1 go get -d -v ./...
buildah run $container1 go build -v ./...


# Create runtime container
container2=$(buildah from $RUNTIME)


# Copy files from the builder container
buildah copy --chown=1001:1001 \
    --from=$container1 $container2 \
    '/go/src/hello-world/hello-world' '/'


# Configure exposed ports
buildah config --port 8080 $container2


# Configure default CMD
buildah config --cmd /hello-world $container2


# Configure default user
buildah config --user=1001 $container2


# Commit final image
buildah commit $container2 hello-world


# Remove build containers
buildah rm $container1 $container2
```

In the preceding example, we highlighted the two working containers' creation commands and the related `container1` and `container2` variables that store the container ID.

Also, note the `buildah copy` command, where we have defined the source container with the `--from` option, and used the `--chown` option to define user and group owners of the copied resource. This approach proves to be more flexible than the Dockerfile-based workflow, since we can enrich our script with variables, conditionals, and loops.

For instance, we have tested with the `if` condition in the Bash script to check the existence of the `go.mod` and `main.go` files before copying them inside the working container dedicated to the build.

Let's now add an extra feature to the script. In the following example, we evolved the previous one by adding a semantic versioning for the build and creating a version archive before starting the build of the final runtime image:

> **Important Note**
>
> The concept of semantic versioning is aimed to provide a clear and standardized way to manage software versioning and dependency management. It is a set of standard rules whose purpose is to define how software release versions are applied and follows the **X.Y.Z** versioning pattern, where **X** is the major version, **Y** is the minor version, and **Z** is the patch version. For more information, check out the official specifications: `https://semver.org/`.

```bash
#!/bin/bash
# Define builder and runtime images
BUILDER=docker.io/library/golang
RUNTIME=registry.access.redhat.com/ubi8/ubi-micro:latest
RELEASE=1.0.0

# Create builder container
container1=$(buildah from $BUILDER)

# Copy files from host
if [ -f go.mod ]; then
    buildah copy $container1 'go.mod' '/go/src/hello-world/'
else
    exit 1
fi
if [ -f main.go ]; then
    buildah copy $container1 'main.go' '/go/src/hello-world/'
else
    exit 1
fi

# Configure and start build
buildah config --workingdir /go/src/hello-world $container1
buildah run $container1 go get -d -v ./...
```

```
buildah run $container1 go build -v ./...
# Extract build artifact and create a version archive
buildah unshare --mount mnt=$container1 \
    sh -c 'cp $mnt/go/src/hello-world/hello-world .'
cat > README << EOF
Version $RELEASE release notes:
- Implement basic features
EOF
tar zcf hello-world-${RELEASE}.tar.gz hello-world README
rm -f hello-world README


# Create runtime container
container2=$(buildah from $RUNTIME)


# Copy files from the builder container
buildah copy --chown=1001:1001 \
    --from=$container1 $container2 \
    '/go/src/hello-world/hello-world' '/'


# Configure exposed ports
buildah config --port 8080 $container2


# Configure default CMD
buildah config --cmd /hello-world $container2


# Configure default user
buildah  config--user=1001 $container2


# Commit final image
buildah commit $container2 hello-world:$RELEASE


# Remove build containers
buildah rm $container1 $container2
```

The key changes in the script are again highlighted in bold. First, we added a `RELEASE` variable that tracks the release version of the application. Then, we extracted the build artifact using the `buildah unshare` command, followed by the `--mount` option to pass the container mount point. The user namespace unshare was necessary to make the script capable of running rootless.

After extracting the artifact, we created a gzipped archive using the `$RELEASE` variable inside the archive name and removed the temporary files.

Finally, we started the build of the runtime image and committed using the `$RELEASE` variable again as the image tag.

In this section, we have learned how to run multistage builds with Buildah using both Dockerfiles/Containerfiles and native commands. In the next section, we will learn how to isolate Buildah builds inside a container.

Running Buildah inside a container

Podman and Buildah follow a fork/exec approach that makes them very easy to run inside a container, including rootless containers scenarios.

There are many use cases that imply the need for containerized builds. Nowadays, one of the most common adoption scenarios is the application build workflow running on top of a **Kubernetes** cluster.

Kubernetes is basically a container orchestrator that manages the scheduling of containers from a control plane over a set of worker nodes that run a container engine compatible with the **Container Runtime Interface** (**CRI**). Its design allows great flexibility in customizing networking, storage, and runtimes, and leads to the great flourishing of side projects that are now incubating or matured inside the **Cloud Native Computing Foundation** (**CNCF**).

Vanilla Kubernetes (which is the basic community release without any customization or add-ons) doesn't have any native build feature but offers the proper framework to implement one. Over time, many solutions appeared trying to address this need.

For example, Red Hat **OpenShift** introduced, way back when Kubernetes 1.0 was released, its own build APIs and the *Source-to-Image* toolkit to create container images from source code directly on top of the OpenShift cluster.

Another interesting solution is Google's **kaniko**, which is a build tool to create container images inside a Kubernetes cluster that runs every build step inside user space.

Besides using already implemented solutions, we can design our own running Buildah inside containers that are orchestrated by Kubernetes. We can also leverage the rootless-ready design to implement secure build workflows.

It is possible to run CI/CD pipelines on top of a Kubernetes cluster and embed containerized builds within a pipeline. One of the most interesting CNCF projects, **Tekton Pipelines**, offers a cloud-native approach to accomplish this goal. Tekton allows running pipelines that are driven by Kubernetes' custom resources – special APIs that extend the basic API set.

Tekton Pipelines are made up of many different tasks, and users can either create their own or grab them from **Tekton Hub** (`https://hub.tekton.dev/`), a free repository where many pre-baked tasks are available to be consumed immediately, including examples from Buildah (`https://hub.tekton.dev/tekton/task/buildah`).

The preceding examples are useful to understand why containerized builds are important. In this book, we want to focus on the details of running builds within containers, with special attention paid to security-related constraints.

Running rootless Buildah containers with volume stores

For the examples in this subsection, the stable upstream `quay.io/buildah/stable` Buildah image will be used. This image already embeds the latest stable Buildah binary.

Let's run our first example with a rootless container that builds the contents of the `~/build` directory in the host and stores the output in a local volume named `storevol`:

```
$ podman run --device /dev/fuse \
    -v ~/build:/build:z \
    -v storevol:/var/lib/containers quay.io/buildah/stable \
    buildah build -t build_test1 /build
```

This example brings some peculiar options that deserve attention, as follows:

- The `--device /dev/fuse` option, which loads the fuse kernel module in the container, which is necessary to run fuse-overlay commands
- The `-v ~/build:/build:z` option, which bind-mounts the `/root/build` directory inside the container, assigning proper SELinux labeling with the `:z` suffix
- The `-v storevol:/var/lib/containers` option, which creates a fresh volume mounted on the default container store where all the layers are created

When the build is complete, we can run a new container using the same volume and inspect or manipulate the built image:

```
$ podman run --rm -v storevol:/var/lib/containers quay.io/
buildah/stable buildah images
REPOSITORY                  TAG       IMAGE ID      CREATED
SIZE
localhost/build_test1                 latest    cd36bf58daff    12
minutes ago    283
docker.io/library/fedora    latest    b080de8a4da3    4 days ago
159 MB
```

We have successfully built an image whose layers have been stored inside the `storevol` volume. To recursively list the content of the store, we can extract the volume mount point with the `podman volume inspect` command:

```
$ ls -alR \
$(podman volume inspect storevol --format '{{.Mountpoint}}')
```

From now on, it is possible to launch a new Buildah container to authenticate to the remote registry, and tag and push the image. In the next example, Buildah tags the resulting image, authenticates to the remote registry, and finally pushes the image:

```
$ podman run --rm -v storevol:/var/lib/containers \
  quay.io/buildah/stable \
  sh -c 'buildah tag build_test1 \
    registry.example.com/build_test1 \
    && buildah login -u=<USERNAME> -p=<PASSWORD> \
    registry.example.com && \
    buildah push registry.example.com/build_test1'
```

When the image is successfully pushed, it is finally safe to remove the volume:

```
# podman volume rm storevol
```

Despite working perfectly, this approach has some limits that are worth discussing.

The first limit we can notice is that the store volume is not isolated, and thus any other container can access its contents. To overcome this issue, we can use SELinux's **Multi-Category Security** (**MCS**) with the `:z` suffix in order to apply categories to the volume and make it accessible exclusively to the running container.

However, since a second container would run by default with different category labels, we should grab the volume categories and run the second tag/push container with the `--security-opt label=level:s0:<CAT1>,<CAT2>` option.

Alternatively, we can just run build, tag, and push commands in one single container, as shown in the following example:

```
$ podman run --device /dev/fuse \
    -v ~/build:/build \
    -v secure_storevol:/var/lib/containers:Z \
    quay.io/buildah/stable \
    sh -c 'buildah build -t test2 /build && \
      buildah tag test2 registry.example.com/build_test2 && \
      buildah login -u=<USERNAME> \
      -p=<PASSWORD> \
      registry.example.com && \
      buildah push registry.example.com/build_test2'
```

> **Important Note**
>
> In the preceding examples, we used the Buildah login by directly passing the username and password in the command. Needless to say, this is far from being an acceptable security practice.

Instead of passing sensitive data in the command line, we can mount the authentication file that contains a valid session token as a volume inside the container.

The next example mounts a valid `auth.json` file, stored under the `/run/user/<UID>` tmpfs, inside the build container, and the `--authfile /auth.json` option is then passed to the `buildah push` command:

```
$ podman run --device /dev/fuse \
    -v ~/build:/build \
    -v /run/user/<UID>/containers/auth.json:/auth.json:z \
    -v secure_storevol:/var/lib/containers:Z \
    quay.io/buildah/stable \
    sh -c 'buildah build -t test3 /build && \
      buildah tag test3 registry.example.com/build_test3 && \
      buildah push --authfile /auth.json \
      registry.example.com/build_test3'
```

Finally, we have a working example that avoids exposing clear credentials in the commands passed to the container.

To provide a working authentication file, we need to authenticate from the host that will run the containerized build or copy a valid authentication file. To authenticate with Podman, we'll use the following command:

```
$ podman login -u <USERNAME> -p <PASSWORD> <REGISTRY>
```

If the authentication process succeeds, the obtained token is stored in the /run/user/<UID>/containers/auth.json file, which stores a JSON-encoded object with a structure similar to the following example:

```
{
        "auths": {
                "registry.example.com": {
                        "auth": "<base64_encoded_token>"
                }
        }
}
```

> **Security Alert!**
> If the authentication file mounted inside the container has multiple authentication records for different registries, they will be exposed inside the build container. This can lead to potential security issues, since the container will be able to authenticate on those registries using the tokens specified in the file.

The volume-based approach we just described has some small impact on the performance when compared to a native host build but provides better isolation of the build process, a reduced attack surface, thanks to the rootless execution and standardization of the build environment across different hosts.

Let's now inspect how to run containerized builds using bind-mounted stores.

Running Buildah containers with bind-mounted stores

In the highest isolation scenario, where DevOps teams follow a zero-trust approach, every build container should have its own isolated store populated at the beginning of the build and destroyed upon completion. Isolation can be easily achieved with SELinux MCS security.

To test this approach, let's start by creating a temporary directory that will host the build layers. We also want to generate a random suffix for a name in order to host multiple builds without conflicts:

```
# BUILD_STORE=/var/lib/containers-$(echo $RANDOM | md5sum |
head -c 8)
# mkdir $BUILD_STORE
```

> **Important Note**
>
> The preceding example and the next builds are executed as root.

We can now run the build and bind-mount the new directory to the /var/lib/ containers folder inside the container and add the :z suffix to ensure multi-category security isolation:

```
# podman run --device /dev/fuse \
    -v ./build:/build:z \
    -v $BUILD_STORE:/var/lib/containers:Z \
    -v /run/containers/0/auth.json:/auth.json \
    quay.io/buildah/stable \
    bash -c 'set -euo pipefail; \
        buildah build -t registry.example.com/test4 /build; \
        buildah push --authfile /auth.json \
        registry.example.com/test4'
```

The MCS isolation guarantees isolation from other containers. Every build container will have its own custom store, and this implies the need to re-pull the base image layers on every execution, since they are never cached.

Despite being the most secure in terms of isolation, this approach also offers the slowest performance because of the continuous pulls on the build run.

On the other hand, the less secure approach does not expect any store isolation, and all the build containers mount the default host store under `/var/lib/containers`. This approach provides better performance, since it allows the reuse of cached layers from the host store.

SELinux will not allow a containerized process to access the host store; therefore, we need to relax SELinux security restrictions to run the following example using the `--security-opt label=disable` option.

The following example runs another build using the default host store:

```
# podman run --device /dev/fuse \
  -v ./build:/build:z
  -v /var/lib/containers:/var/lib/containers \
  --security-opt label=disable \
  -v /run/containers/0/auth.json:/auth.json \
  quay.io/buildah/stable \
  bash -c 'set -euo pipefail; \
    buildah build -t registry.example.com/test5 /build; \
    buildah push --authfile /auth.json \
    registry.example.com/test5'
```

The approach described in this example is the opposite of the previous one – better performances but worse security isolation.

A good compromise between the two implies the usage of a secondary, read-only image store to provide access to the cached layers. Buildah supports the usage of multiple image stores, and the `/etc/containers/storage.conf` file *inside the Buildah stable image* already configures the `/var/lib/shared` folder for this purpose.

To prove this, we can inspect the content of the `/etc/containers/storage.conf` file, where the following section is defined:

```
# AdditionalImageStores is used to pass paths to additional
Read/Only image stores
# Must be comma separated list.
additionalimagestores = [
"/var/lib/shared",
]
```

This way, we can get good isolation and better performance, since cached images from the host will be already available in the read-only store. The read-only store can be prepopulated with the most used images to speed up builds or can be mounted from a network share.

The following example shows this approach, by bind-mounting the read-only store to the container and executing the build with the advantage of reusing pre-pulled images:

```
# podman run --device /dev/fuse \
  -v ./build:/build:z \
  -v $BUILD_STORE:/var/lib/containers:Z \
  -v /var/lib/containers/storage:/var/lib/shared:ro \
  -v /run/containers/0/auth.json:/auth.json:z \
  quay.io/buildah/stable \
  bash -c 'set -euo pipefail; \
  buildah build -t registry.example.com/test6 /build; \
  buildah push --authfile /auth.json \
  registry.example.com/test6'
```

The examples showed in this subsection are also inspired by a great technical article written by *Dan Walsh* (one of the leads of the Buildah and Podman projects) on the *Red Hat Developer* blog; refer to the *Further reading* section for the original article link. Let's close this section with an example of native Buildah commands.

Running native Buildah commands inside containers

We have so far illustrated examples using Dockerfiles/Containerfiles, but nothing prevents us from running containerized native Buildah commands. The following example creates a custom Python image built from a Fedora base image:

```
# BUILD_STORE=/var/lib/containers-$(echo $RANDOM | md5sum |
head -c 8)# mkdir $BUILD_STORE
```

```
# podman run --device /dev/fuse \
  -e REGISTRY=<USER_DEFINED_REGISTRY:PORT> \
  --security-opt label=disable \
  -v $BUILD_STORE:/var/lib/containers:Z \
```

```
 -v /var/lib/containers/storage:/var/lib/shared:ro \
 -v /run/containers/0:/run/containers/0 \
 quay.io/buildah/stable \
 bash -c 'set -euo pipefail; \
   container=$(buildah from fedora); \
   buildah run $container dnf install -y python3 python3; \
   buildah commit $container $REGISTRY/python_demo; \
   buildah push -authfile \
   /run/containers/0/auth.json $REGISTRY/python_demo'
```

From a performance standpoint as well as the build process, nothing changes from the previous examples. As already stated, this approach provides more flexibility in the build operations.

If the commands to be passed are too many, a good workaround can be to create a shell script and inject it into the Buildah image using a dedicated volume:

```
# BUILD_STORE=/var/lib/containers-$(echo $RANDOM | md5sum | head -c 8)
# PATH_TO_SCRIPT=/path/to/script
# REGISTRY=<USER_DEFINED_REGISTRY:PORT>
# mkdir $BUILD_STORE
# podman run --device /dev/fuse \
  -v $BUILD_STORE:/var/lib/containers:Z \
  -v /var/lib/containers/storage:/var/lib/shared:ro \
  -v /run/containers/0:/run/containers/0 \
  -v $PATH_TO_SCRIPT:/root:z \
  quay.io/buildah/stable /root/build.sh
```

build.sh is the name of the shell script file containing all the build custom commands.

In this section, we have learned how to run Buildah in containers covering both volume mounts and bind mounts. We have learned how to run rootless build containers that can be easily integrated into pipelines or Kubernetes clusters to provide an end-to-end application life cycle workflow. This is due to the flexible nature of Buildah, and for the same reason, it is very easy to embed Buildah inside custom builders, as we will see in the next section.

Integrating Buildah in custom builders

As we saw in the previous section of this chapter, Buildah is a key component of Podman's container ecosystem. Buildah is a dynamic and flexible tool that can be adapted to different scenarios to build brand-new containers. It has several options and configurations available, but our exploration is not yet finished.

Podman and all the projects developed around it have been built with extensibility in mind, making every programmable interface available to be reused from the outside world.

Podman, for example, inherits Buildah capabilities for building brand-new containers through the `podman build` command; with the same principle, we can embed Buildah interfaces and its engine in our custom builder.

Let's see how to build a custom builder in the Go language; we will see that the process is pretty straightforward, because Podman, Buildah, and many other projects in this ecosystem are actually written in the Go language.

Including Buildah in our Go build tool

As a first step, we need to prepare our development environment, downloading and installing all the required tools and libraries for creating our custom build tool.

In *Chapter 3*, *Running the First Container*, we saw various Podman installation methods. In the following section, we will use a similar procedure while going through the preliminary steps for building a Buildah project from scratch, downloading its source file to include in our custom builder.

First of all, let's ensure we have all the needed packages installed on our development host system:

```
# dnf install -y golang git go-md2man btrfs-progs-devel \
gpgme-devel device-mapper-devel
Last metadata expiration check: 0:43:05 ago on mar 9 nov 2021,
17:21:23.
Package git-2.33.1-1.fc35.x86_64 is already installed.
Dependencies resolved.
================================================================
================================================================
===============================================
```

```
Package
Architecture                        Version
Repository                          Size

================================================================
================================================================
============================================

Installing:
btrfs-progs-devel                                       x86_64
5.14.2-1.fc35                       updates
50 k
device-mapper-devel                                     x86_64
1.02.175-6.fc35                     fedora
45 k
golang                                                  x86_64
1.16.8-2.fc35                       fedora
608 k
golang-github-cpuguy83-md2man                           x86_64
2.0.1-1.fc35                        fedora
818 k
gpgme-devel                                             x86_64
1.15.1-6.fc35                       updates
163 k
Installing dependencies:
[... omitted output]
```

After installing the Go language core libraries and some other development tools, we are ready to create the directory structure for our project and initialize it:

```
$ mkdir ~/custombuilder
$ cd ~/custombuilder
[custombuilder]$ export GOPATH=`pwd`
```

As shown in the previous example, we followed these steps:

1. Created the project root directory
2. Defined the Go language root path that we are going to use

We are now ready to create our Go module that will create our customized container image with a few easy steps.

To speed up the example and avoid any writing errors, we can download the Go language code that we are going to use for this test from the official GitHub repository of this book:

1. Go to `https://github.com/PacktPublishing/Podman-for-DevOps` or run the following command:

    ```
    $ git clone https://github.com/PacktPublishing/Podman-
    for-DevOps
    ```

2. After that, copy the files provided in the `Chapter07/*` directory into the newly created `~/custombuilder/` directory.

You should have the following files in your directory at this point:

```
$ cd ~/custombuilder/src/builder
$ ls -latotal 148
drwxrwxr-x. 1 alex alex      74 9 nov 15.22 .
drwxrwxr-x. 1 alex alex      14 9 nov 14.10 ..
-rw-rw-r--. 1 alex alex    1466 9 nov 14.10 custombuilder.go
-rw-rw-r--. 1 alex alex     161 9 nov 15.22 go.mod
-rw-rw-r--. 1 alex alex  135471 9 nov 15.22 go.sum
-rw-rw-r--. 1 alex alex     337 9 nov 14.17 script.js
```

At this point, we can run the following command to let the Go tools acquire all the needed dependencies to ready the module for execution:

```
$ go mod tidy
go: finding module for package github.com/containers/storage/
pkg/unshare
go: finding module for package github.com/containers/image/v5/
storage
go: finding module for package github.com/containers/storage
go: finding module for package github.com/containers/image/v5/
types
go: finding module for package github.com/containers/buildah/
define
go: finding module for package github.com/containers/buildah
go: found github.com/containers/buildah in github.com/
containers/buildah v1.23.1
go: found github.com/containers/buildah/define in github.com/
containers/buildah v1.23.1
```

```
go: found github.com/containers/image/v5/storage in github.com/
containers/image/v5 v5.16.1
```

```
go: found github.com/containers/image/v5/types in github.com/
containers/image/v5 v5.16.1
```

```
go: found github.com/containers/storage in github.com/
containers/storage v1.37.0
```

```
go: found github.com/containers/storage/pkg/unshare in github.
com/containers/storage v1.37.0
```

The tool analyzed the provided custombuilder.go file, and it found all the required libraries, populating the go.mod file.

> **Important Note**
> Please be aware that the previous command will verify whether a module is available, and if it is not, the tool will start downloading it from the internet. So, be patient during this step!

We can check that the previous commands downloaded all the required packages by inspecting the directory structure we created earlier:

```
$ cd ~/custombuilder
[custombuilder]$ ls
pkg  src
[custombuilder]$ ls -la pkg/
total 0
drwxrwxr-x. 1 alex alex  28  9 nov 18.27 .
drwxrwxr-x. 1 alex alex  12  9 nov 18.18 ..
drwxrwxr-x. 1 alex alex  20  9 nov 18.27 linux_amd64
drwxrwxr-x. 1 alex alex 196  9 nov 18.27 mod
[custombuilder]$ ls -la pkg/mod/
total 0
drwxrwxr-x. 1 alex alex 196  9 nov 18.27 .
drwxrwxr-x. 1 alex alex  28  9 nov 18.27 ..
drwxrwxr-x. 1 alex alex  22  9 nov 18.18 cache
drwxrwxr-x. 1 alex alex 918  9 nov 18.27 github.com
drwxrwxr-x. 1 alex alex  24  9 nov 18.27 go.etcd.io
drwxrwxr-x. 1 alex alex   2  9 nov 18.27 golang.org
[... omitted output]
```

```
[custombuilder]$ ls -la pkg/mod/github.com/
[... omitted output]
drwxrwxr-x. 1 alex alex  98  9 nov 18.27   containerd
drwxrwxr-x. 1 alex alex  20  9 nov 18.27   containernetworking
drwxrwxr-x. 1 alex alex 184  9 nov 18.27   containers
drwxrwxr-x. 1 alex alex 110  9 nov 18.27   coreos
[... omitted output]
```

We are now ready to run our custom builder module, but before going forward, let's take a look at the key elements contained in the Go source file.

If we start looking at the `custombuilder.go` file, just after defining the package and the libraries to use, we defined the main function of our module.

In the main function, at the beginning of the definition, we inserted a fundamental code block:

```
if buildah.InitReexec() {
   return
}
unshare.MaybeReexecUsingUserNamespace(false)
```

This piece of code enables the usage of **rootless** mode by leveraging the Go `unshare` package, available through `github.com/containers/storage/pkg/unshare`.

To leverage the build features of Buildah, we have to instantiate `buildah.Builder`. This object has all the methods to define the build steps, configure the build, and finally run it.

To create `Builder`, we need an object called `storage.Store` from the `github.com/containers/storage` package. This element is responsible for storing the intermediate and resultant container images. Let's see the code block we are discussing:

```
buildStoreOptions, err := storage.DefaultStoreOptions(unshare.
IsRootless(), unshare.GetRootlessUID())
buildStore, err := storage.GetStore(buildStoreOptions)
```

As you can see from the previous example, we are getting the default options and passing them to the `storage` module to request a `Store` object.

Another element we need for creating `Builder` is the `BuilderOptions` object. This element contains all the default and custom options we might assign to Buildah's `Builder`. Let's see how to define it:

```
builderOpts := buildah.BuilderOptions{
    FromImage:          "node:12-alpine", // Starting image
    Isolation:          define.IsolationChroot, // Isolation
environment
    CommonBuildOpts:    &define.CommonBuildOptions{},
    ConfigureNetwork:   define.NetworkDefault,
    SystemContext:      &types.SystemContext {},
}
```

In the previous code block, we defined a `BuilderOptions` object that contains the following:

- An initial image that we are going to use to build our target container image:

  - In this case, we chose the Node.js image based on Alpine Linux distribution. This is because, in our example, we are simulating the build process of a Node.js application.

- Isolation mode to adopt once the build starts. In this case, we are going to use chroot isolation that fits a lot of build scenarios well – less isolation but fewer requirements.

- Some default options for the build, network, and system contexts:

  - `SystemContext` objects define the information contained in configuration files as parameters.

Now that we have all the necessary data for instantiating `Builder`, let's do it:

```
builder, err := buildah.NewBuilder(context.TODO(), buildStore,
builderOpts)
```

As you can see, we are calling the `NewBuilder` function, with all the required options that we created in code earlier in this section, to get `Builder` ready to create our custom container image.

Now that we are ready to instruct `Builder` with the required options to create the custom image, let's first add into the container image the **JavaScript** file containing our application, for which we are creating this container image:

```
err = builder.Add("/home/node/", false, buildah.
AddAndCopyOptions{}, "script.js")
```

We are assuming that the JavaScript main file is stored next to the Go module that we are writing and using in this example, and we are copying this file into the `/home/node` directory, which is the default path where the base container image expects to find this kind of data.

The JavaScript program that we are going to copy into the container image and use for this test is really simple – let's inspect it:

```
var http = require("http");
http.createServer(function(request, response) {
  response.writeHead(200, {"Content-Type": "text/plain"});
  response.write("Hello Podman and Buildah friends. This page
is provided to you through a container running Node.js version:
");
  response.write(process.version);
  response.end();
}).listen(8080);
```

Without going deep into the JavaScript language syntax and its concepts, we can note looking at the JavaScript file that we are using the HTTP library for listening on port `8080` for incoming requests, responding to these requests with a default welcome message: `Hello Podman and Buildah friends. This page is provided to you through a container running Node.js`. We also append the Node.js version to the response string.

> **Important Note**
>
> Please consider that JavaScript, also known as **JS**, is a high-level programming language that is compiled just in time. As we stated earlier, we are neither going deep into the definition of the JavaScript language nor its most famous runtime environment, Node.js.

After that, we configure the default command to run for our custom container image:

```
builder.SetCmd([]string{"node", "/home/node/script.js"})
```

We just set the command to execute the Node.js execution runtime, referring to the JavaScript program that we just added to the container image.

For committing the changes we made, we need to get the image reference that we are working on. At the same time, we will also define the container image name that `Builder` will create:

```
imageRef, err := is.Transport.ParseStoreReference(buildStore,
"podmanbook/nodejs-welcome")
```

Now, we are ready to commit the changes and call the `commit` function of `Builder`:

```
imageId, _, _, err := builder.Commit(context.TODO(), imageRef,
define.CommitOptions{})
```
```
fmt.Printf("Image built! %s\n", imageId)
```

As we can see, we just requested `Builder` to commit the changes, passing the image reference we obtained earlier, and then we finally print it as a reference.

We are now ready to run our program! Let's execute it:

```
[builder]$ go run custombuilder.go
```
```
Image built!
e60fa98051522a51f4585e46829ad6a18df704dde774634dbc010baae440
4849
```

We can now test the custom container image we just built:

```
[builder]$ podman run -dt -p 8080:8080/tcp podmanbook/nodejs-
welcome:latest
```
```
747805c1b59558a70c4a2f1a1d258913cae5ffc08cc026c74ad3ac21aab1
8974
```
```
[builder]$ curl localhost:8080
```
```
Hello Podman and Buildah friends. This page is provided to you
through a container running Node.js version: v12.22.7
```

As we can see in the previous code block, we are running the container image we just created with the following options:

- `-d`: Detached mode, which runs the container in the background
- `-t`: Allocates a new pseudo-TTY
- `-p`: Publishes the container port to the host system
- `podmanbook/nodejs-welcome:latest`: The name of our custom container image

Finally, we use the `curl` command-line tool for requesting and printing the HTTP response provided by our JavaScript program, which is containerized in the custom container image that we created!

> **Important Note**
>
> The example described in this section is just a simple overview of all the great features that the Buildah Go module can enable for our custom image builders. To learn more about the various functions, variables, and code documentation, you can refer to the docs at `https://pkg.go.dev/github.com/containers/buildah`.

As we saw in this section, Buildah is a really flexible tool, and with its libraries, it can support custom builders in many different scenarios.

If we try to search on the internet, we can find many examples of Buildah supporting the creation of custom container images. Let's see some of them.

Quarkus-native executables in containers

Quarkus is defined as the Kubernetes-native Java stack leveraging OpenJDK (the open Java development kit) project and the GraalVM project. GraalVM is a Java virtual machine that has many special features, such as the compilation of Java applications for fast startup and low memory footprint.

> **Important note**
>
> We will not go into the details of Quarkus, GraalVM, and any other companion projects. The example that we will deep-dive into is only for your reference. We encourage you to learn more about these projects by going through their web pages and reading the related documentation.

If we take a look at the Quarkus documentation web page, we can easily find that, after a long tutorial in which we can learn how to build a Quarkus-native executable, we can then pack and execute this executable in a container image.

The steps provided in the Quarkus documentation leverage a Maven wrapper with a special option. Maven was born as a Java build automation tool, but then it was also extended to other programming languages. If we take a quick look at this command, we will note the name of Podman inside:

```
$ ./mvnw package -Pnative -Dquarkus.native.container-build=true
-Dquarkus.native.container-runtime=podman
```

This means that the Maven wrapper program will invoke a Podman build to create a container image with the preconfigured environment shipped by the Quarkus project and the binary application that we are developing.

We saw the name of Podman inside the option. This is because, as we saw in *Chapter 6, Meet Buildah – Building Containers from Scratch*, Podman borrows Buildah's build logic by vendoring its libraries.

To explore this example further, we can take a look at `https://quarkus.io/guides/building-native-image`.

A Buildah wrapper for the Rust language

Another cool example of build tools made through the Buildah library or CLI is the Buildah wrapper for the **Rust** programming language. Rust is a programming language similar to C++, designed for performance and safe concurrency. The main project page is available at this URL: `https://github.com/Dennis-Krasnov/Buildah-Rust`.

This Buildah wrapper leverages the Rust package manager names **Cargo** for downloading the needed dependencies, compiles it in a package, and makes it distributable.

> **Important Note**
>
> We will not go into the details of Rust, Cargo, and any other companion projects. The example that we will deep-dive into is only for your reference. We encourage you to learn more about these projects by going through their web pages and reading the related documentation.

The example in the project homepage is really simple, as you can see in the following code block:

```
$ cd examples/
$ cargo run --example nginx
$ podman run --rm -it -p 8080:80 nginx_rust
```

The first command, after selecting the directory named `examples`, executes a simple block of code that is needed to create a container, while the second tests the container image that the Buildah wrapper has just made through Buildah itself.

We can take a look at the Rust code used in the first command of the previous code block. The first command executes the small piece of code in the `nginx.rs` file:

```
use buildah_rs::container::Container;
fn main() {
    let mut container = Container::from("nginx:1.21");
    container.copy("html", "/usr/share/nginx/html").unwrap();
    container.commit("nginx_rust").unwrap();
}
```

As stated before, we will not dive deep into the code syntax or into the library itself; anyway, the code is pretty simple, and it just imports the Buildah wrapper library, creates a container image starting from `nginx:1.21`, and finally, copies the local `html` directory to the container image's destination path.

To explore this example further, take a look at `https://github.com/Dennis-Krasnov/Buildah-Rust`.

This concludes this section. We have learned, through a lot of useful examples, about how to integrate Buildah in different scenarios to support custom builders of the container images of our projects.

Summary

In this chapter, we have learned how to leverage Podman's companion, Buildah, in some advanced scenarios to support our development projects.

We saw how to use Buildah for multistage container image creation, which allows us to create builds with multiple stages using different FROM instructions and, subsequently, to have images that grab contents from the previous ones.

Then, we discovered that there are many use cases that imply the need for containerized builds. Nowadays, one of the most common adoption scenarios is the application build workflow running on top of a Kubernetes cluster. For this reason, we went into the details of containerizing Buildah.

Finally, we learned through a lot of interesting examples how to integrate Buildah to create custom builders for container images. As we saw in this chapter, there are several options and methods to actually build a container image with the Podman ecosystem tools, and most of the time, we usually start from a base image for customizing and extending a previous OS layer to fit our use cases.

In the next chapter, we will learn more about container base images, how to choose them, and what to look out for when we are making our choice.

Further readings

- A list of CNCF projects: `https://landscape.cncf.io/`

- *Best practices for running Buildah in a container*: `https://developers.redhat.com/blog/2019/08/14/best-practices-for-running-buildah-in-a-container`

- The Buildah Go module documentation: `https://pkg.go.dev/github.com/containers/buildah`

- Quarkus-native executables: `https://quarkus.io/guides/building-native-image`

- The Buildah wrapper for the Rust language: `https://github.com/Dennis-Krasnov/Buildah-Rust`

8

Choosing the Container Base Image

The fastest and easiest way to learn about and get some experience with containers is to start working with pre-built container images, as we saw in the previous chapters. After a deep dive into container management, we discovered that sometimes, the available service, its configuration, or even the application version is not the one that our project requires. Then, we introduced Buildah and its feature for building custom container images. In this chapter, we are going to address another important topic that is often questioned in community and enterprise projects: the choice of a **container base image**.

Choosing the right container base image is an important task of the container journey: a container base image is the underlying operating system layer that our system's service, application, or code will rely on. Due to this, we should choose one that fits our best practices concerning security and updates.

In this chapter, we're going to cover the following main topics:

- The Open Container Initiative image format
- Where do container images come from?

- Trusted container image sources
- Introducing Universal Base Image

Technical requirements

To complete this chapter, you will need a machine with a working Podman installation. As stated in *Chapter 3*, *Running the First Container*, all the examples in this book have been executed on a Fedora 34 system or later but can be reproduced on an operating system of your choice.

Having a good understanding of the topics that we covered in *Chapter 4*, *Managing Running Containers*, will help you easily grasp concepts regarding container images.

The Open Container Initiative image format

As we described in *Chapter 1*, *Introduction to Container Technology*, back in 2013, Docker was introduced in the container landscape and became very popular rapidly.

At a high level, the Docker team introduced the concept of container images and container registries, which was a game-changer. Another important step was being able to *extract* containerd projects from Docker and donate them to the **Cloud Native Computing Foundation** (**CNCF**). This motivated the open source community to start working seriously on container engines that could be injected into an orchestration layer, such as Kubernetes.

Similarly, in 2015, Docker, with the help of many other companies (Red Hat, AWS, Google, Microsoft, IBM, and others), started the **Open Container Initiative** (**OCI**) under the Linux Foundation umbrella.

These contributors developed the Runtime Specification (runtime-spec) and the Image Specification (image-spec) to describe how the API and the architecture for new container engines should be created in the future.

After a few months of work, the OCI team released its first implementation of a container engine that adhered to the OCI's specifications; the project was named `runc`.

It's worth looking at the container image specification in detail and going over some theory behind the practice, which we introduced in *Chapter 2*, *Comparing Podman and Docker*.

The specification defines an OCI container image that consists of the following:

- **Manifest**: This contains the metadata of the contents and dependencies of the image. This also includes the ability to identify one or more filesystem archives that will be unpacked to get the final runnable filesystem.

- **Image Index (optional)**: This represents a list of manifests and descriptors that can provide different implementations of the image, depending on the target platform.

- **Set of Filesystem Layers**: The actual set of layers that should be merged to build the final container filesystem.

- **Configuration**: This contains all the information that's required by the container runtime engine to effectively run the application, such as arguments, environment variables, and so on.

We will not deep dive into every element of the OCI Image Specification, but the Image Manifest deserves a closer look.

OCI Image Manifest

The Image Manifest defines a set of layers and the configuration for a single container image that is built for a specific architecture and an operating system.

Let's explore the details of the OCI Image Manifest by looking at the following example:

```
{
  "schemaVersion": 2,
  "config": {
    "mediaType": "application/vnd.oci.image.config.v1+json",
    "size": 7023,
    "digest":
"sha256:b5b2b2c507a0944348e0303114d8d93aaaa081732b86451d9bce1f
432a537bc7"
  },
  "layers": [
    {
      "mediaType": "application/vnd.oci.image.layer.
v1.tar+gzip",
      "size": 32654,
      "digest":
"sha256:9834876dcfb05cb167a5c24953eba58c4ac89b1adf57f28f2f9d09a
f107ee8f0"
    }
  ],
  "annotations": {
    "com.example.key1": "value1",
```

```
    "com.example.key2":  "value2"
  }
}
```

Here, we are using the following keywords:

- `schemaVersion`: A property that must be set to a value of 2. This ensures backward compatibility with Docker.

- `config`: A property that references a container's configuration through a digest:

  - `mediaType`: This property defines the actual configuration format (just one currently).

- `layers`: This property provides an array of descriptor objects:

  - `MediaType`: In this case, this descriptor should be one of the media types that's allowed for the layer's descriptors.

- `annotations`: This property defines additional metadata for the image manifest.

To summarize, the main goal of the specification is to make interoperable tools for building, transporting, and preparing a container image to be run.

The Image Manifest Specification has three main goals:

- To enable hashing for the image's configuration, thereby generating a unique ID

- To allow multi-architecture images due to its high-level manifest (image index) that references platform-specific versions of the image manifest

- To be able to easily translate the container image into the OCI Runtime Specification

Now, let's learn where these container images come from.

Where do container images come from?

In the previous chapters, we used pre-built images to run, build, or manage a container, but where do these container images come from?

How can we dig into their source commands or into the Dockerfile/ContainerFile that's used to build it?

Well, as we've mentioned previously, Docker introduced the concept of container image and Container Registry for storing these images – even publicly. The most famous Container Registry is Docker Hub but after Docker's introduction, other cloud container registries were released too.

We can choose between the following cloud container registries:

- **Docker Hub**: This is the hosted registry solution by Docker Inc. This registry also hosts official repositories and security verified images for some popular open source projects.

- **Quay**: This is the hosted registry solution that was born under the CoreOS company, though it is now part of Red Hat. It offers private and public repositories, automated scanning for security purposes, image builds, and integration with popular Git public repositories.

- **Linux Distribution Registries**: Popular Linux distributions are typically community-based, such as Fedora Linux, or enterprise-based, such as **Red Hat Enterprise Linux** (RHEL). They usually offer public container registries, though these are often only available for projects or packages that have already been provided as system packages. These registries are not available to end users and they are fed by the Linux distributions' maintainers.

- **Public Cloud Registries**: Amazon, Google, Microsoft, and other public cloud providers offer private container registries for their customers.

We will explore these registries in more detail in *Chapter 9, Pushing Images to a Container Registry*.

Docker Hub, as well as Quay.io, are public container registries where we can find container images that have been created by anyone. These registries are full of useful custom images that we can use as starting points for testing container images quickly and easily.

Just downloading and running a container image is not always the best thing to do – we could hit very old and outdated software that could be vulnerable to some known public vulnerability or, even worse, we could download and execute some malicious code that could compromise our whole infrastructure.

For this reason, Docker Hub and Quay.io usually offer features to underline where such images come from. Let's inspect them.

Docker Hub container registry service

As we introduced earlier, Docker Hub is the most famous Container Registry available. It hosts multiple container images for community and enterprise products.

By looking at the detail page of a container image, we can easily discover all the required information about that project and its container images. The following screenshot shows Alpine Linux's Docker Hub page:

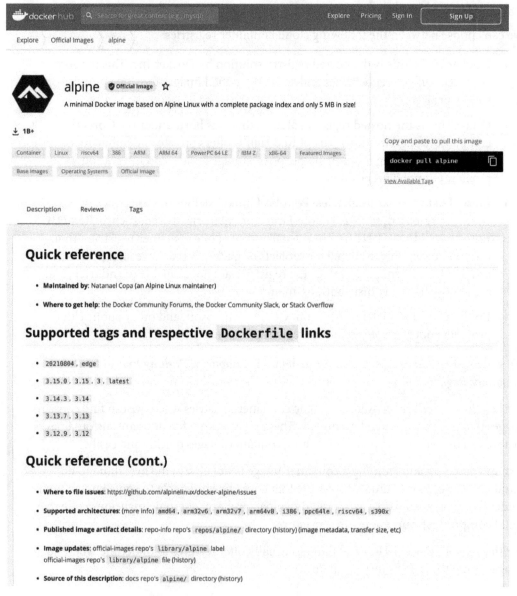

Figure 8.1 – Alpine Linux container image on Docker Hub

As you can see, at the top of the page, we can find helpful information, the latest tags, the supported architectures, and useful links to the project's documentation and the issue-reporting system.

On the Docker Hub page, we can find the *Official Image* tag, just after the image's name, when that image is part of Docker's Official Images program. The images in this program are curated directly by the Docker team in collaboration with the upstream projects' maintainers.

> **Important note**
> If you want to look at this page in more depth, point your web browser to
> `https://hub.docker.com/_/alpine`.

Another important feature that's offered by Docker Hub (not only for official images) is the ability to look into the Dockerfile that was used to create a certain image.

If we click on one of the available tags on the container image page, we can easily look at the Dockerfile of that container image tag.

Clicking on the tag named `20210804, edge` on that page will redirect us to the GitHub page of the `docker-alpine` project, which is defined as the following Dockerfile: `https://github.com/alpinelinux/docker-alpine/blob/edge/x86_64/Dockerfile`.

We should always pay attention and prefer official images. If an official image is not available or it does not fit our needs, then we need to inspect the Dockerfile that the content creator published, as well as the container image.

Quay container registry service

Quay is a container registry service that was acquired by CoreOS in 2014 and is now part of the Red Hat ecosystem.

The registry allows its users to be more cautious once they've chosen a container image by providing security scanning software.

Quay adopts the Clair project, a leading container vulnerability scanner that displays reports on the repository tags web page, as shown in the following screenshot:

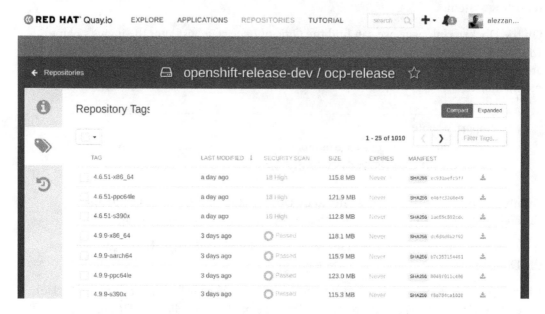

Figure 8.2 – Quay vulnerability Security Scan page

On this page, we can click on **Security Scan** to inspect the details of that security scan. If you want to learn more about this feature, please go to `https://quay.io/repository/openshift-release-dev/ocp-release?tab=tags`.

As we've seen, using a public registry that offers every user the security scan feature could help ensure that we choose the right and most secure flavor of the container image we are searching for.

Red Hat Ecosystem Catalog

The Red Hat Ecosystem Catalog is the default container registry for **Red Hat Enterprise Linux** (**RHEL**) and Red Hat **OpenShift Container Platform** (**OCP**) users. The web interface of this registry is publicly accessible to any users, whether they are authenticated or not, although almost all the images that are provided are reserved for paid users (RHEL or OCP users).

We are talking about this registry because it combines all the features we talked about previously. This registry offers the following to its users:

- Official container images by Red Hat
- ContainerFile/Dockerfile sources to inspect the content of the image
- Security reports (index) about every container image that's distributed

The following screenshot shows what this information looks like on the **Red Hat Ecosystem Catalog** page:

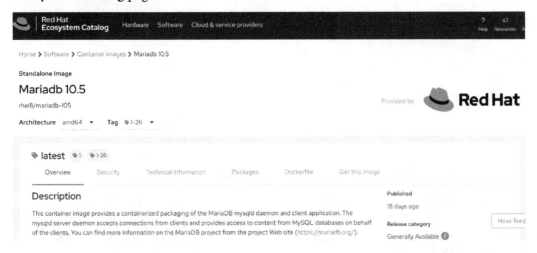

Figure 8.3 – MariaDB container image description page on the Red Hat Ecosystem Catalog

As we can see, the page shows the description of the container image we have selected (MariaDB database), the version, the available architectures, and various tags that can be selected from the respective drop-down menu. Some tabs also mention the keywords we are interested in: *Security* and *Dockerfile*.

By clicking on the **Security** tab, we can see the status of the vulnerability scan that was executed for that image tag, as shown in the following screenshot:

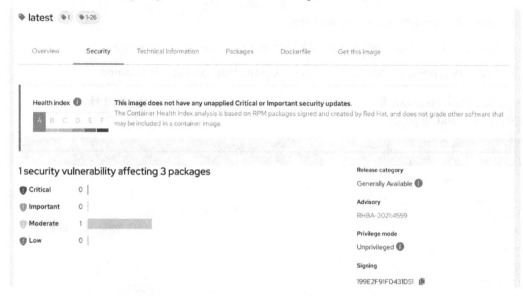

Figure 8.4 – MariaDB container image Security page on the Red Hat Ecosystem Catalog

As we can see, at the time of writing, for this latest image tag, a security vulnerability has already been identified that's affecting three packages. To the right, we can find the Red Hat Advisory ID, which is linked to the public **Common Vulnerabilities and Exposures (CVEs)**.

By clicking on the **Dockerfile** tab, we can look at the source ContainerFile that was used to build that container image:

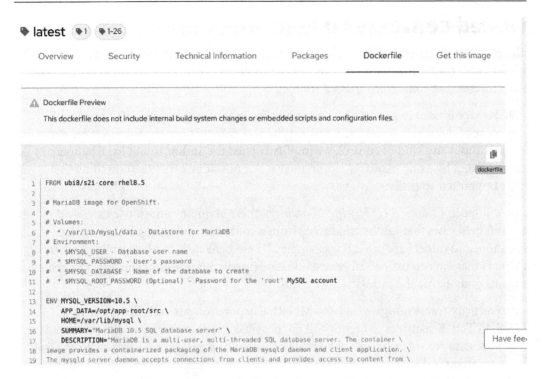

Figure 8.5 – MariaDB container image Dockerfile page on Red Hat Ecosystem Catalog

As we can see, we can look at the source ContainerFile that was used to build the container image we are going to pull and run. This is a great feature that we can access by clicking on the same description page of the container image we are looking for.

If we take a closer look at the preceding screenshot, we can see that the MariaDB container image was built using a very special container base image: UBI8.

UBI stands for **Universal Base Image**. It is an initiative that was launched by Red Hat that lets every user (Red Hat customers or not) open Red Hat container images. This allows the Red Hat ecosystem to expand by leveraging all the previously mentioned services that are offered by the Red Hat Ecosystem Catalog, as well as by leveraging the updated packages that are directly from Red Hat.

We will talk more about UBI and its container images later in this chapter.

Trusted container image sources

In the previous section, we defined the central role of the image registry as a source of truth for valid, usable images. In this section, we want to stress the importance of adopting trusted images that come from trusted sources.

An OCI image is used to package binaries and runtimes in a structured filesystem with the purpose of delivering a specific service. When we pull that image and run it on our systems without any kind of control, we implicitly trust the author to not have tampered with its content by using malicious components. But nowadays, trust is something that cannot be granted so easily.

As we will see in *Chapter 11, Securing Containers*, there are many attack use cases and malicious behaviors that can be conducted from a container: privilege escalation, data exfiltration, and miners are just a few examples. These behaviors can be amplified when containers that are run inside Kubernetes clusters (many thousands of clusters) can spawn malicious pods across the infrastructure easily.

To help security teams mitigate this, the MITRE Corporation periodically releases **MITRE ATT&CK** matrices to identify all the possible attack strategies and their related techniques, with real-life use cases, and their detection and mitigation best practices. One of these matrixes is dedicated to containers, where many techniques are implemented based on insecure images where malicious behaviors can be conducted successfully.

> **Important Note**
> You should prefer images that come from a registry that supports vulnerability scans. If the scan results are available, check them carefully and avoid using images that spot critical vulnerabilities.

With this in mind, what is the first step for creating a secure cloud-native infrastructure? The answer is choosing images that only come from trusted sources, and the first step is to configure trusted registries and patterns to block disallowed ones. We will cover this in the following subsection.

Managing trusted registries

As shown in *Chapter 3, Running the First Container*, in the *Preparing your environment* section, Podman can manage trusted registries with config files.

The `/etc/containers/registries.conf` file (overridden by the user-related `$HOME/.config/containers/registries.conf` file, if present) manages a list of trusted registries that Podman can safely contact to search and pull images.

Let's look at an example of this file:

```
unqualified-search-registries = ["docker.io", "quay.io"]


[[registry]]
location = "registry.example.com:5000"
insecure = false
```

This file helps us define the trusted registries that can be used by Podman, so it deserves a detailed analysis.

Podman accepts both **unqualified** and **fully-qualified** images. The difference is quite simple and can be illustrated as follows:

- A fully-qualified image includes a registry server FQDN, namespace, image name, and tag. For example, `docker.io/library/nginx:latest` is a fully-qualified image. It has a full name that cannot be confused with any other Nginx image.

- An unqualified image only includes the image's name. For example, the `nginx` image can have multiple instances in the searched registries. The majority of the images that result from the basic `podman search nginx` command will not be official and should be analyzed in detail to ensure they're trusted. The output can be filtered by the `OFFICIAL` flag and by the number of `STARS` (more is better).

The first global setting of the registries configuration file is the `unqualified-search-registry` array, which defines the search list of registries for unqualified images. When the user runs the `podman search <image_name>` command, Podman will search across the registries defined in this list.

By removing a registry from the list, Podman will stop searching the registry. However, Podman will still be able to pull a fully qualified image from a foreign registry.

To manage single registries and create matching patterns for specific images, we can use the `[[registry]]` **Tom's Obvious, Minimal Language** (TOML) tables. The main settings of these tables are as follows:

- `prefix`: This is used to define the image names and can support multiple formats. In general, we can define images by following the `host[:port]/namespace[/_namespace_...]/repo(:_tag|@digest)` pattern, though simpler patterns such as `host[:port]`, `host[:port]/namespace`, and even `[*.]host` can be applied. Following this approach, users can define a generic prefix for a registry or a more detailed prefix to match a specific image or tag. Given a fully qualified image, if two `[[registry]]` tables have a prefix with a partial match, the longest matching pattern will be used.

- `insecure`: This is a Boolean (`true` or `false`) that allows unencrypted HTTP connections or TLS connections based on untrusted certificates.

- `blocked`: This is a Boolean (`true` or `false`) that's used to define blocked registries. If it's set to true, the registries or images that match the prefix are blocked.

- `location`: This field defines the registry's location. By default, it is equal to `prefix`, but it can have a different value. In that case, a pattern that matches a custom prefix namespace will resolve to the `location` value.

Along with the main `[[registry]]` table, we can define an array of `[[registry.mirror]]` TOML tables to provide alternate paths to the main registry or registry namespace.

When multiple mirrors are provided, Podman will search across them first and then fall back to the location that's defined in the main `[[registry]]` table.

The following example extends the previous one by defining a namespaced registry entry and its mirror:

```
unqualified-search-registries = ["docker.io", "quay.io"]

[[registry]]
location = "registry.example.com:5000/foo"
insecure = false
[[registry.mirror]]
location = "mirror1.example.com:5000/bar"
[[registry.mirror]]
location = "mirror2.example.com:5000/bar"
```

According to this example, if a user tries to pull the image tagged as `registry.example.com:5000/foo/app:latest`, Podman will try `mirror1.example.com:5000/bar/app:latest`, then `mirror2.example.com:5000/bar/app:latest`, and fall back to `registry.example.com:5000/foo/app:latest` in case a failure occurs.

Using a prefix provides even more flexibility. In the following example, all the images that match `example.com/foo` will be redirected to mirror locations and fall back to the main location at the end:

```
unqualified-search-registries = ["docker.io", "quay.io"]
[[registry]]
prefix = "example.com/foo"
location = "registry.example.com:5000/foo"
insecure = false
[[registry.mirror]]
location = "mirror1.example.com:5000/bar"
[[registry.mirror]]
location = "mirror2.example.com:5000/bar"
```

In this example, when we pull the `example.com/foo/app:latest` image, Podman will attempt `mirror1.example.com:5000/bar/app:latest`, followed by `mirror2.example.com:5000/bar/app:latest` and `registry.example.com:5000/foo/app:latest`.

It is possible to use mirroring in a more advanced way, such as replacing public registries with private mirrors in disconnected environments. The following example remaps the `docker.io` and `quay.io` registries to a private mirror with different namespaces:

```
[[registry]]
prefix="quay.io"
location="mirror-internal.example.com/quay"
[[registry]]
prefix="docker.io"
location="mirror-internal.example.com/docker"
```

> **Important Note**
> Mirror registries should be kept up-to-date with mirrored repositories. For this reason, administrators or SRE teams should implement an image sync policy to keep the repositories updated.

Finally, we are going to learn how to block a source that is not considered trusted. This behavior could impact a single image, a namespace, or a whole registry.

The following example tells Podman to not search for or pull images from a blocked registry:

```
[[registry]]
location = "registry.rogue.io"
blocked = true
```

It is possible to refine the blocking policy by passing a specific namespace without blocking the whole registry. In the following example, every image search or pull that matches the `quay.io/foo` namespace pattern defined in the `prefix` field is blocked:

```
[[registry]]
prefix = "quay.io/foo/"
location = "docker.io"
blocked = true
```

According to this pattern, if the user tries to pull an image called `quay.io/foo/nginx:latest` or `quay.io/foo/httpd:v2.4`, the prefix is matched, and the pull is blocked. No blocking action occurs when the `quay.io/bar/fedora:latest` image is pulled.

Users can also define a very specific blocking rule for a single image or even a single tag by using the same approach that was described for namespaces. The following example blocks a specific image tag:

```
[[registry]]
prefix = "internal-registry.example.com/dev/app:v0.1"
location = "internal-registry.example.com "
blocked = true
```

It is possible to combine many blocking rules and add mirror tables on top of them.

> **Important Note**
>
> In a complex infrastructure with many machines running Podman (for example, developer workstations), a clever idea would be to keep the registry's configuration file updated using configuration management tools and declaratively apply the registry's filters.

Fully qualified image names can become quite long if we sum up the registry FQDN, namespace(s), repository, and tags. It is possible to create aliases using the [aliases] table to allow short image names to be used. This approach can simplify image management and reduce human error. However, aliases do not handle image tags or digests.

The following example defines a series of aliases for commonly used images:

```
[aliases]
"fedora" = "registry.fedoraproject.org/fedora"
"debian" = "docker.io/library/debian"
```

When an alias matches a short name, it is immediately used without the registries defined in the unqualified-search-registries list being searched.

> **Important Note**
> We can create custom files inside the /etc/containers/ registries.conf.d/ folder to define aliases without bloating the main configuration file.

With that, we have learned how to manage trusted sources and block unwanted images, registries, or namespaces. This is a security best practice but it does not relieve us from the responsibility of choosing a valid image that fits our needs while being trustworthy and having the lowest attack surface possible. This is also true when we're building a new application, where base images must be lightweight and secure. Red Hat UBI images can be a helpful solution for this problem.

Introducing Universal Base Image

When working on enterprise environments, many users and companies adopt RHEL as the operating system of choice to execute workloads reliably and securely. RHEL-based container images are available too, and they take advantage of the same package versioning as the OS release. All the security updates that are released for RHEL are immediately applied to OCI images, making them wealthy, secure images to build production-grade applications with.

Unfortunately, RHEL images are not publicly available without a Red Hat subscription. Users who have activated a valid subscription can use them freely on their RHEL systems and build custom images on top of them, but they are not freely redistributable without breaking the Red Hat enterprise agreement.

So, why worry? There are plenty of commonly used images that can replace them. This is true, but when it comes to reliability and security, many companies choose to stick to an enterprise-grade solution and this is not an exception for containers.

For these reasons, and to address the redistribution limitations of RHEL images, Red Hat created the **Universal Base Image**, also known as **UBI**. UBI images are freely redistributable, can be used to build containerized applications, middleware, and utilities, and are constantly maintained and upgraded by Red Hat.

UBI images are based on the currently supported versions of RHEL: at the time of writing, the **UBI7** and **UBI8** images are currently available (based on RHEL7 and RHEL8, respectively), along with the **UBI9-beta** image, which is based on RHEL9-beta. In general, we can consider UBI images as a subset of the RHEL operating system.

All UBI images are available on the public Red Hat registry (`registry.access.redhat.com`) and Docker Hub (`docker.io`).

There are currently four different flavors of UBI images, each one specialized for a particular use case:

- **Standard**: This is the standard UBI image. It has the most features and packages availability.

- **Minimal**: This is a stripped-down version of the standard image with minimalistic package management.

- **Micro**: This is a UBI version with a smaller footprint, without a package manager.

- **Init**: This is a UBI image that includes the `systemd` init system so that you can manage the execution of multiple services in a single container.

All of these are **free to use and redistribute** inside custom images. Let's describe each in detail, starting with the UBI Standard image.

The UBI Standard image

The UBI Standard image is the most complete UBI image version and the closest one to standard RHEL images. It includes the **YUM** package manager, which is available in RHEL, and can be customized by installing the packages that are available in its dedicated software repositories; that is, *ubi-8-baseos* and *ubi-8-appstream*.

The following example shows a Dockerfile/ContainerFile that uses a standard UBI8 image to build a minimal `httpd` server:

```
FROM registry.access.redhat.com/ubi8

# Update image and install httpd
RUN yum update -y && yum install -y httpd && yum clean all -y

# Expose the default httpd port 80
EXPOSE 80

# Run the httpd
CMD ["/usr/sbin/httpd", "-DFOREGROUND"]
```

The UBI Standard image was designed for generic applications and packages that are available on RHEL and already includes a curated list of basic system tools (including `curl`, `tar`, `vi`, `sed`, and `gzip`) and OpenSSL libraries while still retaining a small size (around 230 MiB): fewer packages means more lightweight images and a smaller attack surface.

If the UBI Standard image is still considered too big, the UBI Minimal image might be a good fit.

The UBI Minimal image

The UBI Minimal image is a stripped-down version of the UBI Standard image and was designed for self-consistent applications and their runtimes (Python, Ruby, Node.js, and so on). For this reason, it's smaller in size, has a small selection of packages, and doesn't include the YUM package manager; this has been replaced with a minimal tool called `microdnf`. The UBI Minimal image is smaller than the UBI Standard image and is roughly half its size.

The following example shows a Dockerfile/ContainerFile using a UBI 8 Minimal image to build a proof-of-concept Python web server:

```
# Based on the UBI8 Minimal image

FROM registry.access.redhat.com/ubi8-minimal

# Upgrade and install Python 3.6
RUN microdnf upgrade && microdnf install python3
```

```
# Copy source code
COPY entrypoint.sh http_server.py /
```

```
# Expose the default httpd port 80
EXPOSE 8080
```

```
# Configure the container entrypoint
ENTRYPOINT ["/entrypoint.sh"]
```

```
# Run the httpd
CMD ["/usr/bin/python3", "-u", "/http_server.py"]
```

By looking at the source code of the Python web server that's been executed by the container, we can see that the web server handler prints a *Hello World!* string when an HTTP GET request is received. The server also manages signal termination using the Python `signal` module, allowing the container to be stopped gracefully:

```python
#!/usr/bin/python3
import http.server
import socketserver
import logging
import sys
import signal
from http import HTTPStatus


port = 8080
message = b'Hello World!\n'
logging.basicConfig(
    stream = sys.stdout,
    level = logging.INFO
)


def signal_handler(signum, frame):
    sys.exit(0)
```

```
class Handler(http.server.SimpleHTTPRequestHandler):
  def do_GET(self):
    self.send_response(HTTPStatus.OK)
    self.end_headers()
    self.wfile.write(message)

if __name__ == "__main__":
  signal.signal(signal.SIGTERM, signal_handler)
  signal.signal(signal.SIGINT, signal_handler)
  try:
    httpd = socketserver.TCPServer(('', port), Handler)
    logging.info("Serving on port %s", port)
    httpd.serve_forever()
  except SystemExit:
    httpd.shutdown()
    httpd.server_close()
```

Finally, the Python executable is called by a minimal entry point script:

```
#!/bin/bash
set -e
exec $@
```

The script launches the command that's passed by the array in the CMD instruction. Also, notice the -u option that's passed to the Python executable in the command array. This enables unbuffered output and has the container print access logs in real time.

Let's try to build and run the container to see what happens:

```
$ buildah build -t python_httpd .
```

```
$ podman run -p 8080:8080 python_httpd
INFO:root:Serving on port 8080
```

With that, our minimal Python httpd server is ready to operate and serve a lot of barely useful but warming *Hello World!* responses.

UBI Minimal works best for these kinds of use cases. However, an even smaller image may be necessary. This is the perfect use case for the UBI Micro image.

The UBI Micro image

The UBI Micro image is the latest arrival to the UBI family. Its basic idea was to provide a distroless image, a stripped-down package manager without all the unnecessary packages, to provide a very small image that could also offer a minimal attack surface. Reducing the attack surface is required to achieve secure, minimal images that are more complex to exploit.

The UBI 8 Micro image is great in multi-stage builds, where the first stage creates the finished artifact(s) and the second stage copies them inside the final image. The following example shows a basic multi-stage Dockerfile/ContainerFile where a minimal Golang application is being built inside a UBI Standard container while the final artifact is copied inside a UBI Micro image:

```
# Builder image
FROM registry.access.redhat.com/ubi8-minimal AS builder

# Install Golang packages
RUN microdnf upgrade && \
    microdnf install golang && \
    microdnf clean all

# Copy files for build
COPY go.mod /go/src/hello-world/
COPY main.go /go/src/hello-world/

# Set the working directory
WORKDIR /go/src/hello-world

# Download dependencies
RUN go get -d -v ./...

# Install the package
RUN go build -v ./...

# Runtime image
FROM registry.access.redhat.com/ubi8/ubi-micro:latest
COPY --from=builder /go/src/hello-world/hello-world /
```

```
EXPOSE 8080
```

```
CMD ["/hello-world"]
```

The build's output results in an image that's approximately 45 MB in size.

The UBI Micro image has no built-in package manager, but it is still possible to install additional packages using Buildah native commands. This works effectively on an RHEL system, where all the Red Hat GPG certificates are installed.

The following example shows a build script that can be executed on RHEL 8. Its purpose is to install additional Python packages using the host's yum package manager, on top of a UBI Micro image:

```
#!/bin/bash

set -euo pipefail

if [ $UID -ne 0 ]; then
    echo "This script must be run as root"
    exit 1
fi

container=$(buildah from registry.access.redhat.com/ubi8/ubi-micro)
mount=$(buildah mount $container)

yum install -y \
  --installroot $mount \
  --setopt install_weak_deps=false \
  --nodocs \
  --noplugins \
  --releasever 8 \
  python3

yum clean all --installroot $mount

buildah umount $container
buildah commit $container micro_httpd
```

Notice that the `yum install` command is executed by passing the `--installroot $mount` option, which tells the installer to use the working container mount point as the temporary root to install the packages.

UBI Minimal and UBI Micro images are great for implementing microservices architectures where we need to orchestrate multiple containers together, with each running a specific microservice.

Now, let's look at the UBI Init image, which allows us to coordinate the execution of multiple services inside a container.

The UBI Init image

A common pattern in container development is to create highly specialized images with a single component running inside them.

To implement multi-tier applications, such as those with a frontend, middleware, and a backend, the best practice is to create and orchestrate multiple containers, each one running a specific component. The goal is to have minimal and very specialized containers, each one running its own service/process while following the **Keep It Simple, Stupid** (**KISS**) philosophy, which has been implemented in UNIX systems since their inception.

Despite being great for most use cases, this approach does not always suit certain special scenarios where many processes need to be orchestrated together. An example is when we need to share all the container namespaces across processes, or when we just want a single, *uber* image.

Container images are normally created without an init system and the process that's executed inside the container (invoked by the CMD instruction) usually gets **PID 1**.

For this reason, Red Hat introduced the UBI Init image, which runs a minimal **Systemd** init process inside the container, allowing multiple Systemd units that are governed by the Systemd process with a PID of 1 to be executed.

The UBI Init image is slightly smaller than the Standard image but has more packages available than the Minimal image.

The default CMD is set to `/sbin/init`, which corresponds to the Systemd process. Systemd ignores the `SIGTERM` and `SIGKILL` signals, which are used by Podman to stop running containers. For this reason, the image is configured to send `SIGRTMIN+3` signals for termination by passing the `STOPSIGNAL SIGRTMIN+3` instruction inside the image Dockerfile.

The following example shows a Dockerfile/ContainerFile that installs the `httpd` package and configures a `systemd` unit to run the `httpd` service:

```
FROM registry.access.redhat.com/ubi8/ubi-init

RUN yum -y install httpd && \
        yum clean all && \
        systemctl enable httpd

RUN echo "Successful Web Server Test" > /var/www/html/index.html

RUN mkdir /etc/systemd/system/httpd.service.d/ && \
        echo -e '[Service]\nRestart=always' > /etc/systemd/system/httpd.service.d/httpd.conf

EXPOSE 80
CMD [ "/sbin/init" ]
```

Notice the RUN instruction, where we create the `/etc/systemd/system/httpd.service.d/` folder and the Systemd unit file. This minimal example could be replaced with a COPY of pre-edited unit files, which is particularly useful when multiple services must be created.

We can build and run the image and inspect the behavior of the `init` system inside the container using the `ps` command:

```
$ buildah build -t init_httpd .
$ podman run -d --name httpd_init -p 8080:80 init_httpd
$ podman exec -ti httpd_init /bin/bash
[root@b4fb727f1907 /]# ps aux
USER         PID %CPU %MEM    VSZ   RSS TTY        STAT START
TIME COMMAND
root           1  0.1  0.0  89844  9404 ?          Ss   10:30
0:00 /sbin/init
root          10  0.0  0.0  95552 10636 ?          Ss   10:30
0:00 /usr/lib/systemd/systemd-journald
root          20  0.1  0.0 258068 10700 ?          Ss   10:30
0:00 /usr/sbin/httpd -DFOREGROUND
dbus          21  0.0  0.0  54056  4856 ?          Ss   10:30
```

```
0:00 /usr/bin/dbus-daemon --system --address=systemd: --nofork
--nopidfile --systemd-activation --syslog-only
apache        23  0.0  0.0 260652   7884 ?          S    10:30
0:00 /usr/sbin/httpd -DFOREGROUND
apache        24  0.0  0.0 2760308 9512 ?           Sl   10:30
0:00 /usr/sbin/httpd -DFOREGROUND
apache        25  0.0  0.0 2563636 9748 ?           Sl   10:30
0:00 /usr/sbin/httpd -DFOREGROUND
apache        26  0.0  0.0 2563636 9516 ?           Sl   10:30
0:00 /usr/sbin/httpd -DFOREGROUND
root         238  0.0  0.0  19240   3564 pts/0       Ss   10:30
0:00 /bin/bash
root         247  0.0  0.0  51864   3728 pts/0       R+   10:30
0:00 ps aux
```

Note that the /sbin/init process is executed with a PID of 1 and that it spawns the httpd processes. The container also executed dbus-daemon, which is used by Systemd to expose its API, along with systemd-journald to handle logs.

Following this approach, we can add multiple services that are supposed to work together in the same container and have them orchestrated by Systemd.

So far, we have looked at the four currently available UBI images and demonstrated how they can be used to create custom applications. Many public Red Hat images are based on UBI. Let's take a look.

Other UBI-based images

Red Hat uses UBI images to produce many pre-built specialized images, especially for runtimes. They are usually expected to not have redistribution limitations.

This allows runtime images to be created for languages, runtimes, and frameworks such as Python, Quarkus, Golang, Perl, PDP, .NET, Node.js, Ruby, and OpenJDK.

UBI is also used as the base image for the **Source-to-Image** (**s2i**) framework, which is used to build applications natively in OpenShift without the use of Dockerfiles. With s2i, it is possible to assemble images from user-defined custom scripts and, obviously, application source code.

Last but not least, Red Hat's supported releases of Buildah, Podman, and Skopeo are packaged using UBI 8 images.

Moving beyond Red Hat's offering, other vendors use UBI images to release their images too – Intel, IBM, Isovalent, Cisco, Aqua Security, and many others adopt UBI as the base for their official images on Red Hat Marketplace.

Summary

In this chapter, we learned about the OCI image specifications and the role of container registries.

After that, we learned how to adopt secure image registries and how to filter out those registries using custom policies that allow us to block specific registries, namespaces, and images.

Finally, we introduced UBI as a solution to create lightweight, reliable, and redistributable images based on RHEL packages.

With the knowledge you've gained in this chapter, you should be able to understand OCI image specifications in more detail and manage image registries securely.

In the next chapter, we will explore the difference between private and public registries and how to create a private registry locally. Finally, we will learn how to manage container images with the specialized **Skopeo** tool.

Further reading

To learn more about the topics that were covered in this chapter, take a look at the following resources:

- MITRE ATT&CK® Matrix: `https://attack.mitre.org/matrices/enterprise/containers/`

- Things You Should Know on Kubernetes Threat Matrix: `https://cloud.redhat.com/blog/2021-kubernetes-threat-matrix-updates-things-you-should-know`

- How to manage Linux container registries: `https://www.redhat.com/sysadmin/manage-container-registries`

- Introducing the Red Hat Universal Base Image: `https://www.redhat.com/en/blog/introducing-red-hat-universal-base-image`

- Introduction to Red Hat's UBI Micro: `https://www.redhat.com/en/blog/introduction-ubi-micro`

9

Pushing Images to a Container Registry

In the previous chapter, we went through the very important concept of the container base image. As we saw, it is really important to choose the base image wisely for our containers, using official container images from trusted container registries and development communities.

But once we choose the preferred base image and then build our final container image, we need a way to further distribute our work to the various target hosts that we plan to let it run on.

The best option to distribute a container image is to push it to a container registry and after that, let all the target hosts pull the container image and run it.

For this reason, in this chapter, we're going to cover the following main topics:

- What is a container registry?
- Cloud-based and on-premise container registries
- Managing container images with Skopeo
- Running a local container registry

Technical requirements

Before proceeding with the chapter and its examples, a machine with a working Podman installation is required. As stated in *Chapter 3*, *Running the First Container*, all the examples in the book are executed on a Fedora 34 system or later but can be reproduced on your OS of choice.

A good understanding of the topics covered in *Chapter 4*, *Managing Running Containers*, and *Chapter 8*, *Choosing the Container Base Image*, is useful to easily grasp concepts regarding container registries.

What is a container registry?

A container registry is just a collection of container images' repositories, used in conjunction with systems that need to pull and run container images in a dynamic way.

The main features available on a container registry are the following:

- Repository management
- Pushing container images
- Tag management
- Pulling container images
- Authentication management

Let's look at every feature in detail in the following sections.

Repository management

One of the most important features of container registries is managing container images through repositories. Depending on the container registry implementation that we choose, we will be sure to find a web interface or a command-line interface that will let us handle the creation of a sort of *folder* that will act as a repository for our container images.

According to the **Open Container Initiative (OCI)** Distribution Specification *[1]*, the container images are organized in a repository that is identified by name. A repository name is usually composed of a user/organization name and the container image name in this way: *myorganization/mycontainerimage*, and it must respect the following regular expression check:

```
[a-z0-9]+([._-][a-z0-9]+)*(/[a-z0-9]+([._-][a-z0-9]+)*)*
```

> **Important Definition**
>
> A **regular expression (regex)** is a search pattern defined by a sequence of characters. This pattern definition leverages several notations that let the user define in detail the target keyword, line, or multiple lines to find in a text document.

Once we've created a repository on our container registry, we should be able to start pushing, pulling, and handling different versions (identified by a label) of our container images.

Pushing container images

The act of pushing container images to a container registry is handled by the container tool that we are using, which respects the OCI Distribution Specification.

In this process, the blobs, which are the binary form of the content, are uploaded first and, usually at the end, the manifest is then uploaded. This order is not strict and mandatory by the specification, but a registry may refuse a manifest that references blobs that it does not know.

Using a container management tool to push a container image to a registry, we must specify again the name of the repository in the form shown before and the container image's tag we want to upload.

Tag management

As we introduced starting in *Chapter 4, Managing Running Containers*, the container images are identified by a name and a tag. Thanks to the tag mechanism, we can store several different versions of the container images on a system's local cache or on a container registry.

The container registry should be able to expose the feature of content discovery, providing the list of the container images' tags to the client requesting it. This feature can give the opportunity to the container registry's users to choose the right container image to pull and run to the target systems.

Pulling container images

In the process of pulling container images, the client should first request the manifest to know which blobs, which are the binary form of the content, to pull to get the final container image. The order is strict because without pulling and parsing the manifest file of the container image, the client would not be able to know which binary data it has to request from the registry.

Using a container management tool to pull a container image from a registry, we must specify again the name of the repository in the form shown before and the container image's tag we want to download.

Authentication management

All the previous operations may require authentication. In many cases, public container registries may allow anonymous pulling and content discovery but for pushing container images they require a valid authentication.

Depending on the container registry chosen, we might find basic or advanced features to authenticate to a container registry, let our client store a token, and then use it for every operation that could require it.

This ends up our brief deep dive into container registry theory. If you want to know more about the OCI Distribution Specification, you can investigate the URL *[1]* available at the end of this chapter in the *Further reading* section.

> **Nice to Know**
> The OCI Distribution Specification also defines a set of conformance tests that anyone could run against a container registry to check if that particular implementation respects all the rules defined in the specification: `https://github.com/opencontainers/distribution-spec/tree/main/conformance`.

The various implementations of a container registry available on the web, in addition to the basic functions we described before, also add more features that we will discover soon in the next section.

Cloud-based and on-premise container registries

As we introduced in the previous sections, the OCI defined a standard to adhere to for container registries. This initiative allowed the rise of many other container registries apart from the initial Docker Registry and its online service, Docker Hub.

We can group the available container registries into two main categories:

- Cloud-based container registries
- On-premise container registries

Let's see these two categories in detail in the following subsections.

On-premise container registries

On-premise container registries are often used for creating a private repository for enterprise purposes. The main use cases include the following:

- Distributing images in a private or isolated network
- Deploying a new container image at a large scale over several machines
- Keeping any sensitive data in our own data center
- Improving the speed of pulling and pushing images using an internal network

Of course, running an on-premise registry requires several skills to ensure availability, monitoring, logging, and security.

This is a non-comprehensive list of the available container registries that we can install on-premises:

- **Docker Registry**: Docker's project, which is currently at version 2, provides all the basic features described in the earlier sections and we will learn how to run it in the last section of this chapter, *Running a local container registry*.

- **Harbor**: This is a VMware open source project that provides high availability, image auditing, and integration with authentication systems.

- **GitLab Container Registry**: This is strongly integrated with the GitLab product, so it requires minimal setup, but it depends on the main project.

- **JFrog Artifactory**: This manages more than just containers; it provides management for any artifact.

- **Quay**: This is the open source distribution of the Red Hat product called Quay. This project offers a fully-featured web UI, a service for image vulnerability scanning, data storage, and protection.

We will not go into every detail of these container registries. What we can suggest for sure is to pay attention and choose the product or project that fits better with your use cases and support needs. Many of these products have support plans or enterprise editions (license required) that could easily save your skin in the event of a disaster.

Let's now see what the cloud-based container registries are that could make our life easier, offering a complete managed service, with which our operational skills could be reduced to zero.

Cloud-based container registries

As anticipated in the previous section, cloud-based container registries could be the fastest way to start working with container images through a registry.

As described in *Chapter 8*, *Choosing the Container Base Image*, there are several cloud-based container registry services on the web. We will concentrate only on a small subset, taking out of the analysis the ones provided by a public cloud provider and the ones offered by the Linux distribution, which usually are only available to pull images, preloaded by the distribution maintainers.

We will take a look at these cloud container registries:

- **Docker Hub**: This is a hosted registry solution by Docker Inc. This registry also hosts official repositories and security verified images for some popular open source projects.

- **Quay**: This is the hosted registry solution born under the CoreOS company, now part of Red Hat. It offers private and public repositories, automated scanning for security purposes, image builds, and integration with popular Git public repositories.

Docker Hub cloud registry

Docker Hub cloud registry was born together with the Docker project and it represented one of the greatest features added to this project and containers in general, the right attention they deserved.

Talking about features, Docker Hub has free and paid plans:

- Anonymous access: Only 100 image pulls in 6 hours.

- A registered user account with the free tier: 200 image pulls in 6 hours and unlimited public repositories. With the free tier we do not get builds or security scans.

- Pro, Team, and Business accounts: Thousands of image pulls per day, automated builds, security scans, RBAC, and so on.

As we just reported, if we try to log in with a registered user account with the free tier, we can only create public repositories. This could be enough for communities or individual developers, but once you start using it at the enterprise level, you may need the additional features provided by the paid plans.

To avoid a big limitation in terms of image pulls, we should at least use a registered user account and log in to the web portal and to the container registry with our beloved container engine: Podman. We will see in the following sections how to authenticate to a registry and ensure 200 image pulls every 6 hours using Docker Hub.

Red Hat Quay cloud registry

Quay cloud registry is the Red Hat on-premise registry but offered as **Software-as-a-Service (SaaS)**.

Quay cloud registry, like Docker Hub, offers paid plans as well to unlock additional features.

But the nice news is that Quay's free tier has a lot of features included:

- Build from a Dockerfile, manually uploaded or even linked through GitHub/ Bitbucket/Gitlab or any Git repository.

- Security scans for images pushed on the registry.

- Usage/auditing logs.

- Robot user account/tokens for integrating any external software.

- There is no limit on image pulls.

On the other hand, the paid plans will unlock private repositories and team-based permissions.

Let's look at the Quay cloud registry by creating a public repository and linking it to a GitHub repository in which we pushed a Dockerfile to build our target container image:

1. First, we need to register or log in to the Quay portal at `https://quay.io`.

   After that, we can click on the **+ Create New Repository** button in the upper-right corner:

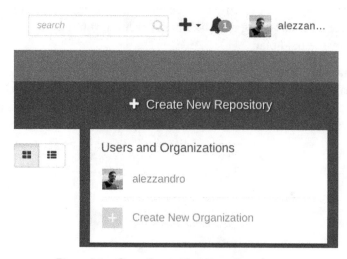

Figure 9.1 – Quay Create New Repository button

2. Once done, the web portal will request some basic information about the new repository we want to create:

   - A name

   - A description

   - Public or private (we are using a free account, so public is fine)

   - How to initialize the repository:

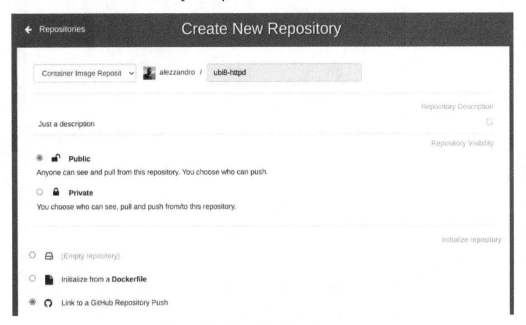

Figure 9.2 – Create New Repository page

We just defined a name for our repo, `ubi8-httpd`, and we chose to link this repository to a GitHub repository push.

3. Once confirmed, the Quay registry cloud portal will redirect us to GitHub to allow the authorization and then it will ask us to select the right organization and GitHub repository to link with:

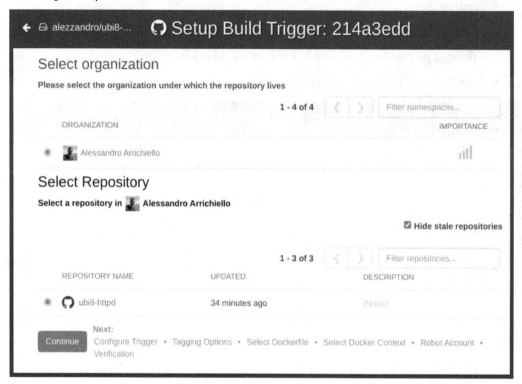

Figure 9.3 – Select the GitHub repository to link with our container repo

We just selected the default organization and the Git repository we created holding our Dockerfile. The Git repository is named `ubi8-httpd` and it is available here: `https://github.com/alezzandro/ubi8-httpd`.

> **Important Note**
> The repository used in this example belongs to the author's own project. You can fork the repository on GitHub and make your own copy with read/write permissions in order to be able to make changes and experiment with commits and automated builds.

4. Finally, it will ask us to further configure the trigger:

Figure 9.4 – Build trigger customization

We just left the default option, which will trigger a new build every time a push is made on the Git repository for any branches and tags.

5.   Once done, we will be redirected to the main repository page:

Figure 9.5 – Main repository page

Once created, the repository is empty with no information or activity, of course.

6. On the left bar, we can easily access the build section. It's the fourth icon starting from the top. In the following figure, we just executed two pushes on our Git repository, which triggered two different builds:

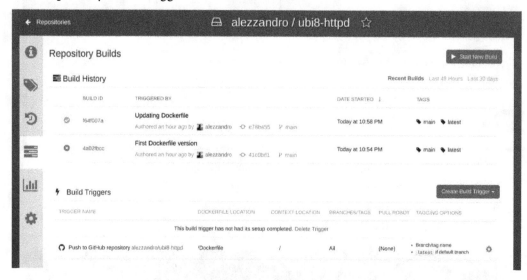

Figure 9.6 – Container image build section

7. If we try clicking on one of the builds, the cloud registry will show the details of the build:

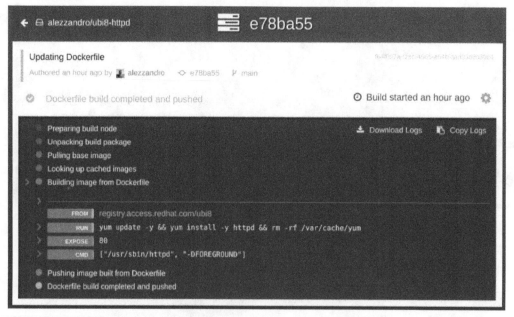

Figure 9.7 – Container image build details

As we can see, the build worked as expected, connecting to the GitHub repository, downloading the Dockerfile and executing the build, and finally, pushing the image to the container registry, all in an automated way. The Dockerfile contains just a few commands for installing an httpd server on a UBI8 base image, as we learned in *Chapter 8, Choosing the Container Base Image.*

8. Finally, the last section that is worth mentioning is the included security scanning functionality. This feature is accessible by clicking the *Tag* icon, the second from the top in the left panel:

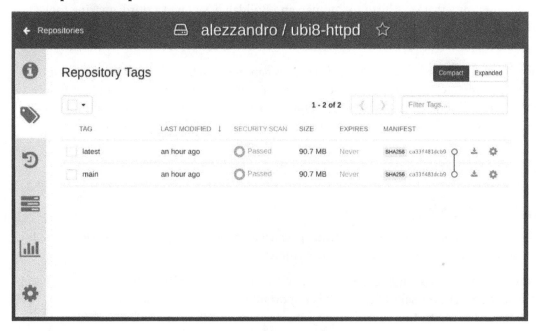

Figure 9.8 – Container image tags page

As you will notice, there is a SECURITY SCAN column (the third) reporting the status of the scan executed on that particular container image associated with the tag name reported in the first column. By clicking on the value of that column (in the previous screenshot, it is Passed), we can obtain further details.

We just got some experience leveraging a container registry offered as a managed service. This could make our life easier, reducing our operational skills, but they are not always the best option for our projects or companies.

In the next section, we will explore more in detail how to manage container images with Podman's companion Skopeo, and then we'll learn how to configure and run a container registry on-premises.

Managing container images with Skopeo

So far, we have learned about many container registry concepts, including the differences between private and public registries, their compliance with OCI image specifications, and how to consume images with Podman and Buildah to build and run containers.

However, sometimes we need to implement simple image manipulation tasks such as moving an image from a registry to a mirror, inspecting a remote image without the need to pull it locally, or even signing images.

The community that gave birth to Podman and Buildah developed a third amazing tool, **Skopeo** (`https://github.com/containers/skopeo`), which exactly implements the features described previously.

Skopeo was designed as an image and registry manipulation tool for DevOps teams and is not intended to run containers (the main role of Podman) nor build OCI images (the main role of Buildah). Instead, it offers a minimal and straightforward command-line interface with basic image manipulation commands that will prove to be extremely useful in different contexts.

Let's inspect the most interesting features in the next subsections.

Installing Skopeo

Skopeo is a Go binary tool that is already packaged and available for many distributions. It can also be built and installed from source directly.

This section provides a non-exhaustive list of installation examples on the major distributions. For the sake of clarity, it is important to reiterate that the book lab environments were all based on Fedora 34:

- **Fedora**: To install Skopeo on Fedora, run the following `dnf` command:

```
$ sudo dnf -y install skopeo
```

- **Debian**: To install Skopeo on Debian Bullseye, Testing and Unstable (Sid), run the following `apt-get` commands:

```
$ sudo apt-get update
$ sudo apt-get -y install skopeo
```

- **RHEL 8/9, CentOS 8 and CentOS Stream 8/9**: To install Skopeo on RHEL, CentOS, and CentOS Stream, run the following `dnf` command:

```
$ sudo dnf -y install skopeo
```

- **RHEL 7 and CentOS 7**: To install Skopeo on earlier releases of RHEL and CentOS, run the following `yum` command:

```
$ sudo yum -y install skopeo
```

- **Ubuntu**: To install Skopeo on Ubuntu 20.10 and newer, run the following command:

```
$ sudo apt-get -y update
$ sudo apt-get -y install skopeo
```

- **Arch Linux**: To install Skopeo on Arch Linux, run the following `pacman` command:

```
$ sudo pacman -S skopeo
```

- **openSUSE**: To install Skopeo on openSUSE, run the following `zypper` command:

```
$ sudo zypper install skopeo
```

- **macOS**: To install Skopeo on macOS, run the following `brew` command:

```
$ brew install skopeo
```

- **Building from source**: Skopeo can also be built from source. As for Buildah, for the purposes of this book, we will keep the focus on simple deployment methods but if you're curious, you can find a dedicated install section in the main project repository that illustrates how to build Skopeo from source: `https://github.com/containers/skopeo/blob/main/install.md#building-from-source`.

  The preceding link shows examples of containerized and non-containerized builds.

- **Running Skopeo in a container**: Skopeo is also released as a container image that can be executed with Podman. To pull and run the latest version of Skopeo as a container, use the following `podman` command:

```
$ podman run quay.io/skopeo/stable:latest <command>
<options>
```

- **Windows**: At the time of writing of this book, there is no build available for Microsoft Windows.

Skopeo uses the same system and local configuration files described for Podman and Buildah, therefore we can immediately focus on the installation verification and the analysis of the most common use cases.

Verifying the installation

To verify the correct installation, simply run the `skopeo` command with the `-h` or `--help` option to view all available commands, as in the following example:

```
$ skopeo -h
```

The expected output will show, among the utility options, all the available commands, each one with a description of the command scope. The full list of commands is as follows:

- `copy`: Copy an image across locations, using different transports, such as the Docker Registry, local directories, OCI, tarballs, OSTree, and OCI archives.
- `delete`: Delete an image from a target location.
- `help`: Print help commands.
- `inspect`: Inspect the metadata, tags, and configuration of an image in a target location.
- `list-tags`: Shows the available tags for a specific image repository.
- `login`: Authenticates to a remote registry.
- `logout`: Log out from a remote registry.
- `manifest-digest`: Produce a manifest digest for a file.
- `standalone-sign`: A debugging tool to publish and sign an image using local files.
- `standalone-verify`: Verify an image signature using local files.
- `sync`: Synchronizes one or more images across locations.

Let's now inspect in greater detail some of the most interesting Skopeo commands.

Copying images across locations

Podman, just like Docker, can be used not only to run containers but also to pull images locally and push them to other locations. However, one of the main caveats is the need to run two commands, one to pull and one to push, while the local image store remains filled with the pulled images. Therefore, users should periodically clean up the local store.

Skopeo offers a smarter and simpler way to achieve this goal with the `skopeo copy` command. The command implements the following syntax:

```
skopeo copy [command options] SOURCE-IMAGE DESTINATION-IMAGE
```

In this generic description, SOURCE-IMAGE and DESTINATION-IMAGE are images belonging to local or remote locations and reachable using one of the following **transports**:

- `docker://docker-reference`: This transport is related to images stored in registries implementing the *Docker Registry HTTP API V2*.

  This setting uses the `/etc/containers/registries.conf` or `$HOME/.config/containers/registries.conf` file to obtain further registry configurations.

  The `docker-reference` field follows the format `name[:tag|@digest]`.

- `containers-storage:[[storage-specifier]]{image-id|docker-reference[@image-id]}`: This setting refers to an image in local container storage.

  The `storage-specifier` field is in the format `[[driver@]root[+run-root][:options]]`.

- `dir:path`: This setting refers to an existing local directory that holds manifests, layers (in tarball format), and signatures.

- `docker-archive:path[:{docker-reference|@source-index}]`: This setting refers to a Docker archive obtained with the `docker save` or `podman save` commands.

- `docker-daemon:docker-reference|algo:digest`: This setting refers to image storage in the Docker daemon's internal storage.

- `oci:path[:tag]`: This setting refers to an image stored in a local path compliant with the OCI layout specifications.

- `oci-archive:path[:tag]`: This setting refers to an OCI layout specification compliant image stored in tarball format.

- `ostree:docker-reference[@/absolute/repo/path]`: This setting refers to an image stored in a local `ostree` repository. OSTree is a tool to manage multiple versioned filesystem trees. It allows you to manage operating systems in an atomic and immutable way. Check out `man ostree` for more details.

Let's inspect some usage examples of the `skopeo copy` command in real-world scenarios. The first example shows how to copy an image from a remote registry to another remote registry:

```
$ skopeo copy \
    docker://docker.io/library/nginx:latest \
    docker://private-registry.example.com/lab/nginx:latest
```

The preceding example does not take care of registry authentication, which is usually a requirement to push images to the remote repository. In the next example, we show a variant where both source and target registry are decorated with authentication options:

```
$ skopeo copy \
    --src-creds USERNAME:PASSWORD \
    --dest-creds USERNAME:PASSWORD \
    docker://registry1.example.com/mirror/nginx:latest \
    docker://registry2.example.com/lab/nginx:latest
```

The previous approach, despite working perfectly, has the limitation of passing username and password strings as clear text strings. To avoid this, we can use the `skopeo login` command to authenticate to our registries before running `skopeo copy`.

The third example shows a pre-authentication to the destination registry, assuming that the source registry is publicly accessible for pulls:

```
$ skopeo login private-registry.example.com
$ skopeo copy \
    docker://docker.io/library/nginx:latest \
    docker://private-registry.example.com/lab/nginx:latest
```

When we log in to the source/target registries, the system persists the registry-provided auth tokens in dedicated auth files that we can reuse later for further access.

By default, Skopeo looks at the `${XDG_RUNTIME_DIR}/containers/auth.json` path, but we can provide a custom location for the auth file. For example, in case we used Docker container runtime before, we could find it in the path `${HOME}/.docker/config.json`. This file contains a simple JSON object that holds, for every used registry, the token obtained upon authentication. The client (Podman, Skopeo, or Buildah) will use this token to directly access the registry.

The following example shows the usage of the auth file, provided with a custom path:

```
$ skopeo copy \
   --authfile ${HOME}/.docker/config.json \
   docker://docker.io/library/nginx:latest \
   docker://private-registry.example.com/lab/nginx:latest
```

Another common issue that can be encountered when working with a private registry is the lack of certificates signed by a known **certification authority** (**CA**) or the lack of HTTPS communication (which means that all traffic is completely unencrypted). If we consider these totally non-secure scenarios safe to trust in a lab environment, we can skip the TLS verification with the `--dest-tls-verify` and `--src-tls-verify` options, which accept a simple Boolean value.

The following example shows how to skip the TLS verification on the target registry:

```
$ skopeo copy \
   --authfile ${HOME}/.docker/config.json \
   --dest-tls-verify false \
   docker://docker.io/library/nginx:latest \
   docker://private-registry.example.com/lab/nginx:latest
```

So far, we've seen how to move images across public and private registries, but we can use Skopeo to move images to and from local stores easily. For example, we can use Skopeo as a highly specialized push/pull tool for images inside our build pipelines.

The next example shows how to push a locally built image to a public registry:

```
$ skopeo copy \
   --authfile ${HOME}/.docker/config.json \
   containers-storage:quay.io/<namespace>/python_httpd \
   docker://quay.io/<namespace>/python_httpd:latest
```

This is an amazing way to manage an image push with total control over the push/pull process and shows how the three tools – Podman, Buildah, and Skopeo – can fulfill specialized tasks in our DevOps environment, each one accomplishing the purpose it was designed for at its best.

Let's see another example, this time showing how to pull an image from a remote registry to an OCI-compliant local store:

```
$ skopeo copy \
  --authfile ${HOME}/.docker/config.json \
  docker://docker.io/library/nginx:latest \
  oci:/tmp/nginx
```

The output folder is compliant with the OCI image specifications and will have the following structure (blob hashes cut for layout reasons):

```
$ tree /tmp/nginx
/tmp/nginx/
├── blobs
│   └─sha256
│       ├──21e0df283cd68384e5e8dff7e6be1774c86ea3110c1b1e932[...]
│       ├──44be98c0fab60b6cef9887dbad59e69139cab789304964a19[...]
│       ├──77700c52c9695053293be96f9cbcf42c91c5e097daa382933[...]
│       ├──81d15e9a49818539edb3116c72fbad1df1241088116a7363a[...]
│       ├──881ff011f1c9c14982afc6e95ae70c25e38809843bb7d42ab[...]
│       ├──d86da3a6c06fb46bc76d6dc7b591e87a73cb456c990d814fd[...]
│       ├──e5ae68f740265288a4888db98d2999a638fdcb6d725f42767[...]
│       └──ed835de16acd8f5821cf3f3ef77a66922510ee6349730d89a[...]
├── index.json
└── oci-layout
```

The files inside the blobs/sha256 folder include the image manifest (in JSON format) and the image layers, as compressed tarballs.

It's interesting to know that Podman can seamlessly run a container based on a local folder compliant with the OCI image specifications. The next example shows how to run an NGINX container from the previously downloaded image:

```
$ podman run -d oci:/tmp/nginx
Getting image source signatures
Copying blob e5ae68f74026 done
Copying blob 21e0df283cd6 done
Copying blob ed835de16acd done
Copying blob 881ff011f1c9 done
Copying blob 77700c52c969 done
```

```
Copying blob 44be98c0fab6 done
Copying config 81d15e9a49 done
Writing manifest to image destination
Storing signatures
90493fe89f024cfffda3f626acb5ba8735cadd827be6c-
26fa44971108e09b54f
```

Notice the `oci:` prefix before the image path, necessary to specify that the path provided is OCI compliant.

Besides, it is interesting to show that Podman copies and extracts the blobs inside its local store (under `$HOME/.local/share/containers/storage` for a rootless container like the one in the example).

After learning how to copy images with Skopeo, let's see how to inspect remote images without the need to pull them locally.

Inspecting remote images

Sometimes we need to verify the configurations, tags, or metadata of an image before pulling and executing it locally. For this purpose, Skopeo offers the useful `skopeo inspect` command to inspect images over supported transports.

The first example shows how to inspect the official NGINX image repository:

```
$ skopeo inspect docker://docker.io/library/nginx
```

The `skopeo copy` command creates a JSON-formatted output with the following fields:

- `Name`: The name of the image repository.

- `Digest`: The SHA256 calculated digest.

- `RepoTags`: The full list of available image tags in the repository. This list will be empty when inspecting local transports such as `containers-storage:` or `oci:` since they will be referred to as a single image.

- `Created`: The creation date of the repository or image.

- `DockerVersion`: The version of Docker used to create the image. This value is empty for images created with Podman, Buildah, or other tools.

- `Labels`: Additional labels applied to the image at build time.

- `Architecture`: The target system architecture the image was built for. This value is `amd64` for x86-64 systems.

- `Os`: The target operating system the image was built for.

- `Layers`: The list of layers that compose the image, along with their SHA256 digest.

- `Env`: Additional environment variables defined in the image at build time.

The same considerations illustrated previously about authentication and TLS verification apply to the `skopeo inspect` command: it is possible to inspect images on a private registry upon authentication and skip the TLS verification. The next example shows this use case:

```
$ skopeo inspect \
    --authfile ${HOME}/.docker/config.json \
    --tls-verify false \
    registry.example.com/library/test-image
```

Inspecting local images is possible by passing the correct transport. The next example shows how to inspect a local OCI image:

```
$ skopeo inspect oci:/tmp/custom_image
```

The output of this command will have an empty `RepoTags` field.

In addition, it is possible to use the `--no-tags` option to intentionally skip the repository tags, like in the following example:

```
$ skopeo inspect --no-tags docker://docker.io/library/nginx
```

On the other hand, if we need to print only the available repository tags, we can use the `skopeo list-tags` command. The next example prints all the available tags of the official Nginx repository:

```
$ skopeo list-tags docker://docker.io/library/nginx
```

The third use case we are going to analyze is the synchronization of images across registries and local stores.

Synchronizing registries and local directories

When working with disconnected environments, a quite common scenario is the need to synchronize repositories from a remote registry locally.

To serve this purpose, Skopeo introduced the `skopeo sync` command, which helps synchronize content between a source and destination, supporting different transport kinds.

We can use this command to synchronize a whole repository, with all the available tags inside it, between a source and a destination. Alternatively, it is possible to synchronize only a specific image tag.

The first example shows how to synchronize the official busybox repository from a private registry to the local filesystem. This command pulls all the tags contained in the remote repository to the local destination (the target directory must already exist):

```
$ mkdir /tmp/images
$ skopeo sync \
  --src docker --dest dir \
  registry.example.com/lab/busybox /tmp/images
```

Notice the use of the `--src` and `--dest` options to define the kind of transport. Supported transport types are as follows:

- *Source*: `docker`, `dir`, and `yaml` (covered later in this section)
- *Destination*: `docker` and `dir`

By default, Skopeo syncs the repository content to the destination without the whole image source path. This could represent a limitation when we need to sync repositories with the same name from multiple sources. To solve this limitation, we can add the `--scoped` option and get the full image source path copied in the destination tree.

The second example shows a scoped synchronization of the busybox repository:

```
$ skopeo sync \
  --src docker --dest dir --scoped \
  registry.example.com/lab/busybox /tmp/images
```

The resulting path in the destination directory will contain the registry name and the related namespace, with a new folder named after the image tag.

The next example shows the directory structure of the destination after a successful synchronization:

```
ls -A1 /tmp/images/docker.io/library/
busybox:1
busybox:1.21.0-ubuntu
busybox:1.21-ubuntu
busybox:1.23
busybox:1.23.2
```

```
busybox:1-glibc
busybox:1-musl
busybox:1-ubuntu
busybox:1-uclibc
[...omitted output...]
```

If we need to synchronize only a specific image tag, it is possible to specify the tag name in the source argument, like in this third example:

```
$ skopeo sync --src docker --dest dir docker.io/library/
busybox:latest /tmp/images
```

We can directly synchronize two registries using Docker both for the source and destination transport. This is especially useful in disconnected environments where systems are allowed to reach a local registry only. The local registry can mirror repositories from other public or private registries and the task can be scheduled periodically to keep the mirror updated.

The next example shows how to synchronize the UBI8 image and all its tags from the public Red Hat repository to a local mirror registry:

```
$ skopeo sync \
    --src docker --dest docker \
    --dest-tls-verify=false \
    registry.access.redhat.com/ubi8 \
    mirror-registry.example.com
```

The preceding command will mirror all the UBI8 image tags to the target registry.

Notice the `--dest-tls-verify=false` option to disable TLS certificate checks on the destination.

The `skopeo sync` command is great to mirror repositories and single images between locations but when it comes to mirroring full registries or a large set of repositories, we should run the command many times, passing different source arguments.

To avoid this limitation, the source transport can be defined as a YAML file to include an exhaustive list of registries, repositories, and images. It is also possible to use regular expressions to capture only selected subsets of image tags.

The following is an example of a custom YAML file that will be passed as a source argument to Skopeo:

Chapter09/example_sync.yaml

```
docker.io:
  tls-verify: true
  images:
    alpine: []
    nginx:
      - "latest"
  images-by-tag-regex:
    httpd: ^2\.4\.[0-9]*-alpine$
quay.io:
  tls-verify: true
  images:
    fedora/fedora:
      - latest
registry.access.redhat.com:
  tls-verify: true
  images:
    ubi8:
      - "8.4"
      - "8.5"
```

In the preceding example, different images and repositories are defined and therefore the file content deserves a detailed description.

The whole `alpine` repository is pulled from `docker.io`, along with the `nginx:latest` image tag. Also, a regular expression is used to define a pattern of tags for the `httpd` image, in order to pull Alpine-based image version 2.4.z only.

The file also defines a specific tag (`latest`) for the `fedora` image stored under `https://quay.io/` and the `8.4` and `8.5` tags for the `ubi8` image stored under the `registry.access.redhat.com` registry.

Once defined, the file is passed as an argument to Skopeo, along with the destination:

```
$ skopeo sync \
  --src yaml --dest dir \
  --scoped example_sync.yaml /tmp/images
```

All the contents listed in the `example_sync.yaml` file will be copied to the destination directory, following the previously mentioned filtering rules.

The next example shows a larger mirroring use case, applied to the OpenShift release images. The following `openshift_sync.yaml` file defines a regular expression to sync all the images for version 4.9.z of OpenShift built for the x86_64 architecture:

Chapter09/openshift_sync.yaml

```
quay.io:
  tls-verify: true
  images-by-tag-regex:
    openshift-release-dev/ocp-release: ^4\.9\..*-x86_64$
```

We can use this file to mirror a whole minor release of OpenShift to an internal registry accessible from disconnected environments and use this mirror to successfully conduct an air-gapped installation of OpenShift Container Platform. The next command example shows this use case:

```
$ skopeo sync \
  --src yaml --dest docker \
  --dest-tls-verify=false \
  --src-authfile pull_secret.json \
  openshift_sync.yaml mirror-registry.example.com:5000
```

It is worth noticing the usage of a pull secret file, passed with the `--src-authfile` option, to authenticate on the Quay public registry and pull images from the `ocp-release` repository.

There is a final Skopeo feature that captures our interest: the remote deletion of images, covered in the next subsection.

Deleting images

A registry can be imagined as a specialized object store that implements a set of HTTP APIs to manipulate its content and push/pull objects in the form of image layers and metadata.

The **Docker Registry v2** protocol is a standard API specification that is widely adopted among many registry projects. This set of API specifications covers all the registry functions that are expected to be exposed to an external client through standard HTTP GET, PUT, DELETE, POST, and PATCH methods.

This means that we could interact with a registry with any kind of HTTP client capable of managing the requests correctly, for example, the curl command.

Any container engine uses, at a lower level, HTTP client libraries to execute the various methods against the registry (for example, for an image pull).

The Docker v2 protocol also supports the remote deletion of images, and any registry that implements this protocol supports the following DELETE request for images:

```
DELETE /v2/<name>/manifests/<reference>
```

The following example represents a theoretical delete command issued with the curl command against a local registry:

```
$ curl -v --silent \
    -H "Accept: application/vnd.docker.distribution.manifest.
v2+json" \
    -X DELETE http://127.0.0.1:5000/v2/<name>/manifests/
sha256:<image_tag_digest>
```

The preceding example intentionally avoids including the management of authorization tokens for readability.

Podman or Docker, designed to work as registry engines, do not implement a remote delete feature in their command interfaces.

Fortunately, Skopeo comes to the rescue with its built-in skopeo delete command to manage remote image deletion with a simple and user-friendly syntax.

The following example deletes an image on a hypothetical internal mirror-registry. example.com:5000 registry:

```
$ skopeo delete \
    docker://mirror-registry.example.com:5000/foo:bar
```

The command immediately deletes the image tag references in the remote registry.

> **Important Note**
> When deleting images with Skopeo, it is necessary to enable image deletion in the remote registry, as covered in the next section, *Running a local container registry*.

In this section, we have learned how to use Skopeo to copy, delete, inspect, and sync images or even whole repositories across different transports, including private local registries, gaining control over daily image manipulation operations.

In the next section, we will learn how to run and configure a local container registry to directly manage image storage in our lab or development environments.

Running a local container registry

Most companies and organizations adopt enterprise-grade registries to rely on secure and resilient solutions for their container image storage. Most enterprise registries also offer advanced features such as **role-based access control** (**RBAC**), an image vulnerability scanner, mirroring, geo-replication, and high availability, becoming the default choice for production and mission-critical environments.

However, sometimes it is very useful to run a simple local registry, for example, in development environments or training labs. Local registries can also be helpful in disconnected environments to mirror main public or private registries.

This section aims to illustrate how to run a simple local registry and how to apply basic configuration settings.

Running a containerized registry

Like every application, a local registry can be installed on the host by its administrators. Alternatively, a commonly preferred approach is to run the registry itself inside a container.

The most used containerized registry solution is based on the official **Docker Registry 2.0** image, which offers all the necessary functionalities for a basic registry and is very easy to use.

When running a local registry, containerized or not, we must define a destination directory to host all image layers and metadata. The next example shows the first execution of a containerized registry, with the `/var/lib/registry` folder created and bind-mounted to hold image data:

```
# mkdir /var/lib/registry
# podman run -d \
    --name local_registry \
    -p 5000:5000 \
    -v /var/lib/registry:/var/lib/registry:z \
    --restart=always registry:2
```

The registry will be reachable at the host address on port `5000/tcp`, which is also the default port for this service. If we run the registry on our local workstation, it will be reachable at `localhost:5000`, and exposed to the external connection using the assigned IP address or its **Fully Qualified Domain Name (FQDN)** if the workstation/laptop is resolved by a local DNS service.

For, example, if a host has the IP address `10.10.2.30` and FQDN `registry.example.com` correctly resolved by DNS queries, the registry service will be reachable at `10.10.2.30:5000` or at `registry.example.com:5000`.

> **Important Note**
> If the host runs a local firewall service or is behind a corporate firewall, do not forget to open the correct ports to expose the registry externally.

We can try to build and push a test image to the new registry. The following Containerfile builds a basic UBI-based httpd server:

Chapter09/local_registry/minimal_httpd/Containerfile

```
FROM registry.access.redhat.com/ubi8:latest
RUN dnf install -y httpd && dnf clean all -y
COPY index.html /var/www/html
RUN dnf install -y git && dnf clean all -y
CMD ["/usr/sbin/httpd", "-DFOREGROUND"]
```

We can build the new image with Buildah:

```
$ buildah build -t minimal_httpd .
```

To push the image to the local registry, we can use Podman or its companion tools Buildah or Skopeo. Skopeo is very handy for these use cases since we do not even need to scope the image name with the registry name.

The next command shows how to push the new image on the registry:

```
$ skopeo copy --dest-tls-verify=false \
  containers-storage:localhost/minimal_httpd \
  docker://localhost:5000/minimal_httpd
```

Notice the use of --dest-tls-verify=false: it was necessary since the local registry provides an HTTP transport by default.

Despite being simple to implement, the default registry configuration has some limitations that must be addressed. To illustrate one of those limitations, let's try to delete the just uploaded image:

```
$ skopeo delete \
  --tls-verify=false \
  docker://localhost:5000/minimal_httpd
```

```
FATA[0000] Failed to delete /v2/minimal_httpd/manifests/
sha256:f8c0c374cf124e728e20045f327de30ce1f3c552b307945de9b-
911cbee103522: {"errors":[{"code":"UNSUPPORTED","message":"The
operation is unsupported."}]}
(405 Method Not Allowed)
```

As we can see in the previous output, the registry did not allow us to delete the image, returning an HTTP 405 error message. To alter this behavior, we need to edit the registry configuration.

Customizing the registry configuration

The registry configuration file /etc/docker/registry/config.yml can be modified to alter its behavior. The default content of this file is the following:

```
version: 0.1
log:
  fields:
    service: registry
storage:
  cache:
```

```
    blobdescriptor: inmemory
  filesystem:
    rootdirectory: /var/lib/registry
http:
  addr: :5000
  headers:
    X-Content-Type-Options: [nosniff]
health:
  storagedriver:
    enabled: true
    interval: 10s
    threshold: 3
```

We soon realize that this is an extremely basic configuration with no authentication, no deletion of images allowed, and no TLS encryption. Our custom version will try to address those limitations.

> **Important Note**
>
> The full documentation about the registry configuration has a wide range of options that we're not mentioning here since it is out of the scope of this book. More configuration options can be found at this link: https://docs.docker.com/registry/configuration/.

The following file contains a modified version of the registry config.yml:

Chapter09/local_registry/customizations/config.yml

```
version: 0.1
log:
  fields:
    service: registry
storage:
  cache:
    blobdescriptor: inmemory
  filesystem:
    rootdirectory: /var/lib/registry
  delete:
    enabled: true
```

```
auth:
  htpasswd:
    realm: basic-realm
    path: /var/lib/htpasswd
http:
  addr: :5000
  headers:
    X-Content-Type-Options: [nosniff]
  tls:
    certificate: /etc/pki/certs/tls.crt
    key: /etc/pki/certs/tls.key
health:
  storagedriver:
    enabled: true
    interval: 10s
    threshold: 3
```

The highlighted sections in the previous example emphasize the added features:

- **Image deletion**: By default, this setting is disabled.

- **Basic authentication** using an htpasswd file. This approach is acceptable in a development and lab environment while a token-based authentication relying on an external issuer would be best suited for production use cases.

- **HTTPS transport** using self-signed certificates.

Before running the registry again with our custom configuration, we need to generate a htpasswd file that holds at least one valid login and the self-signed certificates for TLS encryption. Let's start with the htpasswd file – we can generate it using the htpasswd utility, like in the following example:

```
htpasswd -cBb ./htpasswd admin p0dman4Dev0ps#
```

The -cBb option enables batch mode (useful to provide the password non-interactively), creates the file if it does not exist, and enables the **bcrypt** hashing function *[2]*. In this example, we create the user admin with the password p0dman4Dev0ps#.

Finally, we need to create a self-signed server certificate with its related private key, to be used for HTTPS connections. As an example, a certificate associated with the *localhost* **Common Name** (**CN**) will be created.

> **Important Note**
> Bounding certificates to the *localhost* CN is a frequent practice in development environments. However, if the registry is meant to be exposed externally, the CN and SubjectAltName fields should map to the host FQDN and alternate names.

The following example shows how to create a self-signed certificate with the openssl utility:

```
$ mkdir certs
$ openssl req -newkey rsa:4096 -x509 -sha256 -nodes \
  -days 365 \
  -out certs/tls.crt \
  -keyout certs/tls.key \
  -subj '/CN=localhost' \
  -addext "subjectAltName=DNS:localhost"
```

The command will issue non-interactive certificate generation, without any extra information about the certificate subject. The private key tls.key is generated using a 4096-bit RSA algorithm. The certificate, named tls.crt, is set to expire after 1 year. Both the key and certificate are written inside the certs directory.

To inspect the content of the generated certificate, we can run the following command:

```
$ openssl x509 -in certs/tls.crt -text -noout
```

The command will produce a human-readable dump of the certificate data and validity.

> **Hint**
> For the purpose of this example, the self-signed certificate is acceptable, but it should be avoided in production scenarios.
>
> Solutions such as **Let's Encrypt** provide a free CA service for everybody and can be used to reliably secure the registry or any other HTTPS service. For further details, visit https://letsencrypt.org/.

We now have all the requirements to run our custom registry. Before creating the new container, make sure the previous instance has been stopped and removed:

```
# podman stop local_registry && podman rm local_registry
```

The next command shows how to run the new custom registry using bind mounts to pass the certificates folder, the `htpasswd` file, the registry store, and, obviously, the custom config file:

```
# podman run -d --name local_registry \
    -p 5000:5000 \
    -v $PWD/htpasswd:/var/lib/htpasswd:z \
    -v $PWD/config.yml:/etc/docker/registry/config.yml:z \
    -v /var/lib/registry:/var/lib/registry:z \
    -v $PWD/certs:/etc/pki/certs:z \
    --restart=always \
    registry:2
```

We can now test the login to the remote registry using the previously defined credentials:

```
$ skopeo login -u admin -p p0dman4DevOps# --tls-verify=false
localhost:5000
Login Succeeded!
```

Notice the `--tls-verify=false` option to skip TLS certificate validation. Since it is a self-signed certificate, we need to bypass checks that would produce the error message *x509: certificate signed by unknown authority*.

We can try again to delete the image pushed before:

```
$ skopeo delete \
    --tls-verify=false \
    docker://localhost:5000/minimal_httpd
```

This time, the command will succeed since the deletion feature was enabled in the config file.

A local registry can be used to mirror images from an external public registry. In the next subsection, we will see an example of registry mirroring using our local registry and a selected set of repositories and images.

Using a local registry to sync repositories

Mirroring images and repositories to a local registry can be very useful on disconnected environments. This can also be very useful to keep an async copy of selected images and be able to keep pulling them during public service outages.

The next example shows simple mirroring using the `skopeo sync` command with a list of images provided by a YAML file and our local registry as the destination:

```
$ skopeo sync \
   --src yaml --dest docker \
   --dest-tls-verify=false \
   kube_sync.yaml localhost:5000
```

The YAML file contains a list of the images that compose a Kubernetes control plane for a specific release. Again, we take advantage of regular expressions to customize the images to pull:

Chapter09/kube_sync.yaml

```
k8s.gcr.io:
  tls-verify: true
  images-by-tag-regex:
    kube-apiserver: ^v1\.22\..*
    kube-controller-manager: ^v1\.22\..*
    kube-proxy: ^v1\.22\..*
    kube-scheduler: ^v1\.22\..*
    coredns/coredns: ^v1\.8\..*
    etcd: 3\.4.[0-9]*-[0-9]*
```

When synchronizing a remote and local registry, a lot of layers can be mirrored in the process. For this reason, it is important to monitor the storage used by the registry (`/var/lib/registry` in our example) to avoid filling up the filesystem.

When the filesystem is filled, deleting older and unused images with Skopeo is not enough and an extra garbage collection action is necessary to free space. The next subsection illustrates this process.

Managing registry garbage collection

When a delete command is issued on a container registry, it only deletes the image manifests that reference a set of blobs (which could be layers or further manifests), while keeping the blobs in the filesystem.

If a blob is no longer referenced by any manifest, it can be eligible for garbage collection by the registry. The garbage collection process is managed with a dedicated command, `registry garbage-collect`, issued inside the registry container. This is not an automatic process and should be executed manually or scheduled.

In the next example, we will run a simple garbage collection. The `--dry-run` flag only prints the eligible blobs that are no longer referenced by a manifest and thus they can be safely deleted:

```
# podman exec -it local_registry \
  registry garbage-collect --dry-run \
  /etc/docker/registry/config.yml
```

To delete the blobs, simply remove the `--dry-run` option:

```
# podman exec -it local_registry \
  registry garbage-collect /etc/docker/registry/config.yml
```

Garbage collection is helpful to keep the registry cleaned of unused blobs and save space. On the other hand, we must keep in mind that an unreferenced blob could still be reused in the future by another image. If deleted, it could be necessary to upload it again eventually.

Summary

In this chapter, we explored how to interact with container registries, which are the fundamental storage services for our images. We started with a high-level description of what a container registry is and how it works and interacts with our container engines and tools. We then moved on to a more detailed description of the differences between public, cloud-based registries and private registries, usually executed on-premises. It was especially useful to understand the benefits and limitations of both and to help us to understand the best approach for our needs.

To manage container images on registries, we introduced the Skopeo tool, which is part of the Podman companion tools family, and illustrated how it can be used to copy, sync, delete, or simply inspect images over registries, giving users a higher degree of control over their images.

Finally, we learned how to run a local containerized registry using the official community image of the Docker Registry v2. After showing a basic usage, we went deeper into more advanced configuration details by showing how to enable authentication, image deletion, and HTTPS encryption. The local registry proved to be useful to sync local images as well as remote registries. The registry garbage collection process was illustrated to keep things tidy inside the registry store.

With the knowledge gained in this chapter, you will be able to manage images over registries and even local registry instances with a higher degree of awareness of what happens under the hood. Container registries are a crucial part of a successful container adoption strategy and should be understood very well: with this chapter's concepts in mind, you should also be able to understand and design the best fitting solutions and gain deep control over the tools to manipulate images.

With this chapter, we have also completed the exploration of all the basic tasks related to container management. We can now move on to more advanced topics, such as container troubleshooting and monitoring, covered in the next chapter.

Further reading

- [1] **Open Container Initiative (OCI)** Distribution Specification: `https://github.com/opencontainers/distribution-spec/blob/main/spec.md`

- [2] Bcrypt description: `https://en.wikipedia.org/wiki/Bcrypt`

- [3] Docker Registry v2 API specifications: `https://docs.docker.com/registry/spec/api/`

Section 3: Managing and Integrating Containers Securely

In this part of the book, you will learn how to troubleshoot, monitor, and create an advanced configuration for the running containers on the operating system host.

This part of the book comprises the following chapters:

10

Troubleshooting and Monitoring Containers

Running a container could be mistaken as the ultimate goal for a DevOps team, but instead, this is only the first step of a long journey. System administrators should ensure that their systems are working properly to keep the services up and running; in the same way, the DevOps team should ensure that their containers are working properly.

In container management activities, having the right knowledge of troubleshooting techniques could really help minimize any impact on the final services, reducing downtime. Talking of issues and troubleshooting, a good practice is to keep monitoring containers to easily intercept any issues or errors to speed up recovery.

In this chapter, we're going to cover the following main topics:

- Troubleshooting running containers
- Monitoring containers with health checks
- Inspecting our container build results
- Advanced troubleshooting with `nsenter`

Technical requirements

Before proceeding with the chapter information and examples, a machine with a working Podman installation is required. As stated in *Chapter 3, Running the First Container*, all the examples in the book are executed on a Fedora 34 system or later, but can be reproduced on your OS of choice.

A good understanding of the topics covered in *Chapter 4, Managing Running Containers*, and *Chapter 5, Implementing Storage for the Container's Data*, will be useful to easily grasp concepts relating to container registries.

Troubleshooting running containers

Troubleshooting containers is an important practice that we need experience with to solve common issues and investigate any bugs we may encounter on the container layer or in the application running inside our containers.

Starting from *Chapter 3, Running the First Container*, we started working with basic Podman commands for running and then inspecting containers on our host system. We saw how we can collect logs with the `podman logs` command, and we also learned how to use the information provided by the `podman inspect` command. Finally, we should also consider taking a look at the output of the useful `podman system df` command, which will report storage usage for our containers and images, and also the useful `podman system info` command, which will show useful information on the host where we are running Podman.

In general, we should always consider that the running container is just a process on the host system so we always have available all the tools and commands for troubleshooting the underlying OS and its available resources.

A best practice for troubleshooting containers could be a top-down approach, analyzing the application layer first, then moving to the container layer, down finally to the base host system.

At the container level, many of the issues that we may encounter have been summarized by the Podman project team in a comprehensive list on the project page. We will cover some of the more useful ones in the following sections.

Permission denied while using storage volumes

A very common issue that we may encounter during our activities on RHEL, Fedora, or any Linux distribution that uses the SELinux security subsystem is related to storage permission. The error described as follows is triggered when SELinux is set to `Enforcing` mode, which is also the suggested approach to fully guarantee the mandatory access security features of SELinux.

We can try to test this on our Fedora workstation, first creating a directory and then trying to use this as a volume in our container:

```
$ mkdir ~/mycontent
$ podman run -v ~/mycontent:/content fedora \
touch /content/file
touch: cannot touch '/content/file': Permission denied
```

As we can see, the `touch` command reports a `Permission denied` error, because actually, it cannot write in the filesystem.

As we saw in detail in *Chapter 5, Implementing Storage for the Container's Data*, SELinux recursively applies labels to files and directories to define their context. Those labels are usually stored as extended filesystem attributes. SELinux uses contexts to manage policies and define which processes can access a specific resource.

The container we just ran got its own Linux namespace and an SELinux label that is completely different from the local user in the Fedora workstation, which is why we actually got that error before.

Without a proper label, the SELinux system prevents the processes running in the container from accessing the content. This is also because Podman does not change the labels set by the OS if not explicitly requested through a command option.

To let Podman change the label for a container, we can use either of two suffixes, `:z` or `:Z`, for the volume mount. These options tell Podman to relabel file objects on the volume.

The `:z` option is used to instruct Podman that two containers share a storage volume. So, in this case, Podman will label the content with a shared content label that will allow two or more containers to read/write content on that volume.

The `:Z` option is used to instruct Podman to label the volume's content with a private unshared label that can only be used by the current container.

The command would result in something like this:

```
$ podman run -v ~/mycontent:/content:Z fedora \
touch /content/file
```

As we can see, the command didn't report any error; it worked.

Issues with the ping command in rootless containers

On some hardened Linux systems, the `ping` command execution could be limited to only a restricted group of users. This could cause the failure of the `ping` command used in a container.

As we saw in *Chapter 3, Running the First Container*, when starting the container, the base OS will associate with it a different user ID from the one used in the container itself. The user ID associated to the container could fall outside the allowed range of user's IDs enabled to use the `ping` command.

In a Fedora workstation installation, the default configuration will allow any container to run the `ping` command without issues. To manage restrictions on the usage of the `ping` command, Fedora uses the `ping_group_range` kernel parameter, which defines the allowed system groups that can execute the `ping` command.

If we take a look at a just-installed Fedora workstation, the default range is the following one:

```
$ cat /proc/sys/net/ipv4/ping_group_range
0       2147483647
```

So, nothing to worry about for a brand-new Fedora system. But what about if the range is smaller than this one?

Well, we test this behavior by changing the allowed range with a simple command. In this example, we are going to restrict the range and see that the `ping` command will actually fail then:

```
$ sudo sysctl -w "net.ipv4.ping_group_range=0 0"
```

Just in case the range is smaller than the one reported in the previous output, we can make it persistent by adding a file to `/etc/sysctl.d` that contains `net.ipv4.ping_group_range=0 0`.

The applied change in the `ping` group range will impact the mapped user privileges to run the `ping` command inside the container.

Let's start by building a Fedora-based image with the `iputils` package (not included by default) using Buildah:

```
$ container=$(buildah from docker.io/library/fedora) && \
  buildah run $container -- dnf install -y iputils && \
  buildah commit $container ping_example
```

We can test it by running the following command inside a container:

```
$ podman run --rm ping_example ping -W10 -c1 redhat.com
PING redhat.com (209.132.183.105): 56 data bytes
--- redhat.com ping statistics ---
1 packets transmitted, 0 packets received, 100% packet loss
```

The command, executed on a system with a restricted range, produces a 100% packet loss since the `ping` command is not able to send packets over a raw socket.

The example demonstrates how a restriction in `ping_group_range` impacts the execution of `ping` inside a rootless container. By setting the range to a value large enough to include the user private group GID (or one of the user's secondary groups), the `ping` command will be able to send ICMP packets correctly.

> **Important Note**
>
> Do not forget to restore the original `ping_group_range` before proceeding with the next examples. On Fedora, the default configuration can be restored with the `sudo sysctl -w "net.ipv4.ping_group_range=0 2147483647"` command and by removing any persistent configuration applied under `/etc/sysctl.d` during the exercise. For a base container image that we are building through a Dockerfile, we may need to add a brand-new user with a large UID/GID. This will create a large, sparse `/var/log/lastlog` file and this can cause the build to hang forever. This issue is related to the Go language, which does not correctly support sparse files, leading to the creation of this huge file in the container image.

> **Good to Know**
>
> The `/var/log/lastlog` file is a binary and sparse file that contains information about the last time that the users logged in to the system. The apparent size of a sparse file reported by `ls -l` is larger than the actual disk usage. A sparse file attempts to use filesystem space in a more efficient way, writing the metadata that represents the empty blocks to disk instead of the empty space that should be stored in the block. This will use less disk space.

If we need to add a brand-new user to our base container image with a high UID number, the best way would be to append the `--no-log-init` option to the Dockerfile command, as shown here:

```
RUN useradd --no-log-init -u 99999000 -g users myuser
```

This option instructs the `useradd` command to stop creating the lastlog file, solving the issue we may encounter.

As mentioned in the early paragraphs of this section, the Podman team has created a long but non-comprehensive list of common issues. We strongly suggest taking a look at it if any issues are encountered: `https://github.com/containers/podman/blob/main/troubleshooting.md`.

Troubleshooting could be tricky, but the first step is always the identification of an issue. For this reason, a monitoring tool could help in alerting as soon as possible in the case of issues. Let's see how to monitor containers with health checks in the next section.

Monitoring containers with health checks

Starting with version 1.2, Podman supports the option to add a health check to containers. We will go in depth in this section into these health checks and how to use them.

A health check is a Podman feature that can help determine the health or readiness of the process running in a container. It could be as simple as checking that the container's process is running but also more sophisticated, such as verifying that both the container and its applications are responsive using, for example, network connections.

A health check is made up of five core components. The first is the main element that will instruct Podman on the particular check to execute; the others are used for configuring the schedule of the health check. Let's see these elements in detail:

- **Command**: This is the command that Podman will execute inside the target container. The health of the container and its process will be determined through the wait for either a success (return code 0) or a failure (with other exit codes).

  If our container provides a web server, for example, our health check command could be something really simple, such as a `curl` command that will try to connect to the web server port to make sure it is responsive.

- **Retries**: This defines the number of consecutive failed commands that Podman has to execute before the container will be marked as unhealthy. If a command executes successfully, Podman will reset the retry counter.

- **Interval**: This option defines the interval time within which Podman will run the health check command.

  Finding the right interval time could be really difficult and requires some trial and error. If we set it to a small value, then our system may spend a lot of time running the health checks. But if we set it to a large value, we may struggle and catch timeouts. This value can be defined with a widely used time format: 30s or 1h5m.

- **Start period**: This describes the time after which the health checks will be started by Podman. In this period, Podman will ignore health check failures.

  We can consider this as a grace period that should be used to allow our application to successfully be up and start replying correctly to any clients as well as to our health checks.

- **Timeout**: This defines the period of time the health check itself must complete before being considered unsuccessful.

Let's take a look at a real example, supposing we want to define a health check for a container and run that health check manually:

```
$ podman run -dt --name healthtest1 --healthcheck-command \
'CMD-SHELL curl http://localhost || exit 1' \
--healthcheck-interval=0 quay.io/libpod/alpine_nginx:latest

Trying to pull quay.io/libpod/alpine_nginx:latest...
Getting image source signatures
Copying blob ac35fae19c6c done
Copying blob 4c0d98bf9879 done
Copying blob 5b0fccc9c35f done
Copying config 7397e078c6 done
Writing manifest to image destination
Storing signatures
1faae6c46839b9076f68bee467f9d56751db6ab45dd149f249b0790e05
c55b58
$ podman healthcheck run healthtest1
$ echo $?
0
```

As we can see from the previous code block, we just started a brand-new container named `checktest1`, defining a `healthcheck-command` that will run the `curl` command on the `localhost` address inside the target container. Once the container started, we manually ran `healthcheck` and verified that the exit code was `0`, meaning that the check completed successfully and our container is healthy. In the previous example, we also used the `--healthcheck-interval=0` option to actually disable the run interval and make the health check manual.

Podman uses **systemd** timers to schedule health checks. For this reason, it is mandatory if we want to schedule a health check for our containers. Of course, if some of our systems do not use systemd as the default daemon manager, we could use different tools, such as `cron`, to schedule the health checks, but these should be set manually.

Let's inspect how this automatic integration with systemd works by creating an health check with an interval:

```
$ podman run -dt --name healthtest2 --healthcheck-command
'CMD-SHELL curl http://localhost || exit 1' --healthcheck-
interval=10s quay.io/libpod/alpine_nginx:latest
70e7d3f0b4363759fc66ae4903625e5f451d3af6795a96586bc1328c1b149
ce5
$ podman ps
CONTAINER ID   IMAGE                                      COMMAND
CREATED         STATUS                      PORTS        NAMES
70e7d3f0b436   quay.io/libpod/alpine_nginx:latest   nginx
-g daemon o...   7 seconds ago   Up 7 seconds ago  (healthy)
healthtest2
```

As we can see from the previous code block, we just started a brand-new container named `checktest2`, defining the same `healthcheck-command` of the previous example but now specifying the `--healthcheck-interval=10s` option to actually schedule the check every 10 seconds.

After the `podman run` command, we also ran the `podman ps` command to actually inspect whether the health check is working properly, and as we can see in the output, we have the `healthy` status for our brand-new container.

But how does this integration work? Let's grab the container ID and search for it in the following directory:

```
$ ls /run/user/$UID/systemd/transient/70e*
/run/user/1000/systemd/transient/70e7d3f0b4363759fc66ae4903625
e5f451d3af6795a96586bc1328c1b149ce5.service
```

```
/run/user/1000/systemd/transient/70e7d3f0b4363759fc66ae4903625
e5f451d3af6795a96586bc1328c1b149ce5.timer
```

The directory shown in the previous code block holds all the systemd resources in use for our current user. In particular, we looked into the `transient` directory, which holds temporary unit files for our current user.

When we start a container with a health check and a schedule interval, Podman will perform a transient setup of a systemd service and timer unit file. This means that these unit files are not permanent and can be lost on reboot.

Let's inspect what is defined inside these files:

```
$ cat /run/user/$UID/systemd/transient/70e7d3f0b4363759fc66a
e4903625e5f451d3af6795a96586bc1328c1b149ce5.service
# This is a transient unit file, created programmatically via
the systemd API. Do not edit.
[Unit]
Description=/usr/bin/podman healthcheck run 70e7d3f0b4363759
fc66ae4903625e5f451d3af6795a96586bc1328c1b149ce5


[Service]
Environment="PATH=/home/alex/.local/bin:/home/alex/bin:/usr/
local/bin:/usr/local/sbin:/usr/bin:/usr/sbin:/var/lib/snapd/
snap/bin"
ExecStart=
ExecStart="/usr/bin/podman" "healthcheck" "run" "70e7d3f0b
4363759fc66ae4903625e5f451d3af6795a96586bc1328c1b149ce5"


$ cat /run/user/$UID/systemd/transient/70e7d3f0b4363759fc66
ae4903625e5f451d3af6795a96586bc1328c1b149ce5.timer
# This is a transient unit file, created programmatically via
the systemd API. Do not edit.
[Unit]
Description=/usr/bin/podman healthcheck run 70e7d3f0b4363759
fc66ae4903625e5f451d3af6795a96586bc1328c1b149ce5


[Timer]
OnUnitInactiveSec=10s
AccuracySec=1s
RemainAfterElapse=no
```

As we can see from the previous code block, the service unit file contains the Podman health check command, while the timer unit file defines the scheduling interval.

Finally, just because we may want a quick way to identify healthy or unhealthy containers, we can use the following command to quickly output them:

```
$ podman ps -a --filter health=healthy
CONTAINER ID  IMAGE                                     COMMAND
CREATED          STATUS                                 PORTS
NAMES
1faae6c46839  quay.io/libpod/alpine_nginx:latest  nginx -g
daemon o...  36 minutes ago  Exited (137) 19 minutes ago
(healthy)                    healthtest1
70e7d3f0b436  quay.io/libpod/alpine_nginx:latest  nginx -g
daemon o...  13 minutes ago  Up 13 minutes ago (healthy)
healthtest2
```

In this example, we used the `--filter health=healthy` option to display only the healthy containers with the `podman ps` command.

We learned how to troubleshoot and monitor our containers in the previous sections, but what about the container build process? Let's discover more about container build inspection in the next section.

Inspecting your container build results

In previous chapters, we discussed in detail the container build process and learned how to create custom images using Dockerfiles/Containerfiles or Buildah-native commands. We also illustrated how the second approach helps achieve a greater degree of control of the build workflow.

This section helps provide some best practices to inspect the build results and understand potentially related issues.

Troubleshooting builds from Dockerfiles

When using Podman or Buildah to run a build based on a Dockerfile/Containerfile, the build process prints all the instructions' outputs and related errors on the terminal stdout. For all RUN instructions, errors generated from the executed commands are propagated and printed for debugging purposes.

Let's now try to test some potential build issues. This is not an exhaustive list of errors; the purpose is to provide a method to analyze the root cause.

The first example shows a minimal build where a RUN instruction fails due to an error in the executed command. Errors in RUN instructions can cover a wide range of cases but the general rule of thumb is the following: the executed command returns an exit code and if this is non-zero, the build fails and the error, along with the exit status, is printed.

In the next example, we use the yum command to install the httpd package, but we have intentionally made a typo in the package name to generate an error. Here is the Dockerfile transcript:

Chapter10/RUN_command_error/Dockerfile

```
FROM registry.access.redhat.com/ubi8

# Update image and install httpd
RUN yum install -y htpd && yum clean all -y

# Expose the default httpd port 80
EXPOSE 80

# Run the httpd
CMD ["/usr/sbin/httpd", "-DFOREGROUND"]
```

If we try to execute the command, we will get an error generated by the yum command not being able to find the missing htpd package:

```
$ buildah build -t custom_httpd .
STEP 1/4: FROM registry.access.redhat.com/ubi8
STEP 2/4: RUN yum install -y htpd && yum clean all -y
Updating Subscription Management repositories.
Unable to read consumer identity

This system is not registered with an entitlement server. You
can use subscription-manager to register.

Red Hat Universal Base Image 8 (RPMs) - BaseOS  3.9 MB/s |
796kB     00:00
Red Hat Universal Base Image 8 (RPMs) - AppStre 6.2 MB/s | 2.6
MB     00:00
```

```
Red Hat Universal Base Image 8 (RPMs) - CodeRea 171 kB/s |  16
kB      00:00
```

```
No match for argument: htpd
Error: Unable to find a match: htpd
error building at STEP "RUN yum install -y htpd && yum clean
all -y": error while running runtime: exit status 1
ERRO[0004] exit status 1
```

The first two lines print the error message generated by the yum command, as in a standard command-line environment.

Next, Buildah (and, in the same way, Podman) produces a message to inform us about the step that generated the error. This message is managed in the imagebuildah package by the stage executor, which handles, as the name indicates, the execution of the build stages and their statuses. The source code can be inspected in the Buildah repository on GitHub: https://github.com/containers/buildah/blob/main/imagebuildah/stage_executor.go.

The message includes the Dockerfile instruction and the generated error, along with the exit status.

The last line includes the ERRO[0004] error code and the final exit status 1, related to the buildah command execution.

Solution: Use the error message to find the RUN instruction that contains the failing command and fix or troubleshoot the command error.

Another very common failure reason in builds is the missing parent image. It could be related to a misspelled repository name, a missing tag, or an unreachable registry.

The next example shows another variation of the previous Dockerfile, where the image repository name is mistyped and thus does not exist in the remote registry:

Chapter10/FROM_repo_not_found/Dockerfile

```
FROM registry.access.redhat.com/ubi_8
```

```
# Update image and install httpd
RUN yum install -y httpd && yum clean all -y
```

```
# Expose the default httpd port 80
```

```
EXPOSE 80
```

```
# Run the httpd
CMD ["/usr/sbin/httpd", "-DFOREGROUND"]
```

When running a build from this Dockerfile, we will encounter an error caused by the missing image repository, as in the next example:

```
$ buildah build -t custom_httpd .
STEP 1/4: FROM registry.access.redhat.com/ubi_8
Trying to pull registry.access.redhat.com/ubi_8:latest...
error creating build container: initializing source docker://
registry.access.redhat.com/ubi_8:latest: reading manifest
latest in registry.access.redhat.com/ubi_8: name unknown: Repo
not found
ERRO[0001] exit status 125
```

The last line produces a different error code, ERRO[0001], and an exit status, 125. This is a very easy error to troubleshoot and only requires passing a valid repository to the FROM instruction.

Solution: Fix the repository name and relaunch the build process. Alternatively, verify that the target registry holds the wanted repository.

What happens if we misspell the image tag? The next Dockerfile snippet shows an invalid tag for the official Fedora image:

Chapter10/FROM_tag_not_found/Dockerfile

```
FROM docker.io/library/fedora:sometag
```

```
# Update image and install httpd
RUN dnf install -y httpd && dnf clean all -y
```

```
# Expose the default httpd port 80
EXPOSE 80
```

```
# Run the httpd
CMD ["/usr/sbin/httpd", "-DFOREGROUND"]
```

This time, when we build the image, we will get a 404 error produced by the registry, which is unable to find an associated manifest for the `sometag` tag:

```
$ buildah build -t custom_httpd .
STEP 1/4: FROM docker.io/library/fedora:sometag
Trying to pull docker.io/library/fedora:sometag...
error creating build container: initializing source docker://
fedora:sometag: reading manifest sometag in docker.io/library/
fedora: manifest unknown: manifest unknown
ERRO[0001] exit status 125
```

The missing tag will generate an `ERRO[0001]` error, while the exit status will be set to `125` again.

Solution: Find a valid tag to be used for the build process. Use `skopeo list-tags` to find all the available tags in a given repository.

Sometimes, the error caught from the FROM instruction is caused by the attempt to access a private registry without authentication. This is a very common mistake and simply requires an authenticating step on the target registry before any build action takes place.

In the next example, we have a Dockerfile that uses an image from a generic private registry running using Docker Registry v2 APIs:

Chapter10/FROM_auth_error/Dockerfile

```
FROM local-registry.example.com/ubi8

# Update image and install httpd
RUN yum install -y httpd && yum clean all -y

# Expose the default httpd port 80
EXPOSE 80

# Run the httpd
CMD ["/usr/sbin/httpd", "-DFOREGROUND"]
```

Let's try to build the image and see what happens:

```
$ buildah build -t test3 .
STEP 1/4: FROM local-registry.example.com/ubi8
Trying to pull local-registry.example.com/ubi8:latest...
error creating build container: initializing source docker://
local-registry.example.com/ubi8:latest: reading manifest
latest in local-registry.example.com/ubi8: unauthorized:
authentication required
ERRO[0000] exit status 125
```

In this use case, the error is very clear. We are not authorized to pull the image from the target registry and thus, we need to authenticate with a valid auth token to access it.

Solution: Authenticate with `podman login` or `buildah login` to the registry to retrieve the token or provide an authentication file with a valid token.

So far, we have inspected errors generated by builds with Dockerfiles. Let's now see the behavior of Buildah in the case of errors when using its command-line instructions.

Troubleshooting builds with Buildah-native commands

When running Buildah commands, it is a common practice to put them inside a shell script or a pipeline.

In this example, we will use Bash as the interpreter. By default, Bash executes the script up to the end, regardless of intermediate errors. This behavior can generate unexpected errors if a Buildah instruction inside the script fails. For this reason, the best practice is to add the following command at the beginning of the script:

```
set -euo pipefail
```

The resulting configuration is a sort of safety net that blocks the execution of the script as soon as we encounter an error and avoids common mistakes, such as unset variables.

The `set` command is a Bash internal instruction that configures the shell for the script execution. The `-e` option inside this instruction tells the shell to exit immediately if a pipeline or a single command fails and the `-o pipefail` option tells the shell to exit with the error code of the rightmost command of a failing pipeline that produced a non-zero exit code. The `-u` option tells the shell to treat unset variables and parameters as an error during parameter expansion. This keeps us safe from the missing expansion of unset variables.

The next script embeds the logic of a simple build of an `httpd` server on top of the Fedora image:

```
#!/bin/bash


set -euo pipefail
# Trying to pull a non-existing tag of Fedora official image
container=$(buildah from docker.io/library/fedora:non-existing-tag)
buildah run $container -- dnf install -y httpd; dnf clean all -y
buildah config --cmd "httpd -DFOREGROUND" $container
buildah config --port 80 $container
buildah commit $container custom-httpd
buildah tag custom-httpd registry.example.com/custom-httpd:v0.0.1
```

The image tag was set wrong on purpose. Let's see the results of the script execution:

```
$ ./custom-httpd.sh
Trying to pull docker.io/library/fedora:non-existing-tag...
initializing source docker://fedora:non-existing-tag: reading
manifest non-existing-tag in docker.io/library/fedora: manifest
unknown: manifest unknown
ERRO[0001] exit status 125
```

The build produces a `manifest unknown` error with the `ERRO[0001]` error code and the `125` exit status, just like the similar attempt with the Dockerfile.

From this output, we can also learn that Buildah (and Podman, which uses Buildah libraries for its build implementation) produces the same messages as a standard build with a Dockerfile/Containerfile, with the only exception of not mentioning the build step, which is obvious since we are running free commands inside a script.

Solution: Find a valid tag to be used for the build process. Use `skopeo list-tags` to find all the available tags in a given repository.

In this section, we have learned how to analyze and troubleshoot build errors, but what can we do when the errors happen at runtime inside the container and we do not have the proper tools for troubleshooting inside the image? For this purpose, we have a native Linux tool that can be considered the real Swiss Army knife of namespaces: `nsenter`.

Advanced troubleshooting with nsenter

Let's start with a dramatic sentence: troubleshooting issues at runtime can sometimes be complex.

Also, understanding and troubleshooting runtime issues inside a container implies an understanding of how containers work in GNU/Linux. We explained these concepts in *Chapter 1, Introduction to Container Technology*.

Sometimes, troubleshooting can be very easy and, as stated in the previous sections, the usage of basic commands, such as podman logs, podman inspect, and podman exec, along with the usage of tailored health checks, can help us to gain access to the necessary information to complete our analysis successfully.

Images nowadays tend to be as small as possible. What happens when we need more specialized troubleshooting tools, and they are not available inside the image? You could think to exec a shell process inside the container and install the missing tool but sometimes (and this is a growing security pattern), package managers are not available inside container images, sometimes not even the curl or wget commands!

We may feel a bit lost but we must remember that containers are processes executed within dedicated namespaces and cgroups. What if we had a tool that could let us exec inside one or more namespaces while keeping our access to the host tools? That tool exists and is called nsenter (access the manual page with man nsenter). It is not affiliated with any container engine or runtime and provides a simple way to execute commands inside one or multiple namespaces unshared for a process (the main container process).

Before diving into real examples, let's discuss the main nsenter options and arguments by running it with the --help option:

```
$ nsenter --help


Usage:
 nsenter [options] [<program> [<argument>...]]


Run a program with namespaces of other processes.


Options:
 -a, --all                 enter all namespaces
 -t, --target <pid>        target process to get namespaces from
 -m, --mount[=<file>]      enter mount namespace
```

```
-u, --uts[=<file>]        enter UTS namespace (hostname etc)
-i, --ipc[=<file>]        enter System V IPC namespace
-n, --net[=<file>]        enter network namespace
-p, --pid[=<file>]        enter pid namespace
-C, --cgroup[=<file>]     enter cgroup namespace
-U, --user[=<file>]       enter user namespace
-T, --time[=<file>]       enter time namespace
-S, --setuid <uid>        set uid in entered namespace
-G, --setgid <gid>        set gid in entered namespace
      --preserve-credentials do not touch uids or gids
-r, --root[=<dir>]        set the root directory
-w, --wd[=<dir>]          set the working directory
-F, --no-fork             do not fork before exec'ing <program>
-Z, --follow-context      set SELinux context according to
--target PID

-h, --help                display this help
-V, --version             display version


For more details see nsenter(1).
```

From the output of this command, it is easy to spot that there are as many options as the number of available namespaces.

Thanks to nsenter, we can capture the PID of the main process of a container and then exec commands (including a shell) inside the related namespaces.

To extract the container's main PID, we use can use the following command:

```
$ podman inspect <Container_Name> --format '{{ .State.Pid }}'
```

The output can be inserted inside a variable for easier access:

```
$ CNT_PID=$(podman inspect <Container_Name> \
   --format '{{ .State.Pid }}')
```

> **Hint**
>
> All namespaces associated with a process are represented inside the `/proc/` `[pid]/ns` directory. This directory contains a series of symbolic links mapping to a namespace type and its corresponding inode number.
>
> The following command shows the namespaces associated with the process executed by the container: `ls -al /proc/$CNT_PID/ns`.

We are going to learn how to use `nsenter` with a practical example. In the next subsection, we will try to network troubleshoot a database client application that returns an HTTP internal server error without mentioning any useful information in the application logs.

Troubleshooting a database client with nsenter

It is not uncommon to work on alpha applications that still do not have logging correctly implemented or that have poor handling of log messages.

The following example is a web application that extracts fields from a Postgres database and prints out a JSON object with all the occurrences. The verbosity of the application logs has been intentionally left to a minimum and no connection or query errors are produced.

For the sake of space, we will not print the application source code in the book; however, it is available at the following URL for inspection: `https://github.com/` `PacktPublishing/Podman-for-DevOps/tree/main/Chapter10/students`.

The folder also contains a SQL script to populate a sample database. The application is built using the following Dockerfile:

Chapter10/students/Dockerfile

```
FROM docker.io/library/golang AS builder


# Copy files for build
RUN mkdir -p /go/src/students/models
COPY go.mod main.go /go/src/students
COPY models/main.go /go/src/students/models


# Set the working directory
WORKDIR /go/src/students

```

```
# Download dependencies
RUN go get -d -v ./...

# Install the package
RUN go build -v

# Runtime image
FROM registry.access.redhat.com/ubi8/ubi-minimal:latest as bin
COPY --from=builder /go/src/students /usr/local/bin
COPY entrypoint.sh /

EXPOSE 8080

ENTRYPOINT ["/entrypoint.sh"]
```

As usual, we are going to build the container with Buildah:

```
$ buildah build -t students .
```

The container accepts a set of custom flags to define the database, host, port, and credentials. To see the help information, simply run the following command:

```
$ podman run students students -help
%!(EXTRA string=students)
-database string
      Default application database (default "students")
-host string      Default host running the database (default
"localhost")
-password string      Default database password (default
"password"
-port string      Default database port (default "5432")
-username string      Default database username (default
"admin")
```

We have been informed that the database is running on host pghost.example.com on port 5432, with username students and password Podman_R0cks#.

The next command runs the students web application with the custom arguments:

```
$ podman run --rm -d -p 8080:8080 \
    --name students_app students \
    students -host pghost.example.com \
    -port 5432 \
    -username students \
    -password Podman_R0cks#
```

The container starts successfully, and the only log message printed is the following:

```
$ podman logs students_app
2021/12/27 21:51:31 Connecting to host pghost.example.com:5432,
database students
```

It is now time to test the application and see what happens when we run a query:

```
$ curl localhost:8080/students
Internal Server Error
```

The application can take some time to answer but after a while, it will print an internal server error (500) HTTP message. We will find the reason in the following paragraphs. Logs are not useful since nothing else other than the first boot message is printed. Besides, the container was built with the UBI minimal image, which has a small footprint of pre-installed binaries and no utilities for troubleshooting. We can use nsenter to inspect the container behavior, especially from a networking point of view, by attaching our current shell program to the container network namespace while keeping access to our host binaries.

We can now find out the main process PID and populate a variable with its value:

```
$ CNT_PID=$(podman inspect students_app --format '{{ .State.Pid
}}')
```

The following example runs Bash in the container network namespace, while retaining all the other host namespaces (notice the sudo command to run it with elevated privileges):

```
$ sudo nsenter -t $CNT_PID -n /bin/bash
```

> **Important Note**
>
> It is possible to run any host binary directly from `nsenter`. A command such as the following is perfectly legitimate: `$ sudo nsenter -t $CNT_PID -n ip addr show`.

To demonstrate that we are really executing a shell attached to the container network namespace, we can launch the `ip addr show` command:

```
# ip addr show
1: lo: <LOOPBACK,UP,LOWER_UP> mtu 65536 qdisc noqueue state
UNKNOWN group default qlen 1000
    link/loopback 00:00:00:00:00:00 brd 00:00:00:00:00:00
    inet 127.0.0.1/8 scope host lo
       valid_lft forever preferred_lft forever
    inet6 ::1/128 scope host
       valid_lft forever preferred_lft forever
2: tap0: <BROADCAST,UP,LOWER_UP> mtu 65520 qdisc fq_codel state
UNKNOWN group default qlen 1000
    link/ether fa:0b:50:ed:9d:37 brd ff:ff:ff:ff:ff:ff
    inet 10.0.2.100/24 brd 10.0.2.255 scope global tap0
       valid_lft forever preferred_lft forever
    inet6 fe80::f80b:50ff:feed:9d37/64 scope link
       valid_lft forever preferred_lft forever
# ip route
default via 10.0.2.2 dev tap0
10.0.2.0/24 dev tap0 proto kernel scope link src 10.0.2.100
```

The first command, `ip addr show`, prints the IP configuration, with a basic `tap0` interface connected to the host and the loopback interface.

The second command, `ip route`, shows the default routing table inside the container network namespace.

We can take a first look at the active connections using the `ss` tool, already available on our Fedora host:

```
# ss -atunp
Netid State      Recv-Q Send-Q Local Address:Port   Peer
Address:PortProcess
```

```
tcp   TIME-WAIT 0       0            10.0.2.100:50728
10.0.2.100:8080
tcp   LISTEN    0       128                *:8080
*:*    users⊗"("studen"s",pid=402788,fd=3))
```

We immediately spot that there are no established connections between the application and the database host, which tells us that the issue is probably related to routing, firewall rules, or name resolution causes that prevent us from reaching the host correctly.

The next step is to try to manually connect to the database with the psql client tool, available from the rpm postgresql package:

```
# psql -h pghost.example.com
psql: error: could not translate host name "pghost.example.com"
to address: Name or service not known
```

This message is quite clear: the host is not resolved by the DNS service and causes the application to fail. To finally confirm it, we can run the dig command, which returns an NXDOMAIN error, a typical message from a DNS server to say that the domain cannot be resolved and does not exist:

```
# dig pghost.example.com

; <<>> DiG 9.16.23-RH <<>> pghost.example.com
;; global options: +cmd
;; Got answer:
;; ->>HEADER<<- opcode: QUERY, status: NXDOMAIN, id: 40669
;; flags: qr rd ra; QUERY: 1, ANSWER: 0, AUTHORITY: 0,
ADDITIONAL: 1

;; OPT PSEUDOSECTION:
; EDNS: version: 0, flags:; udp: 4096
;; QUESTION SECTION:
;pghost.example.com.            IN    A

;; Query time: 0 msec
;; SERVER: 192.168.200.1#53(192.168.200.1)
;; WHEN: Mon Dec 27 23:26:47 CET 2021
;; MSG SIZE  rcvd: 47
```

After checking with the development team, we discovered that the database name had a missing dash that was misspelled, and the correct name was `pg-host.example.com`. We can now fix the issue by running the container with the correct name.

We expect now to see the correct results when launching the query again:

```
$ curl localhost:8080/students
{"Id":10149,"FirstName":"Frank","MiddleName":"Vincent",
"LastName":"Zappa","Class":"3A","Course":"Composition"}
```

In this example, we have focused on network namespace troubleshooting, but it is possible to attach our current shell program to multiple namespaces by simply adding the related flags.

We can also simulate `podman exec` by running the command with the `-a` option:

```
$ sudo nsenter -t $CNT_PID -a /bin/bash
```

This command attaches the process to all the unshared namespaces, including the mount namespace, thus giving the same filesystem tree view that is seen by processes inside the container.

Summary

In this chapter, we focused on container troubleshooting, trying to provide a set of best practices and tools to find and fix issues inside a container at build time or runtime.

We started by showing off some common use cases during container execution and build stages and their related solutions.

Afterward, we introduced the concept of health checks and illustrated how to implement solid probes on containers to monitor their statuses, while showing the architectural concepts behind them.

In the third section, we learned about a series of common error scenarios related to builds and showed how to solve them quickly.

In the final section, we introduced the `nsenter` command and simulated a web frontend application that needed network troubleshooting to find out the cause of an internal server error. Thanks to this example, we learned how to conduct advanced troubleshooting inside the container namespaces.

In the next chapter, we are going to discuss container security, a crucial concept that deserves great attention. We will learn how to secure containers with a series of best practices, the difference between rootless and rootful containers, and how to sign container images to make them publicly available.

Further reading

- Podman troubleshooting guidelines: `https://github.com/containers/podman/blob/main/troubleshooting.md`

11
Securing Containers

Security is becoming the hottest topic of current times. Enterprises and companies all over the world are making huge investments in security practices and tools that should help protect their systems from internal or external attacks.

As we saw in *Chapter 1*, *Introduction to Container Technology*, containers and their host systems can be considered a medium to execute and keep a target application running. Security should be applied to all levels of the service architecture, from the base infrastructure to the target application code, all while passing through the virtualization or containerization layer.

In this chapter, we will look at the best practices and tools that could help improve the overall security of our containerization layer. In particular, we're going to cover the following main topics:

- Running rootless containers with Podman
- Do not run containers with UID 0
- Signing our container images
- Customizing Linux kernel capabilities
- SELinux interaction with containers

Technical requirements

To complete this chapter's examples, you will need a machine with a working Podman installation. As we mentioned in *Chapter 3, Running the First Container*, all the examples in this book have been executed on a Fedora 34 system or later, but they can be reproduced on your OS of choice.

Having a good understanding of the topics that were covered in *Chapter 4, Managing Running Containers, Chapter 5, Implementing Storage for the Container's Data*, and *Chapter 9, Pushing Images to a Container Registry*, will help you understand the container security topics we'll be discussing here.

Running rootless containers with Podman

As we briefly saw in *Chapter 4, Managing Running Containers*, it is possible for Podman to let standard users without administrative privileges run containers in a Linux host. These containers are often referred to as "rootless containers."

Rootless containers have many advantages, including the following:

- They create an additional security layer that could block attackers trying to get root privileges on the host, even if the container engine, runtime, or orchestrator has been compromised.

- They can allow many unprivileged users to run containers on the same host, making the most of high-performance computing environments.

Let's think about the approach that's used by any Linux system to handle traditional process services. Usually, the package maintainers tend to create a dedicated user for scheduling and running the target process. If we try to install an Apache web server on our favorite Linux distribution through the default package manager, then we can find out that the installed service will run through a dedicated user named "apache."

This approach has been the best practice for years because, from a security perspective, allowing fewer privileges improves security.

Using the same approach but with a rootless container allows us to run the container process without the need for additional privileges escalation. Additionally, Podman is daemonless, so it will just create a child process.

Running rootless containers in Podman is pretty straightforward and, as we saw in the previous chapters, many of the examples in this book can be run as standard unprivileged users. Now, let's learn what's behind the execution of a rootless container.

The Podman Swiss Army knife – subuid and subgid

Modern Linux distributions use a version of the shadow-utils package that leverages two files: /etc/subuid and /etc/subgid. These files are used to determine which UIDs and GIDs can be used to map a user namespace.

The default allocation for every user is 65536 UIDs and 65536 GIDs.

We can run the following simple command to check how the subuid and subgid allocation works in rootless containers:

```
$ id
uid=1000(alex) gid=1000(alex) groups=1000(alex),10(wheel)
$ podman run alpine cat /proc/self/uid_map /proc/self/gid_map
Resolved "alpine" as an alias (/etc/containers/registries.
conf.d/000-shortnames.conf)
Trying to pull docker.io/library/alpine:latest...
Getting image source signatures
Copying blob 59bf1c3509f3 done
Copying config c059bfaa84 done
Writing manifest to image destination
Storing signatures
         0        1000             1
         1      100000         65536
         0        1000             1
         1      100000         65536
```

As we can see, both files indicate that they start mapping UID and GID 0 with the current user's UID/GID that we just run the container with; that is, 1000. After that, it maps UID and GID 1, starting from 100000 and arriving at 165536. This is calculated by summing the starting point, 100000, and the default range, 65536.

Using rootless containers is not the only best practice we can implement for our container environments. In the next section, we'll learn why we shouldn't run a container with UID 0.

Do not run containers with UID 0

Container runtimes can be instructed to perform running processes inside a container with a user ID that's different from the one that initially created the container, similar to what we saw for rootless containers. Running the container's processes as a non-root user can be helpful for security purposes. For example, using an unprivileged user in a container could limit the attack surface inside and outside that container.

By default, a Dockerfile and Containerfile may set the default user as root (that is, UID=0). To avoid this, we can leverage the USER instruction in those build files – for example, USER 1001 – to instruct Buildah or other container build tools to build and run the container image using that particular user (with UID 1001).

If we want to force a specific UID, we need to adjust the permissions of any file, folder, or mount we plan to use with our running containers.

Now, let's learn how to adapt an existing image so that it can be run with a standard user.

We can leverage some prebuilt images on DockerHub or pick one of the official Nginx container images. First, we need to create a basic nginx configuration file:

```
$ cat hello-podman.conf
server {
    listen 80;

    location / {
        default_type text/plain;
        expires -1;
        return 200 'Hello Podman user!\nServer address:
$server_addr:$server_port\n';
    }
}
```

The nginx configuration file is really simple: we define the listening port (80) and the content message to return once a request arrives on the server.

Then, we can create a simple Dockerfile to leverage one of the official Nginx container images:

```
$ cat Dockerfile
FROM docker.io/library/nginx:mainline-alpine
RUN rm /etc/nginx/conf.d/*
ADD hello-podman.conf /etc/nginx/conf.d/
```

The Dockerfile contains three instructions:

- FROM: For selecting the official Nginx image
- RUN: For cleaning the configuration directory from any default config example
- ADD: For copying the configuration file we just created

Now, let's build the container image with Buildah:

```
$ buildah bud -t nginx-root:latest -f .
STEP 1/3: FROM docker.io/library/nginx:mainline-alpine
STEP 2/3: RUN rm /etc/nginx/conf.d/*
STEP 3/3: ADD hello-podman.conf /etc/nginx/conf.d/
COMMIT nginx-root:latest
Getting image source signatures
Copying blob 8d3ac3489996 done
. . .
Copying config 21c5f7d8d7 done
Writing manifest to image destination
Storing signatures
--> 21c5f7d8d70
Successfully tagged localhost/nginx-root:latest
21c5f7d8d709e7cfdf764a14fd6e95fb4611b2cde52b57aa46d43262a
6489f41
```

Once you've built the image, name it nginx-root. Now, we are ready to run
our container:

```
$ podman run --name myrootnginx -p 127.0.0.1::80 -d nginx-root
364ec7f5979a5059ba841715484b7238db3313c78c5c577629364aa46b6d
9bdc
```

Here, we used the –p option to publish the port and make it reachable from the host. Let's
find out what local port has been chosen, randomly, in the host system:

```
$ podman port myrootnginx 80
127.0.0.1:38029
```

Finally, let's call our containerized web server:

```
$ curl localhost:38029
Hello Podman user!
Server address: 10.0.2.100:80
```

The container is finally running, but what user is using our container? Let's find out:

```
$ podman ps | grep root
364ec7f5979a  localhost/nginx-root:latest   nginx -g daemon
o...  55 minutes ago  Up 55 minutes ago  0.0.0.0:38029->80/tcp
myrootnginx
$ podman exec 364ec7f5979a id
uid=0(root) gid=0(root)
```

As expected, the container is running as root!

Now, let's make a few edits to change the user. First, we need to change the listening port in the Nginx server configuration:

```
$ cat hello-podman.conf
server {
    listen 8080;

    location / {
        default_type text/plain;
        expires -1;
        return 200 'Hello Podman user!\nServer address:
$server_addr:$server_port\n';
    }
}
```

Here, we replaced the listening port (80) with 8080; we cannot use a port that's below 1024 with unprivileged users.

Then, we need to edit our Dockerfile:

```
$ cat Dockerfile
FROM docker.io/library/nginx:mainline-alpine
RUN rm /etc/nginx/conf.d/*
```

```
ADD hello-podman.conf /etc/nginx/conf.d/
```

```
RUN chmod -R a+w /var/cache/nginx/ \
        && touch /var/run/nginx.pid \
        && chmod a+w /var/run/nginx.pid
EXPOSE 8080
USER nginx
```

As you can see, we fixed the permissions for the main file and folder on the Nginx server, exposed the new 8080 port, and set the default user to an Nginx one.

Now, we are ready to build a brand-new container image. Let's call it nginx-user:

```
$ buildah bud -t nginx-user:latest -f .
STEP 1/6: FROM docker.io/library/nginx:mainline-alpine
STEP 2/6: RUN rm /etc/nginx/conf.d/*
STEP 3/6: ADD hello-podman.conf /etc/nginx/conf.d/
STEP 4/6: RUN chmod -R a+w /var/cache/nginx/         && touch /
var/run/nginx.pid         && chmod a+w /var/run/nginx.pid
STEP 5/6: EXPOSE 8080
STEP 6/6: USER nginx
COMMIT nginx-user:latest
Getting image source signatures
Copying blob 8d3ac3489996 done
...
Copying config 7628852470 done
Writing manifest to image destination
Storing signatures
--> 76288524704
Successfully tagged localhost/nginx-user:latest
762885247041fd233c7b66029020c4da8e1e254288e1443b356cbee4d73
adf3e
```

Now, we can run the container:

```
$ podman run --name myusernginx -p 127.0.0.1::8080 -d nginx-
user
299e0fb727f339d87dd7ea67eac419905b10e36181dc1ca7e35dc7d0a
9316243
```

Find the associated random host port and check whether the web server is working:

```
$ podman port myusernginx 8080
127.0.0.1:42209
$ curl 127.0.0.1:42209
Hello Podman user!
Server address: 10.0.2.100:8080
```

Finally, let's see whether we changed the user that's running the target process in our container:

```
$ podman ps | grep user
299e0fb727f3  localhost/nginx-user:latest  nginx -g daemon o...
38 minutes ago  Up 38 minutes ago  127.0.0.1:42209->8080/tcp
myusernginx
$ podman exec 299e0fb727f3 id
uid=101(nginx) gid=101(nginx) groups=101(nginx)
```

As you can see, our container is running as an unprivileged user, which is what we wanted.

If you want to look at a ready-to-use example of this, please go to this book's GitHub repository: `https://github.com/PacktPublishing/Podman-for-DevOps`.

Unfortunately, security is not all about permissions and users – we also need to take care of the base image and its source and check container image signatures. We'll learn about this in the next section.

Signing our container images

When we're dealing with images that have been pulled from external registries, we will have some security concerns related to the potential attack tactics that have been conducted on the containers (see [1] in the *Further reading* section), especially masquerading techniques, which help the attacker manipulate image components to make them appear legitimate. This could also happen due to a **man-in-the-middle** (**MITM**) attack being conducted by an attacker over the wire.

To prevent certain kinds of attacks while you're managing containers, the best solution is to use a detached image signature to trust the image provider and guarantee its reliability.

GNU Privacy Guard (**GPG**) is a free implementation of the OpenPGP standard and can be used, together with Podman, to sign images and check their valid signatures once they've been pulled.

When an image is pulled, Podman can verify the validity of the signatures and reject images without valid signatures.

Now, let's learn how to implement a basic image signature workflow.

Signing images with GPG and Podman

In this section, we will create a basic GPG key pair and configure Podman to push and sign the image while storing the signature in a staging store. For the sake of clarity, we will run a registry using the basic Docker Registry V2 container image without any customization.

Before testing the image pull and signature validation workflow, we will expose a basic web server to publish the detached signature.

To create image signatures with GPG, we need to create a valid GPG key pair or use an existing one. For this reason, we will provide a short recap on GPG key pairs to help you understand how image signatures work.

A key pair is composed of a private key and a public key. The public key can be shared universally, while the private key is kept private and never shared with anybody. The public key that belongs to the receiver can be used by the sender of a file or message to sign it. In this way, only the owner of the private key (that is, the receiver) will be able to decrypt the message.

We can easily translate this concept into container images: the image owner that pushes it to the remote registry can sign it using a key pair and store the detached signature on a store (from now on, *sigstore*) that is publicly accessible by users. Here, the signature is separated by the image itself – the registry will store the image blobs while the sigstore will hold and expose the image signatures.

Users who are pulling the image will be able to validate the image signature using the previously shared public key.

Now, let's go back to creating the GPG key pair. We are going to create a simple one with the following command:

```
$ gpg --full-gen-key
```

The preceding command will ask you a series of questions and provide a passphrase to help you generate the key pair. By default, this will be stored in the $HOME/.gnupg folder.

The key pair's output should be similar to the following:

```
$ gpg --list-keys
/home/vagrant/.gnupg/pubring.kbx
pub    rsa3072 2022-01-05 [SC]
       2EA4850C32D29DA22B7659FEC38D92C0F18764AC
uid            [ultimate] Foo Bar foobar@example.com
sub    rsa3072 2022-01-05 [E]
```

It is also possible to export generated key pairs. The following command will export the public key to a file:

```
$ gpg --armor --export foobar@example.com > pubkey.pem
```

This command will be useful later when we define the image signature's verification.

The following command can be used to export the private key:

```
$ gpg --armor \
  --export-secret-keys foobar@example.com > privkey.pem
```

In both examples, the --armor option has been used to export the keys in **Privacy Enhanced Mail (PEM)** format.

Once the key pair has been generated, we can create a basic registry that will host our container images. To do so, we will reuse the basic example from *Chapter 9, Pushing Images to a Container Registry*, and run the following command as root:

```
# mkdir /var/lib/registry
# podman run -d \
  --name local_registry \
  -p 5000:5000 \
  -v /var/lib/registry:/var/lib/registry:z \
  --restart=always registry:2
```

We now have a local registry without authentication that can be used to push the test images. As we mentioned previously, the registry is unaware of the image's detached signature.

Podman must be able to write signatures on a staging sigstore. There is already a default configuration in the /etc/containers/registries.d/default.yaml file, which looks as follows:

```
default-docker:
#  sigstore: file:///var/lib/containers/sigstore
   sigstore-staging: file:///var/lib/containers/sigstore
```

The sigstore-staging path is where Podman writes image signatures; it must write them to a writable folder. It is possible to customize this path or keep the default configuration as-is.

If we want to create multiple user-related sigstores, we can create the $HOME/.config/containers/registries.d/default.yaml files and define a custom sigstore-staging path in the user's home directory, following the same syntax that was shown in the previous example. This will allow users to run Podman in rootless mode and successfully write to their sigstore.

> **Important**
>
> It is not a good idea to share the default sigstore across all users by allowing general write permissions. This is because every user in the host would have write access to the existing signatures.

Since we want to use the default sigstore while still using the default GPG key pair under the user's home directory, we will run Podman by elevating privileges with sudo, an exception to the approach that this book follows.

The following example shows the Dockerfile of a custom httpd image that's been built using UBI 8:

Chapter11/image_signature/Dockerfile

```
FROM registry.access.redhat.com/ubi8
# Update image and install httpd
RUN yum install -y httpd && yum clean all -y
# Expose the default httpd port 80
EXPOSE 80
# Run the httpd
CMD ["/usr/sbin/httpd", "-DFOREGROUND"]
```

To build the image, we can run the following command:

```
$ cd Chapter11/image_signature
$ sudo podman build -t custom_httpd .
```

Now, we can tag the image with the local registry name:

```
$ sudo podman tag custom_httpd localhost:5000/custom_httpd
```

Finally, it's time to push the image on the temporary registry and sign it using the generated key pair. The --sign-by option allows users to pass a valid key pair that's been identified by the user's email:

```
$ sudo GNUPGHOME=$HOME/.gnupg podman \
    push --tls-verify=false \
    --sign-by foobar@example.com \
    localhost:5000/custom_httpd
Getting image source signatures
Copying blob 3ba8c926eef9 done
Copying blob a59107c02e1f done
Copying blob 352ba846236b done
Copying config 569b015109 done
Writing manifest to image destination
Signing manifest
Storing signatures
```

The preceding code successfully pushed the image blobs to the registry and stored the image signature. Notice the GNUPGHOME variable, which was passed at the beginning of the command to define the GPG keystore path that's accessed by Podman.

> **Warning**
> The --sign-by option is not supported on the remote Podman client.

To verify that the image has been signed correctly and that its signature is being saved in the sigstore, we can check the content of /var/lib/containers/sigstore:

```
$ ls -al /var/lib/containers/sigstore/
drwxr-xr-x. 6 root     root     4096 Jan  5 18:58 .
drwxr-xr-x. 5 root     root     4096 Jan  5 13:29 ..
```

```
drwxr-xr-x. 2 root     root     4096 Jan  5 18:58 'custom_httpd@
sha256=573c1eb93857c0169a606f1820271b143ac5073456f844255c3c7a9e
308bf639'
```

As you will see, the new directory contains the image signature file:

```
$ ls -al /var/lib/containers/sigstore/'custom_httpd@
sha256=573c1eb93857c0169a606f1820271b143ac5073456f844255c3c7a9
e308bf639'
total 12
drwxr-xr-x. 2 root root 4096 Jan  5 18:58 .
drwxr-xr-x. 6 root root 4096 Jan  5 18:58 ..
-rw-r--r--. 1 root root  730 Jan  5 18:58 signature-1
```

With that, we have successfully pushed and signed the image, making it more secure for future use. Now, let's learn how to configure Podman to retrieve signed images.

Configuring Podman to pull signed images

To successfully pull a signed image, Podman must be able to retrieve the signature from a sigstore and have access to a public key to verify the signature.

Here, we are dealing with detached signatures, and we have already learned that the registry doesn't hold any information about image signatures. For this reason, we need to make them available to users with a publicly accessible sigstore: a web server (Nginx, Apache httpd, and so on) will be a good fit.

Since the signing host will be the same as the one used to test image pulls, we will run an Apache httpd server that exposes the sigstore staging folder as the server document root. In a real-life scenario, we would move the signatures to a dedicated web server.

For this example, we will use the standard docker.io/library/httpd image and run the container with root privileges to grant access to the sigstore folder:

```
# podman run -d -p 8080:80 \
  --name sigstore_server \
  -v /var/lib/containers/sigstore:/usr/local/apache2/htdocs:z \
  docker.io/library/httpd
```

The web server is now available at http://localhost:8080 and can be used by Podman to retrieve image signatures.

Now, let's configure Podman for image pulling. First, we must configure the default image sigstore. We have already defined the staging sigstore that's used by Podman to write a signature, so now, we need to define the sigstore that's used to read image signatures.

To do so, we must edit the `/etc/containers/registries.d/default.yaml` file one more time and add a reference to the default sigstore web server that's running on `http://localhost:8080`:

```
default-docker:
  sigstore: http://localhost:8080
  sigstore-staging: file:///var/lib/containers/sigstore
```

The preceding code configures the sigstore that's used by Podman for all images. However, it is possible to add more sigstores for specific registries by populating the *docker* field of the file. The following code configures the sigstore for the public Red Hat registry:

```
docker:
  registry.access.redhat.com:
    sigstore: https://access.redhat.com/webassets/docker/
content/sigstore
```

Before we test the image pulls, we must implement the public key that's used by Podman to verify the signatures. This public key must be stored in the host that pulls the image and belongs to the key pair that's used to sign the image.

The configuration file that's used to define the public key's path is `/etc/containers/policy.json`.

The following code shows the `/etc/containers/policy.json` file with a custom configuration for the registry's `localhost:5000`:

```
{
    "default": [
        {
            "type": "insecureAcceptAnything"
        }
    ],
    "transports": {
        "docker": {
            "localhost:5000": [
                {
```

```
                    "type": "signedBy",
                    "keyType": "GPGKeys",
                    "keyPath": "/tmp/pubkey.gpg"
                }
            ]
        },
        "docker-daemon": {
            "": [
                {
                    "type": "insecureAcceptAnything"
                }
            ]
        }
    }
}
```

To verify the signatures of images that have been pulled from `localhost:5000`, we can use a public key that's stored in the path defined by the `keyPath` field. The public key must exist in the defined path and be readable by Podman.

If we need to extract the public key from the example key pair that was generated at the beginning of this section, we can use the following GPG command:

```
$ gpg --armor --export foobar@example.com > /tmp/pubkey.gpg
```

Now, we are ready to test the image pull and verify its signature:

```
$ podman pull --tls-verify=false localhost:5000/custom_httpd
Getting image source signatures
Checking if image destination supports signatures
Copying blob 23fdb56daf15 skipped: already exists
Copying blob d4f13fad8263 skipped: already exists
Copying blob 96b0fdd0552f done
Copying config 569b015109 done
Writing manifest to image destination
Storing signatures
569b015109d457ae5fabb969fd0dc3cce10a3e6683ab60dc10505fc2d68
e769f
```

The image was successfully pulled into the local store after signature verification using the public key provided.

Now, let's see how Podman behaves when it is unable to correctly verify the signature.

Testing signature verification failures

What if we make the sigstore unavailable? Will Podman still succeed in pulling the image if it's unable to verify the signature? Let's try to stop the local httpd server that exposes the sigstore:

```
# podman stop sigstore_server
```

Before pulling it again, let's remove the previously cached image to avoid false positives:

```
$ podman rmi localhost:5000/custom_httpd
```

Now, we can try to pull the image again:

```
$ podman pull --tls-verify=false localhost:5000/custom_httpd
Trying to pull localhost:5000/custom_httpd:latest...
WARN[0000] failed, retrying in 1s ... (1/3). Error: Source
image rejected: Get "http://localhost:8080/custom_httpd@
sha256=573c1eb93857c0169a606f1820271b143ac5073456f844255c3c7a9
e308bf639/signature-1": dial tcp [::1]:8080: connect:
connection refused
WARN[0001] failed, retrying in 1s ... (2/3). Error: Source
image rejected: Get "http://localhost:8080/custom_httpd@
sha256=573c1eb93857c0169a606f1820271b143ac5073456f844255c3c7a9
e308bf639/signature-1": dial tcp [::1]:8080: connect:
connection refused
WARN[0002] failed, retrying in 1s ... (3/3). Error: Source
image rejected: Get "http://localhost:8080/custom_httpd@
sha256=573c1eb93857c0169a606f1820271b143ac5073456f844255c3c7a9
e308bf639/signature-1": dial tcp [::1]:8080: connect:
connection refused
Error: Source image rejected: Get "http://localhost:8080/
custom_httpd@sha256=573c1eb93857c0169a606f1820271b143ac5073456f
844255c3c7a9e308bf639/signature-1": dial tcp [::1]:8080:
connect: connection refused
```

The preceding error demonstrates that Podman is trying to connect to the web server that exposes the sigstore and failed. This error blocked the whole image pull process.

A different error occurs when the public key we use to verify the signature is not valid or not part of the key pair that was used to sign the image. To test this, let's replace the public key with another one from a different key pair – in this example, the public Fedora 34 RPM-GPG key, which has been taken from the /etc/pki/rpm-gpg directory (any other public key can be used):

```
$ mv /tmp/pubkey.gpg /tmp/pubkey.gpg.bak
$ cp /etc/pki/rpm-gpg/RPM-GPG-KEY-fedora-34-x86_64 \
     /tmp/pubkey.gpg
```

The previously stopped httpd server must be restarted; we want to make the signatures available and focus on the wrong public key error:

```
# podman start sigstore_server
```

Now, we can pull the image again and inspect the generated errors:

```
$ podman pull --tls-verify=false localhost:5000/custom_httpd
Trying to pull localhost:5000/custom_httpd:latest...
Error: Source image rejected: Invalid GPG
signature: gpgme.Signature{Summary:128,
Fingerprint:"2EA4850C32D29DA22B7659FEC38D92C0F18764AC",
Status:gpgme.Error{err:0x9}, Timestamp:time.Time{wall:0x0,
ext:63777026489, loc:(*time.Location)(0x560e17e5d680)},
ExpTimestamp:time.Time{wall:0x0, ext:62135596800, loc:(*time.
Location)(0x560e17e5d680)}, WrongKeyUsage:false, PKATrust:0x0,
ChainModel:false, Validity:0, ValidityReason:error(nil),
PubkeyAlgo:1, HashAlgo:8}
```

Here, Podman generates an error that's caused by an invalid GPG signature, which is correct since the public key that's being used does not belong to the correct key pair.

> **Important**
> Do not forget to restore the valid public key before proceeding with the following examples.

Podman can manage multiple registries and sigstores, and also offers dedicated commands to help you customize security policies, as we'll see in the next subsection.

Managing keys with Podman image trust commands

It is possible to edit the `/etc/containers/policy.json` file and modify its JSON objects to add or remove configurations for dedicated registries. However, manual editing can be prone to errors and hard to automate.

Alternatively, we can use the `podman image trust` command to dump or modify the current configuration.

The following code shows how to print the current configuration with the `podman image trust show` command:

```
$
default          accept
localhost:5000   signedBy                    foobar@example.com
http://localhost:8080
                 insecureAcceptAnything
http://localhost:8080
```

It is also possible to configure new trusts. For example, we can add the Red Hat public GPG key to check the signature of UBI images.

First, we need to download the Red Hat public key:

```
$ sudo wget -O /etc/pki/rpm-gpg/RPM-GPG-KEY-redhat \
  https://www.redhat.com/security/data/fd431d51.txt
```

> **Note**
> Red Hat's product signing keys, including the one that was used in this example, can be found at `https://access.redhat.com/security/team/key`.

After downloading the key, we must configure the image trust for UBI 8 images that have been pulled from *registry.access.redhat.com* using the `podman image trust set` command:

```
$ sudo podman image trust set -f /etc/pki/rpm-gpg/RPM-GPG-KEY-redhat registry.access.redhat.com/ubi8
```

After running the preceding command, the `/etc/containers/policy.json` file will change, as follows:

```json
{
    "default": [
        {
            "type": "insecureAcceptAnything"
        }
    ],
    "transports": {
        "docker": {
            "localhost:5000": [
                {
                    "type": "signedBy",
                    "keyType": "GPGKeys",
                    "keyPath": "/tmp/pubkey.gpg"
                }
            ],
            "registry.access.redhat.com/ubi8": [
                {
                    "type": "signedBy",
                    "keyType": "GPGKeys",
                    "keyPath": "/etc/pki/rpm-gpg/RPM-GPG-KEY-redhat"
                }
            ]
        },
        "docker-daemon": {
            "": [
                {
                    "type": "insecureAcceptAnything"
                }
            ]
        }
    }
}
```

Note that the entry that's related to *registry.access.redhat.com/ubi8* and the public key that was used to verify the image signatures have been added to the file.

To complete the configuration, we need to add the Red Hat sigstore configuration to the `/etc/containers/registries.d/default.yaml` configuration file:

```
docker:
  registry.access.redhat.com:
    sigstore: https://access.redhat.com/webassets/docker/
content/sigstore
```

> **Tip**
>
> It is possible to create custom registry configuration files for different providers in the `/etc/containers/registries.d` folder. For example, the preceding example could be defined in a dedicated `/etc/containers/registries.d/redhat.yaml` file. This allows you to easily maintain and version registry sigstore configurations.

From now on, every time a UBI8 image is pulled from *registry.access.redhat.com*, its signature will be pulled from the Red Hat sigstore and validated using the provided public key.

So far, we have looked at examples of managing keys concerning Podman, but it is also possible to manage signature verification with Skopeo. In the next subsection, we are going to look at some basic examples.

Managing signatures with Skopeo

We can verify an image signature using Skopeo when we're pulling an image from a valid transport.

The following example uses the `skopeo copy` command to pull the image from our registry to the local store. This command has the same effects as using a `podman pull` command but allows more control over the source and destination transports:

```
$ skopeo copy --src-tls-verify=false \
  docker://localhost:5000/custom_httpd \
  containers-storage:localhost:5000/custom_httpd
```

Skopeo does not need any further configuration since the previously modified configuration files already define the sigstore and public key path.

We can also use Skopeo to sign an image before copying it to a transport:

```
$ sudo GNUPGHOME=$HOME/.gnupg skopeo copy \
    --dest-tls-verify=false \
    --sign-by foobar@example.com \
    containers-storage:localhost:5000/custom_httpd \
    docker://localhost:5000/custom_httpd
```

Once again, the configuration files that are used by Podman are still valid for Skopeo, which uses the same sigstore to write the signatures and the same GPG store to retrieve the key that's used to generate the signature.

In this section, we learned how to verify image signatures and avoid potential MITM attacks. In the next section, we'll shift focus and learn how to execute the container runtime by customizing Linux kernel capabilities.

Customizing Linux kernel capabilities

Capabilities are features that were introduced in Linux kernel 2.2 with the purpose of splitting elevated privileges into single units that can be arbitrarily assigned to a process or thread.

Instead of running a process as a fully privileged instance with effective UID 0, we can assign a limited subset of specific capabilities to an unprivileged process. By providing more granular control over the security context of the process's execution, this approach helps mitigate potential attack tactics.

Before we discuss the capabilities of containers, let's recap on how they work in a Linux system so that we understand their inner logic.

Capabilities quickstart guide

Capabilities are associated with the file executables using extended attributes (see man xattr) and are automatically inherited by the process that's executed with an execve() system call.

The list of available capabilities is quite large and still growing; it includes very specific actions that can be performed by a thread. Some basic examples are as follows:

- **CAP_CHOWN**: This capability allows a thread to modify a file's UID and GID.
- **CAP_KILL:** This capability allows you to bypass the permission checks to send a signal to a process.

- **CAP_MKNOD**: This capability allows you to create a special file with the `mknod()` syscall.

- **CAP_NET_ADMIN**: This capability allows you to operate various privileged actions on the system's network configuration, including changing the interface configuration, enabling/disabling promiscuous mode for an interface, editing routing tables, and enabling/disabling multicasting.

- **CAP_NET_RAW**: This capability allows a thread to use RAW and PACKET sockets. This capability can be used by programs such as ping to send ICMP packets without the need for elevated privileges.

- **CAP_SYS_CHROOT**: This capability allows you to use the `chroot()` syscall and change mount namespaces with the `setns()` syscall.

- **CAP_DAC_OVERRIDE**: This capability allows you to bypass **discretionary access control (DAC)** checks for file read, write, and execution.

For more details and an extensive list of available capabilities, see the relevant man page (`man capabilities`).

To assign a capability to an executable, we can use the `setcap` command, as shown in the following example, where `CAP_NET_ADMIN` and `CAP_NET_RAW` are being permitted in the `/usr/bin/ping` executable:

```
$ sudo setcap 'cap_net_admin,cap_net_raw+p' /usr/bin/ping
```

The '+*p*' flag in the preceding command indicates that the capabilities have been set to *Permitted*.

To inspect the capabilities of a file, we can use the `getcap` command:

```
$ getcap /usr/bin/ping
/usr/bin/ping cap_net_admin,cap_net_raw=p
```

See `man getcap` and `man setcap` for more details about these utilities.

We can inspect the active capabilities of a running process by looking at the `/proc/<PID>/status` file. In the following code, we are launching a `ping` command after setting the `CAP_NET_ADMIN` and `CAP_NET_RAW` capabilities. We want to launch the process in the background and check its current capabilities:

```
$ ping example.com > /dev/null 2>&1 &
$ grep 'Cap.*' /proc/$(pgrep ping)/status
CapInh: 0000000000000000
```

```
CapPrm:  0000000000003000
CapEff:  0000000000000000
CapBnd:  000000ffffffffff
CapAmb:  0000000000000000
```

Here, we are interested in evaluating the bitmap in the `CapPrm` field, which represents the permitted capabilities. To get a user-friendly value, we can use the `capsh` command to decode the bitmap hex value:

```
$ capsh --decode=0000000000003000
0x0000000000003000=cap_net_admin,cap_net_raw
```

The result is similar to the output of the `getcap` command in the `/usr/bin/ping` file, demonstrating that executing the command propagated the file's permitted capabilities to its process instance.

For a full list of the constants that were used to set the bitmaps, as well as their capabilities, see the following kernel header file: `https://github.com/torvalds/linux/blob/master/include/uapi/linux/capability.h`.

> **Tip**
>
> Distributions such as RHEL and CentOS use the preceding configuration to allow the ping to send ICMP packets with access from all users without them being executed as privileged processes with *setuid 0*. This is an insecure approach where an attacker could leverage a vulnerability or bug in the executable to escalate privileges and gain control of the system.
>
> Fedora introduced a new and more secure approach in version 31 that's based on using the `net.ipv4.ping_group_range` Linux kernel parameter. By setting an extensive range that covers all system groups, this parameter allows users to send ICMP packets without the need to enable the CAP_NET_ADMIN and CAP_NET_RAW capabilities.
>
> For more details, see the following wiki page from the Fedora Project: `https://fedoraproject.org/wiki/Changes/EnableSysctlPingGroupRange`.

Now that we've provided a high-level description of the Linux kernel's capabilities, let's learn how they are applied to containers.

Capabilities in containers

Capabilities can be applied inside containers to allow targeted actions to take place. By default, Podman runs containers using a set of Linux kernel capabilities that are defined in the `/usr/share/containers/containers.conf` file. At the time of writing, the following capabilities are enabled inside this file:

```
default_capabilities = [
    "CHOWN",
    "DAC_OVERRIDE",
    "FOWNER",
    "FSETID",
    "KILL",
    "NET_BIND_SERVICE",
    "SETFCAP",
    "SETGID",
    "SETPCAP",
    "SETUID",
    "SYS_CHROOT"
]
```

We can run a simple test to verify that those capabilities have been effectively applied to a process running inside a container. For this test, we will use the official Nginx image:

```
$ podman run -d --name cap_test docker.io/library/nginx
$ podman exec -it cap_test sh -c 'grep Cap /proc/1/status'
CapInh: 00000000800405fb
CapPrm: 00000000800405fb
CapEff: 00000000800405fb
CapBnd: 00000000800405fb
CapAmb: 0000000000000000
```

Here, we have extracted the current capabilities from the parent Nginx process (running with PID 1 inside the container). Now, we can check the bitmap with the `capsh` utility:

```
$ capsh --decode=00000000800405fb
0x00000000800405fb=cap_chown,cap_dac_override,cap_fowner,cap_
fsetid,cap_kill,cap_setgid,cap_setuid,cap_setpcap,cap_net_bind_
service,cap_sys_chroot,cap_setfcap
```

The preceding list of capabilities is the same as the list that was defined in the default Podman configuration. Note that the capabilities are applied in both rootless and rootful mode.

> **Note**
>
> If you're curious, the capabilities for the containerized process(es) are set up by the container runtime, which is either `runc` or `crun`, based on the distribution.

Now that we know how capabilities are configured and applied inside containers, let's learn how to customize a container's capabilities.

Customizing a container's capabilities

We can add or drop capabilities either at runtime or statically.

To statically change the default capabilities, we can simply edit the *default_capabilities* field in the `/usr/share/containers/containers.conf` file and add or remove them according to our desired results.

To modify capabilities at runtime, we can use the `-cap-add` and `-cap-drop` options, both of which are provided by the `podman run` command.

The following code removes the `CAP_DAC_OVERRIDE` capability from a container:

```
$ podman run -d --name cap_test2 --cap-drop=DAC_OVERRIDE
docker.io/library/nginx
```

If we look at the capability bitmaps again, we will see that they were updated accordingly:

```
$ podman exec cap_test2 sh -c 'grep Cap /proc/1/status'
CapInh: 00000000800405f9
CapPrm: 00000000800405f9
CapEff: 00000000800405f9
CapBnd: 00000000800405f9
CapAmb: 0000000000000000
$ capsh --decode=00000000800405f9
0x00000000800405f9=cap_chown,cap_fowner,cap_fsetid,cap_
kill,cap_setgid,cap_setuid,cap_setpcap,cap_net_bind_
service,cap_sys_chroot,cap_setfcap
```

It is possible to pass the --cap-add and --cap-drop options multiple times:

```
$ podman run -d --name cap_test3 \
    --cap-drop=KILL \
    --cap-drop=DAC_OVERRIDE \
    --cap-add=NET_RAW \
    --cap-add=NET_ADMIN \
    docker.io/library/nginx
```

When we're dealing with capabilities, we must be careful while dropping a default capability. The following code shows an error in the Nginx container when dropping the CAP_CHOWN capability:

```
$ podman run --name cap_test4 \
    --cap-drop=CHOWN \
    docker.io/library/nginx
/docker-entrypoint.sh: /docker-entrypoint.d/ is not empty, will attempt to perform configuration
/docker-entrypoint.sh: Looking for shell scripts in /docker-entrypoint.d/
/docker-entrypoint.sh: Launching /docker-entrypoint.d/10-listen-on-ipv6-by-default.sh
10-listen-on-ipv6-by-default.sh: info: Getting the checksum of /etc/nginx/conf.d/default.conf
10-listen-on-ipv6-by-default.sh: info: Enabled listen on IPv6 in /etc/nginx/conf.d/default.conf
/docker-entrypoint.sh: Launching /docker-entrypoint.d/20-envsubst-on-templates.sh
/docker-entrypoint.sh: Launching /docker-entrypoint.d/30-tune-worker-processes.sh
/docker-entrypoint.sh: Configuration complete; ready for start up
2022/01/06 23:19:39 [emerg] 1#1: chown("/var/cache/nginx/client_temp", 101) failed (1: Operation not permitted)
nginx: [emerg] chown("/var/cache/nginx/client_temp", 101) failed (1: Operation not permitted)
```

Here, the container fails. From the output, we can see that the Nginx process was unable to show the /var/cache/nginx/client_temp directory. This is a direct consequence of the CAP_CHOWN capability being removed.

Not all capabilities can be applied to rootless containers. For example, if we try to apply the CAP_MKNOD capability to a rootless container, any attempt to create a special file inside a rootless container won't be allowed by the kernel:

```
$ podman run -it --cap-add=MKNOD \
  docker.io/library/busybox /bin/sh
/ # mkdir -p /test/dev
/ # mknod -m 666 /test/dev/urandom c 1 8
mknod: /test/dev/urandom: Operation not permitted
```

Instead, if we run the container with elevated root privileges, the capability can be assigned successfully:

```
# podman run -it --cap-add=MKNOD \
  docker.io/library/busybox /bin/sh
/ # mkdir -p /test/dev
/ # mknod -m 666 /test/dev/urandom c 1 8
/ # stat /test/dev/urandom
File: /test/dev/urandom
  Size: 0          Blocks: 0          IO Block: 4096
character special file
Device: 31h/49d Inode: 530019       Links: 1      Device type:
1,8
Access: (0666/crw-rw-rw-)  Uid: (    0/    root)  Gid: (    0/
root)
Access: 2022-01-06 23:50:06.056650747 +0000
Modify: 2022-01-06 23:50:06.056650747 +0000
Change: 2022-01-06 23:50:06.056650747 +0000
```

> **Note**
> Generally, adding capabilities to containers implies enlarging the potential attack surface that a malicious attacker could use. If it's not necessary, it is a good practice to keep the default capabilities and drop the unwanted ones once the potential side effects have been analyzed.

In this section, we learned how to manage capabilities inside containers. However, capabilities are not the only security aspect to consider when you're securing containers. SELinux, as we will learn in the next section, has a crucial role in guaranteeing container isolation.

SELinux interaction with containers

In this section, we will discuss SELinux policies and introduce **Udica**, a tool that's used to generate SELinux profiles for containers.

SELinux works directly in kernel space and manages object isolation while following a least-privilege model that contains a series of **policies** that can handle enforcing or exceptions. To define these objects, SELinux uses labels that define **types**. By default, SELinux works in **Enforcing** mode, denying access to resources with a series of exceptions defined by policies. To disable Enforcing mode, SELinux can be put in **Permissive** mode, where violations are only audited, without them being blocked.

> **Security Alert**
>
> As we mentioned previously, switching SELinux to Permissive mode or completely disabling it is *not a good practice* as it opens you up to potential security threats. Instead of doing that, users should create custom policies to manage the necessary exceptions.

By default, SELinux uses a **targeted** policy type, which tries to target and confine specific object types (processes, files, devices, and so on) using a set of predefined policies.

SELinux allows different kinds of access control. They can be summarized as follows:

- **Type Enforcement** (TE): This controls access to resources according to process and file types. This is the main use case of SELinux access control.

- **Role-Based Access Control** (RBAC): This controls access to resources using SELinux users (which can be mapped to real system users) and their associated SELinux roles.

- **Multi-Level Security** (MLS): This grants all processes with the same sensitivity level read/write access to the resources.

- **Multi-Category Security** (MCS): This controls access using **categories**, which are plain text labels that are applied to resources. Categories are used to create compartments of objects, along with the other SELinux labels. Only processes that belong to the same category can access a given resource. In *Chapter 5*, *Implementing Storage for the Container's Data*, we discussed MCS and how we can map categories to resources that have been accessed by containers.

With Type Enforcement, the system files receive labels called **types**, while processes receive labels called **domains**. A process that belongs to a domain can be allowed to access a file that belongs to a given type, and this access can be audited by SELinux.

For example, according to SELinux, the Apache `httpd` process, which is labeled with the `httpd_t` domain, can access files or directories with `httpd_sys_content_t` labels.

An SELinux-type policy is based on the following pattern:

```
POLICY DOMAIN TYPE:CLASS OPERATION;
```

Here, `POLICY` is the kind of policy (`allow`, `allowxperm`, `auditallow`, `neverallow`, `dontaudit`, and so on), `DOMAIN` is the process domain, `TYPE` is the resource type context, `CLASS` is the object category (for example, `file`, `dir`, `lnk_file`, `chr_file`, `blk_file`, `sock_file`, or `fifo_file`), and `OPERATION` is a list of actions that are handled by the policy (for example, `open`, `read`, `use`, `lock`, `getattr`, or `revc`).

The following example shows a basic `allow` rule:

```
allow myapp_t myapp_log_t:file { read_file_perms append_file_
perms };
```

In this example, the process that's running in the `myapp_t` domain is allowed to access files of the `myapp_log_t` type and perform the `read_file_perms` and `append_file_perms` actions.

SELinux manages policies in a modular fashion, allowing you to dynamically load and unload policy modules without the need to recompile the whole policy set every time. Policies can be loaded and unloaded using the `semodule` utility, as shown in the following example, which shows an example of loading a custom policy:

```
# semodule -i custompolicy.pp
```

The `semodule` utility can also be used to view all the loaded policies:

```
# semodule -l
```

On Fedora, CentOS, RHEL, and derivate distributions, the current binary policy is installed under the `/etc/selinux/targeted/policy` directory in a file named `polixy.XX`, with XX representing the policy version.

On the same distributions, container policies are defined inside the `container-selinux` package, which contains the already compiled SELinux module. The source code of the package is available on GitHub if you wish to look at it in more detail: `https://github.com/containers/container-selinux`.

By looking at the repository's content, we will find the three most important policy source files for developing any module:

- `container.fc`: This file defines the files and directories that are bound to the types defined in the module.

- `container.te`: This file defines the policy rules, attributes, and aliases.

- `container.if`: This file defines the module interface. It contains a set of public macro functions that are exposed by the module.

A process that's running inside a container is labeled with the `container_t` domain. It has read/write access to resources labeled with the `container_file_t` type context and read/execute access to resources labeled with the `container_share_t` type context.

When a container is executed, the `podman` process, as well as the container runtime and the `conmon` process, run with the `container_runtime_t` domain type and are allowed to execute processes that transition only to specific types. Those types are grouped in the `container_domain` attribute and can be inspected with the `seinfo` utility (installed with the `setools-console` package on Fedora), as shown in the following code:

```
$ seinfo -a container_domain -x
Type Attributes: 1
    attribute container_domain;
container_engine_t
container_init_t
container_kvm_t
container_logreader_t
container_t
container_userns_t
spc_t
```

The `container_domain` attribute is declared in the `container.te` source file in the `container-policy` repository using the **attribute** keyword:

```
attribute container_domain;
attribute container_user_domain;
attribute container_net_domain;
```

The preceding attributes are mapped to the `container_t` type using a `typeattribute` declaration:

```
typeattribute container_t container_domain, container_net_
domain, container_user_domain;
```

Using this approach, SELinux guarantees process isolations across containers and between a container and its host. In this way, a process escaping the container (maybe exploiting a vulnerability) cannot access resources on the host or inside other containers.

When a container is created, the image's read-only layers, which form the OverlayFS set of LowerDirs, are labeled with the `container_ro_file_t` type, which prevents the container from writing inside those directories. At the same time, MergedDir, which is the sum of LowerDirs and UpperDir, is writable and labeled as `container_file_t`.

To prove this, let's run a **rootful** container with the `c1` and `c2` MCS categories:

```
# podman run -d --name selinux_test1 --security-opt
label=level:s0:c1,c2 nginx
```

Now, we can find all the files labeled as `container_file_t:s0:c1,c2` under the host filesystem:

```
# find /var/lib/containers/storage/overlay -type f -context
'*container_file_t:s0:c1,c2*' -printf '%-50Z%p\n'
system_u:object_r:container_
file_t:s0:c1,c2        /var/lib/containers/storage/
overlay/4b147975bb5c336b10e71d21c49fe88ddb00d0569b77ddab1
d7737f80056677b/merged/lib/x86_64-linux-gnu/libreadline.so.8.1
system_u:object_r:container_
file_t:s0:c1,c2        /var/lib/containers/storage/
overlay/4b147975bb5c336b10e71d21c49fe88ddb00d0569b77ddab1
d7737f80056677b/merged/lib/x86_64-linux-gnu/libhistory.so.8.1
system_u:object_r:container_
file_t:s0:c1,c2        /var/lib/containers/storage/
overlay/4b147975bb5c336b10e71d21c49fe88ddb00d0569b77ddab1
d7737f80056677b/merged/lib/x86_64-linux-gnu/libexpat.so.1.6.12
system_u:object_r:container_
file_t:s0:c1,c2        /var/lib/containers/storage/
overlay/4b147975bb5c336b10e71d21c49fe88ddb00d0569b77ddab1
d7737f80056677b/merged/lib/udev/rules.d/96-e2scrub.rules
```

```
system_u:object_r:container_
file_t:s0:c1,c2        /var/lib/containers/storage/
overlay/4b147975bb5c336b10e71d21c49fe88ddb00d0569b77ddab1
d7737f80056677b/merged/lib/terminfo/r/rxvt-unicode-256color
```

```
system_u:object_r:container_
file_t:s0:c1,c2        /var/lib/containers/storage/
overlay/4b147975bb5c336b10e71d21c49fe88ddb00d0569b77ddab1
d7737f80056677b/merged/lib/terminfo/r/rxvt-unicode
```

```
[...output omitted...]
```

As expected, the container_file_t label, which is associated with the c1 and c2 categories, is applied to all the files under the MergedDir container.

At the same time, we can demonstrate that the container's LowerDirs are labeled as container_ro_file_t. First, we need to extract the container's LowerDirs list:

```
# podman inspect selinux_test1 \
    --format '{{.GraphDriver.Data.LowerDir}}'
/var/lib/containers/storage/
overlay/9566cbcf1773eac59951c14c52156a6164db1b0d8026d015
e193774029db18a5/diff:/var/lib/containers/storage/
overlay/24de59cced7931bbcc0c4a34d4369c15119a0b8b180f98a0434
fa76a6dfcd490/diff:/var/lib/containers/storage/
overlay/1bb84245b98b7e861c91ed4319972ed3287bdd2ef02a8657c696
a76621854f3b/diff:/var/lib/containers/storage/
overlay/97f26271fef21bda129ac431b5f0faa03ae0b2b50bda6af
969315308fc16735b/diff:/var/lib/containers/storage/
overlay/768ef71c8c91e4df0aa1caf96764ceec999d7eb0aa584
e241246815c1fa85435/diff:/var/lib/containers/storage/
overlay/2edcec3590a4ec7f40cf0743c15d78fb39d8326bc029073
b41ef9727da6c851f/diff
```

The rightmost directory represents the container's lowest layer and is usually the base filesystem tree of the image. Let's inspect the type context of this directory:

```
# ls -alZ /var/lib/containers/storage/
overlay/2edcec3590a4ec7f40
cf0743c15d78fb39d8326bc029073b41ef9727da6c851f/diff
total 84
dr-xr-xr-x. 21 root root unconfined_u:object_r:container_ro_
file_t:s0 4096 Jan  5 23:16 .
drwx------.  6 root root unconfined_u:object_r:container_ro_
file_t:s0 4096 Jan  5 23:16 ..
```

```
drwxr-xr-x.  2 root root unconfined_u:object_r:container_ro_
file_t:s0 4096 Dec 20 00:00 bin

drwxr-xr-x.  2 root root unconfined_u:object_r:container_ro_
file_t:s0 4096 Dec 11 17:25 boot

drwxr-xr-x.  2 root root unconfined_u:object_r:container_ro_
file_t:s0 4096 Dec 20 00:00 dev

drwxr-xr-x. 30 root root unconfined_u:object_r:container_ro_
file_t:s0 4096 Dec 20 00:00 etc

drwxr-xr-x.  2 root root unconfined_u:object_r:container_ro_
file_t:s0 4096 Dec 11 17:25 home

drwxr-xr-x.  8 root root unconfined_u:object_r:container_ro_
file_t:s0 4096 Dec 20 00:00 lib
[...omitted output...]
```

The preceding output also shows another interesting aspect: since the LowerDir layers are shared across multiple containers that use the same image, we won't find any MCS categories that have been applied here.

Containers do not have read/write access to files or directories that are not labeled as container_file_t. Previously, we saw that it is possible to relabel those files by applying the :z suffix to mounted volumes or by manually relabeling them in advance before running the containers.

However, relabeling crucial directories such as /home or /var/logs is a very bad idea since many other non-containerized processes won't be able to access them anymore.

The only solution is to manually create custom policies that override the default behavior. However, this is too complex to manage in everyday use and production environments.

Luckily, we can solve this limitation with a tool that generates custom SELinux security profiles for our containers: **Udica**.

Introducing Udica

Udica is an open source project (https://github.com/containers/udica) that was created by Lukas Vrabec, SELinux evangelist and team leader of the SELinux and Security Special Projects engineering teams at Red Hat.

Udica aims to overcome the rigid policy limitations that were described previously by generating SELinux profiles for containers and allowing them to access resources that would normally be prevented with the common container_t domain.

To install Udica on Fedora, simply run the following command:

```
$ sudo dnf install -y udica setools-console container-selinux
```

On other distributions, Udica can be installed from its source by running the following commands:

```
$ sudo dnf install -y setools-console git container-selinux
$ git clone
$ cd udica && sudo python3 ./setup.py install
```

To demonstrate how Udica works, we are going to create a container that writes to the /var/log directory of the host, which is bind-mounted when the container is created. By default, the process with the container_t domain would not be able to write a directory labeled with the var_log_t type.

The following script, which has been executed inside the container, is an endless loop that writes a log line composed of the current date and a counter:

Chapter11/custom_logger/logger.sh

```bash
#!/bin/bash
set -euo pipefail
trap "echo Exited; exit;" SIGINT SIGTERM

# Run an endless loop writing a simple log entry with date
count=1
while true; do
echo "$(date +%y/%m/%d_%H:%M:%S) - Line #$count" | tee -a /var/
log/custom.log
    count=$((count+1))
    sleep 2
done
```

The preceding script uses the set -euo pipefail option, to exit immediately in case an error occurs, and the tee utility, to write both to standard output and the /var/log/custom.log file in append mode. The count variable increments on each loop cycle.

The Dockerfile for this container is kept minimal – it just copies the logger script and executes it at container startup:

Chapter11/custom_logger/Dockerfile

```
FROM docker.io/library/fedora
# Copy the logger.sh script
COPY logger.sh /
# Exec the logger.sh script
CMD ["/logger.sh"]
```

> **Important**
> The `logger.sh` script must be executed before the build so that it can be launched correctly at container startup.

The container image is built with the name `custom_logger`:

```
# cd /Chapter11/custom_logger
# buildah build -t custom_logger .
```

Now, it's time to test the container and see how it behaves. The `/var/log` directory is bind-mounted with `rw` permissions to the container's `/var/log`, without this altering its type context. We should keep the execution in the foreground to see the immediate output:

```
# podman run -v /var/log:/var/log:rw \
  --name custom_logger1 custom_logger
tee: /var/log/custom.log: Permission denied
22/01/08_09:09:33 - Custom log event #1
```

As expected, the script failed to write to the target file. We could fix this by changing the directory type context to `container_file_t` but, as we learned previously, this is a poor idea since it would prevent other processes from writing their logs.

Instead, we can use Udica to generate a custom SELinux security profile for the container. In the following code, the container specs are exported to a `container.json` file and then parsed by Udica to generate a custom profile called *custom_logger*:

```
# podman inspect custom_logger1 > container.json
# udica -j container.json custom_logger
```

```
Policy custom_logger created!
```

```
Please load these modules using:
# semodule -i custom_logger.cil /usr/share/udica/templates/
{base_container.cil,log_container.cil}
Restart the container with: "--security-opt label=type:custom_
logger.process" parameter
```

Once the profile has been generated, Udica outputs the instructions to configure the container. First, we need to load the new custom policy using the `semodule` utility. The generated file is in **Common Intermediate Language (CIL)** format, an intermediate policy language for SELinux. Along with the generated CIL file, the example loads some Udica templates, `/usr/share/udica/templates/base_container.cil` and `/usr/share/udica/templates/log_container.cil`, whose rules are inherited in the custom container policy file.

Let's load the modules using the suggested command:

```
# semodule -i custom_logger.cil /usr/share/udica/templates/
{base_container.cil,log_container.cil}
```

After loading the modules in SELinux, we are ready to run the container with the custom `custom_logger.process` label, passing it as an argument to the Podman `--security-opt` option. The other container option was kept identical, except for its name, which has been updated to `custom_logger2` to differentiate it from the previous instance:

```
# podman run -v /var/log:/var/log:rw \
  --name custom_logger2 \
  --security-opt label=type:custom_logger.process \
  custom_logger
22/01/08_09:05:19 - Line #1
22/01/08_09:05:21 - Line #2
22/01/08_09:05:23 - Line #3
22/01/08_09:05:25 - Line #5
[...Omitted output...]
```

This time, the script successfully wrote to the /var/log/custom.log file thanks to the custom profile that was generated with Udica.

Note that the container processes are not running with the container_t domain, but with the new custom_logger.process superset, which includes additional rules on top of the default.

We can confirm this by running the following command on the host:

```
# ps auxZ | grep 'custom_logger.process'
unconfined_u:system_r:container_runtime_t:s0-s0:c0.c1023 root
26546 0.1  0.6 1365088 53768 pts/0 Sl+ 09:16   0:00 podman
run -v /var/log:/var/log:rw --security-opt label=type:custom_
logger.process custom_logger system_u:system_r:custom_logger.
process:s0:c159,c258 root 26633 0.0  0.0 4180 3136 ? Ss 09:16
0:00 /bin/bash /logger.sh
```

```
system_u:system_r:custom_logger.process:s0:c159,c258 root 26881
0.0  0.0 2640 1104 ? S 09:18   0:00 sleep 2
```

Udica creates the custom policy by parsing the JSON spec file and looking for the container mount points, ports, and capabilities. Let's look at the content of the generated custom_logger.cil file from our example:

```
(block custom_logger
    (blockinherit container)
    (allow process process ( capability ( chown dac_override
fowner fsetid kill net_bind_service setfcap setgid setpcap
setuid sys_chroot )))


    (blockinherit log_rw_container)
```

The CIL language syntax is beyond the scope of this book, but we still can notice some interesting things:

- The *custom_logger* profile is defined by a block statement.
- The allow rule enables the default capabilities for the container.
- The policy inherits the container and log_rw_container blocks with the blockinherit statements.

The generated CIL file inherits the blocks that have been defined in the available Udica templates, each one focused on specific actions. On Fedora, the templates are installed via the `container-selinux` package and are available in the `/usr/share/udica/templates/` folder:

```
# ls -1 /usr/share/udica/templates/
base_container.cil
config_container.cil
home_container.cil
log_container.cil
net_container.cil
tmp_container.cil
tty_container.cil
virt_container.cil
x_container.cil
```

The available templates are implemented for common scenarios, such as accessing log directories or user homes, or even for opening network ports. Among them, the `base_container.cil` template is always included by all the Udica-generated policies as the base building block that's used to generate the custom policies.

According to the behavior of the container that's derived from the spec file, other templates are included. For example, the policy inherited the `log_rw_container` block from the `log_container.cil` template to let the custom logger container access the `/var/log` directory.

Udica is a great tool for addressing container isolation issues and helps administrators address SELinux confinement use cases by overcoming the complexity of writing rules manually.

Generated security profiles can also be versioned inside a GitHub repository and reused for similar containers on different hosts.

Summary

In this chapter, we learned how to develop and apply techniques to improve the overall security of our container-based service architecture. We learned how leveraging rootless containers and avoiding UID 0 can reduce the attack surface of our services. Then, we learned how to sign and trust container images to avoid MITM attacks. Finally, we went under the hood of a containers' tools and looked at the Linux kernel's capabilities and the SELinux subsystem, which can help us fine-tune various security aspects for our running containers.

Now that we've done a deep dive into security, we are ready to move on to the next chapter, where we will take an advanced look at networking for containers.

Further reading

For more information about the topics that were covered in this chapter, take a look at the following resources:

- MITRE ATT&CK Container Matrix: `https://attack.mitre.org/matrices/enterprise/containers/`

- GNU Privacy Guard: `https://gnupg.org/`

- RFC4880 – OpenPGP standard: `https://www.rfc-editor.org/info/rfc4880`

- Podman image signing tutorial: `https://github.com/containers/podman/blob/main/docs/tutorials/image_signing.md`

- Lukas Vrabec's blog: `https://lukas-vrabec.com/`

- CIL introduction and design principles: `https://github.com/SELinuxProject/cl/wiki`

- Udica introduction on Red Hat's blog: `https://www.redhat.com/en/blog/generate-selinux-policies-containers-with-udica`

12

Implementing Container Networking Concepts

Container network isolation leverages network namespaces to provide separate network stacks for each container. Without a container runtime, managing network interfaces across multiple namespaces would be complex. Podman provides flexible network management that allows users to customize how containers communicate with external containers and other containers inside the same host.

In this chapter, we will learn about the common configuration practices for managing container networking, along with the differences between rootless and rootfull containers.

In this chapter, we're going to cover the following main topics:

- Container networking and Podman setup
- Interconnecting two or more containers
- Exposing containers outside our underlying host
- Rootless container network behavior

Technical requirements

To complete this chapter, you will need a machine with a working Podman installation. As we mentioned in *Chapter 3, Running the First Container*, all the examples in this book can be executed on a Fedora 34 system or later but can be reproduced on your **operating system (OS)** of choice. The examples in this chapter will be related to both Podman v3.4.z and Podman v4.0.0 since they provide different network implementations.

A good understanding of the topics that were covered in *Chapter 4, Managing Running Containers, Chapter 5, Implementing Storage for the Container's Data*, and *Chapter 9, Pushing Images to a Container Registry*, will help you grasp the container networking topics we'll be covering.

You must also have a good understanding of basic networking concepts to understand topics such as routing, the IP protocol, DNS, and firewalling.

Container networking and Podman setup

In this section, we'll cover Podman's networking implementation and how to configure networks. Podman 4.0.0 introduced an important change to the network stack. However, Podman 3 is still widely used in the community. For this reason, we will cover both implementations.

Podman 3 leverages the **Container Network Interface** (**CNI**) to manage local networks that are created on the host. The CNI provides a standard set of specifications and libraries to create and configure plugin-based network interfaces in a container environment.

CNI specifications were created for Kubernetes to provide a network configuration format that's used by the container runtime to set up the defined plugins, as well as an execution protocol between plugin binaries and runtimes. The great advantage of this plugin-based approach is that vendors and communities can develop third-party plugins that satisfy the CNI's specifications.

The Podman 4 network stack is based on a brand new project called **Netavark**, a container-native networking implementation completely written in Rust and designed to work with Podman. Rust is a great programming language for developing system and network components thanks to its efficient memory management and high performance, similar to the C programming language. Netavark provides better support for dual-stack networking (IPv4/IPv6) and inter-container DNS resolution, along with a tighter bond with the Podman project development roadmap.

Important Note

Users upgrading from Podman 3 to Podman 4 will continue to use CNI by default and preserve their previous configuration. New Podman 4 installations will use Netavark by default. Users can revert to the CNI network backend by upgrading the `network_backend` field in the `/usr/share/containers/containers.conf` file.

In the next subsection, we'll focus on the CNI configuration that's used by Podman 3 to orchestrate container networking.

CNI configuration quick start

A typical CNI configuration file defines a list of plugins and their related configuration. The following example shows the default CNI configuration of a fresh Podman installation on Fedora:

Chapter12/podman_cni_conf.json

```
"cniVersion": "0.4.0",
"name": "podman",
"plugins": [
  {
    "type": "bridge",
    "bridge": "cni-podman0",
    "isGateway": true,
    "ipMasq": true,
    "hairpinMode": true,
    "ipam": {
      "type": "host-local",
```

```json
        "routes": [{ "dst": "0.0.0.0/0" }],
        "ranges": [
          [
            {
              "subnet": "10.88.0.0/16",
              "gateway": "10.88.0.1"
            }
          ]
        ]
      }
    },
    {
      "type": "portmap",
      "capabilities": {
        "portMappings": true
      }
    },
    {
      "type": "firewall"
    },
    {
      "type": "tuning"
    }
  ]
}
```

As we can see, the `plugins` list in this file contains a set of plugins that are used by the runtime to orchestrate container networking.

The CNI community curates a repository of reference plugins that can be used by container runtimes. CNI reference plugins are organized into **interface-creating**, **IP address management (IPAM)**, and **Meta** plugins. Interface-creating plugins can make use of IPAM and Meta plugins.

The following non-exhaustive list describes the most commonly used interface-creating plugins:

- `bridge`: This plugin creates a dedicated Linux bridge on the host for the network. Container interfaces are attached to the managed bridge to communicate between each other and with the external systems. This plugin is currently supported by Podman and by the `podman network` CLI tools and is the default interface-creating plugin that's configured when Podman is installed or a new network is created.

- `ipvlan`: This plugin allows you to attach an IPVLAN interface to the container. The IPVLAN solution is an alternative to the traditional Linux bridge networking solution for containers, where a single parent interface is shared across multiple sub-interfaces, each with an IP address. This plugin is currently supported by Podman but you can still manually create and edit the CNI configuration file if necessary.

- `macvlan`: This plugin allows a MACVLAN configuration, which is an approach similar to IPVLAN with one main difference: in this configuration, each container sub-interface also gets a MAC address. This plugin is currently supported by Podman and by the `podman network` CLI tools.

- `host-device`: This plugin allows you to directly pass an existing interface into a container. This is currently not supported by Podman.

CNI IPAM plugins are related to the IP address management inside containers. There are only three reference IPAM plugins:

- dhcp: This plugin lets you execute a daemon on the host that manages the dhcp leases on behalf of the running containers. It also implies that a running dhcp server is already running on the host network.

- host-local: This plugin is used to allocate IP addresses to containers using a defined address range. The allocation data is stored in the host filesystem. It is optimal for local container execution and is the default IPAM plugin that's used by Podman in the network bridge.

- `static`: This is a basic plugin that manages a discrete list of static addresses that are assigned to containers.

NI Meta plugins are used to configure specific behaviors in the host, such as tuning, firewall rules, and port mapping, and are executed as chained plugins along with the interface-creating plugins. The current Meta plugins that are maintained in the reference plugins repository are as follows:

- `portmap`: This plugin is used to manage port mapping between the container and the host. It applies configuration using the host firewall (`iptables`) and is responsible for creating **Source NAT (SNAT)** and **Destination Nat (DNAT)** rules. This plugin is enabled by default in Podman.

- `firewall`: This plugin configures firewall rules to allow container ingress and egress traffic. It's enabled by default in Podman.

- `tuning`: This plugin customizes system tuning (using `sysctl` parameters) and interface attributes in the network namespace. It's enabled by default in Podman.

- `bandwidth`: This plugin can be used to configure traffic rate limiting on containers using the Linux traffic control subsystem.

- `sbr`: This plugin is used to configure **source-based routing (SBR)** on interfaces.

> **Important Note**
> On a Fedora system, all the CNI plugin binaries are located in the `/usr/libexec/cni` folder and are provided by the `containernetworking-plugins` package, installed as a Podman dependency.

Going back to the CNI configuration example, we can see that the default Podman configuration uses a `bridge` plugin with `host-local` IP address management and that the `portmap`, `tuning`, and `firewall` plugins are chained together with it.

In the default network that was created for Podman, the subnet that's been allocated for container networking is `10.88.0.0/16` and the bridge, called `cni-podman0`, acts as the default gateway to containers on `10.88.0.1`, implying that all outbound traffic from a container is directed to the bridge's interface.

> **Important Note**
> This configuration is applied to rootfull containers only. Later in this chapter, we'll learn that Podman uses a different networking approach for rootless containers to overcome the user's limited privileges. We will see that this approach has many limitations on host interfaces and IP address management.

Now, let's see what happens on the host when a new rootfull container is created.

Podman CNI walkthrough

In this subsection, we will investigate the most peculiar network events that occur when a new container is created when CNI is used as a network backend.

> **Important Note**
>
> All the examples in this subsection are executed as the root user. Ensure that you clean up the existing running containers to have a clearer view of the network interfaces and firewall rules.

We will try to run an example using the Nginx container and map its default internal port, 80/tcp, to the host port, 8080/tcp.

Before we begin, we want to verify the current host's IP configuration:

```
# ip addr show
1: lo: <LOOPBACK,UP,LOWER_UP> mtu 65536 qdisc noqueue state UNKNOWN group
default qlen 1000
    link/loopback 00:00:00:00:00:00 brd 00:00:00:00:00:00
    inet 127.0.0.1/8 scope host lo
       valid_lft forever preferred_lft forever
    inet6 ::1/128 scope host
       valid_lft forever preferred_lft forever
2: eth0: <BROADCAST,MULTICAST,UP,LOWER_UP> mtu 1500 qdisc fq_
codel state UP group default qlen 1000
    link/ether 52:54:00:a9:ce:df brd ff:ff:ff:ff:ff:ff
    altname enp0s5
    altname ens5
    inet 192.168.121.189/24 brd 192.168.121.255 scope global
dynamic noprefixroute eth0
       valid_lft 3054sec preferred_lft 3054sec
    inet6 fe80::2fb:9732:a0d9:ac70/64 scope link noprefixroute
valid_lft forever preferred_lft forever
3: cni-podman0: <NO-CARRIER,BROADCAST,MULTICAST,UP> mtu 1500
qdisc noqueue state DOWN group default qlen 1000
    link/ether de:52:45:ae:1a:7f brd ff:ff:ff:ff:ff:ff
```

```
    inet 10.88.0.1/16 brd 10.88.255.255 scope global cni-
podman0
        valid_lft forever preferred_lft forever
    inet6 fe80::dc52:45ff:feae:1a7f/64 scope link
        valid_lft forever preferred_lft forever
```

Along with the host's main interface, eth0, we can see a cni-podman0 bridge interface with an address of 10.88.0.1/16. Also, notice that the bridge's state is set to DOWN.

> **Important**
>
> If the host that's being used for the test is a fresh install and Podman has never been executed before, the cni-podman0 bridge interface will not be listed. This is not a problem – it will be created when a rootfull container is created for the first time.

If no other container is running on the host, we should see no interface attached to the virtual bridge. To verify this, we are going to use the bridge link show command, whose output is expected to be empty:

```
# bridge link show cni-podman0
```

Looking at the firewall rules, we do not expect to see rules related to containers in the filter and nat tables:

```
# iptables -L
# iptables -L -t nat
```

> **Important Note**
>
> The output of the preceding commands has been omitted for the sake of brevity, but it is worth noting that the filter table should already contain two CNI-related chains named CNI-ADMIN and CNI-FORWARD.

Finally, we want to inspect the routing rules for the cni-podman0 interface:

```
# ip route show dev cni-podman0
10.88.0.0/16 proto kernel scope link src 10.88.0.1 linkdown
```

This command says that all traffic going to the 10.88.0.0/16 network goes through the cni-podman0 interface.

Let's run our Nginx container and see what happens to the network interfaces, routing, and firewall configuration:

```
# podman run -d -p 8080:80 \
  --name net_example docker.io/library/nginx
```

The first and most interesting event is a new network interface being created, as shown in the output of the ip addr show command:

```
# ip addr show
[...omitted output...]
3: cni-podman0: <BROADCAST,MULTICAST,UP,LOWER_UP> mtu 1500
qdisc noqueue state UP group default qlen 1000
    link/ether de:52:45:ae:1a:7f brd ff:ff:ff:ff:ff:ff
    inet 10.88.0.1/16 brd 10.88.255.255 scope global cni-
podman0
       valid_lft forever preferred_lft forever
    inet6 fe80::dc52:45ff:feae:1a7f/64 scope link
       valid_lft forever preferred_lft forever
5: vethcf8b2132@if2: <BROADCAST,MULTICAST,UP,LOWER_UP> mtu 1500
qdisc noqueue master cni-podman0 state UP group default
    link/ether b6:4c:1d:06:39:5a brd ff:ff:ff:ff:ff:ff link-
netns cni-df380fb0-b8a6-4f39-0d19-99a0535c2f2d
    inet6 fe80::90e3:98ff:fe6a:acff/64 scope link
       valid_lft forever preferred_lft forever
```

This new interface is part of a **veth pair** (see man 4 veth), a couple of virtual Ethernet devices that act like a local tunnel. Veth pairs are native Linux kernel virtual interfaces that don't depend on a container runtime and can be applied to use cases that go beyond container execution.

The interesting part of veth pairs is that they can be spawned across multiple network namespaces and that a packet that's sent to one side of the pair is immediately received on the other side.

The `vethcf8b2132@if2` interface is linked to a device that resides in a network namespace named `cni-df380fb0-b8a6-4f39-0d19-99a0535c2f2d`. Since Linux offers us the option to inspect network namespaces using the `ip netns` command, we can check if the namespace exists and inspect its network stack:

```
# ip netns
cni-df380fb0-b8a6-4f39-0d19-99a0535c2f2d (id: 0)
```

> **Hint**
>
> When a new network namespace is created, a file with the same name under `/var/run/netns/` is created. This file has also the same inode number that's pointed to by the symlink under `/proc/<PID>/ns/net`. When the file is opened, the returned file descriptor gives access to the namespace.

The preceding command confirms that the network namespace exists. Now, we want to inspect the network interfaces that have been defined inside it:

```
# ip netns exec cni-df380fb0-b8a6-4f39-0d19-99a0535c2f2d ip
addr show
1: lo: <LOOPBACK,UP,LOWER_UP> mtu 65536 qdisc noqueue state
UNKNOWN group default qlen 1000
    link/loopback 00:00:00:00:00:00 brd 00:00:00:00:00:00
    inet 127.0.0.1/8 scope host lo
       valid_lft forever preferred_lft forever
    inet6 ::1/128 scope host
       valid_lft forever preferred_lft forever
2: eth0@if5: <BROADCAST,MULTICAST,UP,LOWER_UP> mtu 1500 qdisc
noqueue state UP group default
    link/ether fa:c9:6e:5c:db:ad brd ff:ff:ff:ff:ff:ff link-
netnsid 0
    inet 10.88.0.3/16 brd 10.88.255.255 scope global eth0
       valid_lft forever preferred_lft forever
    inet6 fe80::f8c9:6eff:fe5c:dbad/64 scope link
       valid_lft forever preferred_lft forever
```

Here, we executed an `ip addr show` command that's nested inside the `ip netns exec` command. The output shows us an interface that is on the other side of our veth pair. This also tells us something valuable: the container's IPv4 address, set to `10.88.0.3`.

> **Hint**
>
> If you're curious, the container IP configuration, when using Podman's default network with the `host-local` IPAM plugin, is persisted to the `/var/lib/cni/networks/podman` folder. Here, a file named after the assigned IP address is created and written with the container-generated ID.
>
> If a new network is created and used by a container, its configuration will be persisted in the `/var/lib/cni/networks/<NETWORK_NAME>` folder.

We can also inspect the container's routing tables:

```
# ip netns exec cni-df380fb0-b8a6-4f39-0d19-99a0535c2f2d ip
route
default via 10.88.0.1 dev eth0
10.88.0.0/16 dev eth0 proto kernel scope link src 10.88.0.3
```

All the outbound traffic that's directed to the external networks will go through the `10.88.0.1` address, which has been assigned to the `cni-podman0` bridge.

When a new container is created, the `firewall` and `portmapper` CNI plugins apply the necessary rules in the host filter and NAT tables. In the following code, we can see the rules that have been applied to the container IP address in the `nat` table, where SNAT, DNAT, and masquerading rules have been applied:

```
# iptables -L -t nat -n | grep -B4 10.88.0.3


Chain POSTROUTING (policy ACCEPT)
target       prot opt source               destination
CNI-HOSTPORT-MASQ  all  --  0.0.0.0/0                 0.0.0.0/0
         /* CNI portfwd requiring masquerade */
CNI-fb51a7bfa5365a8a89e764fd  all  --
10.88.0.3          0.0.0.0/0               /* name: "podman" id:
"a5054cca3436a7bc4dbf78fe4b901ceef0569ced24181d2e7b118232123a5f
e3" */

--
Chain CNI-DN-fb51a7bfa5365a8a89e76 (1 references)
target       prot opt source               destination
CNI-HOSTPORT-SETMARK  tcp  --  10.88.0.0/16             0.0.0.0/0
         tcp dpt:8080
```

```
CNI-HOSTPORT-SETMARK  tcp   --   127.0.0.1              0.0.0.0/0
        tcp dpt:8080
DNAT        tcp   --   0.0.0.0/0               0.0.0.0/0
tcp dpt:8080 to:10.88.0.3:80
```

The bolder line shows a DNAT rule in a custom chain named CNI-DN-fb51a7bfa5365a8a89e76. This rule says that all the TCP packets whose destination is the 8080/tcp port on the host should be redirected to the 10.88.0.3:80 port, which is the network socket that's exposed by the container. This rule matches the-p 8080:80 option that we passed during container creation.

But how does the container communicate with the external world? Let's inspect the cni-podman0 bridge again while looking for notable changes:

```
# bridge link show cni-podman0
5: vethcf8b2132@eth0: <BROADCAST,MULTICAST,UP,LOWER_UP> mtu
1500 master cni-podman0 state forwarding priority 32 cost 2
```

The aforementioned interface is connected to the virtual bridge, which also happens to have an IP address assigned to it (10.88.0.1) that acts as the default gateway for all the containers.

Let's try to trace the path of an ICMP packet from the container to a well-known host, 1.1.1.1 (Cloudflare public DNS). To do so, we must run the traceroute utility from the container network's namespace using the ip netns exec command:

```
# ip netns exec cni-df380fb0-b8a6-4f39-0d19-99a0535c2f2d
traceroute -I 1.1.1.1
traceroute to 1.1.1.1 (1.1.1.1), 30 hops max, 60 byte packets
 1  _gateway (10.88.0.1)  0.071 ms  0.025 ms  0.003 ms
 2  192.168.121.1 (192.168.121.1)  0.206 ms  0.195 ms  0.189 ms
 3  192.168.1.1 (192.168.1.1)  5.326 ms  5.323 ms  5.319 ms
 4  192.168.50.6 (192.168.50.6)  17.598 ms  17.595 ms  17.825 ms
 5  192.168.50.5 (192.168.50.5)  17.821 ms  17.888 ms  17.882 ms
 6  10.177.21.173 (10.177.21.173)  17.998 ms  17.772 ms  24.777 ms
 7  185.210.48.42 (185.210.48.42)  25.963 ms  7.604 ms  7.702 ms
 8  185.210.48.43 (185.210.48.43)  7.906 ms  10.344 ms  10.984 ms
```

```
9   185.210.48.77 (185.210.48.77)   12.212 ms   12.030 ms   12.983
ms
10  1.1.1.1 (1.1.1.1)   12.524 ms   12.160 ms   12.649 ms
```

> **Important Note**
> The traceroute program could be installed on the host by default. To install it
> on Fedora, run the `sudo dnf install traceroute` command.

The preceding output shows a series of **hops**, which are a way to count the number of
routes that a packet must pass to reach a destination. In this example, we have a total
of 10 hops, which is necessary to reach the target node. The first hop goes through the
container's default gateway (`10.88.0.1`), moving to the host's network stack.

The second hop is the host's default gateway (`192.168.121.1`), which is assigned to a
virtual bridge in a hypervisor and connected to our lab's host VM.

The third hop is a private network default gateway (`192.168.1.1`) that's assigned to a
physical router that's connected to the lab's hypervisor network.

This demonstrates that all the traffic goes through the `cni-podman0` bridge interface.

We can create more than one network, either using Podman native commands or our
favorite editor to manage JSON files directly.

Now that we've explored CNI's implementation and configuration details, let's look at the
new Netavark implementation in Podman 4.

Netavark configuration quick start

Podman's 4.0.0 release introduced Netavark as the default network backend. The
advantages of Netavark are as follows:

- Support for dual IPv4/IPv6 stacks
- Support for DNS native resolution using the **aardvark-dns** companion project
- Support for rootless containers
- Support for different firewall implementations, including iptables, firewalld,
  and nftables

The configuration files that are used by Netavark are not very different from the ones
that were shown for CNI. Netavark still uses JSON format to configure networks; files are
stored under the `/etc/containers/networks` path for rootfull containers and the
`~/.local/share/containers/storage/networks` path for rootless containers.

The following configuration file shows an example network that's been created and managed under Netavark:

```
[
    {
        "name": "netavark-example",
        "id":
"d98700453f78ea2fdfe4a1f77eae9e121f3cbf4b6160dab89edf9ce23c
b924d7",
        "driver": "bridge",
        "network_interface": "podman1",
        "created": "2022-02-17T21:37:59.873639361Z",
        "subnets": [
            {
                "subnet": "10.89.4.0/24",
                "gateway": "10.89.4.1"
            }
        ],
        "ipv6_enabled": false,
        "internal": false,
        "dns_enabled": true,
        "ipam_options": {
            "driver": "host-local"
        }
    }
]
```

The first noticeable element is the more compact size of the configuration file compared to a CNI configuration. The following fields are defined:

- name: The name of the network.

- id: The unique network ID.

- driver: This specifies the kind of network driver that's being used. The default is bridge. Netavark also supports MACVLAN drivers.

- network_interface: This is the name of the network interface associated with the network. If bridge is the configured driver, this will be the name of the Linux bridge. In the preceding example, a bridge is created called podman1.

- `created`: The network creation timestamp.

- `subnets`: This provides a list of subnet and gateway objects. Subnets are assigned automatically. However, when you're creating a new network with Podman, users can provide a custom CIDR. Netavark allows you to manage multiple subnets and gateways on a network.

- `ipv6_enabled`: Native support for IPv6 in Netavark can be enabled or disabled with this boolean.

- `internal`: This boolean is used to configure a network for internal use only and to block external routing.

- `dns_enabled`: This boolean enables DNS resolution for the network and is served by the `aardvark-dns` daemon.

- `ipam_options`: This object defines a series of `ipam` parameters. In the preceding example, the only option is the kind of IPAM driver, `host-local`, which behaves in a way similar to the CNI host-local plugin.

The default Podman 4 network, named `podman`, implements a bridge driver (the bridge's name is `podman0`). Here, DNS support is disabled, similar to what happens with the default CNI configuration.

Netavark is also an executable binary that's installed by default in the `/usr/libexec/podman/netavark` path. It has a simple **command-line interface** (**CLI**) that implements the `setup` and `teardown` commands, applying the network configuration to a given network namespace (see `man netavark`).

Now, let's look at the effects of creating a new container with Netavark.

Podman Netavark walkthrough

Like CNI, Netavark manages the creation of network configurations in the container network namespace and the host network namespace, including the creation of veth pairs and the Linux bridge that's defined in the config file.

Before the first container is created in the default Podman network, no bridges are created and the host interfaces are the only ones available, along with the loopback interface:

```
# ip addr show
1: lo: <LOOPBACK,UP,LOWER_UP> mtu 65536 qdisc noqueue state
UNKNOWN group default qlen 1000
    link/loopback 00:00:00:00:00:00 brd 00:00:00:00:00:00
    inet 127.0.0.1/8 scope host lo
```

```
        valid_lft forever preferred_lft forever
    inet6 ::1/128 scope host
        valid_lft forever preferred_lft forever
2: eth0: <BROADCAST,MULTICAST,UP,LOWER_UP> mtu 1500 qdisc fq_
codel state UP group default qlen 1000
    link/ether 52:54:00:9a:ea:f4 brd ff:ff:ff:ff:ff:ff
    altname enp0s5
    altname ens5
    inet 192.168.121.15/24 brd 192.168.121.255 scope global
dynamic noprefixroute eth0
        valid_lft 3293sec preferred_lft 3293sec
    inet6 fe80::d0fb:c0d1:159e:2d54/64 scope link noprefixroute
        valid_lft forever preferred_lft forever
```

Let's run a new Nginx container and see what happens:

```
# podman run -d -p 8080:80 \
  --name nginx-netavark
  docker.io/library/nginx
```

When the container is started, the podman0 bridge and a veth interface appear:

```
# ip addr show
1: lo: <LOOPBACK,UP,LOWER_UP> mtu 65536 qdisc noqueue state
UNKNOWN group default qlen 1000
    link/loopback 00:00:00:00:00:00 brd 00:00:00:00:00:00
    inet 127.0.0.1/8 scope host lo
        valid_lft forever preferred_lft forever
    inet6 ::1/128 scope host
        valid_lft forever preferred_lft forever
2: eth0: <BROADCAST,MULTICAST,UP,LOWER_UP> mtu 1500 qdisc fq_
codel state UP group default qlen 1000
    link/ether 52:54:00:9a:ea:f4 brd ff:ff:ff:ff:ff:ff
    altname enp0s5
    altname ens5
    inet 192.168.121.15/24 brd 192.168.121.255 scope global
dynamic noprefixroute eth0
        valid_lft 3140sec preferred_lft 3140sec
```

```
    inet6 fe80::d0fb:c0d1:159e:2d54/64 scope link noprefixroute
        valid_lft forever preferred_lft forever
3: veth2772d0ea@if2: <BROADCAST,MULTICAST,UP,LOWER_UP> mtu 1500
qdisc noqueue master podman0 state UP group default qlen 1000
    link/ether fa:a3:31:63:21:60 brd ff:ff:ff:ff:ff:ff link-
netns netns-61a5f9f9-9dff-7488-3922-165cdc6cd320
    inet6 fe80::f8a3:31ff:fe63:2160/64 scope link
        valid_lft forever preferred_lft forever
8: podman0: <BROADCAST,MULTICAST,UP,LOWER_UP> mtu 1500 qdisc
noqueue state UP group default qlen 1000
    link/ether ea:b4:9d:dd:2c:d1 brd ff:ff:ff:ff:ff:ff
    inet 10.88.0.1/16 brd 10.88.255.255 scope global podman0
        valid_lft forever preferred_lft forever
    inet6 fe80::24ec:30ff:fe1a:2ca8/64 scope link
        valid_lft forever preferred_lft forever
```

There are no particular changes for the end user in terms of network namespaces, mixing context between version management, firewall rules, or routing compared to the CNI walkthrough provided previously.

Again, a network namespace in the host is created for the nginx-netavark container. Let's inspect the contents of the network namespace:

```
# ip netns exec netns-61a5f9f9-9dff-7488-3922-165cdc6cd320 ip
addr show
1: lo: <LOOPBACK,UP,LOWER_UP> mtu 65536 qdisc noqueue state
UNKNOWN group default qlen 1000
    link/loopback 00:00:00:00:00:00 brd 00:00:00:00:00:00
    inet 127.0.0.1/8 scope host lo
        valid_lft forever preferred_lft forever
    inet6 ::1/128 scope host
        valid_lft forever preferred_lft forever
2: eth0@if3: <BROADCAST,MULTICAST,UP,LOWER_UP> mtu 1500
qdisc noqueue state UP group default qlen 1000    link/ether
ae:9b:7f:07:3f:16 brd ff:ff:ff:ff:ff:ff link-netnsid 0
    inet 10.88.0.4/16 brd 10.88.255.255 scope global eth0
        valid_lft forever preferred_lft forever
    inet6 fe80::ac9b:7fff:fe07:3f16/64 scope link
        valid_lft forever preferred_lft forever
```

Once again, it is possible to find the internal IP address that's been assigned to the container.

If the container is executed in rootless mode, the bridge and veth pairs will be created in a rootless network namespace.

> **Important Note**
>
> The rootless network namespace can be inspected in Podman 4 with the `podman unshare --rootless-netns` command.
>
> Users running Podman 3 and CNI can use the `--rootless-cni` option to obtain the same results.

In the next subsection, we will learn how to manage and customize container networks with the CLI tools that are offered by Podman.

Managing networks with Podman

The `podman network` command provides the necessary tools for managing container networks. The following subcommands are available:

- `create`: Creates a new network
- `connect`: Connects to a given network
- `disconnect`: Disconnects from a network
- `exists`: Checks if a network exists
- `inspect`: Dumps the CNI configuration of a network
- `prune`: Removes unused networks
- `reload`: Reloads container firewall rules
- `rm`: Removes a given network

In this section, you will learn how to create a new network and connect a container to it. For Podman 3, all the generated CNI config files are written to the `/etc/cni/net.d` folder in the host.

For Podman 4, all the generated Netavark config files for rootfull networks are written to `/etc/containers/networks`, while the config files for rootless networks are written to `~/.local/share/containers/storage/networks`.

The following command creates a new network called `example1`:

```
# podman network create \
  --driver bridge \
  --gateway "10.89.0.1" \
  --subnet "10.89.0.0/16" example1
```

Here, we provided subnet and gateway information, along with the driver type that corresponds to the CNI interface-creating plugin. The resulting network configuration is written in the aforementioned paths according to the kind of network backend and can be inspected with the `podman network inspect` command.

The following output shows the configuration for a CNI network backend:

```
# podman network inspect example1
[
    {
        "cniVersion": "0.4.0",
        "name": "example1",
        "plugins": [
            {
                "bridge": "cni-podman1",
                "hairpinMode": true,
                "ipMasq": true,
                "ipam": {
                    "ranges": [
                        [
                            {
                                "gateway": "10.89.0.1",
                                "subnet": "10.89.0.0/16"
                            }
                        ]
                    ],
                    "routes": [
                        {
                            "dst": "0.0.0.0/0"
                        }
                    ],
```

```
                        "type": "host-local"
                    },
                    "isGateway": true,
                    "type": "bridge"
                },
                {
                    "capabilities": {
                        "portMappings": true
                    },
                    "type": "portmap"
                },
                {
                    "backend": "",
                    "type": "firewall"
                },
                {
                    "type": "tuning"
                },
                {
                    "capabilities": {
                        "aliases": true
                    },
                    "domainName": "dns.podman",
                    "type": "dnsname"
                }
            ]
        }
    ]
```

The new network CNI configuration shows that a bridge called `cni-podman1` will be created for this network and that containers will allocate IPs from the `10.89.0.0/16` subnet.

The other fields of the configuration are pretty similar to the default one, except for the `dnsname` plugin (project's repository: `https://github.com/containers/dnsname`), which is used to enable internal container name resolution. This feature provides an advantage in cross-container communication that we will look at in the next subsection.

The following output shows the generated configuration for a Netavark network backend:

```
# podman network inspect example1
[
    {
        "name": "example1",
        "id":
"a8ca04a41ef303e3247097b86d9048750e5f1aa819ec573b0e5f78e3cc8a
971b",
        "driver": "bridge",
        "network_interface": "podman1",
        "created": "2022-02-18T17:56:28.451701452Z",
        "subnets": [
            {
                "subnet": "10.89.0.0/16",
                "gateway": "10.89.0.1"
            }
        ],
        "ipv6_enabled": false,
        "internal": false,
        "dns_enabled": true,
        "ipam_options": {
            "driver": "host-local"
        }
    }
]
```

Notice that the bridge naming convention with Netavark is slightly different since it uses the podmanN pattern, with *N >= 0*.

To list all the existing networks, we can use the podman network ls command:

```
# podman network ls
NETWORK ID     NAME      VERSION   PLUGINS
2f259bab93aa podman   0.4.0     bridge,portmap,firewall,tuning
228b48a56dbc example1 0.4.0
bridge,portmap,firewall,tuning,dnsname
```

The preceding output shows the name, ID, CNI version, and active plugins of each active network.

On Podman 4, the output is slightly more compact since there are no CNI plugins to be shown:

```
# podman network ls
NETWORK ID      NAME        DRIVER
a8ca04a41ef3    example1    bridge
2f259bab93aa    podman      bridge
```

Now, it's time to spin up a container that's attached to the new network. The following code creates a PostgreSQL database that's attached to the example1 network:

```
# podman run -d -p 5432:5432 \
  --network example1 \
  -e POSTGRES_PASSWORD=password \
  --name postgres \
  docker.io/library/postgres
533792e9522fc65371fa6d694526400a3a01f29e6de9b2024e84895f354e
d2bb
```

The new container receives an address from the 10.89.0.0/16 subnet, as shown by the podman inspect command:

```
# podman inspect postgres --format '{{.NetworkSettings.
Networks.example1.IPAddress}}'
10.89.0.3
```

When we're using the CNI network backend, we can double-check this information by looking at the contents of the new /var/lib/cni/networks/example1 folder:

```
# ls -al /var/lib/cni/networks/example1/
total 20
drwxr-xr-x. 2 root root 4096 Jan 23 17:26 .
drwxr-xr-x. 5 root root 4096 Jan 23 16:22 ..
-rw-r--r--. 1 root root   70 Jan 23 16:26 10.89.0.3
-rw-r--r--. 1 root root    9 Jan 23 16:57 last_reserved_ip.0
-rwxr-x---. 1 root root    0 Jan 23 16:22 lock
```

Looking at the content of the `10.89.0.3` file, we find the following:

```
# cat /var/lib/cni/networks/example1/10.89.0.3
533792e9522fc65371fa6d694526400a3a01f29e6de9b2024e84895f354
ed2bb
```

The file holds the container ID of our `postgres` container, which is used to track the mapping with the assigned IP address. As we mentioned previously, this behavior is managed by the `host-local` plugin, the default IPAM choice for Podman networks.

> **Important Note**
> The Netavark network backend tracks IPAM configuration in the `/run/containers/networks/ipam.db` file for rootfull containers.

We can also see that a new Linux bridge has been created (notice the `cni-` prefix that is used for CNI network backends):

```
# ip addr show cni-podman1
8: cni-podman1: <BROADCAST,MULTICAST,UP,LOWER_UP> mtu 1500
qdisc noqueue state UP group default qlen 1000
    link/ether 56:ed:1d:a9:53:54 brd ff:ff:ff:ff:ff:ff
    inet 10.89.0.1/16 brd 10.89.255.255 scope global cni-
podman1
        valid_lft forever preferred_lft forever
    inet6 fe80::54ed:1dff:fea9:5354/64 scope link
        valid_lft forever preferred_lft forever
```

The new device is connected to one peer of the PostgreSQL container's veth pair:

```
# bridge link show
10: vethf03ed735@eth0: <BROADCAST,MULTICAST,UP,LOWER_UP> mtu
1500 master cni-podman1 state forwarding priority 32 cost 2
20: veth23ee4990@eth0: <BROADCAST,MULTICAST,UP,LOWER_UP> mtu
1500 master cni-podman0 state forwarding priority 32 cost 2
```

Here, we can see that `vethf03ed735@eth0` is attached to the `cni-podman1` bridge. The interface has the following configuration:

```
# ip addr show vethf03ed735
10: vethf03ed735@if2: <BROADCAST,MULTICAST,UP,LOWER_UP> mtu
1500 qdisc noqueue master cni-podman1 state UP group default
```

```
    link/ether 86:d1:8c:c9:8c:2b brd ff:ff:ff:ff:ff:ff link-
netns cni-77bfb1c0-af07-1170-4cc8-eb56d15511ac
    inet6 fe80::f889:17ff:fe83:4da2/64 scope link
       valid_lft forever preferred_lft forever
```

The preceding output also shows that the other side of the veth pair is located in the container's network namespace – that is, `cni-77bfb1c0-af07-1170-4cc8-eb56d15511ac`. We can inspect the container's network configuration and confirm the IP address that's been allocated from the new subnet:

```
# ip netns exec cni-77bfb1c0-af07-1170-4cc8-eb56d15511ac ip
addr show
1: lo: <LOOPBACK,UP,LOWER_UP> mtu 65536 qdisc noqueue state
UNKNOWN group default qlen 1000
    link/loopback 00:00:00:00:00:00 brd 00:00:00:00:00:00
    inet 127.0.0.1/8 scope host lo
       valid_lft forever preferred_lft forever
    inet6 ::1/128 scope host
       valid_lft forever preferred_lft forever
2: eth0@if10: <BROADCAST,MULTICAST,UP,LOWER_UP> mtu 1500 qdisc
noqueue state UP group default
    link/ether ba:91:9e:77:30:a1 brd ff:ff:ff:ff:ff:ff link-
netnsid 0
    inet 10.89.0.3/16 brd 10.89.255.255 scope global eth0
       valid_lft forever preferred_lft forever
    inet6 fe80::b891:9eff:fe77:30a1/64 scope link
       valid_lft forever preferred_lft forever
```

> **Important Note**
>
> The network namespace naming pattern for the Netavark backend in Podman 4 is `netns-<UID>`.

It is possible to connect a running container to another network without stopping and restarting it. In this way, the container will keep an interface attached to the original network and a second interface, attached to the new network, will be created. This feature, which is useful for use cases such as reverse proxies, can be achieved with the `podman network connect` command. Let's try to run a new `net_example` container:

```
# podman run -d -p 8080:80 --name net_example docker.io/
library/nginx
# podman network connect example1 net_example
```

To verify that the container has been attached to the new network, we can run the `podman inspect` command and look at the networks:

```
# podman inspect net_example
[...omitted output...]
            "Networks": {
                "example1": {
                    "EndpointID": "",
                    "Gateway": "10.89.0.1",
                    "IPAddress": "10.89.0.10",
                    "IPPrefixLen": 16,
                    "IPv6Gateway": "",
                    "GlobalIPv6Address": "",
                    "GlobalIPv6PrefixLen": 0,
                    "MacAddress": "fa:41:66:0a:25:45",
                    "NetworkID": "example1",
                    "DriverOpts": null,
                    "IPAMConfig": null,
                    "Links": null
                },
                "podman": {
```

```
                    "EndpointID": "",
                    "Gateway": "10.88.0.1",
                    "IPAddress": "10.88.0.7",
                    "IPPrefixLen": 16,
                    "IPv6Gateway": "",
                    "GlobalIPv6Address": "",
                    "GlobalIPv6PrefixLen": 0,
                    "MacAddress": "ba:cd:eb:8d:19:b5",
                    "NetworkID": "podman",
                    "DriverOpts": null,
                    "IPAMConfig": null,
                    "Links": null
              }
         }
[...omitted output...]
```

Here, we can see that the container now has two interfaces attached to the podman and example1 networks, with IP addresses allocated from each network's subnet.

To disconnect a container from a network, we can use the podman network disconnect command:

```
# podman network disconnect example1 net_example
```

When a network is not necessary anymore and is disconnected from running containers, we can delete it with the podman network rm command:

```
# podman network rm example1
example1
```

The command's output shows the list of removed networks. Here, the network's CNI configuration is removed from the host's /etc/cni/net.d directory.

> **Important Note**
> If the network has associated containers that are either running or have been stopped, the previous message will fail with Error: "example1" has associated containers with it. To work around this issue, remove or disconnect the associated containers before using the command.

The podman network rm command is useful when we need to remove a specific network. To remove all unused networks, the podman network prune command is a better choice:

```
# podman network prune
WARNING! This will remove all networks not used by at least one
container.
Are you sure you want to continue? [y/N] y
example2
db_network
```

In this section, we learned about the CNI specification and how Podman leverages its interface to simplify container networking. In a multi-tier or microservices scenario, we need to let containers communicate with each other. In the next section, we will learn how to manage container-to-container communication.

Interconnecting two or more containers

Using our knowledge from the previous section, we should be aware that two or more containers that have been created inside the same network can reach each other on the same subnet without the need for external routing.

At the same time, two or more containers that belong to different networks will be able to reach each other on different subnets by routing packets through their networks.

To demonstrate this, let's create a couple of busybox containers in the same default network:

```
# podman run -d --name endpoint1 \
    --cap-add=net_admin,net_raw busybox /bin/sleep 10000
# podman run -d --name endpoint2 \
    --cap-add=net_admin,net_raw busybox /bin/sleep 10000
```

In our lab, the two containers have 10.88.0.14 (endpoint1) and 10.88.0.15 (endpoint2) as their addresses. These two addresses are subject to change and can be collected using the methods illustrated previously with the podman inspect or the nsenter commands.

Regarding capabilities customization, we added the CAP_NET_ADMIN and CAP_NET_RAW capabilities to let the containers run commands such as ping or traceroute seamlessly.

Let's try to run a `traceroute` command from `endpoint1` to `endpoint2` to see the path of a packet:

```
# podman exec -it endpoint1 traceroute 10.88.0.14
traceroute to 10.88.0.14 (10.88.0.14), 30 hops max, 46 byte
packets
 1  10.88.0.14 (10.88.0.14)  0.013 ms  0.004 ms  0.002 ms
```

As we can see, the packet stays on the internal network and reaches the node without additional hops.

Now, let's create a new network, `net1`, and connect a container called `endpoint3` to it:

```
# podman network create --driver bridge --gateway "10.90.0.1"
--subnet "10.90.0.0/16" net1
# podman run -d --name endpoint3 --network=net1 --cap-add=net_
admin,net_raw busybox /bin/sleep 10000
```

The container in our lab gets an IP address of `10.90.0.2`. Let's see the network path from `endpoint1` to `endpoint3`:

```
# podman exec -it endpoint1 traceroute 10.90.0.2
traceroute to 10.90.0.2 (10.90.0.2), 30 hops max, 46 byte
packets
 1  host.containers.internal (10.88.0.1)  0.003 ms  0.001 ms
0.006 ms
 2  10.90.0.2 (10.90.0.2)  0.001 ms  0.002 ms  0.002 ms
```

This time, the packet has traversed the `endpoint1` container's default gateway (`10.88.0.1`) and reached the `endpoint3` container, which is routed from the host to the associated `net1` Linux bridge.

Connectivity across containers in the same host is very easy to manage and understand. However, we are still missing an important aspect for container-to-container communication: DNS resolution.

Let's learn how to leverage this feature with Podman networks.

Container DNS resolution

Despite its many configuration caveats, DNS resolution is a very simple concept: a service is queried to provide the IP address associated with a given hostname. The amount of information that can be provided by a DNS server is far richer than this, but we want to focus on simple IP resolution in this example.

For example, let's imagine a scenario where a web application running on a container named `webapp` needs read/write access to a database running on a second container named `db`. DNS resolution enables `webapp` to query for the `db` container's IP address before contacting it.

Previously, we learned that Podman's default network does not provide DNS resolution, while new user-created networks have DNS resolution enabled by default. On a CNI network backend, the `dnsname` plugin automatically configures a `dnsmasq` service, which is started when containers are connected to the network, to provide DNS resolution. On a Netavark network backend, the DNS resolution is delivered by `aarvark-dns`.

To test this feature, we are going to reuse the **students** web application that we illustrated in *Chapter 10, Troubleshooting and Monitoring Containers*, since it provides an adequate client-server example with a minimal REST service and a database backend based on PostgreSQL.

> **Info**
>
> The source code is available in this book's GitHub repository at `https://github.com/PacktPublishing/Podman-for-DevOps/tree/main/Chapter10/students`.

In this example, the web application simply prints some output in JSON as the result of an HTTP GET that triggers a query to a PostgreSQL database. For our demonstration, we will run both the database and the web application on the same network.

First, we must create the PostgreSQL database pod while providing a generic username and password:

```
# podman run -d \
    --network net1 --name db \
    -e POSTGRES_USER=admin \
    -e POSTGRES_PASSWORD=password \
    -e POSTGRES_DB=students \
    postgres
```

Next, we must restore the data from the SQL dump in the `students` folder to the database:

```
# cd Chapter10/students
# cat db.sql | podman exec -i db psql -U admin students
```

If you haven't already built it in the previous chapters, then you need to build the `students` container image and run it on the host:

```
# buildah build -t students .
# podman run -d \
    --network net1 \
    -p 8080:8080 \
    --name webapp \
    students \
    students -host db -port 5432 \
    -username admin -password
```

Notice the highlighted part of the command: the `students` application accepts the `-host`, `-port`, `-username`, and `-password` options to customize the database's endpoints and credentials.

We did not provide any IP address in the host field. Instead, the Postgres container name, `db`, along with the default `5432` port, were used to identify the database.

Also, notice that the `db` container was created without any kind of port mapping: we expect to directly reach the database over the `net1` container network, where both containers were created.

Let's try to call the `students` application API and see what happens:

```
# curl localhost:8080/students
{"Id":10149,"FirstName":"Frank","MiddleName":
"Vincent","LastName":
"Zappa","Class":"3A","Course":"Composition"}
```

The query worked fine, meaning that the application successfully queried the database. But how did this happen? How did it resolve the container IP address by only knowing its name? In the next section, we'll look at the different behaviors on CNI and Netavark network backends.

DNS resolution on a CNI network backend

On Podman 3 or Podman 4 with a CNI backend, the dnsname plugin is enabled in the net1 network and a dedicated dnsmasq service is spawned that is in charge of resolving container names to their assigned IP addresses. Let's start by finding the container's IP addresses first:

```
# podman inspect db --format '{{.NetworkSettings.Networks.net1.
IPAddress}}'
10.90.0.2
# podman inspect webapp --format '{{.NetworkSettings.Networks.
net1.IPAddress}}'
10.90.0.3
```

We want to look for dnsmasq processes running on the system:

```
# ps aux | grep dnsmasq
root        2703  0.0  0.0  26436  2384 ?          S     16:16
0:00 /usr/sbin/dnsmasq -u root --conf-file=/run/containers/cni/
dnsname/net1/dnsmasq.conf
root        5577  0.0  0.0   6140   832 pts/0      S+    22:00
0:00 grep --color=auto dnsmasq
```

The preceding output shows an instance of the dnsmasq process running with a config file that's been created under the /run/containers/cni/dnsname/net1/ directory. Let's inspect its contents:

```
# ls -al /run/containers/cni/dnsname/net1/
total 12
drwx------. 2 root root 120 Jan 25 16:16 .
drwx------. 3 root root  60 Jan 25 16:16 ..
-rw-r--r--. 1 root root  30 Jan 25 16:28 addnhosts
-rwx------. 1 root root 356 Jan 25 16:16 dnsmasq.conf
-rwxr-x---. 1 root root   0 Jan 25 16:16 lock
-rw-r--r--. 1 root root   5 Jan 25 16:16 pidfile
```

/run/containers/cni/dnsname/net1/dnsmasq.conf defines the dnsmasq configuration:

```
# cat /run/containers/cni/dnsname/net1/dnsmasq.conf
## WARNING: THIS IS AN AUTOGENERATED FILE
```

```
## AND SHOULD NOT BE EDITED MANUALLY AS IT
## LIKELY TO AUTOMATICALLY BE REPLACED.
strict-order
local=/dns.podman/
domain=dns.podman
expand-hosts
pid-file=/run/containers/cni/dnsname/net1/pidfile
except-interface=lo
bind-dynamic
no-hosts
interface=cni-podman1
addn-hosts=/run/containers/cni/dnsname/net1/addnhosts
```

The process listens on the `cni-podman1` interface (the `net1` network bridge, which has an IP address of `10.90.0.1`) and is authoritative for the `dns.podman` domain. The host's records are kept in the `/run/containers/cni/dnsname/net1/addnhosts` file, which contains the following:

```
# cat /run/containers/cni/dnsname/net1/addnhosts
10.90.0.2  db
10.90.0.3  webapp
```

When a container in the `net1` network attempts DNS resolution, it uses its `/etc/resolv.conf` file to find out the DNS server to direct the query to. The file's content in the webapp container is as follows:

```
# podman exec -it webapp cat /etc/resolv.conf
search dns.podman
nameserver 10.90.0.1
```

This shows that the container contacts the `10.90.0.1` address (which is also the container default gateway and the `cni-podman1` bridge) to query hostname resolution.

The search domain allows processes to search for a **Fully Qualified Domain Name (FQDN)**. In the preceding example, db.dns.podman would be resolved correctly by the DNS service. The search domain for a CNI network configuration can be customized by editing the related config file under /etc/cni/net.d/. The default configuration for the dnsname plugin in the net1 config is as follows:

```
{
        "type": "dnsname",
        "domainName": "dns.podman",
        "capabilities": {
            "aliases": true
        }
    }
```

When you update the domainName field to a new value, the changes are not effective immediately. To regenerate the updated dnsmasq.conf, all the containers in the network must be stopped to let the dnsname plugin clean up the current network configuration. When containers are restarted, the dnsmasq configuration is regenerated accordingly.

DNS resolution on a Netavark network backend

If the preceding example was executed on Podman 4 with a Netavark network backend, the aardvark-dns daemon would be responsible for container resolution in a similar way to dnsmasq.

The aardvark-dns project is a companion project of Netavark written in Rust. It is a lightweight authoritative DNS service that can work on both IPv4 A records and IPv6 AAAA records.

When a new network with DNS resolution enabled is created, a new aardvark-dns process is created, as shown in the following code:

```
# ps aux | grep aardvark-dns
root        9115   0.0  0.0 344732   2584 pts/0     Sl    20:15
0:00 /usr/libexec/podman/aardvark-dns --config /run/containers/
networks/aardvark-dns -p 53 run
root       10831   0.0  0.0   6400   2044 pts/0     S+    23:36
0:00 grep --color=auto aardvark-dns
```

The process listens on port 53/udp of the host network namespace for rootfull containers and on port 53/udp of the rootless network namespace for rootless containers.

The output of the ps command also shows the default configuration path – the /run/containers/networks/aardvark-dns directory – where the aardvark-dns process stores the resolution configurations under different files, named after the associated network. For example, for the net1 network, we will find content similar to the following:

```
# cat /run/containers/networks/aardvark-dns/net1
10.90.0.1
dc7fff2ef78e99a2a1a3ea6e29bfb961fc07cd6cf71200d50761e25df30
11636 10.90.0.2   db,dc7fff2ef78e
10c7bbb7006c9b253f9ebe1103234a9af41dced8f12a6d94b7fc46a9a97
5d8cc 10.90.0.2   webapp,10c7bbb7006c
```

The file stores IPv4 addresses (and IPv6 addresses, if present) for every container. Here, we can see the containers' names and short IDs resolved to the IPv4 addresses.

The first line tells us the address where aardvark-dns is listening for incoming requests. Once again, it corresponds to the default gateway address for the network.

Connecting containers across the same network allows for fast and simple communication across different services running in separate network namespaces. However, there are use cases where containers must share the same network namespace. Podman offers a solution to achieve this goal easily: Pods.

Running containers inside a Pod

The concept of a Pod comes from the Kubernetes architecture. According to the official upstream documentation, "*A Pod ... is a group of one or more containers, with shared storage and network resources, and a specification for how to run the containers.*"

A Pod is also the smallest deployable unit in Kubernetes scheduling. All the containers inside a Pod share the same network, UTC, IPC, and (optionally) PID namespace. This means that all the services running on the different containers can refer to each other as **localhost**, while external containers will continue to contact the Pod's IP address. A Pod receives one IP address that is shared across all the containers.

There are many adoption use cases. A very common one is sidecar containers: in this case, a reverse proxy or an OAuth proxy runs alongside the main container to provide authentication or service mesh functionalities.

Podman provides the basic tooling for manipulating Pods with the `podman pod` command. The following example shows how to create a basic Pod with two containers and demonstrates network namespace sharing across the two containers in the Pod.

> **Important Note**
>
> To understand the following example, stop and remove all the running containers and Pods and start with a clean environment.

`podman pod create` initializes a new, empty Pod from scratch:

```
# podman pod create --name example_pod
```

> **Important Note**
>
> When a new, empty Pod is created, Podman also creates an `infra` container, which is used to initialize the namespaces when the Pod is started. This container is based on the `k8s.gcr.io/pause` image for Podman 3 and a locally-built `podman-pause` image for Podman 4.

Now, we can create two basic `busybox` containers inside the Pod:

```
# podman create --name c1 --pod example_pod busybox sh -c
'sleep 10000'
# podman create --name c2 --pod example_pod busybox sh -c
'sleep 10000'
```

Finally, we can start the Pod (and its associated containers) with the `podman pod start` command:

```
# podman pod start example_pod
```

Here, we have a running Pod with two containers (plus an infra one) running. To verify its status, we can use the `podman pod ps` command:

```
# podman pod ps
POD ID          NAME         STATUS       CREATED        INFRA ID
# OF CONTAINERS
8f89f37b8f3b    example_pod  Degraded     8 minutes ago
95589171284a    4
```

With the `podman pod top` command, we can see the resources that are being consumed by each container in the Pod:

```
# podman pod top example_pod
USER        PID          PPID          %CPU        ELAPSED
TTY         TIME         COMMAND
root        1            0             0.000       10.576973703s
?           0s           sleep 1000
0           1            0             0.000       10.577293395s
?           0s           /catatonit -P
root        1            0             0.000       9.577587032s
?           0s           sleep 1000
```

After creating the Pod, we can inspect the network's behavior. First, we will see that only one network namespace has been created in the system:

```
# ip netns
netns-17b9bb67-5ce6-d533-ecf0-9d7f339e6ebd (id: 0)
```

Let's check the IP configuration for this namespace and its related network stack:

```
# ip netns exec netns-17b9bb67-5ce6-d533-ecf0-9d7f339e6ebd ip
addr show
1: lo: <LOOPBACK,UP,LOWER_UP> mtu 65536 qdisc noqueue state
UNKNOWN group default qlen 1000
    link/loopback 00:00:00:00:00:00 brd 00:00:00:00:00:00
    inet 127.0.0.1/8 scope host lo
       valid_lft forever preferred_lft forever
    inet6 ::1/128 scope host
       valid_lft forever preferred_lft forever
2: eth0@if15: <BROADCAST,MULTICAST,UP,LOWER_UP> mtu 1500 qdisc
noqueue state UP group default
    link/ether a6:1b:bc:8e:65:1e brd ff:ff:ff:ff:ff:ff link-
netnsid 0
    inet 10.88.0.3/16 brd 10.88.255.255 scope global eth0
       valid_lft forever preferred_lft forever
    inet6 fe80::a41b:bcff:fe8e:651e/64 scope link
       valid_lft forever preferred_lft forever
```

To verify that the `c1` and `c2` containers share the same network namespace and are running with an IP address of `10.88.0.3`, we can run the same `ip addr show` command inside the containers using the `podman exec` command:

```
# podman exec -it c1 ip addr show
# podman exec -it c2 ip addr show
```

These two containers are expected to return the same output as the `netns-17b9bb67-5ce6-d533-ecf0-9d7f339e6ebd` network namespace.

The example pod can be stopped and removed with the `podman pod stop` and `podman pod rm` commands, respectively:

```
# podman pod stop example_pod
# podman pod rm example_pod
```

We will cover pods in more detail in *Chapter 14, Interacting with systemd and Kubernetes*, where we will also discuss name resolution and multi-pod orchestration.

In this section, we focused on communication across two or more containers inside the same host or Pod, regardless of the number and type of networks involved. However, containers are a platform where you can run services that are generally accessed by the external world. For this reason, in the next section, we will investigate the best practices that can be applied to expose containers outside their hosts and make their services accessible to other clients/consumers.

Exposing containers outside our underlying host

Container adoption in an enterprise company or a community project could be a hard thing to do that could require time. For this reason, we may not have all the required services running as containers during our adoption journey. This is why exposing containers outside our underlying host could be a nice solution for interconnecting services that live in containers to services that run in the legacy world.

As we briefly saw earlier in this chapter, Podman uses two different networking stacks, depending on the container: rootless or rootfull.

Even though the underlying mechanism is slightly different, depending on if you are using a rootless or a rootfull container, Podman's command-line options for exposing network ports are the same for both container types.

> **Good to Know**
>
> Note that the example we are going to see in this section will be executed as a root user. This choice was necessary because the main objective of this section is to show you some of the firewall configurations that could be mandatory for exposing a container service to the outside world.

Exposing a container starts with Port Publishing activities. We'll learn what this is in the next section.

Port Publishing

Port Publishing consists of instructing Podman to create a temporary mapping between the container's ports and some random or custom host's ports.

The option to instruct Podman to publish a port is really simple – it consists of adding the `-p` or `--publish` option to the `run` command. Let's see how it works:

```
-p=ip:hostPort:containerPort
```

The previous option publishes a container's port, or range of ports, to the host. When we are specifying ranges for `hostPort` or `containerPort`, the number must be equal for both ranges.

We can even omit `ip`. In that case, the port will be bound on all the IPs of the underlying host. If we do not set the host port, the container's port will be randomly assigned a port on the host.

Let's look at an example of the port publishing option:

```
# podman run -dt -p 80:80/tcp docker.io/library/httpd
Trying to pull docker.io/library/httpd:latest...
Getting image source signatures
Copying blob 41c22baa66ec done
Copying blob dcc4698797c8 done
Copying blob d982c879c57e done
Copying blob a2abf6c4d29d done
Copying blob 67283bbdd4a0 done
Copying config dabbfbe0c5 done
Writing manifest to image destination
```

```
Storing signatures
ea23dbbeac2ea4cb6d215796e225c0e7c7cf2a979862838ef4299d410c90
ad44
```

As you can see, we have told Podman to run a container starting from the httpd base image. Then, we allocated a pseudo-tty (-t) in detached mode (-d) before setting the port mapping to bind the underlying host port, 80, to port 80 of the container.

Now, we can use the podman port command to see the actual mapping:

```
# podman ps
CONTAINER ID   IMAGE                                  COMMAND
CREATED        STATUS              PORTS               NAMES
ea23dbbeac2e   docker.io/library/httpd:latest   httpd-foreground
3 minutes ago  Up 3 minutes ago  0.0.0.0:80->80/tcp   ecstatic_
chaplygin
# podman port ea23dbbeac2e
80/tcp -> 0.0.0.0:80
```

First, we requested the list of running containers and then passed the correct container ID to the podman port command. We can check if the mapping is working properly like so:

```
# curl localhost:80
<html><body><h1>It works!</h1></body></html>
```

Here, we executed a curl command from the host system and it worked – the httpd process running in the container just replied to us.

If we have multiple ports and we do not care about their assignment on the underlying host system, we can easily leverage the-P or --publish-all option to publish all the ports that are exposed by the container image to random ports on the host interfaces. Podman will run through the container image's metadata looking for the exposed ports. These ports are usually defined in a Dockerfile or Containerfile with the EXPOSE instruction, as shown here:

```
EXPOSE 80/tcp
EXPOSE 80/udp
```

With the previous keyword, we can instruct the container engine that will run the final container of which network ports will be exposed and used by it.

However, we can leverage an easy but insecure alternative, as shown in the next section.

Attaching a host network

To expose a container service to the outside world, we can attach the whole host network to the running container. As you can imagine, this method could lead to the unauthorized use of host resources so, for this reason, it is not recommended and should be used carefully.

As we anticipated, attaching the host network to a running container is quite simple. Using the right Podman option, we can easily get rid of any network isolation:

```
# podman run --network=host -dt docker.io/library/httpd
2cb80369e53761601a41a4c004a485139de280c3738d1b7131c241f4001
f78a6
```

Here, we used the `--network` option while specifying the `host` value. This informs Podman that we want to let the container attach to the host network.

After running the previous command, we can check that the running container is bound to the host system's network interfaces since it can access all of them:

```
# netstat -nap|grep ::80
tcp6        0       0 :::80                          :::*
LISTEN        37304/httpd
# curl localhost:80
<html><body><h1>It works!</h1></body></html>
```

Here, we executed a `curl` command from the host system and it worked – the `httpd` process running in the container just replied to us.

The process of exposing containers outside the underlying host does not stop here. In the next section, we'll learn how to complete this job.

Host firewall configuration

Whether we choose to leverage Port Publishing or attach the host network to the container, the process of exposing containers outside the underlying host does not stop here – we have reached the base OS of our host machine. In most cases, we will also need to allow the incoming connections to flow in the host's underlying machine, which will be interacting with the system firewall.

The following example shows a non-comprehensive way to interact with the base OS firewall. If we're using a Fedora operating system or any other Linux distribution that's leveraging Firewalld as its firewall daemon manager, we can allow incoming connections on port 80 by running the following commands:

```
# firewall-cmd --add-port=80/tcp
success
# firewall-cmd --runtime-to-permanent
success
```

The first command edits the live system rules, while the second command stores the runtime rules in a permanent way that will survive system reboot or service restart.

> **Good to Know**
>
> Firewalld is a firewall service daemon that provides us with an easy and fast way to customize the system firewall. Firewalld is dynamic, which means that it can create, change, and delete the firewall rules without restarting the firewall daemon each time a change is applied.

As we have seen, the process of exposing the container's services is quite simple but should be performed with a bit of consciousness and attention: opening a network port to the outside world should always be done carefully.

Rootless container network behavior

As we saw in the previous sections, Podman relies on CNI plugins or Netavark for containers running as root and has the privileges to alter network configurations in the host network namespace. For rootless containers, Podman uses the `slirp4netns` project, which allows you to create container network configurations without the need for root privileges; the network interfaces are created inside a rootless network namespace where the standard user has sufficient privileges. This approach allows you to transparently and flexibly manage rootless container networking.

In the previous sections, we saw how container network namespaces can be connected to a bridge using a veth pair. Being able to create a veth pair in the host network namespace requires root privileges that are not allowed for standard users.

In the simplest scenario, `slirp4netns` aims to overcome these privilege limitations by allowing a tap device to be created that's attached to a user-mode network namespace. This tap device is created in the rootless network namespace.

For every new rootless container, a new `slirp4netns` process is executed on the host. The process creates a network namespace for the container and a `tap0` device is created and configured with the `10.0.2.100/24` address (from the default slirp4netns `10.0.2.0/24` subnet). This prevents two containers from directly communicating with each other on the same network since there would be an IP address overlap.

The following example demonstrates the network behavior of a rootless `busybox` container:

```
$ podman run -i busybox sh -c 'ip addr show tap0'
2: tap0: <BROADCAST,UP,LOWER_UP> mtu 65520 qdisc fq_codel state
UNKNOWN group default qlen 1000
    link/ether 2a:c7:86:66:e9:20 brd ff:ff:ff:ff:ff:ff
    inet 10.0.2.100/24 brd 10.0.2.255 scope global tap0
        valid_lft forever preferred_lft forever
    inet6 fd00::28c7:86ff:fe66:e920/64 scope global dynamic
mngtmpaddr
        valid_lft 86117sec preferred_lft 14117sec
    inet6 fe80::28c7:86ff:fe66:e920/64 scope link
        valid_lft forever preferred_lft forever
```

It is possible to inspect the rootless network namespace and find the corresponding `tap0` device:

```
$ podman unshare --rootless-netns ip addr show tap0
2: tap0: <BROADCAST,UP,LOWER_UP> mtu 65520 qdisc fq_codel state
UNKNOWN group default qlen 1000
    link/ether 1a:eb:82:6a:82:8d brd ff:ff:ff:ff:ff:ff
    inet 10.0.2.100/24 brd 10.0.2.255 scope global tap0
        valid_lft forever preferred_lft forever
    inet6 fd00::18eb:82ff:fe6a:828d/64 scope global dynamic
mngtmpaddr
        valid_lft 86311sec preferred_lft 14311sec
    inet6 fe80::18eb:82ff:fe6a:828d/64 scope link
        valid_lft forever preferred_lft forever
```

Since rootless containers do not own independent IP addresses, we have two ways to let two or more containers communicate with each other:

- The easiest way could be to put all the containers in a single Pod so that the containers can communicate using the localhost interface, without the need to open any ports.

- The second way is to attach the container to a custom network and have its interfaces managed in the rootless network namespace.

- If we want to keep all the containers independent, we could use the port mapping technique to publish all the necessary ports and then use those ports to let the containers communicate with each other.

Using a Podman 4 network backend, let's quickly focus on the second scenario, where two pods are attached on a rootless network. First, we need to create the network and attach a couple of test containers:

```
$ podman network create rootless-net
$ podman run -d --net rootless-net --name endpoint1 --cap-
add=net_admin,net_raw busybox /bin/sleep 10000
$ podman run -d --net rootless-net --name endpoint2 --cap-
add=net_admin,net_raw busybox /bin/sleep 10000
```

Let's try to ping the endpoint2 container from endpoint1:

```
$ podman exec -it endpoint1 ping -c1 endpoint1
PING endpoint1 (10.89.1.2): 56 data bytes
64 bytes from 10.89.1.2: seq=0 ttl=64 time=0.023 ms
--- endpoint1 ping statistics ---
1 packets transmitted, 1 packets received, 0% packet loss
round-trip min/avg/max = 0.023/0.023/0.023 ms
```

These two containers can communicate on the common network and have different IPv4 addresses. To prove this, we can inspect the contents of the aardvark-dns configuration for the rootless containers:

```
$ cat /run/user/1000/containers/networks/aardvark-dns/rootless-
net
10.89.1.1
fe27f8d653384fc191d5c580d18d874d480a7e8ef74c2626ae21b118eedb
f1e6 10.89.1.2  endpoint1,fe27f8d65338
```

```
19a4307516ce1ece32ce58753e70da5e5abf9cf70feea7b981917ae399ef
934d 10.89.1.3  endpoint2,19a4307516ce
```

Finally, let's demonstrate that the custom network bypasses the `tap0` interface and allows dedicated veth pairs and bridges to be created in the rootless network namespace. The following command will show a Linux bridge for the `rootless-net` network and two attached veth pairs:

```
$ podman unshare --rootless-netns ip link | grep 'podman'
3: podman2: <BROADCAST,MULTICAST,UP,LOWER_UP> mtu 1500 qdisc
noqueue state UP mode DEFAULT group default qlen 1000
4: vethdca7cdc6@if2: <BROADCAST,MULTICAST,UP,LOWER_UP> mtu
1500 qdisc noqueue master podman2 state UP mode DEFAULT group
default qlen 1000
5: veth912bd229@if2: <BROADCAST,MULTICAST,UP,LOWER_UP> mtu
1500 qdisc noqueue master podman2 state UP mode DEFAULT group
default qlen 1000
```

> **Important Note**
>
> If you're running this code on a CNI network backend, use the `podman unshare -rootless-cni` command.

Another limitation of rootless containers is regarding the `ping` command. Usually, on Linux distributions, standard non-root users lack the `CAP_NET_RAW` security capability. This inhibits the execution of the `ping` command, which leverages the send/receive of ICMP packets. If we want to use the `ping` command in a rootless container, we can enable the missing security capability through the `sysctl` command:

```
# sysctl -w "net.ipv4.ping_group_range=0 2000000"
```

Note that this could allow any process that will be executed by a user on these groups to send ping packets.

Finally, while using rootless containers, we also need to consider that the Port Publishing technique can only be used for ports above `1024`. This is because, on Linux operating systems, all the ports below `1024` are privileged and cannot be used by standard non-root users.

Summary

In this chapter, we learned how container network isolation can be leveraged to allow network segregation for each container that's running through network namespaces. These activities seem complex but thankfully, with the help of a container runtime, the steps are almost automated. We learned how to manage container networking with Podman and how to interconnect two or more containers. Finally, we learned how to expose a container's network ports outside of the underlying host and what kind of limitations we can expect while networking for rootless containers.

In the next chapter, we will discover the main differences between Docker and Podman. This will be useful for advanced users, but also for novice ones, to understand what we can expect by comparing these two container engines.

Further reading

To learn more about the topics that were covered in this chapter, take a look at the following resources:

- Container Network Interface: `https://github.com/containernetworking/cni`

- The Netavark project on GitHub: `https://github.com/containers/netavark`

- The Aardvark-dns project on GitHub: `https://github.com/containers/aardvark-dns`

- CNI reference plugins: `https://www.cni.dev/plugins/current/`

- CNI third-party plugins: `https://github.com/containernetworking/cni#3rd-party-plugins`

- Kubernetes Pod definition: `https://kubernetes.io/docs/concepts/workloads/pods/`

- The Slirp4netns project repository: `https://github.com/rootless-containers/slirp4netns`

13
Docker Migration Tips and Tricks

Every technology has a pioneer company, project, and product that, once created and announced, becomes a real game-changer that allowed its base concepts to spread. For containers, this was Docker.

As we learned in *Chapter 1, Introduction to Container Technology*, Docker provided a new approach and great ideas to leveraging existing technologies and creating brand new ones. After a few years, it became the most used technology for containers.

But as usually happens for open source projects, the community and the enterprise started looking for improvements, new architectures, and different implementations. That's where Podman found a place to grow and leverage the standardization that's offered by the **Open Container Initiative** (**OCI**).

Docker was (and still is) the most used container technology. For this reason, in this chapter, we are going to provide some tips and tricks regarding handling the migration process. We will be covering the following topics:

- Migrating existing images and playing with a command's alias
- Podman commands versus Docker commands
- Using Docker Compose with Podman

Technical requirements

Before you proceed with this chapter's lecture and examples, you will need a machine with a working Podman installation. As we mentioned in *Chapter 3*, *Running the First Container*, all the examples in this book have been executed on a Fedora 34 system or later but can be reproduced on your choice of **operating system** (**OS**).

Having a good understanding of the topics that were covered in *Chapter 4*, *Managing Running Containers*, *Chapter 5*, *Implementing Storage for the Container's Data*, and *Chapter 9*, *Pushing Images to a Container Registry*, will help you grasp the concepts that will be covered in this chapter regarding containers.

Migrating existing images and playing with a command's alias

Podman has one great feature that lets any previous Docker user easily adapt and switch to it – complete **command-line interface** (**CLI**) compatibility with Docker.

Let's demonstrate this CLI compatibility with Docker by creating a shell command alias for the `docker` command:

```
# alias docker=podman
# docker
Error: missing command 'podman COMMAND'
Try 'podman --help' for more information.
```

As you can see, we have created a command alias that binds the `podman` command to the `docker` one. If we try to execute the `docker` command after setting the alias, the output is returned from the `podman` command instead.

Let's try this out on the newly created alias by running a container:

```
# docker run --rm -it docker.io/wernight/funbox nyancat
```

We should see something very funny – a running cat, similar to the one shown in the following screenshot:

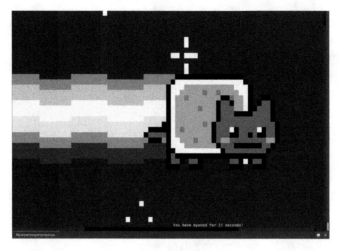

Figure 13.1 – Funny output from running a test container

Let's test something more interesting. Docker, for example, offers a tutorial based on a container image exposing a web server:

```
# docker run -dp 80:80 docker.io/docker/getting-started
Trying to pull docker.io/docker/getting-started:latest...
Getting image source signatures
Copying blob 97518928ae5f done
Copying blob e0bae2ade5ec done
Copying blob a2402c2da473 done
Copying blob e362c27513c3 done
Copying blob a4e156412037 done
Copying blob 3f3577460f48 done
Copying blob 69465e074227 done
Copying blob eb65930377cd done
Copying config 26d80cd96d done
Writing manifest to image destination
Storing signatures
d44a2df41d76b3322e56971d45e92e75f4679e8b620198228fbd9
cc00fe9578f
```

Here, we continued to use the docker alias command with the option for running it by using a daemon, -d, and the option for binding the HTTP port, -p.

If everything worked correctly, then we can point our favorite web browser to `http://`
`localhost:`

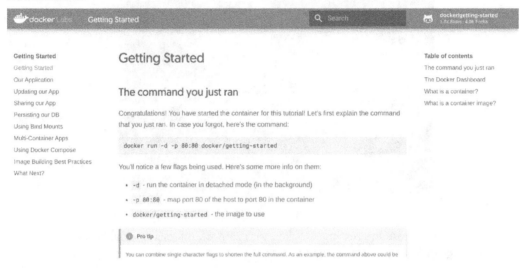

Figure 13.2 – Docker tutorial home page

The first page of Dockerlabs, **Getting Started**, specifies the command that was just run.
From the left column of the page, we can continue with the tutorial.

Let's continue with the tutorial and double-check that the alias will work properly at every
stage.

The tutorial steps are very simple, and they can help you summarize the knowledge that
was shared in the previous chapters, from building a container to using multiple container
applications to create a dedicated network. Please stop before the **Using Docker Compose**
section as we will look at this in more detail shortly.

Don't forget that we are using an alias and that, under the hood, Podman is working
actively to let our containers work as expected, ensuring Docker CLI compatibility.

But what about container migration in the case of swapping Docker in favor of Podman?

Well, a direct way to move existing containers from Docker to Podman does not exist. It is
recommended that you recreate the containers with the respective container images and
reattach any volumes using Podman.

The container images can be exported using the `docker export` command, which will
create a TAR archive file that can be imported into Podman via the `podman import`
command. If you're using a container image registry, you can skip this.

To understand any limitations we may encounter when we're using commands, examples, and resources written for Docker with our Podman installation, let's compare various Podman and Docker commands.

Podman commands versus Docker commands

As we saw in the previous section, as well as in *Chapter 2, Comparing Podman and Docker*, the Podman CLI is based on the Docker CLI. However, because Podman does not require a runtime daemon to work, some of the Docker commands may not be directly available or they could require some workarounds.

The command list is exceptionally long, so the following table only specifies a few:

Docker Command	Podman Command
docker	podman
docker ps	podman ps
docker pull	podman pull
docker push	podman push
docker rename	podman rename
docker restart	podman restart
docker rm	podman rm
docker rmi	podman rmi
docker run	podman run

As you can see, the command's name is the same as comparing the docker command with the podman command. However, even though the name is the same, due to architectural differences between Podman and Docker, some features or behaviors could be different.

Behavioral differences between Podman and Docker

The following commands were intentionally implemented in another way by the Podman development team:

- podman volume create: This command will fail if the volume already exists. In Docker, this command is idempotent, which means that if a volume already exists with the same name, then Docker will just skip this instruction. The actual behavior of Docker does not match the implementations for the other commands.

- podman run -v /tmp/noexist:/tmp: This command will fail if the source volume path does not exist. Instead, Docker will create the folder if it does not exist. Again, the Podman development team considered this a bug and changed it.

- `podman run --restart`: The restart option in Podman will not persist after a system reboot. If required, we can run Podman from a `systemd.unit` file through `podman generate systemd`.

In the next section, we'll see which commands are missing from Podman that exist in Docker.

Missing commands in Podman

The following table shows a non-comprehensive list of Docker commands that, at the time of writing, don't have equivalents in Podman:

Missing Command	Description
`docker container update`	Podman does not support altering any running containers. The Podman development team recommends recreating containers with new arguments.
`docker plugin`	Podman does not support plugins at the time of writing. Its development team recommends using alternative OCI runtimes or OCI runtime hooks to alter its behavior.
`docker swarm`	Podman does not support Docker Swarm, but it does support Kubernetes for orchestration using CRI-O.
`docker trust`	This Docker command has been implemented in the `podman image trust` command.

Now, let's see which commands are missing from Docker.

Missing commands in Docker

Similar to how Podman is missing some Docker commands, Docker is missing some Podman commands.

The following families of commands in Podman don't have respective ones in Docker:

- `podman container`: This command can be used to manage containers.
- `podman generate`: This command can be used to create a structured output (such as a YAML file) for a container, pod, or volume.
- `podman healthcheck`: This command provides you with a set of subcommands that you can use to manage container health checks.

- `podman image`: This command can be used to manage container images.

- `podman init`: This command can be used to initialize a container with all the required steps but without running it.

- `podman machine`: This command lists a set of subcommands for managing Podman's virtual machine on macOS.

- `podman mount`: This command mounts the container's root filesystem in a location that can be accessed by the host.

- `podman network exists/prune/reload`: This command checks and manages the status of a container's network.

- `podman play`: This command creates containers, pods, or volumes based on the input from a structured (such as YAML) file input.

- `podman pod`: This provides a set of subcommands for managing pods or groups of containers.

- `podman system`: This provides a set of subcommands for managing the Podman systems and retrieving information.

- `podman unmount`: This command unmounts a working container's root filesystem.

- `podman unshare`: This command launches a process in a new user namespace (rootless containers).

- `podman untag`: This command removes one or more stored images.

- `podman volume exists`: This command checks if a volume exists.

Of course, if a command is missing, this does not mean that the feature is missing in Docker.

Another useful feature that's available in Docker is Compose. We'll learn how to use it in Podman in the next section.

Using Docker Compose with Podman

When it was first released, Docker quickly gained consensus thanks to its intuitive approach to container management. Along with the main container engine solution, another great feature was introduced to help users orchestrate multiple containers on a single host: **Docker Compose**.

The idea behind Compose is quite simple – it's a tool that can be used to orchestrate multi-container applications that are supposed to interact together on a single host and configured with a declarative file in YAML format. All the applications that are executed in a Compose stack are defined as services that can communicate with the other containers in the stack with a transparent name resolution.

The configuration file is named `docker-compose.yaml` and has a simple syntax where one or more **services** and related **volumes** are created and started.

Development teams can benefit from the stack's automation to quickly test applications on a single host. However, if we need to run our application on a production-like, multi-node environment, the best approach is to adopt a clustered orchestration solution such as Kubernetes.

When Podman was first released, its main purpose was to reach OCI full compatibility and feature parity with Docker CLI commands to become a valid daemonless alternative to the well-known container engine that inspired it. Unfortunately, this Compose compatibility was not supported in the first two major releases. Afterwards, the `podman-compose` project was introduced to fill the gap. The project was a separate development stream that needed to compensate for the lack of native Compose support in Podman.

With Podman v3.0, native support for Docker Compose was finally introduced upstream, leaving users with the choice of using the original `docker-compose` utility or the new `podman-compose` utility.

In this section, we learned how to configure Podman to orchestrate multiple containers with `docker-compose` to provide full compatibility to users migrating from Docker to Podman. In the next subsection, we'll look at an example of using `podman-compose` to leverage rootless container orchestration.

Before we dig into setting up Podman, let's look at a few basic examples of Compose files to understand how they work.

Docker Compose quick start

Compose files can be used to declare one or multiple containers being executed inside a common stack and also to define build instructions for custom applications. The advantage of this approach is that you can fully automate the entire application stack, including frontends, backends, and persistence services such as databases or in-memory caches.

> **Important Note**
>
> The purpose of this section is to provide a quick overview of Compose files to help you understand how Podman can handle them.
>
> For a detailed list of the latest Compose specification, please refer to the following URL: `https://docs.docker.com/compose/compose-file/compose-file-v3/`.
>
> A more extensive list of Compose examples can be found in the Docker Awesome Compose project at `https://github.com/docker/awesome-compose`.

The following is a minimal configuration file that defines a single container running the Docker registry:

Chapter13/registry/docker-compose.yaml

```
services:
  registry:
    ports:
      - "5000:5000"
    volumes:
      - registry_volume:/var/lib/registry
    image: docker.io/library/registry
volumes:
  registry_volume: {}
```

The preceding example can be seen as a more structured and declarative way to define the execution parameters for a container. However, the real value of Docker Compose is its orchestration stacks, which are made up of multiple containers in a single instance.

The following example is even more interesting and shows a configuration file for a WordPress application that uses a MySQL database as its backend:

Chapter13/wordpress/docker-compose.yaml

```
services:
  db:
    image: docker.io/library/mysql:latest
    command: '--default-authentication-plugin=mysql_native_
password'
```

```
    volumes:
        - db_data:/var/lib/mysql
    restart: always
    environment:
        - MYSQL_ROOT_PASSWORD=wordpressroot
        - MYSQL_DATABASE=wordpress
        - MYSQL_USER=wordpress
        - MYSQL_PASSWORD=wordpress
    expose:
        - 3306
        - 33060
  wordpress:
    image: docker.io/library/wordpress:latest
    ports:
        - 8080:80
    restart: always
    environment:
        - WORDPRESS_DB_HOST=db
        - WORDPRESS_DB_USER=wordpress
        - WORDPRESS_DB_PASSWORD=wordpress
        - WORDPRESS_DB_NAME=wordpress
volumes:
  db_data:
```

Here, we can see the two main YAML objects – `services` and `volumes`. Under the `services` part of the code, we have two applications – `db` and `wordpress`. These have been highlighted for clarity.

In the `services` list, there's a set of configuration values that define the container's behavior. These are as follows:

- `image`: The image that's used by the container.

- `command`: Additional commands to be passed to the container's entry point.

- `Volumes`: The list of volumes to be mounted in the container, along with their associated mount points. Along with new dedicated volumes, existing directories in the host can be bind-mounted on container mount points.

- `restart`: Container restart options in case an error occurs.

- `expose`: The list of ports to be exposed by the container.

- `ports`: The list of port mappings between the container and the host.

- `environment`: The list of environment variables to be created in the container. In this example, `WORDPRESS_DB_HOST`, `WORDPRESS_DB_USER`, `WORDPRESS_DB_PASSWORD`, `WORDPRESS_DB_NAME`, are injected into the WordPress container to provide connection parameters to the database.

Together with the service's declaration, we have a list of volumes that are managed by Compose. The engine can create these volumes in the Compose process or use existing volumes that have been labeled as `external`.

The third and final example is a Compose file that builds a minimal REST API application that's been written in Go that writes and retrieves data to a Redis in-memory store:

Chapter13/golang-redis/docker-compose.yaml

```
services:
  web:
    build:
      context: ./app
      labels:
        - "com.example.description=Golang Redis App"
    ports:
      - "8080:8080"
    environment:
      - REDIS_HOST=redis
    depends_on:
      - redis
  redis:
    image: docker.io/library/redis
    deploy:
      replicas: 1
```

In this example, we have new elements that deserve attention:

- A `build` object, which defines the image to be built and also applies custom labels to the build.

- The `context` key holds the path for the build. In this example, the `./app` folder contains all the source code files and the Dockerfile for building the image.

- A `labels` list, which holds a set of labels that are passed as strings in the build process.

- A `depends_on` list that specifies, for the web service, the other services that are considered dependencies; in this case, the `redis` service.

- An `environment` list that defines the name of the `redis` service that's used by the web app.

- A `deploy` object in the `redis` service that lets us define custom configuration parameters, such as the number of container `replicas`.

To bring up Compose applications with Docker, we can run the following command from the `compose` file's folder:

```
$ docker-compose up
```

This command creates all the stack and related volumes while printing the output to `stdout`.

To run in detached mode, simply add the `-d` option to the command:

```
$ docker-compose up -d
```

The following command builds the necessary images and starts the stack:

```
$ docker-compose up --build
```

Alternatively, the `docker-compose build` command can be used to build the applications without starting them.

To shut down a stack running in the foreground, simply hit the *Ctrl + C* keyboard combination. Instead, to shut down a detached application, run the following command:

```
$ docker-compose down
```

To kill an unresponsive container, we can use the `docker-compose kill` command:

```
$ docker-compose kill [SERVICE]
```

This command supports multiple signals with the `-s SIGNAL` option.

Now that we've covered the basic concepts surrounding Docker Compose, let's learn how to configure Podman to run Compose files.

Configuring Podman to interact with docker-compose

To support Compose, Podman needs to expose its REST API service through a local UNIX socket. This service supports both Docker-compatible APIs and the native Libpod APIs.

On a Fedora distribution, the docker-compose (which provides Docker Compose binaries) and podman-docker (which provides aliasing to the docker command) packages must be installed using the following command:

```
$ sudo dnf install docker-compose podman-docker
```

> **Important Note**
>
> The docker-compose package, when installed on a Fedora 34 system, installs version v1.28 at the time of writing, written in Python. The latest version, v2, was completely rewritten in Go and provides a significant performance improvement. It can be downloaded from the GitHub release page at https://github.com/docker/compose/releases.

After installing the packages, we can enable and start the systemd unit that manages the UNIX socket service:

```
$ sudo systemctl enable --now podman.socket
```

This command starts a socket that's listening on /run/podman/podman.sock.

Note that the native docker-compose command looks for a socket file in the /run/docker.sock path by default. For this reason, the podman-docker packages creates a symbolic link on the same path that points to /run/podman/podman.sock, as shown in the following example:

```
# ls -al /run/docker.sock
lrwxrwxrwx. 1 root root 23 Feb  3 21:54 /var/run/docker.sock ->
/run/podman/podman.sock
```

The UNIX socket that's exposed by Podman can be accessed by a process with root privileges only. It is possible to stretch the security restrictions by opening access to the file to all the users in the system or by allowing custom ACLs for a custom group. Later in this chapter, we will see that rootless container stacks can be executed with podman-compose.

For the sake of simplicity, in the next subsection, you'll learn how to run docker-compose commands with Podman in rootfull mode.

Running Compose workloads with Podman and docker-compose

To help you learn how to operate `docker-compose` and create orchestrated multi-container deployments on our host, we will reuse the previous example of the Go REST API with a Redis in-memory store.

We have already inspected the `docker-compose.yaml` file, which builds the web application and deploys one instance of the Redis container.

Let's inspect the Dockerfile that's used to build the application:

Chapter13/golang-redis/Dockerfile

```
FROM docker.io/library/golang AS builder

# Copy files for build
RUN mkdir -p /go/src/golang-redis
COPY go.mod main.go /go/src/golang-redis

# Set the working directory
WORKDIR /go/src/golang-redis

# Download dependencies
RUN go get -d -v ./...

# Install the package
RUN go build -v

# Runtime image
FROM registry.access.redhat.com/ubi8/ubi-minimal:latest as bin
COPY --from=builder /go/src/golang-redis/golang-redis /usr/local/bin
COPY entrypoint.sh /

EXPOSE 8080

ENTRYPOINT ["/entrypoint.sh"]
```

Here, we can see that the Go application is compiled in a multi-stage build and that the Go binary is copied inside a UBI-Minimal image.

The web frontend is minimal – it listens to port 8080/tcp and only implements two endpoints – an HTTP POST method and an HTTP GET method to allow clients to upload and retrieve a JSON object that contains the name, email, and ID of a user. The JSON object is stored inside the Redis database.

> **Important Note**
> If you're curious, the source code for the Go server is available in the Chapter13/golang-redis/app/main.go file. It isn't presented in this book for the sake of space and readability.

To build and run the application, we must change to the project directory and run the docker-compose up command:

```
# cd Chapter13/golang-redis
# docker-compose up --build -d
[...omitted output...]
Successfully tagged localhost/golang-redis_web:latest
6b330224010ed611baba11fc2d66b9e4cfc991312f5166b47b5fcd073
57c6325
Successfully built
6b330224010ed611baba11fc2d66b9e4cfc991312f5166b47b5fcd073
57c6325
Creating golang-redis_redis_1 ... done
Creating golang-redis_web_1   ... done
```

Here, we can see that docker-compose created two containers, whose names always follow the <project_name>_<service_name>_<instance_count> pattern.

The instance count varies when there is more than one replica in the service deployment.

We can inspect the running containers with the usual podman ps command:

```
# podman ps
CONTAINER ID   IMAGE                              COMMAND
CREATED          STATUS            PORTS
NAMES
4a5421c9e7cd   docker.io/library/redis:latest     redis-
server   20 seconds ago  Up 20 seconds ago
golang-redis_redis_1
```

```
8a465d4724ab  localhost/golang-redis_web:latest
20 seconds ago  Up 20 seconds ago  0.0.0.0:8080->8080/tcp
golang-redis_web_1
```

One of the more interesting aspects is that the service names are automatically resolved.

When a Compose stack is created, Podman creates a new network, named with the `<project_name>_default` pattern.

The new network uses the `dnsname` plugin to instantiate a `dnsmasq` process and resolve the containers' IPs to names that have been created after the service names.

We can inspect the network with the following command:

```
# podman network ls | grep golang-redis
49d5a3c3679c  golang-redis_default    0.4.0
bridge,portmap,firewall,tuning,dnsname
```

The `dnsmasq` service can be found using the `ps` command and filtered with `grep`:

```
# ps aux | grep dnsmasq | grep golang
root     2749495  0.0  0.0  26388  2416 ?          S    01:33
0:00 /usr/sbin/dnsmasq -u root --conf-file=/run/containers/cni/
dnsname/golang-redis_default/dnsmasq.conf
```

The `/run/containers/cni/dnsname/golang-redis_default` directory holds the instance's configuration. Inside the `addnhosts` file, we can find the mappings between the service names and the allocated container IPs:

```
# cat /run/containers/cni/dnsname/golang-redis_default/
addnhosts
10.89.3.240      golang-redis_redis_1    4a5421c9e7cd    redis
10.89.3.241       golang-redis_web_1     4298ae9f29c5       web
```

This means that a process inside a container can resolve a service name with a standard DNS query.

When we have multiple container replicas in a service, the resulting resolution that's delivered by `dnsmasq` is similar to a **round-robin DNS**, a simple and minimalistic kind of load balancing that iterates multiple DNS records that are resolved by the same name. When a process calls a service (the `db` service, for example), it will be resolved to as many different IPs as there are service replicas.

Let's go back to the docker-compose.yaml file. In the environment section of the web service configuration, we have the following variable:

```
environment:
  - REDIS_HOST=redis
```

This variable is injected into the running container and represents the name of the redis service. It is used by the Go application to create the connection string to Redis and initialize the connection. When we're using a DNS-resolved service name, the container name and IP address of the redis service are completely irrelevant to our Go application.

We can use the docker-compose exec command to verify that the variable was correctly injected inside the containers running as the web service in the stack:

```
# docker-compose exec web env
Emulate Docker CLI using podman. Create /etc/containers/
nodocker to quiet msg.
PATH=/usr/local/sbin:/usr/local/bin:/usr/sbin:/usr/bin:/sbin:/
bin
TERM=xterm
container=oci
REDIS_HOST=redis
HOME=/root
```

The env command outputs the full list of environment variables in the container. This allows us to verify that the REDIS_HOST variable was created correctly.

Important Note

Storing configurations such as connection strings in a database as constants in the application code is an anti-pattern in general, especially for modern cloud-native applications. The correct approach is to guarantee a strict separation between the application logic and the configuration parameters.

Configurations can be stored as environment variables or inside config/secret files that are injected at runtime in the container that runs the application.

These practices are well-defined in the **Twelve-Factor App** pattern specification, whose URL can be found in the *Further reading* section.

It is finally time to test the application by posting a couple of JSON objects and retrieving one of them with the `curl` command:

```
$ curl -X POST -d \
'{"name":"jim", "email":"jim@example.com", "id":"0001"}' \
localhost:8080
$ curl -X POST -d \
'{"name":"anna", "email":"anna@example.com", "id":"0002"}' \
localhost:8080
```

The web container was successfully written to the Redis backend, which we can see by running the `docker-compose logs` command:

```
# docker-compose logs web
[...omitted output...]
2022/02/06 00:58:06 Storing data:   {"name":"jim","email":"jim@
example.com","id":"0001"}
2022/02/06 00:58:10 Storing data:
{"name":"anna","email":"anna@example.com","id":"0002"}
```

The preceding command captures the logs of all the containers behind the web service.

Finally, we can retrieve the result. The web application reads back the object from the Redis database by looking at its `id`:

```
$ curl -X GET -d '{"id": "0001"}' localhost:8080
{"name":"jim","email":"jim@example.com","id":"0001"}
```

To shut down our application, we can simply use the `docker-compose down` command:

```
# docker-compose down
```

This command destroys the containers and their associated resources, including the custom network, but not volumes. To remove volumes, you must add the `-v` option to the end of the command.

The `docker-compose` utility is a great companion for building and deploying on a single host with Podman. However, in the next chapter, we will learn about some other useful solutions that will let us generate and execute Kubernetes Pod and Service resources, as well as containers that are executed by Systemd units. Before moving on, let's inspect the alternative `podman-compose` tool, which provides support for rootless containers.

Using podman-compose

The podman-compose project started way before version 3.0 of Podman to provide a compatibility layer for users that needed to orchestrate containers with Compose files. In this subsection, we will look at an example of using podman-compose on Fedora.

The podman-compose tool's CLI is written in Python. The package can be installed with dnf or by getting the latest release from the respective GitHub repository (you can find the direct link in *Further reading* section):

```
$ sudo dnf install -y podman-compose
```

Alternatively, it can be installed with Python's package manager, pip3, which supports a broader set of operating systems and distributions:

```
$ pip3 install podman-compose
```

Now, we can run the same Compose stacks from the previous examples with the advantage of the rootless approach that's provided by podman-compose.

The following are all the available commands that are compatible with docker-compose, along with their descriptions and some minor changes that are made by the output of the podman-compose help command:

- help: Shows the tool's help
- version: Shows the command's version
- pull: Pulls the stack images
- push: Pushes the stack images
- build: Builds the stack images
- up: Creates and starts the entire stack or some of its services
- down: Tears down the entire stack
- ps: Show the status of running containers
- run: Creates a container similar to a service to run a one-off command
- exec: Executes a certain command in a running container
- start: Starts specific services
- stop: Stops specific services
- restart: Restarts specific services
- logs: Shows logs from services

The following command creates a stack from a directory containing the necessary configurations and the `docker-compose.yaml` file:

```
$ podman-compose up
```

The command's output is also very similar to the output provided by `docker-compose`.

To shut down the stack, simply run the following command:

```
$ podman-compose down
```

The `podman-compose` project still hasn't reached total feature parity with `docker-compose`. However, it is a very interesting project to follow and contribute to to help implement a Podman-native utility that can evolve independently in the future.

Summary

In this chapter, we learned how to manage a full migration from Docker to Podman.

We covered how to migrate images and create command aliases and we inspected the command compatibility matrix. Here, we provided a detailed overview of the different behaviors of specific commands and the different commands that are implemented in the two container engines – that is, Docker and Podman.

Then, we learned how to migrate Docker Compose by illustrating native Podman 3.0 support for the `docker-compose` command and the `podman-compose` alternative utility.

In the next and final chapter of this book, we will learn how to interact with Systemd by generating custom service units and turning containers into services that are started automatically inside the host. Then, we'll look at Kubernetes-oriented orchestration, where we will learn how to generate Kubernetes resources from running containers and pods and run them in Podman or Kubernetes natively.

Further reading

To learn more about the topics that were covered in this chapter, take a look at the following resources:

- Docker Awesome Compose: `https://github.com/docker/awesome-compose`

- Podman-compose project on GitHub: `https://github.com/containers/podman-compose`

- Red Hat blog introduction to Docker Compose support in Podman: `https://www.redhat.com/sysadmin/podman-docker-compose`

- Twelve-Factor App: `https://12factor.net/`

- Podman man page: `https://github.com/containers/podman/blob/main/docs/source/markdown/podman.1.md`

14
Interacting with systemd and Kubernetes

In the previous chapters, we learned how to initialize and manage containers, starting with simple concepts and arriving at advanced ones. Containers represent a key technology for application development in the latest Linux operating system releases. For this reason, containers are only the starting point for advanced developers and system administrators. Once this technology becomes widely adopted in an enterprise company or a technical project, the next step will be to integrate it with the base operating system and with -system orchestration platforms.

In this chapter, we're going to cover the following main topics:

- Setting up the prerequisites for the host operating system
- Creating the systemd unit files
- Managing container-based systemd services
- Generating Kubernetes YAML resources
- Running Kubernetes resource files in Podman
- Testing the results in Kubernetes

Technical requirements

To complete this chapter, you will need a machine with a working Podman installation. As we mentioned in *Chapter 3*, *Running the First Container*, all the examples in this book were executed on a Fedora 34 system or later but can be reproduced on your choice of **operating system (OS)**.

Having a good understanding of the topics that were covered in *Chapter 4*, *Managing Running Containers*, *Chapter 5*, *Implementing Storage for the Container's Data*, and *Chapter 9*, *Pushing Images to a Container Registry*, will help you grasp the topics we'll cover regarding advanced containers.

You should also have a good understanding of system administration and Kubernetes container orchestration.

For the examples related to the Kubernetes section, you will require Podman version 4.0.0 because of a bug in version 3.4.z that prevents container environment variables from being created (`https://github.com/containers/podman/issues/12781`). This bug was fixed in v4.0.0 but it hasn't been backported to Podman v3 at the time of writing.

Setting up the prerequisites for the host operating system

As we saw in *Chapter 1*, *Introduction to Container Technology*, containers were born to help simplify and create system services that can be distributed on standalone hosts.

In the following sections, we will learn how to run MariaDB and a GIT service in containers while managing those containers like any other service – that is, through Systemd and the `systemctl` command.

First, let's introduce systemd, a system and service manager for Linux that runs as the first process on boot (as PID 1) and acts as an init system that brings up and maintains userspace services. Once a new user logs in to the host system, separate instances are executed to start their services.

The systemd daemon starts services and ensures priority with a dependency system between various entities called *units*. There are 11 different types of units.

Fedora 34 and later has systemd enabled and running by default. We can check if it is running properly by using the following command:

```
# systemctl is-system-running
running
```

In the following sections, we are going to work with system unit files of the `service` type. We can check the current ones by running the following command:

```
# systemctl list-units --type=service | head
  UNIT                        LOAD    ACTIVE SUB      DESCRIPTION
    abrt-journal-core.service  loaded active running Creates ABRT
problems from coredumpctl messages
    abrt-oops.service  loaded active running ABRT kernel log
watcher
    abrt-xorg.service  loaded active running ABRT Xorg log
watcher
    abrtd.service  loaded active running ABRT Automated Bug
Reporting Tool
```

> **Please Note**
> The systemd service and its internals are more complex, so they cannot be summarized in a few lines. For additional information, please refer to the related Linux manual.

In the next section, we are going to learn how to create the systemd unit files for any running container service on our operating system.

Creating the systemd unit files

The unit files on our system define how systemd starts and runs services.

Each unit file represents a single component as a simple text file that describes its behavior, what needs to run before or afterward, and more.

Unit files are stored in a few different places on a system and systemd looks for them in this order:

1. `/etc/systemd/system`
2. `/run/systemd/system`
3. `/usr/lib/systemd/system`

Unit files that are in the earlier directories override the later ones. This lets us change what we need in the `/etc` directory, where configuration is expected, leaving the default configuration files in `/usr`, for example.

But what does a unit file look like? Let's find out.

First, we can get the location of a default unit file by asking systemd about it:

```
# systemctl status sshd
○ sshd.service - OpenSSH server daemon
     Loaded: loaded (/usr/lib/systemd/system/sshd.service;
disabled; vendor preset: disabled)
     Active: inactive (dead)
       Docs: man:sshd(8)
             man:sshd_config(5)
```

Here, we executed the `status` command while passing the `sshd` service name as a filter.

In the systemd output, the default unit file path can be inspected with the following example command:

```
# cat /usr/lib/systemd/system/sshd.service
```

But what about Podman? Well, Podman makes systemd integration easier with its dedicated sub-command:

```
# podman generate systemd -h
Generate systemd units.
Description:
  Generate systemd units for a pod or container.
  The generated units can later be controlled via systemctl(1).
Usage:
  podman generate systemd [options] {CONTAINER|POD}
 ...
```

The `podman generate systemd` command will output a text file representing the unit file that was created. As we can see from the help output, we can set up several options to adjust our settings.

We should always save the generated file and place it on the right path, as described in the previous output. We'll explore this command by providing a full example in the next section.

Managing container-based systemd services

In this section, you will learn how to use the `podman generate systemd` command through a practical example. We will create two system services based on containers to create a GIT repository.

For this example, we will leverage two well-known open source projects:

- **Gitea**: The GIT repository, which also offers a nice web interface for code management
- **MariaDB**: The SQL database for holding the data that's produced by the Gitea service

Let's start with the example. First, we need to generate a password for our database's user:

```
# export MARIADB_PASSWORD=my-secret-pw
# podman secret create --env MARIADB_PASSWORD
53149b678d0dbd34fb56800cc
```

Here, we exported the environment variable with the secret password we are going to use and then leveraged a useful secrets management command that we did not introduce previously: `podman secret create`. Unfortunately, this command holds the secret in plain text, though this is good enough for our purpose. Since we are running these containers as root, these secrets are stored on the filesystem with root-only permissions.

We can inspect the secret with the following commands:

```
# podman secret ls
ID                         NAME             DRIVER
CREATED        UPDATED
53149b678d0dbd34fb56800cc  MARIADB_PASSWORD file          10
hours ago  10 hours ago
# podman secret inspect 53149b678d0dbd34fb56800cc
[
    {
        "ID": "53149b678d0dbd34fb56800cc",
        "CreatedAt": "2022-02-16T00:54:21.01087091+01:00",
        "UpdatedAt": "2022-02-16T00:54:21.01087091+01:00",
        "Spec": {
            "Name": "MARIADB_PASSWORD",
            "Driver": {
                "Name": "file",
```

```
                    "Options": {
                        "path": "/var/lib/containers/storage/
secrets/filedriver"
                    }
                }
            }
        }
]
# cat /var/lib/containers/storage/secrets/filedriver/
secretsdata.json
{
  "53149b678d0dbd34fb56800cc": "bXktc2VjcmV0LXB3"
}
# ls -l /var/lib/containers/storage/secrets/filedriver/
secretsdata.json
-rw-------. 1 root root 53 16 feb 00.54 /var/lib/containers/
storage/secrets/filedriver/secretsdata.json
```

Here, we have asked Podman to list and inspect the secret we created previously and looked at the underlying filesystem for the file holding the secrets.

The file holding the secrets is a file in JSON format and, as we mentioned previously, is in plain text. The first string of the couple is the secret ID, while the second string is the value Base64 encoded. If we try to decode it with the BASE64 algorithm, we would see that it represents the password we just added – that is, my-secret-pw.

Even though the password is stored in plain text, it is good enough for our example because we are using the root user and this filestore has root-only permission, as we can verify with the last command of the previous output.

Now, we can continue setting up the database container. We will start with the database setup because it is a dependency on our GIT server.

We must create a local folder in the host system where we can store container data:

```
# mkdir -p /opt/var/lib/mariadb
```

We can also look at the public documentation of the container image to find out the right volume path and the various environment variables to use to start our container:

```
# podman run -d --network host --name mariadb-service -v \
  /opt/var/lib/mariadb:/var/lib/mysql:Z -e \
```

```
 MARIADB_DATABASE=gitea -e MARIADB_USER=gitea -e \
 MARIADB_RANDOM_ROOT_PASSWORD=true \
 --secret=MARIADB_PASSWORD,type=env docker.io/mariadb:latest
 61ae055ef6512cb34c4b3fe1d8feafe6ec174a25547728873932f0649217
 62d1
```

We are going to run and test the container as standalone first to check if there are any errors; then, we will transform it into a system service.

In the preceding Podman command, we did the following:

- We ran the container in detached mode.
- We assigned it a name – that is, `mariadb-service`.
- We exposed the host network for simplicity; of course, we could limit and filter this connectivity.
- We mapped the storage volume with the newly created local directory while also specifying the `:Z` option to correctly assign the SELinux labels.
- We defined the environment variables to use at runtime by the container's processes, also providing the password's secret with the `--secret` option.
- We used the container image name we want to use – that is, `docker.io/mariadb:latest`.

We can also check if the container is up and running by using the following command:

```
# podman ps
CONTAINER ID    IMAGE                            COMMAND
CREATED           STATUS                PORTS        NAMES
61ae055ef651    docker.io/library/mariadb:latest  mariadbd      56
seconds ago    Up 57 seconds ago                  mariadb-service
```

Now, we are ready to check the output of the `podman generate systemd` command:

```
# podman generate systemd --name mariadb-service
...
[Unit]
Description=Podman container-mariadb-service.service
Documentation=man:podman-generate-systemd(1)
Wants=network-online.target
After=network-online.target
```

```
RequiresMountsFor=/run/containers/storage
[Service]
Environment=PODMAN_SYSTEMD_UNIT=%n
Restart=on-failure
TimeoutStopSec=70
ExecStart=/usr/bin/podman start mariadb-service
ExecStop=/usr/bin/podman stop -t 10 mariadb-service
ExecStopPost=/usr/bin/podman stop -t 10 mariadb-service
PIDFile=/run/containers/storage/overlay-containers/61ae055ef65
12cb34c4b3fe1d8feafe6ec174a25547728873932f064921762d1/userdata/
conmon.pid
Type=forking
[Install]
WantedBy=default.target
```

As you can see, the output has been published directly in the console. Here, we used the --name option to instruct Podman that we want to manage the container with that name through systemd.

Podman generated a unit file with all the required command instructions to integrate our container into the operating system.

In the [Unit] section, we can see that it declared a dependency of this service from the network through the network-online.target unit. It also states the need for the storage mount point for /run/containers/storage containers.

In the [Service] section, Podman defined all the instructions for describing how to start and stop the containerized service.

Now, let's look at the GIT service. First, we will create the storage directory:

```
# mkdir -p /opt/var/lib/gitea/data
```

After that, we can look at the project documentation for any configuration that's needed for the Gitea container image to be built correctly and complete the `podman run` command:

```
# podman run -d --network host --name gitea-service \
-v /opt/var/lib/gitea/data:/data:Z \
docker.io/gitea/gitea:latest
ee96f8276038f750ee3b956cbf9d3700fe46e6e2bae93605a67e623717e
206dd
```

In the previous Podman command, we did the following:

- We ran the container in detached mode.
- We assigned it a name – that is, `gitea-service`.
- We exposed the host network for simplicity; of course, we can limit and filter this connectivity.
- We mapped the storage volume with the newly created local directory while specifying the `:Z` option to correctly assign the SELinux labels.

Finally, we can check if the service is running properly by inspecting its logs:

```
# podman logs gitea-service
Server listening on :: port 22.
Server listening on 0.0.0.0 port 22.
2022/02/16 00:01:55 cmd/web.go:102:runWeb() [I] Starting Gitea
on PID: 12
...
2022/02/16 00:01:56 cmd/web.go:208:listen() [I] Listen:
http://0.0.0.0:3000
2022/02/16 00:01:56 cmd/web.go:212:listen() [I] AppURL(ROOT_
URL): http://localhost:3000/
2022/02/16 00:01:56 ...s/graceful/server.go:61:NewServer() [I]
Starting new Web server: tcp:0.0.0.0:3000 on PID: 12
```

As we can see, the Gitea service is listening on port 3000. Let's point our web browser to http://localhost:3000 to install it with the required configuration:

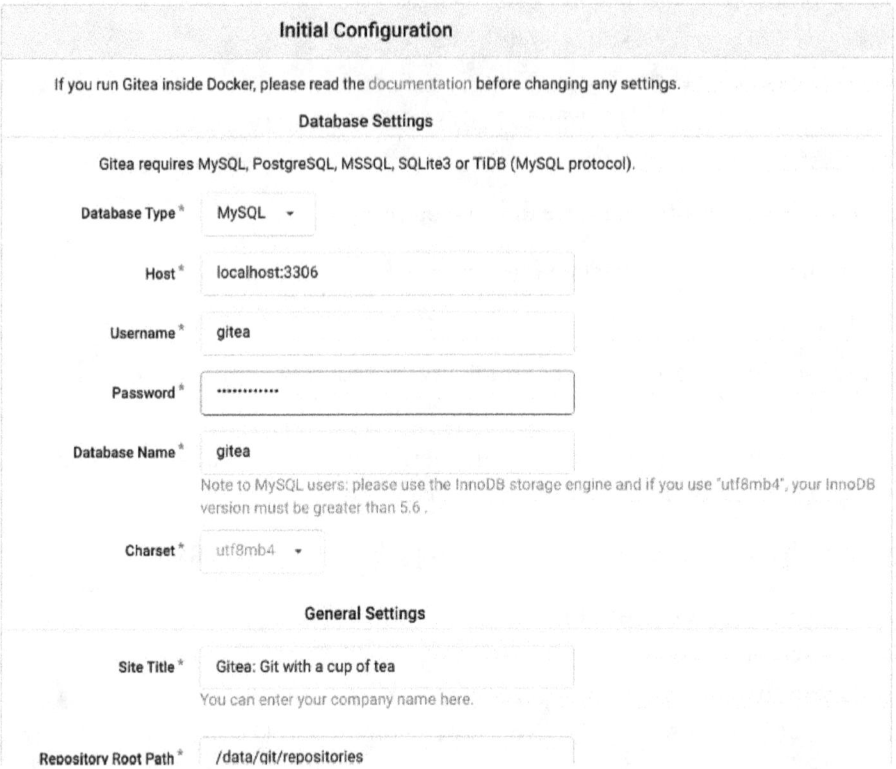

Initial Configuration

If you run Gitea inside Docker, please read the documentation before changing any settings.

Database Settings

Gitea requires MySQL, PostgreSQL, MSSQL, SQLite3 or TiDB (MySQL protocol).

Database Type *	MySQL ▾
Host *	localhost:3306
Username *	gitea
Password *	••••••••••••
Database Name *	gitea

Note to MySQL users: please use the InnoDB storage engine and if you use "utf8mb4", your InnoDB version must be greater than 5.6 .

Charset *	utf8mb4 ▾

General Settings

Site Title *	Gitea: Git with a cup of tea

You can enter your company name here.

Repository Root Path *	/data/git/repositories

Figure 14.1 – Gitea service installation page

In the preceding screenshot, we defined the database's type, address, username, and password to complete the installation. Once done, we should be redirected to the login page, as follows:

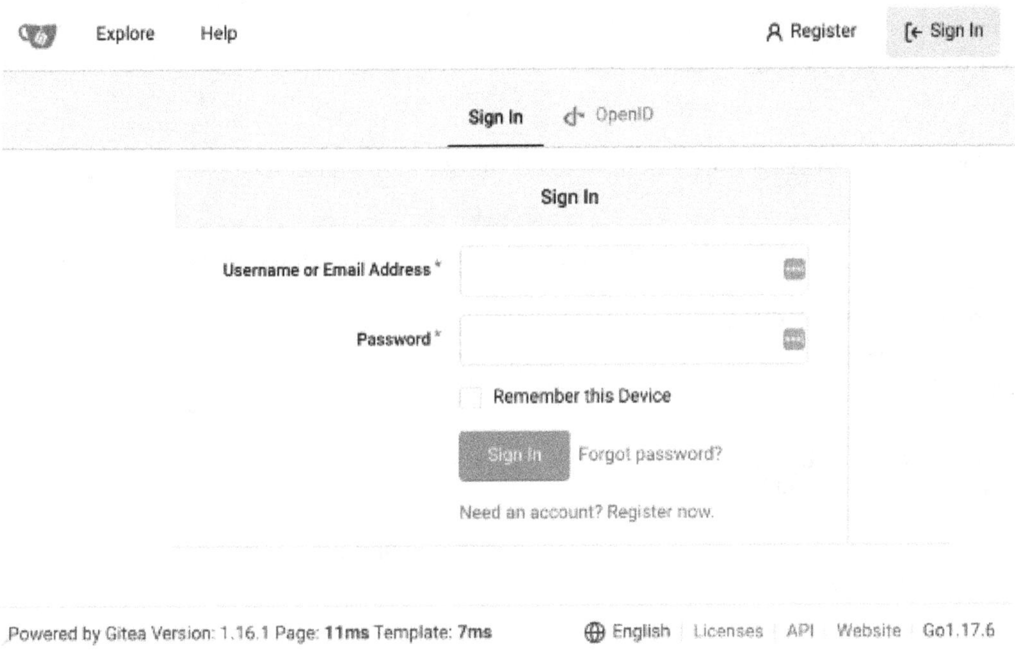

Figure 14.2 – Gitea service login page

Once the configuration is complete, we can generate and add the systemd unit files to the right configuration path:

```
# podman generate systemd --name gitea-service > /etc/systemd/
system/container-gitea-service.service
# podman generate systemd --name mariadb-service > /etc/
systemd/system/container-mariadb-service.service
```

Then, we can manually edit the Gitea service unit file by adding a depending order to the MariaDB service through the special `Requires` instruction:

```
# cat /etc/systemd/system/container-gitea-service.service
...
[Unit]
Description=Podman container-gitea-service.service
Documentation=man:podman-generate-systemd(1)
Wants=network-online.target
After=network-online.target
```

```
RequiresMountsFor=/run/containers/storage
Requires=container-mariadb-service.service
...
```

Thanks to the `Requires` instruction, systemd will start the MariaDB service first, then the Gitea service.

Now, we can stop the containers by starting them through the systemd units:

```
# podman stop mariadb-service gitea-service
mariadb-service
gitea-service
```

Don't worry about the data – previously, we mapped both containers to a dedicated storage volume that holds the data.

We need to let the systemd daemon know about the new unit files we just added. So, first, we need to run the following command:

```
# systemctl daemon-reload
```

After that, we can start the services through systemd and check their statuses:

```
# systemctl start container-mariadb-service.service
# systemctl status container-mariadb-service.service
● container-mariadb-service.service - Podman container-mariadb-
service.service
     Loaded: loaded (/etc/systemd/system/container-mariadb-
service.service; disabled; vendor preset: disabled)
     Active: active (running) since Wed 2022-02-16 01:11:50
CET; 13s ago
...
# systemctl start container-gitea-service.service
# systemctl status container-gitea-service.service
● container-gitea-service.service - Podman container-gitea-
service.service
     Loaded: loaded (/etc/systemd/system/container-gitea-
service.service; disabled; vendor preset: disabled)
     Active: active (running) since Wed 2022-02-16 01:11:57
CET; 18s ago
...
```

Finally, we can enable the service to start them when the OS boots:

```
# systemctl enable container-mariadb-service.service
Created symlink /etc/systemd/system/default.target.wants/
container-mariadb-service.service → /etc/systemd/system/
container-mariadb-service.service.
```

```
# systemctl enable container-gitea-service.service
Created symlink /etc/systemd/system/default.target.wants/
container-gitea-service.service → /etc/systemd/system/
container-gitea-service.service.
```

With that, we have set up and enabled two containerized system services on our host OS. This process is simple and could be useful for leveraging the containers' features and capabilities, extending them to system services.

Now, we are ready to move on to the next advanced topic, where we will learn how to generate Kubernetes resources.

Generating Kubernetes YAML resources

Kubernetes has become the de facto standard for multi-node container orchestration. Kubernetes clusters allow multiple pods to be executed across nodes according to scheduling policies that reflect the node's load, labels, capabilities, or hardware resources (for example, GPUs).

We have already described the concept of a pod – a single execution group of one or more containers that share common namespaces (network, IPC, and, optionally, PID namespaces). In other words, we can think of pods as sandboxes for containers. Containers inside a Pod are executed and thus started, stopped, or paused simultaneously.

One of the most promising features that was introduced by Podman is the capability to generate Kubernetes resources in YAML format. Podman can intercept the configuration of running containers or pods and generate a Pod resource that is compliant with Kubernetes API specifications.

Along with pods, we can generate Service and PersistentVolumeClaim resources as well, which reflect the configurations of the port mappings and volumes that are mounted inside containers.

We can use the generated Kubernetes resources inside Podman itself as an alternative to the Docker Compose stacks or apply them inside a Kubernetes cluster to orchestrate the execution of simple pods.

Kubernetes has many ways to orchestrate how workloads are executed: `Deployments`, `StatefulSets`, `DaemonSets`, `Jobs`, and `CronJobs`. In every case, Pods are their workload-minimal execution units and the orchestration logic changes based on that specific behavior. This means that we can take a Pod resource that's been generated by Podman and easily adapt it to be orchestrated in a more complex object, such as `Deployments`, which manages replicas and version rollouts of our applications, or `DaemonSets`, which guarantees that a singleton pod instance is created for every cluster node.

Now, let's learn how to generate Kubernetes YAML resources with Podman.

Generating basic Pod resources from running containers

The basic command to generate Kubernetes resource from Podman is `podman generate kube`, followed by various options and arguments, as shown in the following code:

```
$ podman generate kube [options] {CONTAINER|POD|VOLUME}
```

We can apply this command to a running container, pod, or existing volume. The command also allows you to use the `-s, --service` option to generate `Service` resources and `-f, --filename` to export contents to a file (the default is to standard output).

Let's start with a basic example of a `Pod` resource that's been generated from a running container. First, we will start a rootless Nginx container:

```
$ podman run -d \
  -p 8080:80 --name nginx \
  docker.io/library/nginx
```

When the container is created, we can generate our Kubernetes `Pod` resource:

```
$ podman generate kube nginx
# Save the output of this file and use kubectl create -f to
import
# it into Kubernetes.
#
# Created with podman-4.0.0-rc4
apiVersion: v1
```

```yaml
kind: Pod
metadata:
  creationTimestamp: "2022-02-10T23:14:25Z"
  labels:
    app: nginxpod
  name: nginx_pod
spec:
  containers:
  - args:
    - nginx
    - -g
    - daemon off;
    image: docker.io/library/nginx:latest
    name: nginx
    ports:
    - containerPort: 80
      hostPort: 8080
    securityContext:
      capabilities:
        drop:
        - CAP_MKNOD
        - CAP_NET_RAW
        - CAP_AUDIT_WRITE
```

Let's describe the generated output. Every new Kubernetes resource is always composed of at least four fields:

- `apiVersion`: This field describes the API version schema of the resource. The `Pod` object belongs to the `v1` version of the `core` APIs of Kubernetes.

- `kind`: This field defines the resource kind, which is `Pod` in our example.

- `metadata`: This field is an object that holds a set of resource metadata that usually includes `name`, `namespace`, `labels`, and `annotations`, along with additional dynamic metadata that's created at runtime, such as `creationTimestamp`, `resourceVersion`, or the resource's `uid`.

- `spec`: This field holds resource specifications and varies among different resources. For example, a `Pod` resource will contain a list of `containers`, along with their startup arguments, volumes, ports, or security contexts.

All the information that's embedded inside a Pod resource is enough to start the pod inside a Kubernetes cluster. Along with the fields described previously, a fifth `status` field is dynamically created when the pod is running to describe its execution status.

From the generated output, we can notice an `args` list for every container, along with their startup commands, arguments, and options.

When you're generating a Pod from a container with mapped ports, the following `ports` list is created inside the Pod resource:

```
ports:
   - containerPort: 80
     hostPort: 8080
```

This means that port `80` must be exposed to the container and port `8080` must be exposed on the host running it. This information will be used by Podman when we create containers and pods with the `podman play kube` command, as we will see in the next section.

The `securityContext` object defines capabilities that must be dropped for this container. This means that the `CAP_MKNOD`, `CAP_NET_RAW`, and `CAP_AUDIT_WRITE` capabilities won't be enabled on a pod that's created from this configuration.

We can apply the output of the `podman generate kube` command directly to a Kubernetes cluster or save it to a file. To save it to a file, we can use the `-f` option:

```
$ podman generate kube nginx -f nginx-pod.yaml
```

To apply the generated output to a running Kubernetes cluster, we can use the Kubernetes CLI tool, `kubectl`. The `kubectl create` command applies a resource object inside the cluster:

```
$ podman generate kube nginx | kubectl create -f -
```

The basic Pod generation command can be enriched by creating the related Kubernetes services, as described in the next subsection.

Generating Pods and services from running containers

Pods running inside a Kubernetes cluster obtain unique IP addresses on a software-defined network that's managed by the default CNI plugin.

These IPs are not routed externally – we can only reach the Pod's IP address from within the cluster. However, we need a layer to balance multiple replicas of the same pods and provide a DNS resolution for a single abstraction frontend. In other words, our application must be able to query for a given service name and receive a unique IP address that abstracts from the pods' IPs, regardless of the number of replicas.

> **Important Note**
>
> Native, cluster-scoped DNS name resolution in Kubernetes is implemented with the **CoreDNS** service, which is started when the cluster's control plane is bootstrapped. CoreDNS is delegated to resolve internal requests and to forward ones for external names to authoritative DNS servers outside the cluster.

The resource that describes the abstraction in one or more pods in Kubernetes is called `Service`.

For example, we can have three replicas of the Nginx pod running inside our cluster and expose them with a unique IP. It belongs to a `ClusterIP` type, and its allocation is dynamic when the service is created. `ClusterIP` services are the default in Kubernetes and their assigned IPs are only local to the cluster.

We can also create `NodePort` type services that use **Network Address Translation (NAT)** so that the service can be reached from the external world. We can do this by mapping the service VIP and port to a local port on the cluster worker nodes.

If we have a cluster running on an infrastructure that allows dynamic load balancing (such as a public cloud provider), we can create `LoadBalancer` type services and have the provider manage ingress traffic load balancing for us.

Podman allows you to create services along with pods by adding the `-s` option to the `podman generate kube` command. This allows them to be potentially reused inside a Kubernetes cluster. The following example is a variation of the previous one and generates the Service resource along with the previously described Pod:

```
$ podman generate kube -s nginx
# Save the output of this file and use kubectl create -f to
import
# it into Kubernetes.
#
# Created with podman-4.0.0-rc4
```

```yaml
apiVersion: v1
kind: Service
metadata:
  creationTimestamp: "2022-02-12T21:54:02Z"
  labels:
    app: nginxpod
  name: nginx_pod
spec:
  ports:
  - name: "80"
    nodePort: 30582
    port: 80
    targetPort: 80
  selector:
    app: nginxpod
  type: NodePort
---
apiVersion: v1
kind: Pod
metadata:
  creationTimestamp: "2022-02-12T21:54:02Z"
  labels:
    app: nginxpod
  name: nginx_pod
spec:
  containers:
  - args:
    - nginx
    - -g
    - daemon off;
    image: docker.io/library/nginx:latest
    name: nginx
    ports:
```

```
       - containerPort: 80
         hostPort: 8080
     securityContext:
       capabilities:
         drop:
         - CAP_MKNOD
         - CAP_NET_RAW
         - CAP_AUDIT_WRITE
```

The generated output contains, along with the Pod resource, a Service resource that exposes the Nginx pod using a selector field. The selector matches all the pods with the `app: nginxpod` label.

When the service is created inside a Kubernetes cluster, an internal, non-routed VIP is allocated for the service. Since this is a `NodePort` type service, a **destination NAT (DNAT)** rule is created to match incoming traffic on all the cluster nodes on port `30582` and forward it to the service IP.

By default, Podman generates `NodePort` type services. Whenever a container or pod is decorated with a port mapping, Podman populates the `ports` object with a list of ports and their related `nodePort` mappings inside the manifest.

In our use case, we created the Nginx container by mapping its port, `80`, to port `8080` on the host. Here, Podman generated a Service that maps the container's port, `80`, to port `30582` on the cluster nodes.

> **Important Note**
> The `nodePort` mapping is applied to Kubernetes cluster nodes only, not to standalone hosts running Podman.

The value of creating Kubernetes services and pods from Podman is the ability to port to a Kubernetes platform.

In many cases, we work with composite, multi-tier applications that need to be exported and recreated together. Podman allows us to export multiple containers into a single Kubernetes Pod object or to create and export multiple pods to gain more control over our application. In the next two subsections, we will see both cases applied to a WordPress application and try to find out what the best approach is.

Generating a composite application in a single Pod

In this first scenario, we will implement a multi-tier application in a single pod. The advantage of this approach is that we can leverage the pod as a single unit that will execute multiple containers and that resource sharing across them is simplified.

We will launch two containers – one for MySQL and one for WordPress – and export them as a single Pod resource. We will learn how to work around some minor adjustments to make it work seamlessly later during run tests.

> **Important Note**
>
> The following examples have been created in a rootless context but can be seamlessly applied to rootfull containers too.
>
> A set of scripts that will be useful for launching the stacks and the generated Kubernetes YAML files are available in this book's GitHub repository at `https://github.com/PacktPublishing/Podman-for-DevOps/tree/main/Chapter14/kube`.

First, we must create two volumes that will be used later by the WordPress and MySQL containers:

```
$ for vol in dbvol wpvol; do podman volume create $vol; done
```

Then, we must create an empty pod named `wordpress-pod` with the necessary pre-defined port mappings:

```
$ podman pod create --name wordpress-pod -p 8080:80
```

Now, we can populate our pod by creating the WordPress and MySQL containers. Let's begin with the MySQL container:

```
$ podman create \
   --pod wordpress-pod --name db \
   -v dbvol:/var/lib/mysql \
   -e MYSQL_ROOT_PASSWORD=myrootpasswd \
   -e MYSQL_DATABASE=wordpress \
   -e MYSQL_USER=wordpress \
   -e MYSQL_PASSWORD=wordpress \
   docker.io/library/mysql
```

Now, we can create the WordPress container:

```
$ podman create \
  --pod wordpress-pod --name wordpress \
  -v wpvol:/var/www/html
  -e WORDPRESS_DB_HOST=127.0.0.1 \
  -e WORDPRESS_DB_USER=wordpress \
  -e WORDPRESS_DB_PASSWORD=wordpress \
  -e WORDPRESS_DB_NAME=wordpress \
  docker.io/library/wordpress
```

Here, we can see that the WORDPRESS_DB_HOST variable has been set to 127.0.0.1 (the address of the loopback device) since the two containers are going to run in the same pod and share the same network namespace. For this reason, we let the WordPress container know that the MySQL service is listening on the same loopback device.

Finally, we can start the pod with the podman pod start command:

```
$ podman pod start wordpress-pod
```

We can inspect the running containers with podman ps:

```
$ podman ps
CONTAINER ID    IMAGE
COMMAND                  CREATED            STATUS
PORTS                    NAMES
19bf706f0eb8    localhost/podman-pause:4.0.0-rc4-1643988335
About an hour ago  Up About an hour ago   0.0.0.0:8080->80/tcp
0400f8770627-infra
f1da755a846c    docker.io/library/mysql:latest
mysqld                   About an hour ago  Up About an hour ago
0.0.0.0:8080->80/tcp    db
1f28ef82d58f    docker.io/library/wordpress:latest
apache2-foregroun...    About an hour ago  Up About an hour ago
0.0.0.0:8080->80/tcp    wordpress
```

Now, we can point our browser to `http://localhost:8080` and confirm the appearance of the WordPress setup dialog screen:

Figure 14.3 – WordPress setup dialog screen

> **Important Note**
>
> The pod also started a third **infra** container. It is based on a minimal `podman-pause` image that initializes the pod's network and the IPC namespaces of our example. The image is built directly in the background on the host the first time a pod is created and executes a `catatonit` process, an `init` micro container written in C that's designed to handle system signals and zombie process reaping.
>
> This behavior of the pod's infra image is directly inherited from Kubernetes's design.

Now, we are ready to generate our Pod YAML manifest with the `podman generate kube` command and save it to a file for reuse:

```
$ podman generate kube wordpress-pod \
  -f wordpress-single-pod.yaml
```

The preceding command generates a file with the following content:

```
# Save the output of this file and use kubectl create -f to
import
# it into Kubernetes.
#
# Created with podman-4.0.0-rc4
apiVersion: v1
kind: Pod
metadata:
  creationTimestamp: "2022-02-13T11:06:38Z"
  labels:
    app: wordpress-pod
  name: wordpress-pod
spec:
  containers:
  - args:
    - mysqld
    env:
    - name: MYSQL_PASSWORD
      value: wordpress
    - name: MYSQL_USER
      value: wordpress
    - name: MYSQL_ROOT_PASSWORD
      value: myrootpasswd
    - name: MYSQL_DATABASE
      value: wordpress
    image: docker.io/library/mysql:latest
    name: db
    ports:
    - containerPort: 80
      hostPort: 8080
```

```yaml
    resources: {}
    securityContext:
      capabilities:
        drop:
          - CAP_MKNOD
          - CAP_NET_RAW
          - CAP_AUDIT_WRITE
    volumeMounts:
    - mountPath: /var/lib/mysql
      name: dbvol-pvc
  - args:
    - apache2-foreground
    env:
    - name: WORDPRESS_DB_HOST
      value: 127.0.0.1
    - name: WORDPRESS_DB_PASSWORD
      value: wordpress
    - name: WORDPRESS_DB_USER
      value: wordpress
    - name: WORDPRESS_DB_NAME
      value: wordpress
    image: docker.io/library/wordpress:latest
    name: wordpress
    resources: {}
    securityContext:
      capabilities:
        drop:
          - CAP_MKNOD
          - CAP_NET_RAW
          - CAP_AUDIT_WRITE
    volumeMounts:
    - mountPath: /var/www/html
      name: wpvol-pvc
  restartPolicy: Never
  volumes:
  - name: wpvol-pvc
```

```
    persistentVolumeClaim:
       claimName: wpvol
  - name: dbvol-pvc
    persistentVolumeClaim:
       claimName: dbvol
status: {}
```

Our YAML file holds a single Pod resource with two containers inside. Note that the previously defined environment variables have been created correctly inside our containers (when using Podman v4.0.0 or later).

Also, notice that the two container volumes have been mapped to PersistentVolumeClaim objects, often referred to as PVC objects.

PVCs are Kubernetes resources that are used to request (in other words, claim) a storage volume resource that satisfies a specific capacity and consumption modes. The attached storage volume resource is called a PersistentVolume (PV) and can be created manually or automatically by a StorageClass resource that leverages a storage driver that's compliant with the **Container Storage Interface** (**CSI**).

When we create a PVC, StorageClass provisions a PersistentVolume that satisfied our storage requests, and the two resources are bound together. This approach decouples the storage request from storage provisioning and makes storage consumption in Kubernetes more portable.

When Podman generates Kubernetes YAML files, PVC resources are not exported by default. However, we can also export the PVC resources to recreate them in Kubernetes with the podman generate kube <VOLUME_NAME> command.

The following command exports the WordPress application, along with its volume definitions, as a PVC:

```
$ podman generate kube wordpress-pod wpvol dbvol
```

The following is an example of the dbvol volume translated into a PersistentVolumeClaim:

```
apiVersion: v1
kind: PersistentVolumeClaim
metadata:
  annotations:
    volume.podman.io/driver: local
  creationTimestamp: "2022-02-13T14:51:05Z"
```

```
   name: dbvol
spec:
  accessModes:
  - ReadWriteOnce
  resources:
    requests:
      storage: 1Gi
status: {}
```

This approach has the advantage of providing the necessary PVC definitions to recreate the whole application in a Kubernetes cluster, but it is not necessary to recreate the volume resources in Podman: if they're not available, an empty volume with the same name will be created automatically.

To recreate all the resource dependencies in a Kubernetes cluster, we can also export the application's `Service` resource.

The following command exports everything in our WordPress example, including pods, services, and volumes:

```
$ podman generate kube -s wordpress-pod wpvol dbvol
```

Before we move on, let's briefly dig into the single pod approach logic that was described in this subsection and look at its advantages and possible limitations.

One great advantage of executing all the containers in a single pod is the simpler networking configuration – one network namespace is shared by all the running containers. This also means we don't have to create a dedicated Podman network to let the containers communicate with each other.

On the other hand, this approach does not reflect the common Kubernetes pattern of executing pods. In Kubernetes, we would prefer to split the WordPress pod and the MySQL pod to manage them independently and have different services associated with them. More separation implies more control and the chance to update independently.

In the next subsection, you'll learn how to replicate this approach and generate multiple pods for every application tier.

Generating composite applications with multiple Pods

One of the features of Docker Compose is that you can create different independent containers that communicate with each other using a service abstraction concept that is decoupled from the container's execution.

The Podman community (and many of its users) believe that a standardization toward Kubernetes YAML manifests to describe complex workloads is useful to get closer to the mainstream orchestration solution.

For this reason, the approach we'll describe in this section can become a full replacement for Docker Compose while providing Kubernetes portability at the same time. First, we will learn how to prepare an environment that can be used to generate the YAML manifests. After that, we can get rid of the workloads and only use the Kubernetes YAML to run our workloads.

The following example can be executed with rootless containers and networks.

> **Important Note**
> Before continuing, make sure that the previous example pod and containers have been completely removed, along with their volumes, to prevent any issues with port assignment or WordPress content initialization. Please refer to the commands in this book's GitHub repository as a reference: `https://github.com/PacktPublishing/Podman-for-DevOps/tree/main/AdditionalMaterial`.

First, we need to create a network. We have chosen the name `kubenet` to identify it easily and leave it with the default configuration for the sake of our example:

```
$ podman network create kubenet
```

Once the network has been created, the two `dbvol` and `wpvol` volumes must be created:

```
$ for vol in wpvol dbvol; do podman volume create $vol; done
```

We want to generate two distinct pods – one for each container. First, we must create the MySQL pod and its related container:

```
$ podman pod create -p 3306:3306 \
   --network kubenet \
   --name mysql-pod
$ podman create --name db \
  --pod mysql-pod \
  -v dbvol:/var/lib/mysql \
  -e MYSQL_ROOT_PASSWORD=myrootpasswd\
  -e MYSQL_DATABASE=wordpress \
  -e MYSQL_USER=wordpress \
```

```
    -e MYSQL_PASSWORD=wordpress \
    docker.io/library/mysql
```

Notice the port mapping, which we can use to access the MySQL service from a client and create the correct port mapping later in the Kubernetes service.

Now, let's create the WordPress pod and container:

```
$ podman pod create -p 8080:80 \
  --network kubenet \
  --name wordpress-pod
$ podman create --name wordpress \
  --pod wordpress-pod \
  -v wpvol:/var/www/html \
  -e WORDPRESS_DB_HOST=mysql-pod \
  -e WORDPRESS_DB_USER=wordpress \
  -e WORDPRESS_DB_PASSWORD=wordpress \
  -e WORDPRESS_DB_NAME=wordpress \
  docker.io/library/wordpress
```

There is a very important variable in the preceding command that can be considered the key to this approach: WORDPRESS_DB_HOST is populated with the mysql-pod string, which is the name that's been given to the MySQL pod.

In Podman, the pod's name will act as the service name of the application and the DNS daemon associated with the network (dnsmasq in Podman 3 or aardvark-dns in Podman 4) will directly resolve the pod name to the associated IP address. This is a key feature that makes multi-pod applications a perfect replacement for Compose stacks.

Now, we can start the two pods and have all the containers up and running:

```
$ podman pod start mysql-pod &&
  podman pod start wordpress-pod
```

Once again, pointing our browsers to http://localhost:8080 should lead us to the WordPress first setup page (if everything was set up correctly).

Now, we are ready to export our Kubernetes YAML manifest. We can choose to simply export the two Pod resources or create a full export that also includes services and volumes. This is useful if you need to import to a Kubernetes cluster.

Let's start with the basic version:

```
$ podman generate kube \
 -f wordpress-multi-pod-basic.yaml \
 wordpress-pod \
 mysql-pod
```

The output of the preceding code will contain nothing but the two Pod resources:

```
# Save the output of this file and use kubectl create -f to
import
# it into Kubernetes.
#
# Created with podman-4.0.0-rc4
apiVersion: v1
kind: Pod
metadata:
  creationTimestamp: "2022-02-13T21:32:48Z"
  labels:
    app: wordpress-pod
  name: wordpress-pod
spec:
  containers:
  - args:
    - apache2-foreground
    env:
    - name: WORDPRESS_DB_NAME
      value: wordpress
    - name: WORDPRESS_DB_HOST
      value: mysql-pod
    - name: WORDPRESS_DB_PASSWORD
      value: wordpress
    - name: WORDPRESS_DB_USER
      value: wordpress
    image: docker.io/library/wordpress:latest
    name: wordpress
    ports:
    - containerPort: 80
```

```yaml
      hostPort: 8080
    resources: {}
    securityContext:
      capabilities:
        drop:
        - CAP_MKNOD
        - CAP_NET_RAW
        - CAP_AUDIT_WRITE
    volumeMounts:
    - mountPath: /var/www/html
      name: wpvol-pvc
  restartPolicy: Never
  volumes:
  - name: wpvol-pvc
    persistentVolumeClaim:
      claimName: wpvol
status: {}
---
apiVersion: v1
kind: Pod
metadata:
  creationTimestamp: "2022-02-13T21:32:48Z"
  labels:
    app: mysql-pod
  name: mysql-pod
spec:
  containers:
  - args:
    - mysqld
    env:
    - name: MYSQL_ROOT_PASSWORD
      value: myrootpasswd
    - name: MYSQL_DATABASE
      value: wordpress
    - name: MYSQL_USER
      value: wordpress
```

```
            - name: MYSQL_PASSWORD
              value: wordpress
            image: docker.io/library/mysql:latest
            name: db
            ports:
            - containerPort: 3306
              hostPort: 3306
            resources: {}
            securityContext:
              capabilities:
                drop:
                - CAP_MKNOD
                - CAP_NET_RAW
                - CAP_AUDIT_WRITE
            volumeMounts:
            - mountPath: /var/lib/mysql
              name: dbvol-pvc
        restartPolicy: Never
        volumes:
        - name: dbvol-pvc
          persistentVolumeClaim:
            claimName: dbvol
status: {}
```

The resulting file is also available in this book's GitHub repository:

```
https://github.com/PacktPublishing/Podman-for-DevOps/blob/
main/Chapter14/kube/wordpress-multi-pod-basic.yaml
```

As we will see in the next section, this YAML file is enough to recreate a fully working WordPress application on Podman from scratch. We can persist and version it on a source control repository such as Git for future reuse.

The following code exports the two `Pod` resources, along with the `PersistentVolumeClaim` and `Service` resources:

```
$ podman generate kube -s \
  -f wordpress-multi-pod-full.yaml \
  wordpress-pod \
```

```
    mysql-pod \
    dbvol \
    wpvol
```

The output of this command is also available in this book's GitHub repository:

`https://github.com/PacktPublishing/Podman-for-DevOps/blob/main/Chapter14/kube/wordpress-multi-pod-full.yaml`

This full manifest is useful for importing and testing our application on a Kubernetes cluster, where the `Service` and `PersistentVolumeClaim` resources are necessary.

Now, we are ready to test our generated resources in Podman and learn how to reproduce full stack deployments with simple operations.

Running Kubernetes resource files in Podman

Now that we've learned how to generate Kubernetes YAML files containing the necessary resources to deploy our applications, we want to test them in a real scenario.

For this book, we will use the WordPress application again, both in its simple form with a single container and in its multi-pod variation.

The following examples are also available in this book's GitHub repository – you can choose to use the resources that have been generated from your labs or use the prepared manifests in this book's repository.

> **Important Note**
> Don't forget to clean up all the previous workloads before testing the creation of Kubernetes resources with Podman.

For all our examples, we will use the `podman play kube` command. It offers us an easy and intuitive interface for managing the execution of complex stacks with a good degree of customization.

The first example will be based on the single-pod manifest:

```
$ podman play kube wordpress-single-pod.yaml
```

The preceding command creates a pod called `wordpress-pod` that's composed of the two containers, along with the necessary volumes. Let's inspect the results and see what happened:

```
$ podman pod ps
POD ID          NAME            STATUS       CREATED         INFRA
ID        # OF CONTAINERS
5f8ecfe66acd    wordpress-pod   Running      4 minutes ago
46b4bdfe6a08    3
```

We can also check the running containers. Here, we expect to see the two WordPress and MySQL containers and the third infra-related `podman-pause`:

```
$ podman ps
CONTAINER ID    IMAGE
COMMAND                 CREATED         STATUS          PORTS
NAMES
46b4bdfe6a08    localhost/podman-pause:4.0.0-rc4-1643988335
4 minutes ago   Up 4 minutes ago   0.0.0.0:8080->80/tcp
5f8ecfe66acd-infra
ef88a5c8d1e5    docker.io/library/mysql:latest
mysqld                  4 minutes ago   Up 4 minutes ago
0.0.0.0:8080->80/tcp   wordpress-pod-db
76c6b6328653    docker.io/library/wordpress:latest
apache2-foregroun...   4 minutes ago   Up 4 minutes ago
0.0.0.0:8080->80/tcp   wordpress-pod-wordpress
```

Finally, we can verify if the `dbvol` and `wpvol` volumes have been created:

```
$ podman volume ls
DRIVER       VOLUME NAME
local        dbvol
local        wpvol
```

Before we look at the more articulated (and interesting) example with the multi-pod manifest, we must clean up the environment. We can do this manually or by using the `--down` option of the `podman play kube` command, which immediately stops and removes the running pods:

```
$ podman play kube --down wordpress-single-pod.yaml
Pods stopped:
5f8ecfe66acd01b705f38cd175fad222890ab612bf572807082f30ab37fd
```

```
0b88
```

```
Pods removed:
```

```
5f8ecfe66acd01b705f38cd175fad222890ab612bf572807082f30ab37fd
0b88
```

> **Important Note**
>
> Volumes are not removed by default since it can be useful to keep them if
> containers have already written data on them. To remove unused volumes, use
> the podman volume prune command.

Now, let's run the multi-pod example using the basic exported manifest:

```
$ podman play kube --network kubenet \
  wordpress-multi-pod-basic.yaml
```

Notice the additional --network argument, which is used to specify the network that
the pods will be attached to. This is necessary information since the Kubernetes YAML file
contains no information about Podman networks. Our pods will be executed in rootless
mode and attached to the rootless kubenet network.

We can check that the two pods have been created correctly by using the following
command:

```
$ podman pod ps
POD ID          NAME           STATUS      CREATED         INFRA
ID        # OF CONTAINERS
c9d775da0379    mysql-pod      Running     8 minutes ago
71c93fa6080b    2
3b497cbaeebc    wordpress-pod  Running     8 minutes ago
0c52ee133f0f    2
```

Now, we can inspect the running containers. The strings that are highlighted in the
following code represent the main workload to differentiate from the infra containers:

```
$ podman ps --format "{{.Image }} {{.Names}}"
localhost/podman-pause:4.0.0-rc5-1644672408 3b497cbaeebc-infra
docker.io/library/wordpress:latest wordpress-pod-wordpress
localhost/podman-pause:4.0.0-rc5-1644672408 c9d775da0379-infra
docker.io/library/mysql:latest mysql-pod-db
```

The `podman volume ls` command confirms the existence of the two volumes:

```
$ podman volume ls
DRIVER       VOLUME NAME
local        dbvol
local        wpvol
```

The rootless network configuration can be inspected with the `podman unshare` command:

```
$ podman unshare --rootless-netns ip addr show
```

> **Important Note**
>
> The `--rootless-netns` option is only available on Podman 4, which is the recommended version for this chapter.

Finally, let's inspect the DNS behavior. On Podman 4, the name resolution for custom networks is managed by the `aardvark-dns` daemon, while on Podman 3, it is managed by `dnsmasq`. Since we assume you're using Podman 4 for these examples, let's look at its DNS configuration. For rootless networks, we can find the managed records in the `/run/user/<UID>/containers/networks/aardvark-dns/<NETWORK_NAME>` file.

In our example, the configuration for the `kubenet` network is as follows:

```
$ cat /run/user/1000/containers/networks/aardvark-dns/kubenet
10.89.0.1
0c52ee133f0fec5084f25bd89ad8bd0f6af2fc46d696e2b8161864567b0a92
0b 10.89.0.4 wordpress-pod,0c52ee133f0f
71c93fa6080b6a3bfe1ebad3e164594c5fa7ea584e180113d2893eb67f6f3b
56 10.89.0.5 mysql-pod,71c93fa6080b
```

The most amazing thing from this output is the confirmation that the name resolution now works at the pod level, not at the container level. This is fair if we think that the pod initialized the namespaces, including the network namespace. For this reason, we can treat the pod name in Podman as a service name.

Here, we demonstrated how the Kubernetes manifests that are generated with Podman can become a great replacement for the Docker Compose approach while being more portable. Now, let's learn how to import our generated resources into a test Kubernetes cluster.

Testing the results in Kubernetes

In this section, we want to import the multi-pod YAML file, which is enriched with the Services and PVC configurations, on Kubernetes.

To provide a repeatable environment, we will use **minikube** (with a lowercase m), a portable solution, to create an all-in-one Kubernetes cluster as the local infrastructure.

The minikube project aims to provide a local Kubernetes cluster on Linux, Windows, and macOS. It uses host virtualization to spin up a VM that runs the all-in-one cluster or containerization to create a control plane that runs inside a container. It also provides a large set of add-ons to extend cluster functionalities, such as ingress controllers, service meshes, registries, logging, and more.

Another widely adopted alternative to spinning up a local Kubernetes cluster is the **Kubernetes in Docker** (**KinD**) project, which is not described in this book. KinD runs a Kubernetes control plane inside a container that's driven by Docker or Podman.

To set up minikube, users need virtualization support (KVM, VirtualBox, Hyper-V, Parallels, or VMware) or a container runtime such as Docker or Podman.

For brevity, we will not cover the technical steps necessary to configure the virtualization support for the different OSs; instead, we will use a GNU/Linux distribution.

> **Important Note**
> If you already own a running Kubernetes cluster or want to set up one in an alternative way, you can skip the next minikube configuration quick start and go to the *Running generated resource files in Kubernetes* subsection.

Setting up minikube

Run the following commands to download and install the latest `minikube` binary:

```
$ curl -LO https://storage.googleapis.com/minikube/releases/
latest/minikube-linux-amd64
```

```
$ sudo install minikube-linux-amd64 /usr/local/bin/minikube
```

You can choose to run minikube with a virtualization or containerization driver. To run minikube as a virtual machine on the KVM driver, you must install the **Qemu/KVM** and **libvirt** packages.

On Fedora, run the following command to install all the mandatory and default packages using the `@virtualization` package group:

```
$ sudo dnf install @virtualization
```

Now, start and enable the `libvirtd` service:

```
$ sudo systemctl enable --now libvirtd
```

To grant the user running minikube the proper permissions, append it to the `libvirt` supplementary group (this operation requires a new login to load the new group):

```
$ sudo usermod -aG libvirt $(whoami)
```

The following command statically configures the `kvm2` driver as the default:

```
$ minikube config set driver kvm2
```

When the preceding command is executed for the first time, minikube will automatically download the proper `kvm2` driver binary before starting the VM.

Alternatively, you can choose to run minikube as a containerized service with Docker or Podman. Assuming Podman is already installed, we only need to ensure that the user running minikube can run passwordless sudo. This is necessary since the Kubernetes cluster must run in a rootfull container, so privilege escalation is necessary. To allow passwordless privilege escalation for Podman, edit the `/etc/sudoers` file with the following command:

```
$ sudo visudo
```

Once opened, add the following line to the end of the file to grant passwordless escalation for the Podman binary and save it. Remember to replace `<username>` with your user's name:

```
<username> ALL=(ALL) NOPASSWD: /usr/bin/podman
```

The following command statically configures the `podman` driver as the default:

```
$ minikube config set driver podman
```

> **Important Note**
> If your host is a virtual machine running on a hypervisor such as KVM and Podman is installed on the host, minikube will detect the environment and set up the default driver as `podman` automatically.

To use minikube, users also need to install the Kubernetes CLI tool, kubectl. The following commands download and install the latest Linux release:

```
$ version=$(curl -L -s https://dl.k8s.io/release/stable.txt)
curl -LO "https://dl.k8s.io/release/${version}/bin/linux/amd64/
kubectl $ sudo install -o root -g root \
  -m 0755 kubectl \
  /usr/local/bin/kubectl
```

Now, we are ready to run our Kubernetes cluster with minikube.

Starting minikube

To start minikube as a VM, use the CRI-O container runtime inside the Kubernetes cluster:

```
$ minikube start --driver=kvm2 --container-runtime=cri-o
```

The --driver option is not necessary if kvm2 has already been configured as the default driver with the minikube config set driver command.

To start minikube with Podman, use the CRI-O container runtime inside the cluster:

```
$ minikube start --driver=podman --container-runtime=cri-o
```

Again, the --driver option is not necessary if podman has been already configured as the default driver with the minikube config set driver command.

To ensure that the cluster has been created correctly, run the following command with the kubectl CLI. All the pods should have the Running status:

```
$ kubectl get pods -A
```

NAMESPACE	NAME	READY	STATUS
RESTARTS	AGE		
kube-system	coredns-64897985d-gqnrn	1/1	
Running 0	19s		
kube-system	etcd-minikube	1/1	
Running 0	27s		
kube-system	kube-apiserver-minikube	1/1	
Running 0	27s		
kube-system	kube-controller-manager-minikube	1/1	
Running 0	27s		

kube-system	kube-proxy-sj7xn	1/1
Running 0	20s	
kube-system	kube-scheduler-minikube	1/1
Running 0	33s	
kube-system	storage-provisioner	1/1
Running 0	30s	

> **Important Note**
>
> If one or more containers still have the `ContainerCreating` status, wait a little longer for the images to be pulled.
>
> Also, notice that the output may differ slightly if you're running minikube with a Podman driver. In that case, an additional pod named `kindnet` will be created to help manage CNI networking inside the cluster.

With that, we have set everything up for a local Kubernetes environment and are ready to test our generated manifests.

Running generated resource files in Kubernetes

In the *Generating a composite application with multiple Pods* section, we learned how to export a manifest file from Podman that included the `Pod` resources, along with the `Service` and `PersistentVolumeClaim` resources. The need to export this set of resources is related to the way Kubernetes handles workloads, storage, and exposed services.

Kubernetes services are needed to provide a resolution mechanism, as well as internal load balancing. In our example, the `mysql-pod` pod will be mapped to a homonymous `mysql-pod` service.

PVCs are required to define a storage claim that starts provisioning persistent volumes for our pods. In minikube, automated provisioning is implemented by a local `StorageClass` named `minikube-hostpath`; it creates local directories in the VM/container filesystem that are later bind-mounted inside the pods' containers.

We can roll out our WordPress stack by using the `kubectl create` command:

```
$ kubectl create -f wordpress-multi-pod-full.yaml
```

If not specified, all the resources will be created in the `default` Kubernetes namespace. Let's wait for the pods to reach the `Running` status and inspect the results.

First, we can inspect the pods and services that have been created:

```
$ kubectl get pods
NAME            READY   STATUS    RESTARTS   AGE
mysql-pod       1/1     Running   0          48m
wordpress-pod   1/1     Running   0          48m
$ kubectl get svc
NAME            TYPE        CLUSTER-IP      EXTERNAL-IP
PORT(S)                 AGE
kubernetes      ClusterIP   10.96.0.1       <none>          443/
TCP             53m
mysql-pod       NodePort    10.108.34.77    <none>
3306:30284/TCP  52m
wordpress-pod   NodePort    10.96.63.142    <none>
80:30408/TCP    52m
```

Notice that the two mysql-pod and wordpress-pod services have been created with the NodePort type and mapped to a port on a 30000 or upper range. We will use the 30408 port to test the WordPress frontend.

The pods are mapped by the services using label matching logic. If the labels that have been defined in the service's selector field exist in the pod, it becomes an endpoint to the service itself. Let's view the current endpoints in our project:

```
$ kubectl get endpoints
NAME            ENDPOINTS           AGE
kubernetes      10.88.0.6:8443      84m
mysql-pod       10.244.0.5:3306     4m9s
wordpress-pod   10.244.0.6:80       4m9s
```

> **Important Note**
>
> The kubernetes service and its related endpoint provide API access to internal workloads. However, it is not part of this book's examples, so it can be ignored in this context.

Let's also inspect the claims and their related volumes:

```
$ kubectl get pvc
NAME      STATUS    VOLUME
CAPACITY    ACCESS MODES    STORAGECLASS    AGE
```

```
dbvol    Bound      pvc-4d4a047b-bd20-4bef-879c-c3d80f96d712    1Gi
RWO                 standard        54m

wpvol    Bound      pvc-accd7947-1499-44b5-bac8-9345da7edc23    1Gi
RWO                 standard        54m
```

```
$ kubectl get pv
NAME                                                      CAPACITY    ACCESS
MODES      RECLAIM POLICY      STATUS     CLAIM                       STORAGECLASS
REASON     AGE
pvc-4d4a047b-bd20-4bef-879c-c3d80f96d712    1Gi              RWO
Delete              Bound       default/dbvol    standard
60m
pvc-accd7947-1499-44b5-bac8-9345da7edc23    1Gi              RWO
Delete              Bound       default/wpvol    standard
60m
```

The two PVC resources have been created and bound to two dynamically provisioned persistent volumes. So long as the PVC objects exist, the related PV will stay untouched, even if the pods are destroyed and recreated.

Now, the WordPress application can be tested. By default, minikube does not deploy an ingress controller (even though this can be enabled with the `minikube addons enable ingress` command), so we will use the simple NodePort service to test the functionalities of our application.

The current minikube VM/container IP must be obtained to reach the exposed NodePort service. Port `30408`, which is associated with the `wordpress-pod` service, listens to the IP address that's produced by the following command:

```
$ minikube ip
10.88.0.6
```

Now, we can point our browser to `http://10.88.0.6:30408` and see the WordPress first setup screen.

To remove the WordPress application and all its related content, use the `kubectl delete` command in the YAML manifest file:

```
$ kubectl delete -f wordpress-multi-pod-full.yaml
```

This command removes all the resources that have been defined in the file, including the generated PVs.

Summary

With that, we have reached the end of this book about Podman and its companion tools.

First, we learned how to generate Systemd unit files and control containerized workloads as Systemd services, which allows us to, for example, automate container execution at system startup.

After that, we learned how to generate Kubernetes YAML resources. Starting with basic concepts and examples, we learned how to generate complex application stacks using both single-pod and multiple pods approaches and illustrated how the latter can provide a great alternative (and Kubernetes compliant) to the Docker Compose methodology.

Finally, we tested our results on Podman and a local Kubernetes cluster that had been created with `minikube` to show the great portability of this approach.

This book's journey finishes here, but Podman's amazing evolution continues thanks to its growing adoption in many contexts and its vibrant and helpful community.

Before you move on, don't forget to join the community on IRC, Matrix, or Discord and subscribe to the relevant mailing lists. Feel free to ask for and give feedback and contribute to help with the growth of the project.

Thank you for your interest and dedication.

Further reading

To learn more about the topics that were covered in this chapter, take a look at the following resources:

- The Catatonit repository on GitHub: `https://github.com/openSUSE/catatonit`
- Kubernetes persistent volumes definition: `https://kubernetes.io/docs/concepts/storage/persistent-volumes/`
- The minikube project's home page: `https://minikube.sigs.k8s.io/`
- The KinD project's home page: `https://kind.sigs.k8s.io/`
- Podman community links: `https://podman.io/community/`

Index

M

N

O

Packt.com

Subscribe to our online digital library for full access to over 7,000 books and videos, as well as industry leading tools to help you plan your personal development and advance your career. For more information, please visit our website.

Why subscribe?

- Spend less time learning and more time coding with practical eBooks and Videos from over 4,000 industry professionals

- Improve your learning with Skill Plans built especially for you

- Get a free eBook or video every month

- Fully searchable for easy access to vital information

- Copy and paste, print, and bookmark content

Did you know that Packt offers eBook versions of every book published, with PDF and ePub files available? You can upgrade to the eBook version at packt.com and as a print book customer, you are entitled to a discount on the eBook copy. Get in touch with us at customercare@packtpub.com for more details.

At www.packt.com, you can also read a collection of free technical articles, sign up for a range of free newsletters, and receive exclusive discounts and offers on Packt books and eBooks.

Other Books You May Enjoy

If you enjoyed this book, you may be interested in these other books by Packt:

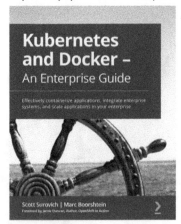

Kubernetes and Docker - An Enterprise Guide

Scott Surovich, Marc Boorshtein

ISBN: 9781839213403

- Create a multinode Kubernetes cluster using kind
- Implement Ingress, MetalLB, and ExternalDNS
- Configure a cluster OIDC using impersonation
- Map enterprise authorization to Kubernetes
- Secure clusters using PSPs and OPA
- Enhance auditing using Falco and EFK
- Back up your workload for disaster recovery and cluster migration
- Deploy to a platform using Tekton, GitLab, and ArgoCD

Learn Docker - Fundamentals of Docker 19.x - Second Edition

Gabriel N. Schenker

ISBN: 9781838827472

- Containerize your traditional or microservice-based applications
- Develop, modify, debug, and test an application running inside a container
- Share or ship your application as an immutable container image
- Build a Docker Swarm and a Kubernetes cluster in the cloud
- Run a highly distributed application using Docker Swarm or Kubernetes
- Update or rollback a distributed application with zero downtime
- Secure your applications with encapsulation, networks, and secrets
- Troubleshoot a containerized, highly distributed application in the cloud

Packt is searching for authors like you

If you're interested in becoming an author for Packt, please visit `authors.packtpub.com` and apply today. We have worked with thousands of developers and tech professionals, just like you, to help them share their insight with the global tech community. You can make a general application, apply for a specific hot topic that we are recruiting an author for, or submit your own idea.

Share Your Thoughts

Now you've finished , we'd love to hear your thoughts! Scan the QR code below to go straight to the Amazon review page for this book and share your feedback or leave a review on the site that you purchased it from.

https://packt.link/r/1-803-24823-8

Your review is important to us and the tech community and will help us make sure we're delivering excellent quality content.